A

DESCRIPTIVE ACCOUNT

OF

ASAM

A

DESCRIPTIVE ACCOUNT

OF

ASAM:

WITH A SKETCH OF

THE LOCAL GEOGRAPHY,

AND A CONCISE HISTORY OF

The Tea-Plant of Asam:

TO WHICH IS ADDED,

A SHORT ACCOUNT OF THE NEIGHBOURING TRIBES,

EXHIBITING THEIR

HISTORY, MANNERS, AND CUSTOMS.

BY WILLIAM ROBINSON

GYAN

Published by

GYAN

Gyan Publishing House
5, Ansari Road
Daryaganj, New Delhi-110002
Phone: 011-47034999, 9811692060
E-mail: books@gyanbooks.com

Distribution Network
gyanbooks.com
India, USA, Canada, UK, Australia

ISBN: 978-81-212-5977-4 (PB)
First Published, 1841

2nd Impression 2024

Printed at: Gyan Press, Delhi.

A DESCRIPTIVE ACCOUNT OF ASAM
Author: WILLIAM ROBINSON

A DESCRIPTIVE ACCOUNT OF ASAM:

WITH A SKETCH OF

THE LOCAL GEOGRAPHY,

AND A CONCISE HISTORY OF

The Tea Plant of Asam:

TO WHICH IS ADDED,

A SHORT ACCOUNT OF THE NEIGHBOURING TRIBES,

EXHIBITING THEIR

HISTORY, MANNERS, AND CUSTOMS.

BY WILLIAM ROBINSON,
GOWHATTI GOVERNMENT SEMINARY.

ILLUSTRATED WITH FOUR MAPS, DRAWN EXPRESSLY FOR THE WORK.

CALCUTTA:
OSTELL AND LEPAGE, BRITISH LIBRARY.
LONDON:
THOMAS OSTELL & Co. 83, LEADENHALL STREET.
MDCCCXLI.

TO WHOM COULD

A WORK OF THIS NATURE BE WITH GREATER PROPRIETY

Dedicated

THAN THE OFFICER, TO WHOSE JUDICIOUS MANAGEMENT

AND PRAISEWORTHY EXERTIONS

THE PROVINCE IS INDEBTED FOR ITS

PRESENT PROSPEROUS CONDITION.

TO MAJOR FRANCIS JENKINS

Agent to the Governor General North-East Frontier &c. &c. &c.

THIS VOLUME

IS

WITH THE WARMEST SENTIMENTS OF GRATITUDE AND ESTEEM

INSCRIBED BY

THE AUTHOR

GOWHATTI,
18th August, 1841.

PREFACE.

In submitting the following work to the public, the author deems it unnecessary to detain the reader by many prefatory remarks.

The subject is one of acknowledged interest at the present time. The daily increasing importance of Asam, and the conspicuous position it begins to hold as the scene of great commercial advantages to British India, render a "Descriptive Account" of the province a great desideratum.

But though no dispute will arise as to the importance of the work, the author has no reason to expect the same unanimity about the fitness of the workman. He delivers this volume to the world, with all the diffidence and anxiety natural to the author of such an undertaking. That there are defects in the work, he will admit; nor can he forget how probable it is, that more impartial, and more discerning eyes will discover many which are invisible to his.

He begs it, however, to be considered, that the

work was undertaken amidst numerous other important and arduous avocations. The sources of his information were further scattered in a great variety of repositories. It sometimes lay in considerable portions, but often in very minute ones; sometimes by itself, but often mixed up with subjects of a very different nature: and even where information relating to his object stood disjoined from other subjects, a small portion of what was useful, commonly lay imbedded in a large mass of what was trifling and insignificant. It was his task to explore this assemblage of heterogeneous things, and to separate, for his own use, what was true, and what was false.

Suffice it, however, to state, that his most strenuous endeavours have not been wanting to render the work, as far as his abilities, attainments, and resources admitted, worthy of the encouragement of a discerning public.

Should it have the effect of bringing this highly valuable province into more general notice; should it afford to inquirers more correct and authentic information than has hitherto been supplied; and, finally, should it even in the most distant manner lead to an improvement in the moral, as well as the temporal condition of the people, he will consider the labour bestowed on it, more than repaid.

It remains to state, that the present work was undertaken at the particular request of the distinguished officer to whom it is, with permission, dedicated. His literary talent, high attainments, and superior knowledge of the province, render him by far the best qualified individual to write on the topics contained in the following pages. His more important duties, however, left him but little leisure for prosecuting such a task. Under these circumstances, the author, in complying with his request, was of opinion, that if no one appeared with higher qualifications to undertake the work, it was better it should be done imperfectly, better it should be done even as he might be capable of doing it, than not be done at all.

The author here begs publicly to acknowledge the obligations he is under to Major Jenkins, for the unreserved communication with him he at all times enjoyed when in quest of information; for the obliging manner in which he was allowed free access to the materials in his possession, as well as to the public documents contained in his office; and likewise for the considerable aid afforded by him in procuring information from other quarters.

His acknowledgments are also due to Mr. C. K. Hudson, for the kind assistance invariably afforded by him. To him he is particularly indebted for the maps, with which the Local Geography is illustrated.

To the Rev. Mr. Mack, and J. O. Voigt, Esq. of Serampore, the author is under peculiar obligation for the very obliging manner in which they undertook to inspect his MSS. and to revise the proof sheets in passing through the press.

To all his other friends, who have on various occasions favoured him with their kind assistance, the author begs to offer his grateful acknowledgments.

Contents.

CHAPTER I.

CHAPTER II.

CHAPTER III.

NATURAL GEOGRAPHY.

Section I.—Geology.

Section II.—Botany.

Section III.---Zoology.

The Tea Plant.

Thea Viridis, Linn. *Chamellia Theifera*, Griff.

CHAPTER IV.

HISTORICAL GEOGRAPHY.

CHAPTER V.

POLITICAL GEOGRAPHY.

CHAPTER VI.

PRODUCTIVE INDUSTRY. Page.

CHAPTER VII.

CIVIL AND SOCIAL STATE.

CHAPTER VIII.

LOCAL GEOGRAPHY.

Section I.—Kamrup, or Lower Asam.

Section II.—Durrung.

Maps.

CHAPTER I.

GENERAL OUTLINE AND ASPECT.

Asam a very interesting country—Derivation of the name—Boundaries—Divided by the Brahmaputra—Ancient Divisions—Beautiful country—Mountain scenery—Physical aspect—Diversity of soil—Hills—Diluvial plains—Alluvial lands—Rivers—The Brahmaputra and its great tributaries.

ASAM is in many points of view a most interesting country. Situated on the north-eastern extremity of the British territory, and bordering on the powerful neighbouring states of Butan, China, and Burma, Asam is the key to the British possessions in this quarter, and deserves therefore the attention of the statesman. It is possessed of rivers in number and extent equal at least to those of any country in the world of the same size. The extraordinary fertility of its soil, its extensive low lands, and its mountain tracts, give it already the productions both of the tropics and of temperate regions, and it requires but further cultivation by a more numerous and enlightened peasantry, to render its produce tenfold more abundant. Its revenue even now shows progressive improvement; and as our communications are opened with the numerous tribes surrounding it, and extended to Butan on the north, and the Shyans on the south-east, new channels of commerce will be obtained, which cannot fail to enrich the country through which they pass, and give a stimulus to its own agricultural and manufacturing industry; it must therefore interest the political economist. Its unexplored mineral treasures, among which gold and iron are abundant; its animal and vegetable productions; the descent, customs, and languages of its numerous mountain tribes, present subjects of inquiry which deserve, and if vigorously prosecuted, will abundantly repay, the researches of the lover of nature and the observer of mankind.

The name Asam is generally supposed to be derived from the Sanskrit term *asama*, a compound word formed from the negative particle अ *a* and सम *sam*, equal, signifying unequalled or unrivalled; but it seems probable that this derivation was merely an invention of the Brahmins, after the conversion of the last dynasty to the Brahminical faith. This dynasty was of a tribe of Shyans, called Ahoms or Asoms, who invaded the country, and from whom it might with greater probability have derived its present appellation. In the Purans, or sacred books of the Hindoos, the western portion of the country is termed Kamrup, and the most eastern Namrup; whilst that portion of it lying between the two, and surrounding the ancient town of Gorganh, or Guerganh, was called the country of Gadha or Gadhagram; whence probably may have originated the general name of the country in Western India, Gor, or, as written by Ptolemy, Corrha.

Asam is bounded on the north and north-east by a range of lofty mountains, rising abruptly to the height of from five to six thousand feet above the level of the adjacent plains, inhabited by Butias, Duflas, Abors, and Mishmis; on the south and south-east by another line of mountainous country, peopled by Khasias, Kacharis, and Nagas; and on the west by the province of Bengal.

The boundary line between Asam and Bengal has constantly varied. The Asamese records claim for the western boundary of Asam the river Kirratiya, running through the Purgunnah of Goraghat. It is certain however, that the kingdom of Asam, under the Ahom dynasty, never extended west beyond Gowalpara; and when the river Kuaratiya is claimed as the boundary, the claim must allude to the western boundary of the old Hindu kingdom of Kamrup, or probably to that river having been the boundary between the Rajas of Gour and the Kuch Rajas, who founded the kingdom of Kuch-Behar, and afterwards conquered all the north-east territory of Rungpore, and the western parts of Asam.

The boundary line between Asam and Bengal, since the former was placed under British control, has been the Monass river on the northern shore of the Brahmaputra, and on its southern bank an imaginary line a little west of the hill of Nagharbera.

From this boundary west, or longitude 90° 40′, to the Mishmi and Singpho hills east, or longitude 97° 20′, a length of about 500 British statute miles, is comprised the country commonly known as Asam. Its breadth between the northern and southern mountains varies considerably, but may be averaged at about sixty miles, covering an area of 30,000 square miles, or 1,58,70,000 purahs of Asam.

This valley is intersected in its whole length by the great river the Brahmaputra, from which it derives its most appropriate name. The two parts thus divided are called the Uttargorah and Dakkingorah, or the north and south bank. These may be termed the geographical divisions of the country; although they at one time likewise divided from each other distinct people, and independent principalities and jurisdictions, until all were subdued under the same authority in the reign of Jaiya Dhwaja Sing, A. D. 1665. All the north bank appears anciently to have been called Kamrup, and the southern bank Namrup, though at present the latter name is confined merely to a small district in the south-east, whilst the former is applied to the whole of Lower Asam.

Of the ancient divisions of the country little is now known. The first line of princes in Asam, of whom we have any authentic record, is the Hindu dynasty of Brahmaputra. The extent of their possessions however is not ascertained, but as to these Rajas are ascribed the great *gars*, or forts, of Baidargar in Kamrup and Pratasspuriagar in Bishnath, and no monuments of their reign are traced elsewhere, it seems probable that the north bank of the river, as far as the latter station only, was held by them. The next race who held Lower Asam were the Kuch Rajas. They possessed themselves of nearly the whole of the present districts of Kamrup and Darang. The names of these two divisions, however they may have originated, have prevailed since the era of their possession of the country.

Whilst the Kuch Rajas were possessing themselves of Lower Asam, the Ahoms had invaded the south-eastern extremity of the valley; and their conquests, together with the settlements of the colonists of this race, led to the permanent distinction of Kamrup from Asam, or Lower from Upper Asam.

Asam is naturally a beautiful tract of country, and enjoys all the advantages requisite for rendering it one of the finest under the sun—though at present, owing to its very thinly populated state, by far the greater portion of it is allowed to run to waste with luxuriance of vegetation. Notwithstanding, it occasionally presents a scenery comparable perhaps to the richest in the world. Its plains decked with a rich verdant robe, and abounding with numerous crystal streams, which winding along the base of a group of beautifully wooded hills, covered to their very summits with trees, interspersed with dark and deep glens, and heaving their swelling ridges into a bright blue sky, constitute altogether a scene of extraordinary magnificence and sublimity, and display a regularity and softness of feature that beggars description. On the other hand, to such as find satisfaction in contemplating nature in her rudest and most gigantic forms, what an inexhaustible fund of delight is here likewise displayed! Mountains beyond mountains hurled together in wild confusion, seem to the spectator like the wrecks of a ruined world; and whilst the eye is gratified with the pleasing panorama, a series of hills innumerable is presented to view, retiring far away in fine perspective, till their blue conical summits are relieved by the proud pinnacles of the Himalaya towering their lofty magazines of tempests and snow midway up to the vertex of the sky, and exhibiting scenes calculated to animate the mind with the sublimest sentiments, and to awaken the most lofty recollections.

In viewing the physical aspect of the country, the beholder is at once struck with the peculiarity of a perfect plain, studded with numerous clumps of hills rising abruptly from the general level, and surrounded by lofty mountains, and intersected in all possible directions by innumerable streams and rivulets, which issuing from the bordering mountains, at length empty themselves into the great channel of the Brahmaputra.

From the length of the valley, as might be conjectured, the soil is very varied; but to enter into any minute detail of its varieties would be foreign to our purpose. Suffice it to say, that the soil of Asam is exceedingly rich, and well adapted to all kinds of agricultural purposes, for the most part composed of a rich black loam, reposing on a grey sandy clay, though occasionally consisting of a light yellow clayey texture.

The lands in Asam may in general be divided into three great classes, with reference to the level of the waters of the Brahmaputra.

The first division is composed of hills, the largest group of which within the valley is that of the Mikir hills, which stand out in the plain, insulated from the southern mountains by the valley of the Jumna river. These extend from east to west to about 63 miles, and are in breadth about 27 miles, occupying an area of 1700 square miles. The hills projecting into the valley at Gowhatti, and extending from Naigang to the Kamakhya Parbut, likewise form another, and the only other considerable interruption of the flat plain of the valley. But these latter are rather prolongations of spurs from the Khassia chain, than isolated groups belonging to the valley. The other hills of Rudrassed, Kaleabar, Singori, Hajie, Sialkuchi, Katimora, &c. are all insulated, of small extent, and excepting for the space they stand upon, not affecting the level of the adjacent plains.

The second division of the lands is what may be termed the diluvial plain of the valley, its level being generally above the ordinary inundations of the Brahmaputra, or of those of its tributary streams. The channels of some of the hill streams, however, are of so little depth that the highest lands in their neighbourhood are often liable to sudden inundations.

On the north bank of the great river, the lands are continuous throughout the whole length of the valley, except where they may be partially interrupted by the alluvial beds of the hill streams. The breadth of these plains is in some places very trifling, whilst in others they comprise a tract of many miles in extent; this however depends in a great measure on the number and the height of the rocks or hills that protect the lands from the devastating aberrations of the great river.

One of these projecting points is at Bishnath, where the rocks rise to a height of about thirty feet above the highest inundations of the Brahmaputra. All the lands from that point, back to the hills, have been thus protected from the encroachments of the river, and now form a high dry plain, extending about twenty-five miles, and then gradually rising in steppes towards the lower ranges of the Butan mountains.

The low hills of Tezpore and Singori, standing on the banks of the Brahmaputra, have in like manner been the means of preventing any encroachments of the river upon the plains of Chardwar and Chutiga, which lie to the west of each of the above hills, thus preserving a large tract of country from the ravages of a periodical inundation.

On the south bank of the river, the width of the diluvial plain is greatest immediately east of the Dhansiri. The great projection to the north of the Mikir hills, and the non-occurrence of rocks on the opposite bank, being the cause of the Brahmaputra at that point taking a northerly direction, a deep plain has in consequence been preserved on its southern bank, extending from the river back to the Naga hills, and comprising a breadth of about thirty miles.

To the west of the Dhansiri, the occurrence of diluvial lands is very uncertain, and when they do occur, they are for the most part of small extent.

The alluvial deposits of the Brahmaputra and of its tributary streams may be considered as another, and the third, general division of lands in Asam. These lands are very extensive, especially so along the channel of the great river, and are of great variety of fertility and elevation, from the vast churs of pure sand subject to annual inundations, to the great islands so raised by drift sand and the accumulated remains of rank vegetable matter, that they are no longer immerged even during the highest inundations of the adjacent streams.

The rapidity with which wastes composed entirely of sand, newly washed forward by the current during floods, become converted into rich pasture is astonishing, and this too independent of any subjacent impervious structure. As the freshes begin to lessen and retire into the deeper channels, the currents form natural embankments on their edges, preventing the return of a small portion of water, which is thus left extended over the sands. These last already saturated, having little capacity for more fluid, that on the surface remains stagnant and exposed to the action of the sun's rays, and slowly evaporates, leaving a thin, impervious crust of animal and vegetable matter. This impregnated with the seeds of Saccharum spontaneum, and other grasses that have been partly transmitted by the winds, and partly left behind by the waters, derives sufficient moisture from the mists and dews, so prevalent along the Brahmaputra during the nights and mornings, to form a non-conducting medium sufficient to protect the germs from the scorching heat to which they would be otherwise exposed in the naked sand. Such places are frequented by numerous flocks of aquatic birds, who resort thither in search of fish and mollusca, and as vegetation begins to appear, herds of wild elephants and buffaloes are attracted by the plentiful supply of food, and the retirement such places afford, and contribute to manure and form the new soil.

All that tract of land between the Kalang Nuddi, a branch of the Brahmaputra, issuing opposite Bishnath, and the great river itself, is, with the exception of very small portions at the foot of a few isolated hills, all one vast field of alluvial ground, extremely rich, and for the most part possessing an extraordinary fertility of soil.

Another similar tract of almost equal extent is the Majuli island, situated between the Brahmaputra and Dihing rivers, and formed chiefly by the silt deposited from the Sulanseri Nuddi.

Besides the above, islands of smaller extent are very numerous along the whole course of the Brahmaputra; and they are generally more or less liable to the destructive deviations of the river.

Other alluvial tracts of no small extent are also formed on the banks of the Barnanddi and the Monass. By their frequent aberrations, and constant inundations, these two rivers have created vast tracts of alluvial lands, which were till very lately almost abandoned and covered with extensive jungles of impenetrable reeds. In the number of its rivers, Asam may be said to exceed every other country of equal extent; including the Brahmaputra and its two great tributaries, sixty-one have been ascertained to exist, of which thirty-four flow from the northern, and twenty-four from the southern mountains, besides numerous others of less consequence. Those issuing from the southern mountains are never rapid. The inundations commence from the northern rivers, filling both the Brahmaputra and the southern streams, these latter having no considerable current till May or June.

But as all the confluents to the Brahmaputra, from their natural direction, belong more properly to sections of the country than to the valley in general, a more particular description of each may be appropriately deferred for the present.

The grand feature, however, of the physical geography of Asam, which belongs to the whole valley, and from which it derives its most appropriate name, is the Brahmaputra. This noble river may be classed amongst the largest in the world, being inferior to but a few in the length of its course, and holding a still higher rank among the great streams, when we calculate its importance by the volume of water it disembogues into the sea, which on a fair computation taken at Gowalpara, during its lowest ebb, amounted to about 1,46,188 cubic feet per second. During the rains, when the river attains a height of from thirty to forty feet above its common level, the body of water it then discharges may fairly be computed at four times the above quantity.

The Brahmaputra is fed principally by three great streams, uniting in latitude 27° 45′, and longitude 95° 30′. The least of these streams is the southernmost, and that which the Hindoos have adopted as the chief branch, having sanctified it by an admission into their mythology. It retains the name of the great river, from its falling straight into the axis of the main trunk. This stream is described as taking its rise from a circular basin, or *well,* towards the eastern extremity of the valley called the Brahmakhund, and situated in the side of the mountains beneath the Snowy range, while behind and above it are stupendous ranges of impracticable transit. It enters the valley rather by a series of cascades, than by a deep defile; and this peculiarity is distinguished by the accumulations of stones of immense size, which have been propelled forward, causing a succession of rapids, which gradually increase in number and difficulty. Impatient of the restraints which it meets with in the hollows among the mountains, it tears up and overturns whatever opposes its progress, till at length tired of uproar and mischief, it quits all that it has swept along, and leaves the opening of the valley strewed with the rejected waste.

This river after its entrance into the valley, receives the waters of the Kundil and Digaru Naddis, which take their rise from the Mishmi hills on the north, and is likewise joined by the Tengapani and Noa Dihing rivers, issuing from the Singpho hills on the north-east.

The other great sources of the Brahmaputra are, the Dihing and Dihong rivers. The source of the Dihong has been hitherto unknown, but it seems probable it must approach, if it do not pass within, the mountains on the frontier of China. It is said to be divided on its issue from the hills into four great branches, which reuniting, form a deep and even stream, though occasionally intersected by rocks. This river forms the natural boundary between the Abor and Mishmi tribes.

The former, the Dihŏng, requires more especial notice from its being the supposed continuation of the Tsanpu, or the great river of Tartary, which, rising in latitude 30° north, longitude 82° east, runs eastward, and passing Lassa penetrates the frontier mountains that divide Thibet from Asam, and enters the valley by a narrow defile in the Abor mountains.

The above supposition has been objected to, on the grounds that the Tsanpu in Thibet, from the length of its course, is necessarily a very large river, and that the Dihŏng, scarcely more than a hundred yards wide, is in consequence by far too small to be the channel of such a stream. Such a conclusion may be granted, but the premises adduced are by no means so satisfactory. A river having its rise in, and flowing through, the arid and elevated region of Thibet, must be very inferior in comparison with one draining a country with a moist climate. Again, supposing the Dihŏng to be but a hundred yards wide (though further within the hills it is said to be of greater width) yet the steep slope of the mountain sides induces an impression that the bed must possess immense depth. The body of water it discharges at its lowest ebb, is computed at fifty thousand cubic feet per second, and supposing the mean velocity of the current to be three miles an hour, the mean depth required to give that discharge is thirty-seven feet. Or even supposing the discharge the same, and the velocity no more than two miles an hour, the mean depth required is fifty-five feet, which also is far within the bounds of probability.

From the circumstance of its hydrographical basin extending amidst snows parallel to the equator from 82° to 98° of longitude, as well as from the position of its course along the elevated plateau of the Himalaya, the Dihong seems very liable to sudden, or at least excessive, periodical inundations.

CHAPTER II.

CLIMATE AND ITS EFFECTS ON MAM.

SECTION I.—CLIMATE.

Acceptation of the term—Causes affecting climate—The action of the sun upon the atmosphere, not the only cause—The elevation of the land—Vicinity of mountain chains—Difference in the radiating and absorbing powers of the land—The climate of Asam approaches to that of Bengal—Modified by the geographical position of the province—Predominant winds in Asam—North-westers—Humidity—Sources of aqueous exhalation—Rains of long continuance—Cold season—Characterized by the appearance of heavy fogs—Probable cause of these mists—Temperate climate—Warm weather—Mean annual temperature—Supposed causes of the equality of temperature.

The term climate in geography comprehends "a portion of the earth's surface contained between two circles parallel to the equator, and of such a breadth, as that the longest day in the parallel nearest the pole, exceeds the longest day in that nearest the equator by some certain space of time." It also expresses "the ordinary state of the atmosphere, with regard to heat and moisture, which prevails in any given portion of the globe." For our purpose we must regard climate in the latter acceptation of the term.

If climate depended solely upon the heat of the sun, all places having the same latitude would have the same mean annual temperature. The motion of the sun in the ecliptic indeed, occasions perpetual variations in the length of the day, and in the direction of the rays with regard to the earth; yet as the cause is periodic, the mean annual temperature, from the sun's motion alone, must be constant in each parallel of latitude.

The distribution of heat, however, in the same parallel, is known to be very irregular in all latitudes, except between the tropics, where the isothermal lines, or the lines passing through places of equal mean annual temperature, are more nearly parallel to the equator. The causes of disturbance are very numerous; but such as have the greatest influence, according to M. de Humboldt, to whom we are indebted for the greater part of what is known on the subject, are, the elevation of the continents; the distribution of land and water over the surface of the globe, exposing different absorbing and radiating powers; the variations in the surface of the land, as forests, sandy deserts, verdant plains, rocks, etc.; mountain chains covered with masses of snow, which tend to diminish the temperature; the reverberation of the sun's rays in the valleys, which increases it; and the interchange of currents both of air and water, which mitigates the rigour of climate. To these may be added cultivation, though its influence extends over but a small portion of the globe.

Cold increases in a very rapid progression with the elevation of the land, as well as with the latitude, being at the rate of one degree to every hundred yards of altitude.

The vicinity of mountain chains has also a great influence upon the temperature. They attract and condense the vapours floating in the air, and send them down in torrents of rain. They likewise radiate heat into the atmosphere at a lower elevation, and increase the temperature of the valleys by the reflection of the sun's rays, and by the shelter they afford against prevailing winds. But, on the contrary, one of the most general and powerful causes of cold arising from the vicinity of mountains, is the freezing currents of wind, which rush from their lofty peaks along the rapid declivities, and chill the surrounding valleys.

The difference in the radiating and absorbing powers of the sea and land, has also a very considerable influence in disturbing the regular distribution of heat. On land the temperature depends upon the nature of the soil and its products, its habitual moisture or dryness. Extensive forests tend in a great measure to cool the air, by shading the ground from the rays of the sun, as well as by evaporation from the boughs. The number of rivers, pools, and marshes, interspersed through a country, produce a like effect in absorbing caloric, and cooling the air by evaporation.

The climate of Asam, in general respects, approaches to that of Bengal, but is considerably modified by the geographical position of the province between two continuous mountain ranges. Their vicinity alters the prevailing winds of Bengal to other points of the compass, and creates local and periodical currents of air unknown to Bengal, and which have at times a considerable effect upon its temperature.

"The united influence of all the elements which constitute physical climate, is variously modified by the prevailing winds, and all their variations depend on the equilibrium of the atmosphere, the heat of one climate, and the cold of another, exercising a continual influence on each other."*

The most prevalent winds in Asam are those that blow in a north-easterly direction, and the whole valley lies exposed to their current. Descending from the Himalaya, the air derives an impetus from its low temperature, and consequent greater specific gravity than that of the heated westerly winds. The air in the vicinity of the mountains having the heat absorbed from it by the snow, and being thus rendered specifically heavier than the general air of the same altitude, consequently sinks, and causes a motion in the warmer air to occupy its place. Thus an upper current is formed, while the lower one descends into the valley, when its diminished temperature renders it sufficient to overcome the heated land-winds which enter from the west, by the great defile of the Brahmaputra.

At the commencement of the rains, the wind frequently

* Dr. J. R. Martin's Topography of Calcutta.

blows from the west, but even then, when the westerly winds may be said to have greatest power, and the influence of opposing currents from the north-east extremity of the valley is most diminished, in consequence of the disappearance of a large proportion of snow in that direction, the westerly winds extend with lessening temperature and velocity as high as Bishnath, in central Asam, beyond which they are seldom known to reach; nor is their power even there sufficient to overcome the influence of the north-east current more than for a few days at a time, during the warmest days of April and May. A strong, warm, westerly wind of any continuance, is almost certain to be followed by a cold north-east wind; and the former in coming in contact with the cool atmosphere in the vicinity of the Snowy range is itself cooled, condensed, and reflected back down the valley.

These alternations of east and west winds are usually accompanied, especially towards the afternoon, by a pretty general haze over the sky, deepening towards the horizon. The calm which intervenes between these changes, sometimes occasions a sensation of very great heat.

The sudden squalls called North-westers, usually occur during this season. They are storms of extreme violence, but of short duration, rarely coming on in the open day, or twice during the absence of the sun, but usually commencing about the time of the evening twilight. They are often preceded for a day or two by the appearance each evening of a dense bank of clouds in the northern horizon, which is occasionally illuminated with faint flashes of lightning, and is dispersed during the night. These storms rage with greatest force between the passage of the sun from the vernal equinox to the summer solstice. His vertical power then loads the air with humidity, and his action diminishing as he goes down, a dense cloud advances from the edge of the horizon. The approach of one of these storms is frequently combined with circumstances of considerable grandeur. The low sharply-defined black clouds, which occupied nearly one-half of the horizon, is towards the centre gradually raised into a gloomy arch, which rapidly extends towards the zenith, its summit resembling the overhanging crest of a gigantic breaking wave; while its lower portion is sloped downwards and forwards into a plane, inclining to the surface of the earth. When the storm is about a mile distant, a dead calm prevails; as it comes nearer, partial eddies of wind catch up the dust and leaves, and whirl them aloft, and the temperature of the atmosphere rapidly sinks. The storm continues to approach with a slow and solemn motion, till it has attained a certain altitude, when a most tremendous gush of wind bursts forth at once with sudden fury, frequently tearing up trees by the roots, and carrying away before it every light substance it can take up, and filling the whole surrounding atmosphere with obscurity. A burst of loud thunder, with flashes of vivid lightning, next succeeds, which seems to clear a passage for a torrent of the heaviest rain, that descends with wonderful impetuosity. After this commotion of the elements, which seldom exceeds half an hour in duration, has subsided, a tranquil temperate season ensues. The face of nature now shines forth with renovated beauty, the green trees being brightly relieved against the deep violet of the departing clouds; the air is cooled and refreshed, and its lower strata, by dilution, purified of the noxious vapours, which had there accumulated before this salutary convulsion.

With regard to humidity, Asam may be considered as enjoying the maximum. In fact, if the theory already adduced to account for the peculiarity of wind during the south-west monsoons be correct, it is difficult to conceive that clouds and showers should not be frequent. On two winds of different temperature and differently saturated, coming into contact, the natural result would be the formation of a cloud, or the precipitation of rain, according to the proportion of moisture contained in the warmer vapour. Add to this the profusion of extensive jheels, which may either be denominated shallow lakes, or deep morasses, so very prevalent in every part of Asam, together with the complete saturation during at least five months in the year of every inch of soil, even that which may not be actually inundated, the extensive sources of aqueous exhalations may be imagined.

The rains are of long continuance; they commence in March, and last till about the middle of October. During the months of March and April the fall is very irregular, but from May to September it is more steady, though not very severe.

The cold season is characterized by the daily presence of very heavy fogs or dense vapours, which arise for the most part from the Brahmaputra, about daylight, and continue to increase for a couple of hours, when they begin gradually to ascend. It is a peculiarity respecting these mists, that they have a tendency to occupy the south side of the valley. As they ascend from the body of the river they are drifted before the north-east wind, which, as we have already noticed, is the most prevalent in Asam; but, from the diminished heat of the valley, it now amounts only to a gentle movement. Its direction is modified, however, in a great measure, by the action of the sun's rays on the upper stratum of mist, causing a more or less powerful dissipation, and exciting a movement in the general mass towards the side on which this action is taking place.

The formation of these mists may be attributed, in part, to the moisture of the surrounding forests; but the circumstance of their making their first appearance on the river, and on such parts of it too as are shallowest and most languid in current, would lead to the more probable supposition that the temperature of the Brahmaputra being higher than that of the surrounding atmosphere, is the cause of the water giving off more vapour than the air can hold suspended in an invisible form; partial condensation then ensues, and the sensible vapour is seen curling over every portion of the river, as steam presents itself to view ascending from the surface of heated water.

Comparatively speaking, Asam enjoys a far more peculiarly temperate climate, with a greater equality of temperature, than is general throughout India. The warm weather is very moderate, and, throughout the year, the nights are cool and refreshing.

The mean annual temperature amounts to 67.2; the mean temperature of the four hottest months amounting to 80, and that of the winter to about 57.

This peculiarity in the climate may in a great measure be attributed to the early setting in, and long continuance of the rains; the former preventing the sudden transition from comparatively cool, to almost intensely hot weather, which occurs in so many parts of the plains of India; and the latter acting in a secondary degree, by preventing any great accumulation of heat. The reduced temperature may also in some measure be attributed to the great evaporation from trees. This is especially the case in the hot dry season; and during the rains the evaporation from trees can add but little to the humidity already existing in the atmosphere. It has been computed that a country covered with trees emits more vapour by one-third than one even covered with water.

Those high altitudes by which Asam is surrounded, occasion likewise a rapid abstraction of heat during the nights of the cold season, in which the waters and the air participate unequally as conductors of different powers. The former retains a higher mean temperature than the latter, and assists, during the cold season to check excessive diurnal variations. On the other hand, in the hot season, when the radiation of heat from extensive masses of sand is prevented by the freshes which cover them, and when, by the melting of the snows the volume of water, as well as the rapidity of the rivers, is increased, the water then presents a temperature much beneath that of the surrounding atmosphere, whose heat it now contributes to lessen, just as it promoted an opposite effect during the cold season.

SECTION II.—EFFECTS OF CLIMATE ON MAN.

Salubrity of the climate of Asam, compared with that of other parts of India —Influenced by certain localities—Causes of relaxing effects of the climate on the southern side of the valley—The northern side more healthy than the southern—Influence of climate on Europeans—Diseases most prevalent among them—Influence of climate on natives of Bengal and Hindosthan—Its influence on the natives of the Province—Prevailing diseases—Their causes and effects—Epidemic diseases—Endemic diseases.

The climate of Asam and its effects on the animal economy, have given rise to a diversity of opinions very contrary in their nature. Some have affirmed the climate to be equal to that of the healthiest provinces in Hindosthan or Bengal; whilst others, on the contrary, have described it as realising in its deleterious effects the reports so prevalent of its bearing a close resemblance to that of Arracan. Were the salubrity of the climate entirely dependant on the physical aspect of the country, the latter assertion might be supposed to carry great weight; but the remarks already offered will, we trust, serve to show that Asam enjoys a far more equable temperature, with fewer atmospheric vicissitudes than is general throughout India; from which circumstance it may be expected to enjoy a greater degree of salubrity, at least as far as temperature alone is concerned, unmodified by other accidents.

The remarkably varied character of the localities throughout the province, may be supposed to exercise a great influence on the general healthiness of the climate, especially with respect to their situation and position in reference to the points of the prevailing winds. This influence is more remarkable in the lower than in the upper portion of the valley, which is mainly attributable to the obstruction the wind receives from the vicinity of the great ranges of hills: for this must prevent the dispersion of the noxious exhalations engendered in the low marshy grounds, and extensive dense forests, abounding in their vicinity, and give rise to those fevers which are regarded as so dangerous and intractable.

The southern side of the upper portion of the valley, though more open to the prevailing winds, is exceedingly moist and damp; which may be attributed to the winds wafting the exhalations arising from the river and marshes in its vicinity to the adjacent hills, where they are frequently known to rest for several successive days. From the relaxing effects of this humid state of the atmosphere, elephantiasis, pulmonary complaints, and hydrocele, are not uncommon, and much more prevalent than on the northern, or even the lower portion of the same side of the valley.

From the frequent occurrence of high table lands on the northern side of the valley, with less jungle and marshy ground, that side has the advantage of a freer circulation of air, and in consequence, is not so productive of the diseases prevalent on the opposite side. Notwithstanding, fevers contracted in the neighbourhood of the jungles are frequently of a malignant nature.

The commencement and cessation of the rains are considered to be the most unhealthy periods of the year.

The influence of the climate on Europeans is not so hurtful as it has frequently been reported to be. Those whose employments do not oblige them to be much exposed to the vicissitudes of the weather, or to travel through uncultivated parts of the country, usually enjoy excellent health, provided they did so previous to their entering the country.

Delicate subjects seldom continue for any length of time in the province without complaining of a sensation of langor and debility, such as they never experienced in Upper India, where the range of the thermometer attains a much greater height; but this languid feeling is probably owing more to the extreme dampness of the climate, and the prevalence of cold north-easterly winds, than to any other cause.

The principal diseases with which Europeans are most liable to be attacked, are fevers, contracted generally in unhealthy parts of the country, or by an immoderate exposure, in seeking pleasure and amusement in the exciting sports of the field. These fevers are generally attended with considerable local congestions of the brain and stomach; but they rarely end fatally, if seen at an early stage.

The immunity from liver and bowel complaints, so characteristic in the influence of the climate of Bengal on the European constitution, may be considered as remarkable. Indeed with the exception of the fevers already mentioned, any other disease is seldom or ever seen; and when assimilated to the climate, Europeans usually enjoy very excellent health.

The above remarks are applicable likewise to the natives of Hindosthan and Bengal, who resort to this province. They in general enjoy good health; but being very liable to indulge in the dissipated habits of the natives, the diseases common to the country frequently occur among them, and prove fatal to a great degree.

The natives of Bengal do not appear to reap any beneficial effects from a change of climate after the attack of any severe disease, as the natives of Hindosthan do; who, on passing beyond the Bengal frontier in progress to their native homes, soon regain their usual strength and vigorous appearance.

European children thrive remarkably well. The disease they are chiefly liable to, is produced by worms.

No certain criterion can be formed of the influence the climate exerts on the natives of the province.

The Asamese in general, or those professing Hinduism, and more especially those in the upper classes, and those not engaged in agricultural pursuits, are for the most part a weak and puny race, extremely predisposed to diseases on the least alteration of the weather, whilst, on the contrary, the bulk of the agricultural population, the Kacharis and other inhabitants of the plains, who are not addicted to the same dissipated habits, enjoy remarkably excellent health. The diseases common to the natives may therefore be attributed more to their habits of indolence and dissipation, than to any pernicious effects of the climate.

The prevailing diseases are fevers, bowel complaints, pulmonic affections, cholera, small pox, verminous diseases, venereal and cutaneous complaints, rheumatism, enlargement of the spleen, goitres, elephantiasis of the leg, and leprosy.

Fevers are exceedingly common between the months of June and October; and a few days warm weather after a short continuance of rain, seldom fail to increase the number of cases. Fevers contracted in the stations are usually very slight; but far different are those malignant fevers contracted in the neighbourhood of the hills and the jungly parts of the country, or where the patient has been exposed to privation and fatigue, without medical assistance, at the commencement of the attack. These fevers are always attended with great prostration of strength and local congestions, especially of the head and stomach. A very large proportion of these cases prove fatal. Such as recover generally need a change of air, either to enable them to regain their strength, or to prevent an obstinate ague, in which it often terminates.

Continued fevers are of extremely rare occurrence, usually passing speedily into a intermittent type. Quotidians are the most numerous, and generally easy of cure; next to them are the tertians. Quartians, though not unfrequent, are of rarer occurrence as a primary affection; and it is astonishing the length of time patients frequently labour under them, without suffering much in outward appearance.

Agues in general yield to the usual mode of treatment; and it is no uncommon occurrence for them to be ushered in with great severity, and not to be succeeded by a second attack, or if at all, by a very mild one; whilst some of the most harassing cases commence very insidiously, and prove very obstinate.

When complicated, as in old cases, they always end with enlargement of the spleen, dropsical effusions, bowel complaints, or painful affections in the bones and joints. The cure is then tedious, and but too often hopeless, and especially so at the commencement of the cold weather, when a large proportion of such patients are carried off by dysentery.

Enlargement of the spleen, consequent on protracted agues, or the result of remittent fevers, are very common. It is, however, surprising to see the good health the patients otherwise enjoy, complaining only when the spleen becomes painful, after an occasional attack of fever.

Dysentery is the disease under which the natives of the country chiefly suffer; it carries off more victims than almost all the other diseases put together. But as an acute affection among the natives of Hindosthan and Bengal, it is not more fatal than elsewhere. Among these latter subjects, it is more likely to attack those who suffer from a broken down constitution, the sequence of protracted fevers and dissipation. When accompanied with a scorbutic diathesis it usually proves fatal, and especially so about the commencement of the cold weather.

Upon the whole, the poorer classes seem to be the greatest sufferers from dysentery. The prevalence of the disease, and the great mortality occasioned by it, may be accounted for in the deficiency of food and proper clothing, the use of putrid fish, indigestible fruits and vegetables, bad water procured from the stagnant pools in the vicinity of their dwellings, the want of the accustomed stimulus of opium, which nearly all partake of, the scantiness of clothing, which renders them peculiarly susceptible of the slightest change of the weather, sleeping on damp floors, and the too frequent practice of keeping on wet clothes. The few that rally and partially recover under such circumstances, often fall victims to relapses, brought on by their own apathy and carelessness. Those addicted to the use of opium are much more liable to the disease than those who abstain from it, and to a large portion of the former it usually proves fatal. The truth is, that in order to procure the drug, the poor people often sell every article they possess; and, were there no other cause, poverty alone, from its distressing influence on both body and mind, would render them liable to all the diseases usually arising from debility.

Dropsical effusion, either in form of anasarca, ascites, or merely a swelling of the hands and feet, is attendant on many cases of bowel complaints; when occurring, as it sometimes does, as a symptom at an advanced stage of the disease, it may in most cases be attributable to general debility. It not unfrequently follows old cases of enlarged spleen.

Pulmonic affections are not so common in the lower as in the upper provinces of Asam, where, especially in the months of February and March, cases of bronchitis and pneumonia are not uncommon.

Asthma is common in Upper Asam, where it spares neither children nor old men, but attacks all ages alike.

Catarrh is very prevalent about the end of January, and usually terminates in bronchitis, if aid be not early obtained.

Scorbutus is frequently seen among the lower classes, arising both from deficiency of nutritious food and from exposure to wet and cold. If associated with dysentery, which is too frequently the case, it proves fatal to great numbers. The natives of Hindosthan suffer greatly from this disease, which may be attributable to a want of sufficient nourishment, as they are constrained to live on rice, the use of their favourite food, *attah* (flour,) usually causing a sensation of extreme heat and indigestion, and not unfrequently bringing on diarrhœa.

The same causes that produce scurvy, render cutaneous diseases extremely common. The natives of hill origin especially are often subject to impetiginous affections, arising from gross neglect of personal cleanliness; whilst, on the other hand, Hindosthanis frequently suffer from ulcerations between the toes and on the soles of the feet, which cause considerable swelling, much pain, and constitutional derangement.

Sloughs soon form, and portions of the thick skin come away. The Asamese are not often attacked in this manner.

Sympathetic bubos in the groin and armpits are common, and if not properly attended to, often suppurate. It is difficult to account for their great frequency, as they are often met with among the young and vigorous, as well as with those bearing marks of a scrofulous habit.

Venereal complaints and gonorrhœa are prevalent at all the stations. The natives say the former disease became common soon after the Burmese invasion, and the name they give it (Maun Bipar) seems to confirm the truth of the assertion.

Obstinate rheumatism, though a rare complaint among the natives of the country, is by no means so uncommon among those of Hindosthan and Bengal.

Goitre, elephantiasis, and leprosy, are met with in many parts of the country, but not so frequently as might be expected. Except close under the hills, goitre is not very common; females however seem to be the chief sufferers from it.

Elephantiasis of the leg is seldom seen in the localities bordering on the banks of the Brahmaputra; but in the neighbourhood of the hills, in the upper portion of the valley, and especially on the southern side of it, it is extremely prevalent.

The natives of the country are very subject to an ephemeral fever, with symptoms closely resembling incipient elephantiasis; but the latter has no tendency to end in suppuration, which this disease usually has: it is consequently said to bear a greater resemblance to erysipelas phlegmonoides. The suppuration generally forms in the ancle and thigh, and but seldom in the leg; it is likewise accompanied by an inflammatory state of the lymphatics as far as the groin. These cases occur periodically.

Sporadic cases of cholera frequently occur; on an average it has hitherto appeared epidemically, every fourth year. Thus in 1825 it raged with uncommon mortality among the troops then on service; again, in 1829, many thousands of the natives were carried off by it; it re-appeared with considerable virulence in 1833, and then again in 1835, but not to so great an extent as during either of the former occasions. In 1838 it again made its appearance, proving fatal to as great an extent as it did in 1829; but fortunately its influence did not extend much beyond the precincts of Lower Asam. In 1839 this disease was very prevalent and fatal in the Muttuck country, and in all the neighbouring hills both north and south.

When this scourge visits the country, several circumstances contribute greatly to increase the mortality than would otherwise attend it. Amongst the principal of these is the fatigue and want of rest endured by the inhabitants, consequent on their assembling in numbers, and sitting up for many nights in succession, singing and clapping their hands by way of Puja to avert the calamity.

It has been remarked that epidemic cholera invariably proceeds from the west. The probable date of its arrival in Upper Asam is from four to five weeks after it has made its appearance in the frontier villages of Bengal; for it travels a hundred miles in sixteen or twenty days, spreading more rapidly on the banks of the great river and the minor streams, than towards the interior, and seldom occurring at the same time on both sides of the stream.

Many of the inhabitants show marks of the small-pox, but it never occurred as an epidemic excepting in 1832, when it raged with uncommon virulency from February to the end of July: the mortality occasioned by it throughout the country, was very considerable.

Generally of late years, the province appears to have been remarkably free from small-pox, and what has occurred has not been of a bad type.

Bhatgoti, a disease closely resembling the aphthæ anginosæ, is peculiar to the province, attacking all classes and all ages. It is generally prevalent during the commencement of the warm weather, and is produced chiefly from the abuse of milk, and too free an indulgence in putrid fish. Aphthæ appear all over the tongue, mouth, and fauces, surrounded by a morbid red inflammation, accompanied by great dyspnoea or hardness of breathing, and pain on pressure over the neck, and attended, with fever and expectoration. If not attended to early, a great prostration of the vital powers ensues, the expectoration becomes copious, mixed with pus, the fever changes into a typhoid form, delirium comes on, and the case terminates fatally.*

The natives are in the habit of using, as a remedy, the nut of the Guilandina Bonduc Lina, (called in Hindosthanee, *Kutkaranja,* in Asamese) *latguti* with a small quantity of pepper and the white of an egg. Three or four doses of this usually arrest the disease, if given in time.

Most of the diseases common to the country however are found to be modifications of the diseases prevalent in Bengal and Hindusthan.†

* A very smiliar disease is often extremely fatal to the cattle of the province, and in 1838-39 vast numbers of cows and bullocks perished from it. At the commencement of the rains, cattle are likewise very subject to sores between the hoofs, which if not properly attended to, end in ulcers and mortification.

† For further particulars, the author begs to refer the medical reader to "Leslie's account of the diseases of Gowhatti," "McLeod's medical topography of Bishnath," and "McCosh's topography of Asam," to which, as well as to the very kind assistance of the medical officers at Gowhatti, he is entirely indebted for the above article.

CHAPTER III.

NATURAL GEOGRAPHY.

SECTION I.—GEOLOGY.

Scarcity of materials—Northern and Southern mountains—Granite—Limestone—Coal—Petroleum—Oil-springs—Mineral and Hot springs—Brine springs—Metals—Iron—Copper—Silver—Gold—Organic remains—Volcanic phenomena—Earthquakes.

Little in detail is known of the Geology of Asam. Were it not from the circumstance of the mountains on the two opposite sides being composed of two very distinct systems, to a mere superficial observer Asam might present itself as an instance of a great valley of denudation. The mountains on the northern side of the valley are, generally speaking, composed of primitive limestone, granite, serpentine, porphyry, and talcose slates; while tertiary sandstones, shell-limestone, and coal, compose the southern group, in conjunction too, with metamorphosed gneiss, greenstone, and syenite.

The rock formations of the scattered clump of hills in Lower Asam are supposed to be uniformly granitic, and chiefly of that variety called gneiss, or stratified granite. The rocks are generally much broken, and seem as though they had suffered from the convulsions of earthquakes or other natural disturbances: but if this were occasioned by the passage of basaltic or other volcanic veins, of which there are traces both in the valley itself and in the bordering mountain ranges of the Khassia country, no such veins or dykes have yet been brought to light.

There is nothing remarkable in the granitic rocks of Asam. The granite is commonly large grained, and frequently contains beds or veins of quartz, together with metamorphosed gneiss. Except the granite and gneiss, there are few varieties of other granitic formations, and if any occur, they are in insulated masses, and not in any extensive formations.

These granitic formations do not contain any metallic beds, nor any minerals of value; and it is not known that they are at present converted to any useful purpose. A small quantity of *Kurum* (Carandam) is procured from some parts of the rocks, by a few petty traders among the Düms, and exported to Bengal. Many parts of the rocks have heretofore yielded handsome and very durable building stones, as may be seen in the frequent remains of ancient edifices about Gowhatti and Tezpore, the carvings and facings of which are still apparently as sharp and distinct as when first executed, notwithstanding the violence with which it is evident the temples they once belonged to have been overthrown, and their subsequent exposure for generations to the ravages of the elements.

Proceeding up the course of the Brahmaputra from Nagarbera to Bishnath, and along the Koliabar hills, the rocks are chiefly of these formations; the only exception known in the plain of the Brahmaputra, is a bed of tufaceous limestone on the banks of the Jai Bareli in Chardwar. The mere circumstance of its existence is, however, all that is at present known. As to its extent, and its situation with regard to the other neighbouring rocks, we have at present no information besides the above. Secondary formations are likewise met with along the line of the Kossilei and Jamuna rivers, containing a shell limestone, very similar in appearance to that of Laour and Chirra, and, as at these places also, accompanied by carboniferous measures, which are known to crop out in several places.

The Mishmi hills, through which the Brahmaputra enters the valley, are also known to abound in limestone rocks, large boulders of which are annually brought down by the floods, and in such quantities as to form a supply equal to all the domestic purposes for which this mineral is required in Upper Asam. These boulders are deposited in a shallow part of the Brahmaputra near Sudiya, a little above its junction with the main trunk, and are so situated as to form a dangerous rapid in the stream. They in general bear a great resemblance to the mottled marbles of China, though some are more of a white crystallized form, and it would appear very well adapted for common statuary purposes.

The coal beds of Asam are of very great extent, and the mineral is itself likely to lead to important results in the future advancement of the country. All along the southern sides of the valley, lie a series of carboniferous formations, unequalled in extent by any yet discovered in India, and, as there is every reason to believe, containing beds of coal of a very superior quality.

In tracing its appearance from the most easterly or remote site of Upper Asam, the first to notice is the coal found on the Noa-Dihing, and its affluent the Dupha Pani, in the hilly country to the south and east of the Bramàkhund. The site of this bed is too remote for it to be of any practical benefit under existing circumstances, as it is beyond the reach of being profitably worked, and introduced to the navigable part of the Brahmaputra.

The next vein of coal to be noticed, is that discovered on the bed of the Manirup river, a small stream that empties itself into the Buri-Dihing. This coal is considerably free from earthy or slaty matter, and exhibits frequently ligneous fibre; though, like the last, it is in too remote a situation to be easily available for useful purposes.

At Boorhat, beds of coal occur in two situations; the first lies close to the channel of the Daising, about a mile from the village of Boorhat. The second bed is about a quarter of a mile distant from that river, at an elevation of about sixty feet. The coal in both these beds appears to be of superior quality, and nothing could well be more favourable than the position for working, nor for the transport of the coal as far as the waters of the Daising admit; for this stream, though barely navigable for laden canoes in the dry weather, in the rains has a depth sufficient for the navigation of large boats, and its stream is no where impetuous.

Another coal bed has been found near Jaipur, about twelve miles to the north-east of Boorhat, and within three miles of the Buri-Dihing, also an excellent river.

The next coal bed that follows in the order proposed, is that situated on the Saffrai, a small tributary of the Daising Nuddi. There is a small range of hills here, which offers some impediment to the easy transmission of the coal. Inferior coals are also known to exist crossing the bed of the stream in different situations; so that, if these last beds should be found to afford good coal, the difficulties would be considerably less in reaching it there, than in the higher situation.

Pieces of coal, of good quality, have been found in the bed of the Nambua, a small stream emptying itself into the Dhansiri, but no correct information has been afforded as to the position of the beds.

The next bed to be noticed is situated at the foot of a small hill, on the east side of a little nullah that runs from the north into the Jumuna river, about three-quarters of a mile above the falls of the latter; the distance of the coal from the Jumuna itself not being more than a hundred yards. The coal here occurs under more favourable circumstances for transmission, than characterize any of the above mentioned localities, the Jamuna being at all times navigable by the common canoes of the country.

The last, and most eastern of the coal beds hitherto discovered, is situated on the Kossilei river, within sixty miles of

Gowhatti. The circumstance of its existence at this most desirable point is all that is at present known.

From the circumstance of a coal field existing in the first mentioned locality, and the re-appearance of the mineral at Namrup, and thence continued to the other southern localities, it seems highly probable that a very extensive coal formation, or series of coal fields, extends from the remote Singpho hills east, along the Naga hills south, to the hills of Kachar, and thence, as there is reason to suppose, crossing somewhere the Jointiah country, and finally connecting itself with the well known coal formation at Chirra, and the lime and coal of Pandua and Laour, in Silhet.

Detached specimens of various kinds of coal have also been found in the Jillundi, Belsiri, and Buruli rivers, that fall into the Brahmaputra from the Bütan mountains, between the 92nd and 93rd degrees of east longitude, at various distances, from fourteen to twenty miles, from their confluence with the main river, and not far from the foot of the mountains. The existence of coal at this situation, connected with the fact of its having been discovered in a similar way by the late Mr. Scott, on the banks of the Tista river, at the foot of the Sikim mountains, three degrees less to the eastward, tends to encourage the hope of finding coal in the lower ranges of the same chain, in some situation in which it may be more available for useful purposes.

These discoveries of coal on the north bank of the Brahmaputra, and over a tract of country fifty miles in length, appear to add greatly to the importance of previous discoveries of coal on the south bank of the river; for it may be presumed that we have by no means obtained a knowledge of the full extent of the coal beds in Asam, and that it is not improbable that they are co-extensive on both sides of the valley, and will be found nearly throughout its whole extent.

Throughout Asam, the coal is generally speaking of a tolerably fair quality, nor is there much variation in the quantity of carbon ascertained to exist in the productions of the several localities. Upon the whole, its mean specific gravity is about 1.288 containing—

Mean volatile and other matter, ...	45.4
Carbon, ...	50.4
Ash, ...	4.2
	100

In the vicinity of some of the above mentioned coal fields, springs, or wells of petroleum, are not of rare occurrence. Oil-springs have likewise been found, but these are of small extent.

The district of Nowgong contains several mineral and hot springs, the waters of which are generally brackish, though those of a few savour of sulphurated hydrogen.

These springs do not appear to have attracted any particular notice, or that degree of veneration from the inhabitants of Asam and of the neighbourhood, as such springs have commonly done in Hindusthan; nor are they at all celebrated for any medicinal properties. Nothing is known of the immediate rocks from which these springs take their rise, though lime and traces of coal, together with an aluminous slate, imbedding large masses of iron pyrites, have occasionally been met with in their vicinity.

Brine-springs are not unfrequent in the low ranges of the Naga hills. In the neighbourhood of Boorhat, Nagahat, and Jaipur, about twenty of these wells are wrought alternately by the Nagas and Asamese, between whom the produce is equally shared. The springs afford a very fair quantity of salt.

The springs most generally known are those of Boorhat and Sudiya. The revenue derived from the latter amounted in 1809 to about 40,000 rupees per annum; and the salt obtained from the springs was said to be purer, and more highly prized, than that imported from Bengal, and which at one time amounted to no less a quantity than 1,00,000 maunds.

The manufacture is commenced in November, and continued till March or April. Being situated in a valley, the wells are subject to inundation during the rains. The process of manufacture is carried on by filling the joints of large bamboos with the water of the wells, and then placing them over a flue to which a fire is applied; the brine in the bamboos is thus evaporated, and dry salt remains. The bamboos are stripped of their woody covering, and only a thin scale of the inner wood is retained; and this being kept damp from the percolation of the brine, is not affected by the heat until the salt is nearly dry, when it is removed. One joint can thus be used over the fire three or four times. From the heavy taxes levied on the manufacture of this salt, as well as from the exceedingly slow and wasteful process of procuring it, it is considered by no means less expensive than the salt imported from Bengal.

In the above localities there are also frequent beds of clay iron-ore, which were at one time evidently worked to a great extent, as appears from the scoria of the furnaces being still found in many parts along the low hills at the foot of the mountain ranges, more especially in the vicinity of Jaipoor and Boorhat, and along the banks of the Suffrai Naddi, at which latter place the Nagas, even at present, occasionally engage in its manufacture.

The only iron-works of any extent now carried on in Asam, are those near Dirgong and Kacharihat; and even these have of late been all but abandoned, owing to injudicious taxes levied on the ore by Raja Purandar Sing, as well as from the inability of the metal to contend with the low priced iron of England, even at this distance from the seat of its manufacture; attributable no doubt to the imperfect and laborious process by which the natives attempt to reduce the ore.

The iron is principally obtained from a ferruginous clay, which after being cleared of a portion of its earthy constituents by washing, is afterwards melted in small clay furnaces.

The Khassia iron, a large quantity of which is annually imported into the country, contributes likewise in no small degree to drive the iron of Asam from its own markets. The Khassias being subject to no taxes, do not in consequence labour under the same disadvantages as the Asamese workmen do; and being more energetic labourers, and possessing furnaces of a far better construction, and more suited to the purpose, they are the better able, by a more economical process, to reduce their ore.

The best iron is found in the Bor-Kangti country, and is there manufactured to great perfection by a wild, barbarous tribe, called Kunungs. The agricultural implements made by that tribe are valued very highly, and are of a superior metal to that commonly produced in Asam.

Neither copper nor silver have as yet been found native in Asam. A small quantity of the former is brought down occasionally by the Abors, a savage and troublesome people, whose visits to the plains are not much encouraged. There is at present no more than one silver mine known to exist amongst the adjacent mountain tribes, in the country of the Bor-Kangtis. This mine is said to produce about eighty thousand rupees a year. The silver formerly used in Asam was in a great measure imported from China in a state of bullion, and was the only article of circulation in the trade between the Asamese and Chinese.

In noticing the metallic produce of Asam, the gold dust of its rivers ought not to be overlooked. Although not connected with any definite sites within the valley, there is scarcely a river throughout its whole extent that does not yield more or less of this precious metal, which seems to be washed down by heavy torrents from the neighbouring hills; the richer deposits being invariably found in the upper courses of the streams, and fresh supplies renewed at every monsoon. It is questionable whether the metal exists in veins in any of the bordering hills; but from what has been ascertained of the production of gold in other countries, it is here likewise very probably disseminated in minute quantities in the clays and disintegrated rocks of the mountains, from which the rains of each successive year gather new supplies to replenish the exhausted sands.

The best gold is said to be found in the most winding streams, having the strongest currents: of these the most noted are the Boroli, the Subaushiri, the Disni, and the Joglo. The two latter contain the purest and best gold; and, in the Joglo, it is said that this precious metal is found in large grains, about the third of an inch in size. The colour of the gold, also, in both the last named rivers is of a deep yellow, and was so much prized, that it is said the jewels of the royal family were invariably made up from what was collected in them.

The most favourable time to wash for gold, is said to be after a rise of the waters in the river, and the most preferable spots are where the beds of the rivers are composed of small rounded pebbles, consisting of quartz and sandstone, with a considerable mixture of sand; and likewise in such spots where, from natural causes, there are extensive deposits of these.

The gold-washers, or sonwals, after selecting a favourable site for their operations, begin the process by passing the sand through a sieve in order to free it from lumps of clay, stones, and other refuse. It is then collected in a wooden trough, with an inclined plane, and having a narrow outlet at one extremity. Water is then thrown over the sand, the coarse and dirty particles of which are thus in a great measure carried off, and the gold, from its gravity, with a considerable mixture of fine sand, lodges in the transverse groves of the trough. To this residue a proportionate quantity of quicksilver is added, and while the gold is uniting with it, water is poured over the sand to keep it in motion. The gold soon adheres to the quicksilver, and forms a little mass at the bottom of the trough; this ball is then put into a shell, and placed over a charcoal fire, by which means the quicksilver is evaporated, and the shell forms into lime: the whole is then thrown into a pot of water, and the pure gold sinks to the bottom.

In closing this meagre sketch of the geology of Asam, it may be proper to notice, that, with the exception of the limestone shells above alluded to, and a quantity of vegetable petrifactions in the neighbourhood of the coal, no organic remains have hitherto been met with. The absence of volcanic dykes has already been remarked; but, as connected with volcanic sources, the frequency and severity of earthquakes may here be noticed. Few months pass over without one or more shocks being experienced; which, owing to the circumstance of their proceeding from north to south, have been supposed to originate in still active volcanoes in Upper Tartary. These earthquakes are commonly preceded by close, calm, and sultry weather, a phenomenon which though commonly remarked in connection with earthquakes in general, would nevertheless rather militate against the supposed distant source of the volcanic shock. Cut off as Asam is from Tartary by the immense intervening and unbroken primary formations of the Himalaya range, it is natural to suppose that the great depth of its foundations would stop all communication by the surface of the earth, and its vast ridge of perpetual snow might likewise, it would be imagined, prevent any atmospheric changes originating at the seat of the volcanic shocks being felt in this deep seated valley.

The sultriness of the atmosphere which so constantly, if not invariably, precedes these rumblings of the earth, as well as the consequent precipitation of rain, might therefore seem to point to some local electric phenomena as their cause, rather than to distant volcanoes. Voltaic electricity it is well known may be elicited by the force of chemical action, as well during the production and condensation of vapour, as from other causes. This electric matter being accumulated in one part of the earth's surface, and on account of the dryness of the season not able easily to diffuse itself, would naturally force its way into the higher regions of the air. The whole surface thus unloaded, would receive a concussion like any other conducting substance, on parting with, or receiving, a quantity of the electric fluid. The rushing noise would likewise sweep over the whole extent of the country, and the fluid in its discharge from the country would likewise naturally follow the course of the rivers, and also take advantage of any eminences to facilitate its ascent into the air; and on its coming in contact with the vapours which float in the atmosphere, the consequence would be the formation of clouds, and the occasion of a sudden shower.

These fancies, however, lead to nothing satisfactory. But where can we seek for the cause or causes of earthquakes? The subject is entirely hypothetical, and we have no means of reaching the seat of these remarkable phenomena.

Certain, however, it is, that these irruptions of the earth have frequently been attended with very alarming consequences; yet strange to say, so readily are such visitations forgotten—for, they are deemed of so little consequence—that whilst the native historians enter into very minute particulars respecting their political history, and are extremely careful in tracing the chronological list of their kings, it is rarely we meet with any allusions to these great natural commotions; we have however found a short account of an earthquake that occurred in 1607, which especially as it was attended with peculiar effects, may here be worth our notice. A number of hills are described as having been variously rent asunder, leaving wide and open chasms; whilst a few others entirely disappeared. The earth is also said to have opened in several places in the plains, throwing up water and mud; and tracts of ground in other parts suddenly sunk, causing the loss of a number of lives.

To similar instances of paroxysmal violence, may probably be attributed many of the changes apparent in the physical features of the country; but whether the changes have been effected by these convulsions alone, or by a slow and gradual perpetuation of elevatory movements, remains for the present uncertain. When the country shall have been further explored by geologists, we may, however, expect to arrive at more exact conclusions.

SECTION II.—BOTANY.

General observations—Timber trees—Bamboos—Canes—Palms—Trees producing gums, varnishes, &c.—Trees used for dyeing and tanning—Plants cultivated for the manufacture of thread or cordage—Trees employed for rearing the silk worm—Trees on which the lac insect feeds—Plants used for chewing and smoking—Plants cultivated for their saccharine juice—Medicinal plants—Flower plants—Parasites—Ferns—Fruit trees—Esculent vegetables—Plants cultivated for their grain—Culmiferous plants—Leguminous grains—Oily seeds.

Asam exhibits over the greater portion of its surface a vegetation very similar to that generally found in Bengal and the adjacent provinces. Instances of irregularity no doubt occur; and those plants which flourish under certain elevations may be expected to straggle down towards, or even to reach, the base of the boundary hills. Almost all valleys, from their configuration, enjoy certain circumstances that admit of such a distribution; and in Asam they are highly favourable, so that a few northern or elevational forms have not unfrequently been found scattered amongst the Flora of Asam. A variety of new species also occur, which have hitherto been unknown to European botanists, and further researches may probably tend to increase their number.

But it does not lie within our province to enter into any lengthened description of the botany of Asam, which, were we even capable of the task, would be an undertaking far beyond the scope of so brief a sketch of the country.

The forests of Asam are upon an extensive scale, but little comparatively speaking has yet been ascertained of the species of trees they contain.

Among those yielding the most valuable and useful *timbers*, are the Gmelina arborea, Roxb., called by the Asamese *Gomári*, and in Bengal *Gumba*. The wood of this tree is used for a variety of economical purposes by the natives, and very much resembles teak. The colour is perhaps a shade or two lighter, and the grain somewhat closer; at the same time that it is fully as light, if not lighter, and may be as easily worked. It bears the effects of weather better than almost any other timber, without shrinking or warping; it derives no injurious effects from being kept in water, and is not readily attacked by insects. The most durable canoes of the country are constructed of this timber, and probably its value may be greatly enhanced should it ever be used for the knees, curved timbers, bottoms, and upper works of vessels, for which purposes it seems admirably adapted. It is used for turnery ware of all kinds; and cylinders of a proper size constructed of it, admit of being turned very thin for drums, and other musical instruments.

Another large and elegant timber indigenous to the forests of Asam, is the Cedrela Toona, Roxb., (Asam, *Pomá*.) It grows to a great size and height, having numerous branches which form a large, beautiful, and shady head. The wood is rather extensively used, being much esteemed for furniture and other purposes. It is a close, hard, but rather brittle wood, of a brown-red colour, and in some respects resembles mahogany, but is lighter, and consequently not so close grained. "The bark is a powerful astringent, and may be used as a tolerably good substitute for Peruvian bark, in the cure of remitting and intermitting fevers."

Artocarpus Chaplasha, Roxb. (Asam, *Chámá* or *Sám*) grows to be a tree of the first magnitude. The trunk is straight, and of an immense size. The wood is serviceable for various purposes, and is reckoned superior to almost every other sort, particularly when employed under water. It is used to a great extent for canoes, for which it is well fitted, being both very buoyant and durable. The tree is found in flower about the months of March and April. When the first flowers appear the tree is destitute of leaves, but these make their appearance before the fruit is formed. The fruits resemble very much what is commonly known by the name of the bread-fruit, Artocarpus incisus, Linn., but is much smaller, and only a little larger in size than a common orange.

The Jak tree (Asam, *Kathál*), Artocarpus integrifolius, Linn. is very common, and is much cultivated in gardens and about villages. It does not in general attain to any great height, but may always be distinguished by its large, ramous, dense, shady head,—more particularly so when it stands detached from other trees. The trunk is short and thick, and the wood in the fineness of its grain resembles mahogany, but is of a pale yellowish texture. It is much used for furniture, and the beams and posts of houses.

There are two species of Lagerstoëmia, and both afford excellent timber. The wood of L. parviflora, Roxb., is close grained, hard, and tough; and makes excellent building timber. L. Reginæ, Roxb., is a larger tree, and is occasionally used for boat building, but the wood is soft, and deficient in toughness. This species is also very common in Bengal; and at Rangoon the timber is used to make knees for ships. When in blossom, its numerous large purple flowers render it very conspicuous.

There are three species of Dillenia.

D. pilosa, Roxb., is a majestic timber tree; the trunk is from six to seven feet in circumference, the wood open, but tough and hard. It is much used for canoes.

D. pentagyna, Roxb., is also a large timber tree. The wood is closer, but in other respects is very like the preceding.

D. speciosa, Thunb., or D. Indica of Linnæus, (Asam, *Aotenga*) is an elegant tree, and when in flower has a beautiful appearance. The trunk is particularly straight, but of no great height, and is about the same thickness as the preceding. The wood is close and hard, but rather brittle. The fleshy leaflets of the calyx, when the fruit is full grown, have an agreeably acid taste, and are much used by the natives in their curries. They likewise make a tolerably pleasant jelly.

Of Jambosa there are two species; the *Jám* which grows to a great size, the trunk being generally from six to eight feet in circumference; it is not much esteemed: and the *Sáljám*, the trunk of which seldom exceeds three cubits in girth. It produces a close, hard, tough wood, used for posts, beams, and planks.

There are two species of Bauhinia, called by the natives *Takra* and *Bakri*. The former affords a close grained, soft, tough wood, of a yellowish colour; the latter, an open grained wood used for furniture.

Callicarpa arborea, Roxb., is a stout, tall tree, the trunk frequently measuring six or seven feet in circumference; the wood is hard, and is used for mortars, pestles, and common furniture. The flowers are small and very numerous, of a lively purple or lilac colour, presenting a very pretty appearance, though possessing rather an offensive smell.

Careya arborea, Roxb., is a tree of immense size. The wood is close, hard, tough, and strong, and well adapted for the stocks of match-locks; for which purpose it is occasionally used.

Chrysophyllum acuminatum, Roxb., (Asam, *Pitakar*,) a middling sized tree. The trunk is about three cubits in girth, the wood is white and tough, and used for common furniture. The fruit ripens in October, and is greedily eaten by the natives. The pulp is almost insipid, and, though tolerably firm, is commonly clammy, adhering to the lips or knife with great tenacity.

Cassia Fistula, Linn., (Asam, *Sonálu*): this tree is uncommonly beautiful when in flower, few surpassing it in the elegance of its numerous long pendulous racemes of large bright yellow flowers, intermixed with the young lively green foliage. The trunk is short and thick, and the wood open, hard, tough, and much used for ploughs. The bark is employed to a considerable extent by tanners; and the leaves are used by the natives as a *ság* (vegetable), and answer the purposes of a mild cathartic.

Croton oblongifolius, Roxb., (Asam, *Parokupi*): a small tree, affording a close grained but rather brittle wood, used for coarse furniture.

Butea frondosa, Roxb., is a small tree very common in Asam, but particularly so on the adjacent mountains. The wood is open, soft, and tough, but not strong, and is but very little used except for coarse furniture. The flowers are large and pendulous, their ground colour is a beautiful deep red, shaded with orange and silver-coloured down, which gives them a most elegant appearance. "From natural fissures and wounds made in the bark of this tree during the hot season, there issues a most beautiful red juice, which soon hardens into a ruby-coloured, brittle, astringent gum, but it soon loses its beautiful colour if exposed to the air.

"This gum held in the flame of a candle, swells and burns away slowly without smell, or the least flame, into a coal, and then into fine light white ashes. Held in the mouth it soon dissolves; its taste is strongly, but simply astringent. Heat does not soften it, but rather renders it more brittle. Pure water dissolves it perfectly, and the solution is of a deep clear red colour. It is in a great measure soluble in spirits, but this solution is paler and a little turbid; the watery solution also becomes turbid when spirit is added, and the alcoholic more clear by the addition of water; diluted vitriolic acid renders both solutions turbid and caustic; vegetable alkali changes the colour of the watery solution to a clean, deep, fiery, blood red; *sal-martis* changes it into a good durable ink.

"Infusions of the flowers, either fresh or dried, dye cotton cloth, previously impregnated with a solution of alum, or alum and tartar, of a most beautiful bright yellow, more or less deep, according to the strength of the infusion. A little alkali added to the infusion, changes it to a deep reddish orange. It then dyes unprepared cotton cloth of the same colour, which the least acid changes to a yellow or lemon. These beautiful colours, however, are not permanent.

"The juice of the fresh flowers, if diluted with alum water and rendered perfectly clear by depuration, then evaporated by the heat of the sun into a soft extract, produces a brighter water colour than any gamboge, and retains its bright colour for a length of time.

"Infusions of the dried flowers yield an extract very little, if any thing inferior to this last mentioned. They yield also a very fine durable yellow lake, and all these in a large proportion.

"The lac insects are frequently found on the small branches and the petioles of the leaves of this tree. Query, whether does the natural juice of its bark contribute to improve the colour of their red nidus, or colouring matter? It would require a set of experiments accurately made on specimens of lac gathered from the various trees it is found on, at the same time, and as near as possible from the same place, to determine this point."*

The natives of Asam make little or no use either of the gum or the flowers of this tree, although they promise fair to be very valuable; the former as a medicine, and the latter as a pigment and dyeing wood.

Terminalia presents three species :—

T. Belerica, Roxb., Corom. pl. 2. n. 198, (Asam, *Bauri*,) grows to be a very large tree, with an erect trunk and a large spreading head. The wood is white, rather soft and durable, but seldom used.

* Vide Roxburgh's Flora Indica, vol. iii. page 244.

From wounds in the bark, large quantities of an insipid gum issue, which much resembles gum arabic, is perfectly soluble in water, and burns away in the flame of a candle, with little smell, into black gritty ashes.

The fruit is used both in medicine and by dyers; and both the bark and fruit are used by tanners.

Unfortunately when in flower the tree emits a most abominable stench.

T. Citrina, Roxb., (Asam, *Hilkha*,) is a very large and tall timber tree, by no means uncommon in the extensive forests of Asam. The trunk is straight, and of a very great size. The wood is much like mahogany, but somewhat finer grained. It is very hard, and said to be free from attacks of insects. The fruit of this tree is occasionally employed as a gentle cathartic.

T. Catappa, Linn., is inferior in size to the two former. The wood is both light and durable, and is used for various economical purposes.

Andrachne trifoliata, Roxb., (Asam, *Ooriam*) : this is a large tree, of quick growth. The trunk is erect, and covered with a smooth olive-coloured bark. The wood is of a dark red when the tree is old, and is preferred to most timbers for posts to houses, and similar purposes.

There are three species of Castanea.

C. Indica, Roxb., is a species of chesnut. The trunk is tolerably straight, about five cubits in circumference, and growing to such a size, as to admit of the wood, which is of a good quality, being used for various purposes. The nuts are oval, of a pretty hard, ligneous texture, and light brown colour, somewhat hairy, particularly round the apex. The kernels are eaten by the natives, and may be compared to indifferent filberts.

The second species, called by the Asamese *Golsinggar*, yields an excellent timber, the wood being close, hard, and tough.

The wood of the third, (Asam, *Kangta Hingoree*) is inferior both in strength and toughness to the preceding.

There are two species of oak (Quercus) indigenous to the forests of Asam, and one grows to be a large and useful timber tree. The wood is light coloured, like the English oak, but harder; and the acorns are entirely covered by an unarmed cup formed of concentric rings.

The other species appears identical with the Quercus lamellata of Roxburgh.

Ehretia serrata, Roxb., (Asam, *Nalshima.*) The wood of this tree is soft and open grained, but rather tough. It yields planks from twelve to eighteen inches wide, but they are not very durable. It is used for posts and other common purposes.

Mallea Rothü, A. Juss., Ekebergia Indica, Roxb., (Asam, *Jiyakohi.*) The wood of this tree is very durable, and much esteemed. The tree delights chiefly in low sloping lands, about the bottom of mountains, where it attains a tolerably good size.

Bridelia, Willdenow, presents one species (B. stipulans?) (Asam, *Kohi*). It is a large timber tree, and affords a close, hard, tough wood, used for chests, stools, and the like.

Icica Indica W. & A., (Asam, *Niyor*), produces a hard, close grained, rather brittle wood, having a resinous scent. This wood is highly esteemed by the natives for furniture.

Shorea robusta, Roxb., (Asam, *Hál,*) is an immense timber tree in the Rungpore forests, but here does not appear to attain any great magnitude. The wood is strong and durable, and is much esteemed for building, and various other economical purposes.

Eugenia Jambolana, Lam., or Syzygium Jambolana, Dek. (Asam, *Kola jám*) grows to be a large tree, and is very common both in its wild and cultivated state. The wood it affords is hard, close grained, and durable; it is used for various purposes. When ripe the fruits are universally eaten; they are of a subacid, astringent taste.

The bark is strongly astringent, and yields an excellent brown dye, partaking of various shades, according to the corrosive employed, or the strength of the decoction. It is also used by tanners.

Eugenia Paniala, Roxb. This is perhaps one of the largest and most robust trees of this very noble genus. Like the former species, it furnishes the natives with a large sized timber, adapted for a variety of purposes.

Tamarindus Indica, Linn. (Asam, *Teteli*). This magnificent tree is common throughout India, and the fruit so generally known as to need no description. Besides producing a fruit which is much used by the natives as an acid in seasoning their food, its timber is excellent for many purposes, and makes good durable furniture. As it is both hard and strong, it is commonly employed for making oil and sugar mills.

Uvaria suberosa, Roxb., (Asam, *Bándor kolá*; Bengal, *Buráchali*) is a small tree, affording a close grained, soft, brittle wood. It is used for posts, beams, and planks.

There are three species of Vitex, Linn.

Vitex Leucoxylon, Linn. (Asam, *Bhodiyá*). This tree will grow on land that is inundated for weeks together. Its flowers are rather large and fragrant, of a whitish straw colour, with the centre of the lower lip densely covered with violet coloured hairs. The wood is chiefly used for making ploughs.

Vitex Acuminata? The trunk is about five feet in circumference, and the wood is very close, hard, and brittle. It is used for the mortars of oil mills, &c.

Vitex Babula? (Asam, *Bubla*) grows to about the same size as the preceding. The wood is close grained, soft, and tough. It is occasionally used for coarse furniture, but is in very little estimation.

Vernonia? (Asam, *Major*). This is the only one of the numerous tribe of corymbiferous plants that grows to be a timber tree. The wood is used for coarse furniture.

Nauclea Cadamba, Roxb., (Asam, *Kadam*) is a noble tree, very common about villages, and is not only highly ornamental, but likewise very useful from the extensive close shade it yields. The wood is of a yellowish tinge, and is used for coarse furniture.

Bombax Malabaricum, Dek., (Asam, *Himolu*). This may justly be ranked amongst the trees of the first class. It grows to a great size, being often found from eighty to a hundred feet high, with a trunk thick and ramous in proportion. When in flower it is one of the most gaudy ornaments of the forests or village, for it is every where common. The wood is considered valuable, and is much employed by the natives for various useful purposes. Canoes made of it, do not last above a year or two.

Sterculia urens, Roxb., (Asam, *Odál*) is a large tree found chiefly among the mountainous parts. The trunk is very straight, with a large and shady head. The wood is soft, and somewhat spongy. Canoes are occasionally made of it. The bark is of a light colour, and very smooth; its outer coat is thin, transparent, covered with a farinaceous substance, and peels off like the exterior pellicle of the birch bark; inwardly it is fibrous and netted. A strong coarse rope is made from the bark, which is used in taking wild elephants, and as cables for rafts of timbers and boats.

The *Gandserai* of Asam, Dr. Wallich supposes to be nearly identical with his "Laurus," now "Camphora glandulifera," Nees., and nearly allied to the Chinese Laurus camphorifera, now known as Camphora officinarum, Bauhin.

From the root of this tree, Professor O'Shaughnessy has extracted an oil by distillation, in all respects similar to the oil of sassapas.

Next in importance to the timber trees, and in this province by far the most useful woody plant, is the *bamboo*. It is the principal, and in most instances the only material of which the houses of the natives are composed. Their furniture, their implements of agriculture, and in fact every article used by them, is entirely, or in part, made from this valuable reed, and not unfrequently is it introduced as an article of food. In this very useful plant, nature seems to have been by no means sparing. It is found on the outskirts of their villages; it encircles the basis of most of the hills; and groves after groves of it are seen in rich luxuriance in all the plains.

It grows from a creeping root, which extending from twelve to twenty feet in diameter, sends up numerous stems, amounting from ten to sometimes a hundred. These rise pretty erect to the height of about eighteen or twenty feet, when their innumerable spreading branches bending gently down, remind one of Moore's date trees—

> ...." Bending,
> Languidly their leaf crown'd heads,
> Like youthful maids, when sleep descending,
> Warns them to their silken beds."

From ten to fifteen bamboos from a clump are cut down annually, while young ones speedily shoot up from the roots to supply their places. The stem perishes whenever it produces seed.

In Asam it is no uncommon thing to see these plants in blossom, but then they are mostly of a considerable age. The period of flowering of the different kinds of bamboos appears to be very various and uncertain. The thin wooded bamboos of the hills appear to flower as the grasses yearly, but the large thick wooded bamboos only flower at long intervals; and with the natives their flowering is considered as a sure sign of a scarcity, as probably the dryness of the season affects their period of producing seed. When in flower the whole plant is destitute of leaves, and forms one immensely, oblong, waving panicle, composed of numerous supra-decompound ramifications. In times of scarcity the seed is boiled, and forms a tolerably good substitute for rice. The young and tender shoots of the plant are also very commonly used by the natives as an ingredient in their curries, and are considered a very good vegetable.

The natives have several specific names for the different varieties of this plant, which in most cases they apply with little or no accuracy.

The most valuable kind, is what is commonly called *Janti bánh*. It grows to a very good size, and is the sort most generally used for posts, beams, and other purposes, where strength is a greater desideratum than dimension.

The next species is *Bháluká bánh*. It is very much esteemed both on account of its size, and strength, and for these reasons is frequently used for the posts of houses. To make it the more serviceable, long immersion in water is requisite, which renders it firmer, and is the means of protecting it from the attacks of those destructive little insects called *Bostrechi* and their larvæ.

There are two varieties of this species, differing considerably in size; the smaller one is called *bháluká* and the larger *makal*.

The *Kátáh bánh*, or thorny bamboo, is a very elegant middling sized species. The joints are from six to twelve inches asunder, armed with strong sharp spines. It grows very straight, and its branches are beautifully feathered, so that it has a very different appearance from the others. It has a much smaller cavity than most other varieties, and some stems are not unfrequently found perfectly solid. It is on that account particularly strong, and well adapted for a variety of purposes. It is occasionally used for the shafts of javelins, or spears.

Bazal bánh. This differs from the other varieties in the length of its joints. Soon after the first rains set in, it sends out new shoots, and as in all the other species, these appear at first in the form of long straight elephant's tusks, invested in strong coriaceous sheaths, one at each joint; these shoots rise simple to their full size, from twenty to seventy feet in height, and from six to twelve inches in circumference, and this in the course of a few weeks; during which period the sheaths drop off, and are soon succeeded by numerous alternate, ramous, and unarmed branches, which shoot out of the joints, but before they make their appearance, the shoots look like so many naked fishing rods of immense size.

Deon bánh. This is a wild, but by no means common species. It is found chiefly on the mountainous regions to the north of Asam, and particularly in those mountains inhabited by the Abors. It grows to no great height. It is much used by this wild tribe for the barbs of their arrows, and for making reeds for their pipes, and other purposes.

Tadlu bánh. This is a common species, and one of the most variously useful. It grows to a tolerably good size, but is not so large a bamboo as most others. The joints are short and thick, which renders it very strong and durable. The roots make very handsome walking sticks.

Bejali bánh. This is very clearly a distinct species from the preceding ones. It is by no means so large, is by far straight, and has a much smaller cavity. Its great strength, solidity, and straightness, render it very generally esteemed. It is used by the natives for cudgels, and is well adapted for the shafts of spears.

The *Nal bánh* is a small species, delighting chiefly in those low marshy situations, so common about the basis of the hills. It is a very thin bamboo, and has proportionately a very large cavity. It is used by basket makers, and when split and well worked together, makes very excellent mats.

Tshágoli bánh. This is a smaller species, and is found on the sides of hills, and in places where the soil is dry. It flowers frequently, and yields an abundance of seeds.

A very thin bamboo, commonly known as the China bamboo, is very common about the Garrow and Kassia hills.

Kánko bánh. This is a very common species, and grows to a tolerably good height; but, owing to its crooked joints, it is not so much esteemed as most of the other species.

Tarvi bánh. This is rather a rare species, being found only on the Garrow hills. It grows from fifty to seventy feet in height, is beautifully erect, and without the least flexure or unevenness of surface, and, different from all the other varieties, is entirely bare of branches, except near the extremity.

It is more than probable that no account of any of these species has yet been published in the writings of any botanist, and it is likewise very possible that most, if not all of them are totally unknown, even in the adjoining province of Bengal. Upon the whole, this genus has been very much neglected, owing probably to its study being attended with numerous difficulties, which are of such a nature as to be formidable even to those who are on the spot where the different species are most numerous.

The same remarks may likewise be applied to those useful plants, which we shall next mention,—*the ratans or canes,* concerning which, modern botanists may be said to have published nothing that is useful in ascertaining the different varieties.

The ratan grows wild, but not the less luxuriantly, throughout all the wastes so extensive in Asam. Though probably not equal to that of the Eastern Archipelago in point of strength and beauty of polish, it is still a most valuable acquisition to the natives, and when split into withes, is converted into "every use, from that of a rope to a thread," and seems to answer all the purposes quite as well.

In Asam there are no less than six varieties commonly known to the natives. These grow spontaneously both in the woods and near villages, where the soil is moist and very rich; two circumstances that appear necessary for every species of this plant.

The most common sort is the *Rángoli bent.* Its leaves resemble those of a cocoanut, (Foliolis acquidistantibus bifaries): the stem is slender, but grows to no great height. The rind of the spines of the leaves is occasionally wrought into mats, but the cortex, which is the most valuable part, is substituted for ropes in all their uses.

The *Jati bent*, very much resembles the former, and is employed for similar purposes. It is probably nothing more than a variety of the same species.

Pákhári bent. This is much like the two former in the structure of its leaves; but the stems, which are far more slender, are employed merely for switches.

The Houka bent, has leaves like those of a date tree (Foliolis fasciculatis squarrosis). The stems are thick, and are generally used for walking sticks; they are also of an immense length, varying from one to two hundred feet, and in mountainous passes are occasionally wrought into suspension bridges.

The Ráidang bent is not quite so thick, but in every other respect resembles the preceding.

Guti Khowá bent. This, as may be inferred from its name, produces an edible fruit. The plant is in general short, and the stem slender. This cane is not used for the purposes to which the others are applied. The nut is sometimes used instead of the Tamul (Betel) nut.

Nearly allied to the canes are the *palms*, those princes of the vegetable kingdom, which administer to so many of the wants and luxuries of the natives, and which, from their graceful appearance, may with truth be ranked among "the grandest features of Indian scenery." In Asam there are no less than five different species of this valuable tribe.

The first we shall mention as the most common and generally esteemed, is the betelnut palm, Areca Catechu, Linn. (Asam, *Tamul.*) This is a most beautiful palm, and scarcely any thing can be more graceful than its high slender pillars, when backed by the dark shade of bamboos and other similar foliage.

It is found in great abundance in all the villages, and the cultivation of it requires but little care and expense. It generally bears fruit on the fifth year, and dies about the twenty-fifth, though occasionally it does not arrive so soon to maturity, but bears fruit for a much longer period, and is of course much longer in dying. The tree is in flower most part of the year; its trunk often rises from forty to fifty feet, but is in general not more than twenty inches in circumference, almost equally thick, and covered with a very smooth whitish bark. The nut is about the size of a hen's egg, enclosed in a membraneous covering of a reddish yellow when ripe. There are two crops in the year; the quantity of nuts yielded by a single tree varies considerably, but the average number may be about three hundred.* Here the betelnut is generally eaten green, and cut into slices, usually four: these slices are wrapped up in the leaf of the *betel-piper*, to which is added a little quicklime. Thus prepared it is chewed and eaten by the natives as a universal luxury. What the benefits are to be derived from this preparation, it would be hard to say; it is, however, probably as defensible as the use of tobacco.†

The Cocoanut palm. *Cocos nucifera* of Linnæus, though supposed not to thrive at any distance from the sea, is not uncommon in Asam; and, what may probably appear still more surprising, it grows luxuriantly on the *Nilachol parbut*, at an elevation of about 800 feet above the level of the sea. It is the tallest palm we have in Asam.

* The nuts may be purchased from 16 to 80 for a pice.

† The natives celebrate the properties, and the uses they derive from it in the following slok—

তাম্বুলং কটুতিক্ত মম্ল মধুরং ক্ষারং কষায়াম্বিতং ।
বাতঘ্নং কৃমিনাশনং কফহরং দুর্গন্ধদোষাপহং ॥
বক্ত্রাস্যাভরণং সুগন্ধিকরণং কামাগ্নিসন্দীপনং ।
তাম্বুলস্যসখে ত্রয়োদশগুণাঃ স্বর্গেপিতৈর্দুর্লভাঃ ইতি ॥

Translation.—The properties of the betel are, that its juice is sharp, bitter, and sweet, salt and astringent: it destroys flatulence and worms in the stomach; it removes phlegm, and all offensive smell in the breath; it beautifies the mouth with its red colour, and produces sweetness in the breath; it also excites heat, and the passions. My friend, the betel possesses these thirteen qualities, which cannot all be found in a single substance, even in heaven itself.

The Caryota urens of Linn., is the Sago palm of Asam, and may well be termed "one of the largest and most charming of this beautiful tribe." It grows about as fast as the cocoanut palm, with a straight columnar trunk, varying from forty to sixty feet in height, and proportionately thick. It is highly valuable in other parts of India, owing to its yielding an immense quantity of toddy or palm wine, which from a tolerably good tree, averages at the rate of from sixty to eighty pints in the course of twenty-four hours. In Asam no wine is extracted from it. The pith or farinaceous part of the trunk of old trees is very little inferior to the best sago. The trunk is very much esteemed for shafts for javelins, for beams, and rafters of houses, and not unfrequently it is cut into walking sticks.

Corypha Taliera, Roxb., (Asam, *Keow*). This is an elegant and stately palm: the trunk is straight, about thirty feet high, and of a tolerably equal thickness throughout. It is of a dark brown colour, somewhat rough, and marked slightly with the annular cicatrices of the fallen leaves. These latter are large, plaited, and subrotund. They are extensively employed by the natives for the covering of their boats. Their *jhapis*, or hats, which very much resemble those worn by the Chinese, are likewise made from this valuable leaf.

Cycas revoluta, Thunb. This is a much smaller palm than any of the preceding, but is no less beautiful. Its growth is very slow. In the space of thirty years it attains to the height of only ten or twelve feet. The fruit, which is a drupa, hangs in immense long racemes, and is eaten by the natives, who also use the fine down from the roots of the leaves as tinder.

The forests of Asam yield a few highly valuable *gums, varnishes, &c.* of which, the first we shall notice, as the most important, is the caoutchouc. The tree that produces this gum is the Ficus elastica of Roxburgh, (Asam, *bargach*); which may justly be ranked amongst the largest known trees, being probably inferior in size only to the banian, which may be said to be capable of infinite extension,

> ...."Branching so broad and long, that in the ground,
> The bending twigs take root, and daughters grow,
> About the mother tree; a pillar'd shade,
> High over-arch'd, and echoing walks between."

Such indeed is the size of the caoutchouc tree, that it may be distinguished from a distance of several miles by its dense, immense and lofty crown. Dr. Griffith in his report on the caoutchouc tree of Asam, gives the following account of it.*

The dimensions of one of the largest were as follows: circumference of main trunk seventy-four feet; ditto of main trunk and the supports 120 feet; ditto of area covered by the branches 610 feet,; estimated height 100 feet.

The trees appear to be, as far at least as I have had opportunities of judging, confined to the *Turai*, the drier parts of which they seem to affect, and they become more abundant towards the hills.

In the tracts of forests traversed by us, estimated to be between seven and eight miles in length, eighty trees were seen, of these by far the greater number were of large size. As we have reason for supposing that they are equally abundant throughout the district of Chardwar, some approximation of their real number may be formed. Thus, taking the length of the belt of the forests to be 30 miles, and its average breadth eight, we may form so many sections, each of the diameter of 100 yards. In the above thirty miles five hundred and twenty eight sections will be formed, and the total number of trees, taking eighty as the average of each section, will be 42,240; and, however over-

* Vide Report on the Caoutchouc tree of Asam, made at the request of Captain T. Jenkins, by William Griffith, Assistant Surgeon; Journal of Asiatic Society, vol. vii. page 132.

estimated this may subsequently prove to be, it is evident that the tree is very abundant, since even in the infancy of the scheme, 300 maunds of juice have been collected in thirty days.

Nothing definitive can be stated of the probable number of trees in the whole valley. It is known to exist about Goalpara, and at Borhath, on the south side of the valley, and I think it will be found to exist along both sides, wherever a belt of *Turai* exists.* I have no doubt but that Asam alone will, when the value of the juice becomes more generally known to the natives, be able to meet all demands.

The geographical range of the tree, as far as has been hitherto ascertained, may be stated to be between 25° 10′, and 27° 20′ north latitude, and between 90° 40′, and 95° 30′ east longitude. Throughout this space, it will be found in the densely wooded tracts, so prevalent along the bases of the hills, and perhaps on their faces, up to an average elevation of 2,250 feet.

The roots of this really noble tree spread out in every direction on reaching the ground, and the larger ones are half uncovered; they occasionally assume the appearance of buttresses, but never to such an extent as those of some other trees. The nature of the trunk of this, and some other species of the same genus, is so extraordinary, that it may not be amiss to make a few remarks on its structure. It differs in the first place from the ordinary form of trunk by its sculptural appearance, and it is from this, that its extremely picturesque appearance arises, which is caused entirely from the tendency of these trees to throw out roots, both from the main trunk as well as from the branches, and from the extreme tendency these have to cohere with the trunk, or with each other. If the roots are thrown out from, or very near the main trunk, they ordinarily run down its surface, and cohere with it firmly, and hence the sculptured

* Captain Veitch, the political agent of Upper Asam, has since ascertained that the tree is as abundant in the district of Naudwar as in that of Chardwar.

appearance; if, as happens in some, they are thrown out from the branches at such a distance from the trunk that they do not come in contact with it, they pass down to the earth, and form what may be called supports. These attain their maximum of development in the banian, and render the growth of that tree quite indefinite. These supports appear never to produce leaf-bearing branches, so long at least as they remain attached to the tree. They are generally perfectly straight at first, becoming conical only by divisions at the apex, when near the earth, and by the natural adhesion of these divisions.

The juice is procured from transverse incisions made in the larger root, which has been already mentioned as being half exposed. The incision reaches the wood, or even penetrates it, but the flow of the juice takes place in these instances from the bark alone.

Beneath the incision a hole is scooped out in the earth, sufficiently deep to hold the jars, or pans, into which the fresh gum is received. By this simple and effectual mode of extracting it, the juice is received into the vessels perfectly free from all impurities. The larger roots are preferred, in addition to their being half exposed, for yielding a richer juice. The fluid on issuing is, when good, nearly of the consistence of cream, and of a very pure white. Its excellence is known by the degree of consistence, and the quality of caoutchouc, on which this would appear to depend, is readily ascertained by rubbing up a few drops in the palm of the hand, when the caoutchouc rapidly becomes separated. By kneading this up again, it soon becomes elastic.

Many incisions are made in one tree. The juice flows rapidly at first, but the rapidity diminishes after a few minutes.

It is said to flow fastest during the night; it continues during two or three days, after which it ceases, owing to the formation of a layer of caoutchouc over the wound. The hole is then covered in again, and it is said that the wound in the root soon heals, and that the tree is in no way injured by the extraction of the gum.

When an attempt is made to bleed the tree beyond what it can healthfully bear, the juice becomes so watery as to be no longer fit for the use of the manufacturers; so that the gum gatherers are obliged to give the trees a due respite and to collect no more gum than the tree can well afford, without sustaining any injury.

The quantity obtainable from a single tree has not yet been exactly ascertained; some of the natives affirm that four or five maunds may be procured; others give only one *ghara* full, or ten seers, as the amount procurable. From the slowness with which it flows, half a maund may be considered a fair average produce of each bleeding. The operation is repeated at the expiration of eighteen or twenty days. Assuming the rate of half a maund to be nearly correct, 20,000 trees will give as the aggregate of four bleedings 12,000 maunds of caoutchouc, that is, if Dr. Roxburgh's proportion of this product to aqueous matter, viz. 15½ oz. to 50, be correct.

There are now in Asam two manufactories of caoutchouc; but the process of cleansing the gum is kept a secret, and all therefore that can be said on this point is, that when prepared it is poured out into wooden moulds about 6 feet in length, and 1½ in breadth, the lower planks being pierced through with holes to allow of the escape of all aqueous and injurious juices, that will not, or should not, coagulate with the pure gum.

If the previous purifying of the gum be properly attended to,—and in this process the whole art of manufacturing the perfectly elastic gum of commerce seems to exist,—the gum should not, by any exposure to the atmosphere, be subject to the least degree of clamminess, or viscidity; and if this important point be not fully attained, the article is of no use in the manufacture of those fine elastic threads, which constitute its chief value in the European markets.

The gum in its best prepared state, is worth from four to six shillings a pound whilst in its worst, when it is only fit for dissolving, for the manufacture of waterproof garments and such like articles, it will not fetch more than as many pence per pound.

The art of obtaining this complete freedom from clamminess, and consequent perfect elasticity, does not appear by any means to have been reduced to a certainty; and, consequently, a far better acquaintance with the article than is yet possessed by the Asam manufacturers, seems requisite before it can be managed with constantly the same results.

The beautiful black Japan varnish, so much admired throughout the world, is the production of a tree which grows as well in the forests of Asam as in Japan. The trees may probably not be the same, but the resemblance between them—the Rhus vernicifera, Dek. of Japan and that of Asam, (Melanorrhœa)?—is very striking. They are both naturally classed with the Terebinthaceæ, to which the chemical qualities of their juice also assimilate them.

The tree is said to possess some resemblance to the ash, with leaves shaped like those of a laurel, of a light green colour, and downy feel.

The tree itself is of no great beauty, but if properly attended to, may prove highly valuable as the source of a very lucrative manufacture.

The Asamese, not generally acquainted with its qualities, make little or no use of it. The hill tribes, but more especially the Khamties, usually employ it for blackening the handles of their daws, knives, &c., to which it gives a beautiful shining lustre.

The tree yields little or no varnish, until the trunk is nearly five inches in diameter, which size it seldom attains before seven or eight years. The liquor distils only at night, and that during the warm weather. To cause the gum to flow, several rows of annular incisions, about an inch apart, are made in the bark of the small twigs and branches. The number of these incisions is of course proportioned to the vigour of the tree. The quantity of gum produced by each tree is very small indeed. It is collected by means of a bamboo spatula.

While the varnish distils, it exhales a malignant vapour, the bad effects of which can only be prevented by preservatives and great precaution, so that very few individuals can be found who are willing to engage in collecting it. The workmen previous to proceeding to their work, are accustomed to rub their bodies well with prepared oil, and wash themselves with a decoction of herbs and bark; and in addition to these precautions, wrap themselves up in thick linen cloth. The labourer who should attempt to collect varnish without using these precautions, would soon be punished for his rashness, and the most dreadful effects would ensue. A kind of tetter appears on the face, and in the course of a few days spreads over the whole body; the skin becomes red and painful; the head swells; and the whole surface of the body is covered with troublesome sores. It is, however, said, that there are men that will handle the tree, and touch the juice with impunity, while others are dreadfully affected, even by being in the way of the wind which carries the effluvia of the tree.

Besides the lustre and beauty which this varnish gives, as is seen in many of the manufactures of China, it has also the property of preserving the wood on which it is laid, especially if no other matter is mixed with it. It prevents it from being hurt either by dampness, or the merciless ravages of insects.

The Dipterocarpus lovis, Hamilt, is the tree that yields the thin liquid balsam commonly known by the name of 'wood oil,' and which is much used in painting. It is common in some parts of eastern Asam. The tree is of immense size, with a remarkably straight trunk. No oil is extracted from it by the Asamese.*

* In the Malay islands, where the tree is abundant, the oil is procured by making an incision in the trunk of the tree, about a couple of feet above the surface of the ground. Here a fire is kept up until the

Canarium bengalense, Roxb., is an immense forest tree, exceedingly tall, and many feet in circumference.

"From fissures, or wounds in the bark, a large quantity of a very pure, clear, amber-coloured resin exudes, which soon becomes hard and brittle, and is not unlike *copal.*" This resin is used by the natives as their *Dhema*, or dammer; it is considered by them of so little consequence, that it fetches but a mere trifle when brought to the market.

Aquilaria Agallocha, Roxb., (Asam *Agará gach.*) The agallochum, or aloe wood. This is an immense tree, and a native of the forests of Asam.

There can be little or no doubt, says Dr. Roxburgh, that this is the tree which furnished the real Colambac, or Agallochum of the ancients, and there seems more reason to think that it was carried to China from our eastern frontier, than to suppose it was carried from Cochin China, or any other country in the vicinity of China, where it has always been in great demand.

The wood is of a light, spongy texture, very porous; and its pores are filled with a soft and fragrant resin. The wood when laid on the fire, melts in great part like resin, and burns away in a few moments with a bright flame, and perfumed smell. Its scent while in the mass, is very fragrant and agreeable, and its taste acrid and bitterish, but very aromatic. The resin, which is so much valued, appears to be created in bunches in the old trees, and probably may be owing to a disease of the tree; the other parts of the timber are almost free from any signs of resin, as is the wood of the young trees. The bark is cut up in long strips,

wound is charred, soon after which, the liquid begins to ooze out. A small notch is cut in the wood to conduct the liquid into the vessel, usually a bamboo, placed beneath to receive it. These operations are performed during the winter months, when the produce of a single tree may be averaged at thirty, or even forty gallons. The old charred surfaces may be cut three or four times during the season, and burnt afresh; when the tree will yield a fresh supply of the liquid.

and much used by the natives as a substitute for paper: their *buranjis*, or chronicles, are usually made of it.

The tree that produces the common marking nut of the natives, Semicarpus anacardium Linn., is also a native of Asam.

The trunk is covered with a gray, scabrous bark, and its inner substance, contains in crevices a quantity of white, soft, almost insipid, gum.

The wood of this tree is reckoned of no use, not only on account of its softness, but also from its containing much acrid juice, which renders it dangerous to cut down, and work upon.

The juice, or resinous balsam, is not soluble in water, and is only diffusible in spirits of wine, for it soon falls to the bottom, unless the menstruum be previously alkalized; the solution is then pretty complete, and of a deep black colour. The natives of Sylhet generally use it as a varnish for their shields, &c., to which it imparts a beautiful black lustre.

The pure, black, acid juice of the cells of the nuts is universally employed to mark all sorts of cotton cloth. The colour is improved, prevented from running, and fixed by a mixture of quicklime and water.

The bark is mildly astringent, and gives out in decoction a deep colour, which dyes brown of various shades.

Of the plants used for *dyeing and tanning*, the following are the most common:—

Morinda tinctoria, Roxb., (Asam, *Asu gach.*) This is a small, but very pretty looking tree, and though only a few feet in height, supports a tolerably large ramous head. The flowers are pure white, jasmine-like, and very fragrant.

The bark of the roots is used by the natives for a red dye, but the colour is neither bright nor durable.*

* In the Circars, the dyers use the bark of the fresh roots, bruised, and gently boiled in water for a short time: the cloth, or yarn, is prepared in a cold infusion of the powdered gall of Terminalia Chebula, in milk and water; it is then dried and moistened with alum water, and again dried, and receives from the above decoction a pretty bright, but fugitive red.

Rubia cordifolia, Linn. Rubia Munjista, Rox., (Asam, *manjit*) usually known by the name of East Indian madder. The root, stems, and larger branches of this little perennial plant are used by the natives to dye red with. The plant is produced in great quantities on all the bordering hills, but the manjit brought from the Abor mountains is the most esteemed.

Symplocos racemosa, Roxb. The bark of this small tree is in request among the dyers, by whom it is used as a mordant only. It is generally employed in dyeing with *manjit*, in which it is an ingredient. The bark is somewhat rough, with a spongy, friable, exterior, grey coat; when fresh it is of a very pale, yellowish colour, and the taste mildly astringent. The abir, (Asam, *phaku*) the red powder used by the natives during the Huli-holidays, is in some places made of the bark of this tree.

Nyctanthes, Arbor tristis, Linn. (Asam, *Harsingár*.) The orange tubes of the flowers dye a most beautiful buff, or orange colour, with the various shades between them, according to the preparation and mode of conducting the operation. The natives occasionally make use of it to dye their clothes, on the celebration of their festivals. But this elegant colour the natives are acquainted with no means of rendering durable.

Butea frondosa. Roxb. Terminalia Belerica. Roxb. Symplocos racemosa. Roxb. Syzggium Janbolana. Dek. Cassia Fistula. Linn. Semecarpus Anacardium. Linn.*

A small quantity of indigo is cultivated by the Asamese, in the vicinity of their villages. But the Mikirs seem to pay more attention to it; and by them it is pretty extensively used.

It is sown on high lands, in very small patches, about the month of April, and the plant is cut in August. It is then tied up in small bundles, and placed in large earthen pots

* These have been already noticed.

filled with water, where it is allowed to ferment, exposed to the heat of the sun for four or five days: the bundles are then removed, a large proportion of lime is thrown into the water, causing it to deposit the fecula, which is laid out on pieces of cloth to dry. In using it as a dye, it is mixed with a dilution of the carbonate of potash, extracted from the plantain tree, and the residue of fermented rice.

With regard to extending the cultivation of this very useful plant, Mr. Hugon, in his remarks on Asam, communicated to the Agricultural Society of Calcutta, states—

"Although the natives do not make use of the large churs of the Brahmaputra to sow indigo, owing to the little of it they require; I am confident these would be as valuable in that respect, as those of Bengal. I have seen chur lands over which no inundation had gone for several years; lands high enough to be worked in June and July, could be procured in any quantity. Upon the whole, I should consider Asam similarly suited as Rungpore and Mymensing."* There seems therefore reason for supposing that indigo might be very successfully cultivated in this province.

The safflower, Carthamus tinctorious, Linn., is cultivated, but to no great extent.

The seed is sown broad-cast in October and November; manure is seldom or never employed, though it often might be used with advantage. The flowers begin to appear in February and March, and are soon after collected; they are then thrown into large pans, and allowed to steep during the night in water, and in the morning the whole is beat up to a pulpy mass.

* See remarks on Asam, communicated by T. Hugon, Esq. Sub-Assistant to the Governor General's Agent, N.E. Frontier. In Transactions of the Agricultural Society of India, vol. ii. page 164, Mr. Hugon further states.—"One pura of indigo, can yield eight or ten maunds of seed on a very ordinary crop.

This is repeatedly washed with clean water and trodden under foot till the liquid comes off clear, and the whole of the yellow dye soluble in water, is separated.

When the washing process is considered complete, the mass is divided into small balls, which are squeezed flat in the hand, and laid out on mats in the sun to dry. It is then considered ready for the hands of the dyer.

The following are the plants commonly used by the natives for the manufacture of *thread* or *cordage*.

The cotton plant, Gossypium herbaceum, Linn. is generally cultivated throughout Asam, but more especially by the adjacent hill tribes.*

Urtica nivea, Linn. (U. tenacissima, Roxb.) called *Rhia* by the Asamese, is pretty generally cultivated for its bark, which abounds in fibres of very great strength and fineness.

Its hemp is considered very valuable ; it is of a good long, fine, and tough staple, and is readily bleached. It is generally stripped off, without steeping, from the stalk recently cut, and when scraped a little clean of the outer bark, may be washed and bleached at pleasure. It is much employed by fishermen in the manufacture of their nets.

There is another species of Urtica, called by the natives *Ban Rhiá.* It is common in the forests, and the hemp produced from it, though inferior to that of the former species, makes good strong cloth.

Crotolaria juncea, Linn. is pretty generally cultivated by the natives, and yields the hemp most commonly employed.

Hibiscus cannabinus, Linn., is cultivated chiefly during the rainy season. The leaves are used as a pot herb, and the bark for hemp.

* The cotton of the eastern districts is more valued than that of the western portions of the country.

Corchorus olitorius, Linn., (Asam, *Pát.*) It is much cultivated for the fibres of its bark, usually termed *jute.* Of this there is a reddish variety, which the natives call *Ban,* or wild *Pát.*

The natives seem to have no idea of the quality of the bark of the common hemp plant, Cannabis sativa, Linn.; the leaves and flowers thereof being the only parts used by them. These they employ as an intoxicating narcotic drug; and a most powerful one it is.

Sterculia urens Roxb.*

Of the plants usually employed by the Asamese for *rearing the silk worms* on, the following are the most important.

Although the Muga moth, (Saturnia) can be reared in houses, it is fed, and thrives best in the open air. The trees which afford it food, are the following:—

Tetranthera quadriflora, Roxb., (Asam, *Addákuri.*) The worms fed on this tree, produce the *Mazankuri mugá,* but the tree is used only when under four years of age. It is a small ramous tree, and generally sprouts up where forests have been cleared for the cultivation of rice or cotton. The worms that are fed on this tree on the first year of its appearance above the ground, produce the best silk; on the second year, the silk is inferior both in quality and quantity; and on the third year it degenerates so much as to be little, if at all, superior to the common *muga.* The leaves are lanceolate, smooth on both sides, and glaucous underneath; from four to six inches long, by one or two broad.

Tetranthera lancifolia, Roxb., (Asam, *Sum*) this is found principally in the forests, on the plains, and about villages, where the plantations of it are pretty extensive. It yields three crops of leaves during the year. The silk

* This has been already noticed.

produced by it is of a light fawn colour, and esteemed next to the *Mazankuri*.

Tetranthera macrophylla, Roxb., (Asam, *Sanábu.*) It is common in most of the forests, and is also found about villages, where in six years it attains its full growth; it is a middling sized, very ramous, evergreen tree. The silk produced from the worm fed on this tree is considered inferior to the preceding, probably more from its darker colour than from any other cause.

Michelia pulnyensis, R. Wight., (Asam, *Champá.*) The silk of the worms fed on this tree is called *Champá putryá mungá*. It is held in the same estimation as the *Mazunkuri*.

Tetranthera Diglotti, Hamilton, (Asam, *Diglutti.*) A tree of small size, and on that account not much used; the silk is equal to that obtained from the preceding. There is a large tree, (Asam, *Kantuloa,*) found both in the hills and the plains, and a few also about the native villages. Its leaves are too hard for young worms; they are therefore reared on the *Sum* till the third moulting, when they are removed to this tree. By this process the silk obtained is stronger than that produced from worms reared entirely on the *Sum*.

Cinnamomum obtusifolium Nees, (Laurus obtusifolia, Roxb.) (Asam, *Pátti shundá*) a pretty large tree, found principally in the forests. The leaves of this are used when those of the *Sum* tree are exhausted.

The mulberry worm, Bombyx mori, is reared on the Morus indica, Linn.

There are hardly any plantations of mulberries in Asam on such a scale as to be worth mentioning. A few men of rank have small patches of it, sufficient to produce silk for their own use. The few *raiats* that sell the silk, generally have not more than a seer to dispose of in the year, the produce of a few plants about their houses, or in the hedges of their fields.

The Eria worm, Phalona Cynthea, is fed principally on the leaves of the *Eri gach*, Ricinus communis, Linn.; it eats the mulberry leaf also, but is said to prefer the former; when the Eri leaves fail, the worm is fed on those of several other trees, known in Asam by the following names:—

Kassul, Hindu ghass, Mikerdál, Akanne, Gamári, Litta Pákori, Barzanolli.

The worm thrives best, and produces most when only fed on the *Eri* tree. It is the only plant which is cultivated purposely for it, and there is scarcely a *raiat* who has not a small patch of it near his house, or on the edges of his field. It requires little or no culture; the ground is turned up lightly with the hoe, and the seeds are thrown in without ploughing. Whilst the plant is yet young it is weeded once or twice, but is afterwards left to itself.

The worms can be reared on the *Hindu ghass* and the *Mikerdál,* but they do not thrive well upon them; many die even after having begun the cocoons, and the few that are got, are small, and yield but little. The leaves of these plants, and those of the others, are used only when the worm is in the fourth or fifth stage, they are then supposed to answer quite as well as the *Eri* leaves. The last mentioned trees are found in the forests, but are not cultivated.

Kántkuri mungá. This worm feeds on many trees besides the *Munga* trees, it is found oftener on the *Bagari* (Zizyphus Jujuba; Lam.) and the *Sirmil* (Bombax malabaricum, Dek.) but not in great quantities. The fibre produced by this worm is stronger than the Munga, and of a lighter colour

Lac is prepared in large quantities; the insect is propagated by tying small baskets filled with the gum upon trees proper for its nourishment, when in the course of three or four months the tree is nearly covered with the family.

The trees on which the insect generally feeds, are the *Juri gach,* Ficus Jooree of Dr. Griffith. It very much resembles the F. religiosa, Linn. but may be readily distinguished from it by the formation of its leaf, wanting that long narrow point which in the leaf of the F. religiosa, occupies nearly one-third of its length.

Zizyphus jujuba, Lam. (Asam, *Bagari,*) this tree is pretty generally known, and the fruit eaten by all classes of people.

Cajanus indicus, Syueag. (Asam, *Gáromáh*) this is found only in a cultivated state, and to appearance is a large shrub of some years duration; yet, with the greatest care, it seldom lives longer than two or three.

The grain it produces holds a high rank amongst the leguminous seeds.

In Asam, as in every part of India, chewing and smoking various vegetable substances, some of them highly intoxicating, is a favourite luxury, and here the people are more than usually addicted to such practices. Under this head opium is by far the most important article.

Papaver somniferum, Linn. The large single white-flowered variety is grown to a very considerable extent. The raising of opium is a business of much delicacy, the poppy being a very tender plant, and liable to injury from various causes. The produce seldom agrees with what might be stated as the average amount, but generally runs in extremes: while one cultivator is disappointed, another is an immense gainer, and while one season will not pay the expenses of culture, another enriches all the cultivators. This circumstance renders the pursuit in the highest degree alluring, from the excitement, uncertainty, and hope connected with it. Probably the uncertainties of this cultivation depend in a great measure on the natural falls of rain, and the qualities and elevation of the soil. The Asamese never have recourse to effectual irrigation, or it is likely their crops of poppy would be equal to those in the western provinces.

The seed is sown in November and in March. When the poppy heads have grown to a proper size, diagonal incisions are made in the pod, and the juice is collected on strips of coarse cloth, about a couple of inches in breadth, and when fully saturated and dried, the cloth is rolled up in little bundles and kept for use.*

The tobacco plant, Nicotiana Tabacum Linn., (Asam *Dhuná pát*,) is pretty generally cultivated, but to no great extent, and the tobacco raised is not adequate to the consumption of the country. It is cultivated in rich spots of land, immediately contiguous to the farmer's house, where, from its situation, the land is abundantly supplied with manure. It is occasionally cultivated in those high lands fit for the growth of sugar cane, and as a crop alternating with that valuable plant. And lastly, it is grown on banks of rivers which are inundated in the rainy season. On the first of these localities it is generally most productive; and on the last it is most scanty. In the beginning of October the plot of ground is well dug up or ploughed, and the young plants that have been sown in a bed in the end of August, are then planted out at the distance of a cubit from each other. The plant is fit for cutting in March and April.

The fruit of the Betelnut palm (Areca Catechu, Linn,) is universally employed, together with the leaf of the Piper Betel, Linn, (Asam *Pān*,) which latter is grown in almost every garden. The plant is raised from slips and cuttings, which are carefully planted in a moist, rich soil, and at first are well enclosed and shaded, so that they are in a great measure protected from both sun and wind. When the plant grows up it is trained to the betelnut palm, though occasionally poles are employed for the purpose.

* Owing to the bad management of the natives, the opium is much dearer in Asam than in the western provinces, even inclusive of the Company's tax, which the drug is not yet subjected to here.

With the betel leaf the natives sometimes use a few carminative seeds. Those raised in the country, are the coriander seed, Coriandrum sativum, Linn. The ripe seed alone is used; it is also employed for medicinal purposes.

Ptychotis Ajowan, Dec. Like the former, this is cultivated, but to no great extent: the seeds, like those of caraway, have an aromatic smell, and warm pungent taste. They are used also both for culinary and medicinal purposes.

In several parts of India various plants are cultivated for the purpose of procuring a saccharine matter from their inspissated juice, and are almost always articles of considerable importance. In Asam, however, besides the Caryota urens, Linn. already mentioned, the only other plant cultivated is the sugar-cane, Saccharum officinarum, Linn. It thrives well, and is cultivated to some extent on the high lands about most of the villages. The season for planting it is in April, and the harvest is reaped in the following February.

The native physicians make use of several plants, of which the following are a few; their medicinal properties, however, as well as the names of various other plants generally employed by them, are in a great measure confined to the faculty.

Croton Tiglium, Linn. (Asam, *Jamalgata,*) a little white-wooded, crooked tree. The taste of the leaves is exceedingly nauseous and of long duration, and the tree itself has a very disagreeable smell. The seed is used as an effectual and easy cathartic; it is also used to cure all venereal complaints.

Calotropis gigantea, Rob. Brown. (Asam, *Madár.*) A large quantity of acrid, milky juice, flows from wounds made in every part of this shrub, which is applied to a variety of medicinal purposes. The plant itself, and preparations made from it, are also used for curing all kinds of fits, epilepsy, hysterics, convulsions, &c. &c.

The bark of the young shoots yields a sort of fine silky flax, which may hereafter prove of some importance.

Piper peepuloides. Roxb. This plant is indigenous in Asam, and is found in great abundance on the hills. It may be considered the long pepper of the country, and as such, is used in medicine.

Jatropha Curcas, Linn. (Asam, *Bágbarinda.)* The leaves of this small tree are occasionally applied by the natives to inflammations, where suppuration is wished for. The seeds taken inwardly, act with very great violence, so as on that account to have been almost exploded from the native materia medica.

Abrus precatorius, Linn. (Asam, *Látalmani.)* This is a very pretty creeping plant. The root is sweet and mucilaginous, and, in these respects, resembles liquorice, for which it may probably be employed as a suitable substitute. The seeds are used as weights by the jewellers in Bengal.

Terminalia Chebula, Linn. The fruit is usually employed as a mild cathartic.

Cassia Fistula, Xantochymus pictorius.*

Hydnocarpus odoratus, (Chaulmoogra odorata, Roxb.,) (Asam, *Chalmugiá*): the natives employ the seeds of this tree in the cure of cutaneous disorders; they are beat up into a soft mass, and in this state applied to the parts affected.

The natives can scarcely be said to possess any *flower* gardens, though their yards frequently contain a variety of pretty flowers, and most of their villages are surrounded by a large number of beautiful flowering trees and shrubs.

Bauhinia purpurea, Linn. (Asam, *Deo kanchan*) is very common about villages, where it is planted for the sake

* These have been already noticed.

of ornament. It is also found wild on the mountains, and grows to be a large tree. The flowers are numerous, of a deep rose colour, and very large.

The plant consecrated to the memory of Sir William Jones, Jonesia Asoca, Roxb., is also a very ornamental tree. The trunk is erect, though not very straight, and the branches are numerous, spreading in every direction so as to form a most elegant, large, shady head. The flowers are pretty large, and very numerous. When they first expand they are of a lively orange colour, gradually changing to red, and presenting a variety of beautiful shades. The flowers are very fragrant during the night.

Roydsia suaveolens, Roxb. This elegant tree is very frequently met with. It is in flower about the month of March, when its numerous blossoms diffuse a strong but pleasant odour through the villages where it grows. The flowers are large, and of a pale yellow colour.

Sphenocarpus grandiflorus, Wall. (Liriodendron grandiflora, Roxb.,) is a middling sized, very ramous tree. It blossoms in April and May, and perfumes the air to a considerable distance, with the fragrance of its fine, large, white flowers.*

Mimusops Elengi, Linn., (*Bokul,*) is a common ornamental tree about villages, where it is generally planted on account of its fragrant white flowers, which are much valued by the natives, as they are well adapted for forming chaplets.

One of the most favourite flowers with the natives, is the *Champá,* Michelia Champaca, Linn. The flowers are yellow, and delightfully fragrant, but their smell is almost too strong and overpowering. The tree is common, but useful only as an ornament.

Mesua ferrea, Linn., (Asam, *Nayessar.*) This is a most elegant tree, the flowers are large, delightfully fragrant,

* In addition to this, there are two other species very common throughout the eastern parts of Upper Asam.

petals pure white, with a large globe of bright gold coloured anthers in the centre. It is found in great abundance about the Hindu temples.

Plumeria acuminata, Dryand. (Asam, *Golanch*), is a very common, middling sized tree, and may be found in great abundance about all the native temples; the flowers are very fragrant.

Agati grandiflorum, Deso. (Asam, *Bok*,) a small delicate looking tree, of only a few years duration. It is generally found in the vicinity of villages, where the natives encourage its growth for the sake of the flowers, which they offer to their gods. The flowers are very large, either red or white.

Harsingar, (Asam,) called Nyctanthes Arbor tristis, Linn. from its flowers spreading at night, and falling at sunrise. It is generally found in the state of a large shrub, or small tree. The flowers are exquisitely fragrant, partaking of the smell of fresh honey. When destitute of flowers, the plant has but an indifferent appearance.

Poinciana pulcherrima, Linn. (Asam, *Dáriá kanchan*,) is a pretty common plant, and is in flower almost the whole of the year.

The genus Hibiscus presents three species. Hibiscus Rosa sinensis, Linn. (Asam, *Jová*). Of this beautiful shrub there are several varieties, the single and double red, single and double yellow and pink. It continues in flower the greatest part of the year.

Hibiscus hirtus, Linn. It flowers chiefly during the rainy season, though more or less the whole year. The flowers are white or red.

H. mutabilis, Linn. said to be a native of China. When the flowers first open in the morning they are nearly white, by night they assume a pretty deep red.

The following are also generally met with—

Gardenia florida, Linn. Talauma pumila, Blume; the flowers are white, and exquisitely fragrant.

Michelia obovata (Magnolia obovata, Thunb.) Flowers, but inodorous.

Michelia fuscata, Blume. Flowers small, of a very pale yellow or cream colour, and exceedingly fragrant.

Gloriosa superba, Linn. A very pretty variegated flower, and is one of the most ornamental plants any country can boast of; the root is said to be a violent poison. This plant grows wild in damp spots.

Canna indica, Linn., the red and the yellow varieties.

Hedychium angustifolium, Roxb.

Kämpfera pandurata, Roxb. Related to this are—

Gastrochilus Jenkinsii, Wall. and G. longiflorus, Wall.

Phajus Wallichii, Lindl.

The liliaceous tribe presents a great many species, of which the following are a few—

Crinum defixum, Ker.; C. amoenum, Roxb.; C. toxicarium, Roxb.; C. zeylanicum, Linn. One or two species of Pancratium.

Cucurligo recurvata, Dryand, and one or two species of Dracœna.

The water lilies are numerous; and amongst them, the most conspicuous are, the

Nymphœa rubra, Roxb., with beautiful large red flowers.

N. pubescens, Willdenow. The white flowered variety is the most common. It blossoms more or less throughout the year.

Nelumbium speciosum, Willdenow. The flowers of this species are large and beautiful beyond description. The tender shoots of the roots between the joints are eaten by the natives, simply boiled, or in their curries. The seeds are eaten raw, roasted, or boiled.

These beautiful aquatics have justly been the admiration of mankind in all countries where they grew, from the earliest ages, and as holy plants are often met with in the religious ceremonies of the Hindus.

Sagittaria sagittifolia, Linn., S. cordifolia, Roxb.

There is a countless variety of creepers, both about villages and in the forests, "whose beauty and perfume would render them valuable acquisitions to the bower, or the parterre."

Amongst these, we may mention a species of honey-suckle, Lonicera, which may justly be ranked with the most odoriferous of the twining shrubs.

There are also great varieties of Jasmines, the flowers of which are mostly white, and highly fragrant: and numerous species of Convolvulus and Ipomæa, are abundantly met with.

The variety of parasitic plants is great, and interesting: under which head we may enumerate the following—

Loranthus pentapetalus, Roxb. The flowers are numerous, small, and red.

L. longiflorus, Poir, the flowers in size and appearance are very much like those of the honey-suckle.

Loranthus involucratus, Roxb., Dendrobium secundum, Lindl.; D. Pierardi. Roxb. The flowers are large, few in number, and of a pale yellow colour.

Saccolabium guttatum; Lindl.; the flowers are numerous, large, and spotted, with a beautiful mixture of red and white.

Aërides suaveolens, Roxb. The flowers are small, and scattered in great profusion round the whole of the raceme; they are also delightfully fragrant.

A. rostratum, Roxb.; A. multiflorum, Roxb. A large and beautiful species, with copious, very long, sub-erect racemes, of numerous pretty large pink coloured flowers.

Micropera pallida, Lindl. The flowers are small, in one variety white, and in another pale yellowish, with a faint tinge of pink.

Cœlogyne nitida, Lindl. Flowers large, and nearly white.

Cymbidium triste, Willd. This is rather a delicate species. The colour of the flower is a dark purple, with a few yellow spots.

Vanda teres, Lindl.; Pholidota imbricata, Lindl.

Most, if not all, of these plants flower during the rains.

The tribe of ferns, so rare in most parts of India, is very numerous, and many of them are very beautiful. The arboreous fern, in the eastern districts, frequently attains the height of from 20 to 30 feet.

The natives have a great number of *fruit* trees about their villages, and most of them are indigenous to the country.

The mango tree, Mangifera indica, Linn., is very abundant, but the fruit is seldom good, and few are found that are not already half-eaten by a species of beetle, of the size of an ordinary spider. These destructive insects commit fearful depredations upon almost every fruit tree, so that great care must be taken to obtain any thing like good fruit.

Averrhoa Carambola, Linn. (Asam, *Hardátengá.*) The fruit is oblong, having five acute angled cells, and is of a pleasant acid flavour. The tree is in blossom during the rains, and the fruit ripens in the cold season.

There are two or three species of Flacourtia, but the most common is F. cataphracta, Roxb. (*Paniala*).

Jambosa vulgaris, Dec. (Asam, *Jam*). Syzygium Jambolana, Dec.*

Artocarpus integrifolius, Linn. jack tree. The *badam* of Bengal; Terminalia Catappa, Linn.

Annona squamosa, Linn. custard apple (Asam, *Atlas katal.*)

A. reticulata, Linn. is also common.

Psidium pomiferum, and P. pyriferum, Linn; the red and the white guava, (Asam, *Maduriám.*)

The pomegranate, Punica Granatum, Linn. (Asam, *Dalim.*) When properly cultivated, the fruit is large and very juicy.

Cicca disticha, Linn. (Asam, *Halfoli tenga)* the *chermella* of the Bengalese.

Carica Papaya, Linn. (Asam, *Amrita.*)

Grewia asiatica, Linn. (Asam, *Phalsá,*)

* These were noticed when treating of timber trees.

Pyrus Malus, Linn., is very common in the hills, but not being improved by culture, the varieties are few.

P. indica, Roxb. (Asam, *Bagori,*) the fruit is round and smooth, a little concave at the base, and from one to two inches in diameter : the taste is exceedingly harsh.

Myrica integrifolia, Roxb., (Asam, *Nagatenga.*) In its raw state this fruit, though inviting to the eye, is almost too sour to be relished; it makes, however, a good jelly, and excellent chutney.

The *jalpai,* (Asam,) a species of the Elæocarpus, has, by some, been compared to the olive, but the affinity is very slight, consisting merely in the fruit being of the same shape and size. The fruit is somewhat acid, and gives a good flavour to curries, which is its principal use. When preserved with oil and salt, it acquires a great resemblance to the olive.

Ficus glomerata, Roxb. (Asam, *Bor Dimoru.*) The fruit is nearly as large as common figs, clothed with a fine soft down, and when ripe is of a rich orange colour.

Aleurites triloba, Forst. A species of walnut usually known as the Butan walnut.

The peach, the pear, and the plum, have been introduced into Asam, and thrive very well.

The varieties, if not species, of citrus or lime, are very numerous. The natives enumerate them by the following names.—

The acid limes are *Nimu tenga; Ghorá nimu tenga.*

The sweet lime is the *Mita nimu tenga.*

The acid limes are *Jámir tenga; Hamir tenga; Páti salung tenga; Bar salang tenga; Cháklą tenga; Narengi tenga.*

The sub-acid lemons are *Cháklá tengá; Nágá Cháklá tengá; Halangá mori tengá; Jota mori tengá; Bor mori tengá.*

There is also a bitter lemon, called *Tita-Karuna Dewa tengá,* and a sweet one called *Páni mori tengá.*

We have two varieties of the shaddock, one with white and the other with red pulp, termed by the natives respectively, *Bogá robab tengá,* and *Ranga robab tengá.*

The citrons are the *Bor jorá tengá*, *Birá jorá tengá*, and *Bon jorá tengá*.

Of the orange, we have the following varieties—*Hintoriá tengá*, *Kamalá tengá*, and *Jendru tengá*.

The varieties of the banana or plantain, are very numerous. The following is a list of the names applied to them by the natives—

Málbog; *Bhimátiá*; *Purákol*; *Montriki*; *Gokhuná*; *Baratmám*; *Bozariá*; *Rámkol*; *Sepátiá*; *Leheti*; *Hágorsini*; *Kerkeriá*; *Súmkol*; *Bogi monuá*; *Digjiá*.

Perhaps no people are better qualified to instruct us in the nature and qualities of esculent vegetables than the Asamese, who are compelled, by their extreme poverty, to search for every edible root and herb the land produces: they, however, occasionally cultivate a few vegetables for the kitchen, but never to any great extent; and the plants that come under this class, may be reduced to four kinds:—

I. Those used as a hot seasoning.

II. Such succulent roots, stems, and fruits, as are included under the general term of *turkari*, and serve as a convenient receptacle for the oil, salt, and other seasoning with which they are dressed.

III. *Sag* or *Hakh*, the leaves and tender stems of plants that are applied to the same purpose.

IV. *Tengá*, or acids used as seasoning.

I. Those plants used as a hot seasoning.

Ginger, Zinziber officinale, Roscoe. This is cultivated in poor high lands. It is planted out in the warm weather, from the middle of April to about the middle of May, and the roots are raised about the end of February, or the beginning of March. Very little more is cultivated than serves for consumption in the country; and, except as a medicine, it is used raw, though occasionally it forms an ingredient in curries.

Turmeric, Curcuma longa, Linn. This plant requires a rich friable soil, and so high as not to be overflowed during the rainy season. It is used raw as a medicine, and not unfrequently as a dye; it enters also into every curry where it can possibly be afforded. It is planted, and the roots are raised about the same time as the ginger, but being more generally used, its cultivation is somewhat more extended.

Chillie, Capsicum frutescens, Linn. (Asam, *Jholokia*); of this the consumption is very great, forming as it does an ingredient in every curry. In Asam there are no fields of this plant, a few bushes about each house being generally found to suffice. The fruit is gathered as it ripens, dried in the sun, and kept in baskets placed on a bamboo stage, raised to a convenient height from the ground.

Onion and garlic, are cultivated in much the same manner as the above, but are perhaps the only produce of gardens artificially watered. Their use is in a great measure confined to Mussulmans, for they are an abomination to the Hindus, although perhaps no seasoning is so well fitted for their insipid food.

Piper nigrum, Linn. The pepper vine grows luxuriantly, and is much cultivated in the gardens of the natives, more particularly in Upper Asam. The pepper is used for culinary purposes, but more frequently as a medicine.

Coriandum sativum, Linn. is not uncommon.

Ptychotis Ajowan, Dec.

To these we must add a peculiar spice, known to the natives by the name of Jabrang. It is very fragrant, very aromatic, and excessively pungent, and if kept in the mouth but a short time, occasions a remarkably tremulous sensation of the tongue and lips. It is the capsule of a species of Xanthoxylum found in great abundance on the mountains to the north-east.

The following, though not cultivated, are indigenous to the country:—

The Cardamum plant, Alpini Cardamomum, Roxb.

Cinnamomum albiflorum, Nees; the *tezpat* of the Hindus, but which from its great resemblance to the bay-leaf, is to Europeans generally known by this name. The tree is found in great abundance on the bordering mountains, and has a very elegant appearance. We have two or three species or varieties of it.

II. *Tarkari*, or such succulent roots, stems, and fruits, as are generally included under the above term.

The sweet potatoe, Batatas edule, Choisy, (Asam *Rangaalu.*) This root was probably the original potatoe known in Europe, and communicated its name to the more valuable plant from America, which latter is not yet generally cultivated by the natives of Asam. The sweet potatoe is much cultivated wherever the soil is free, and is deservedly esteemed by the people as one of their most palatable and nutritious roots. It is sometimes eaten raw, and the leaves are used as greens. It is propagated by planting the smaller and otherwise useless roots in the middle of the rainy season, in October; and it continues until March, and is dug up when required for sale or use.

There is a countless variety of yams, the most esteemed among them are the following—

Dioscorea globosa, Roxb.; D. alata, Linn.; D. purpurea, Roxb., (Asam, *Pasal-alu*); D. rubella, Roxb.; D. aculeata, Linn. (Asam *Hatikhoji-alu*); D. fasciculata, Roxb.

The Arums are also very numerous; the species commonly met with is Arum Colocasia, Linn. (Asam, *Poáti kuchu*). Small offsets from the larger tubers are, like potatoes, planted about the beginning of the rains in a well worked, friable soil, not subject to be inundated, and the roots are taken up about the end of the year.

There are two wild varieties of this species, found generally on the edges of ditches, and other wet places. *Kalá kuchu*, or the dark coloured arum. The leaves and the petioles are more or less tinged with purple, and the roots never attain the size of the cultivated variety, but send out numerous runners. The leaves and their foot stalks are the parts chiefly eaten by the natives.

Ban, or wild *kuchu*. In situation and form this is every way like the preceding, but of an uniform green colour. The roots are rarely eaten where better vegetables are easily procurable.

Arum viviparum, Roxb., (Asam, *Durá dimiá kuchu*). The plant produces annually, in the rainy season, numerous minute bulbs, which are eaten by the natives, and by which the plant is readily propagated.

A. Indicum, Loureiro; (Asam, *Mán kuchu*); this is probably the most stately of the Arum family, the stems generally rising from six to eight feet, and from one to two feet in circumference. The roots are fibrous, intermixed with numerous suckers, which end in little solid edible bulbs, and by which the plant is readily multiplied; the esculent stems and small pendulous bulbs, or tubers, are very generally eaten by the natives of all ranks in their curries.

A. nymphœfolium, Roxb., (Asam, *Bilhá kuchu*). This plant is found in great abundance on the borders of lakes and pools of fresh water. It very much resembles A. Colocasia, and may probably be a very large aquatic variety of this species. Every part of the plant is eaten by the natives.

Butomus lanceolatus, Roxb.; the esculent roots of this plant are eaten.

Lagenaria vulgaris, Seringe; (Asam, *Láu*); this plant is very generally cultivated. The fruit varies considerably in shape, which gives rise to different names; it is needless, however, to enter into these distinctions, as all the kinds are nearly of the same use. The fruit when green, makes an excellent curry.

The shells of the ripe fruit are used by religious mendicants, and by poor persons, as vessels for conveying water. A musical stringed instrument, called by the natives *Láu tokari*, is made of the round variety.

Benincasa cerifera, Savi; Cucurbita maxima, Duchesne.

Cucumis sativus, Linn., the cucumber, (Asam, *Tiya*). This and some of its varieties are pretty generally cultivated, and for the most part eaten raw.

C. utilissimus, Roxb., (Asam, *Kakri*). This is considered by the natives as the most useful species of this most useful genus.

C. Momordica, Roxb., (Asam, *Bangi*), the fruit, when young; is a good substitute for the common cucumber, and when ripe, (after bursting spontaneously) with the addition of a little sugar, is scarcely inferior to the melon, and is reckoned very wholesome.

Solanum Melongena, Linn., (Asam, *Bengená*). Of this universally useful esculent species, the natives reckon many kinds which differ according to the size, shape, and colour of the fruit. The kind most generally esteemed, has the fruit in shape like a pear, and very large quantities are used. The unripe fruit is a very common ingredient in curries; it is also sometimes roasted in ashes, and eaten with rice. The seeds are sown in a small bed about the beginning of the rains, and the seedlings are transplanted in July. The fruit fit for eating, begins to be obtained about the end of September, and continues procurable till the following hot season.

S. longum, Roxb., (Asam, *Ságali hingia bengena*). This plant is in every respect like the former, the fruit excepted, which, in this species is always cylindrical, owing to which circumstance it is considered by Dr. Roxburgh to be clearly a distinct species.

Lycopersicum esculentum, Dun. the Pomum amoris of Rumphus. This, though not indigenous to the country, is now pretty generally cultivated, by the natives for their own use.

Lablab cultratum, Dec. (Asam, *Uroi*). A great many kinds are cultivated, some of them hitherto deemed distinct species, but they run so into each other, that they may probably be considered as mere varieties, although the extremes are often very different; they have all nearly the same qualities, but some are thought better than others. They are either allowed to climb over the roof of the hut, or more usually have a small bamboo stage erected to support them; and almost every house has two or three plants.

Dolichos sinensis, Linn. (Asam, *Lecherá máh*). There are three or more varieties of this species cultivated.

Canavalia gladiata Dec., this species produces a large red bean. The young, tender, half-grown pods are good substitutes for those of the common *Phaseolus*, usually called *French* beans.

Luffa acutangula, Roxb., L. pentandra, Roxb. Both these plants are very generally cultivated, and the unripe fruit is eaten by the natives in their curries. The former is esteemed the better of the two.

Momordica Charantia, Linn. This is generally cultivated for the fruit, which the natives eat unripe in their curries: it is bitter, but reckoned very wholesome.

M. mixta, Roxb.; M. muricata, Willdenow.

Abelmoschus esculentus, Wight and Arn. This is a very good esculent herb, and produces abundance of fruit, the only part which is eaten. It is however very little valued by the natives.

Anethum Sowa, Roxb., *(Sulphá)*. The seeds of this plant are much used by the natives in their curries, and also for medicinal purposes.

The young shoots of the bamboo, the core of the plantain tree, and the green fruits of some of the inferior varieties, are frequently used in curries.

III. *Sag* or *Hakh*, pot herbs.

Rumex vesicarius, Linn., (Asam, *Chuka*), found in a cultivated state and is pretty extensively used.

Beta bengalensis, Roxb., (Asam, *Polang*).

Amarantus gangeticus, Linn. (The *Lall Sag* of the Bengalees). The varieties of this useful species are endless, and are in more general use amongst the natives as pot herbs than probably any other plant.

A. polygonoïdes, Linn. This is found wild in almost every soil and situation. It is reckoned very wholesome.

A. fasciatus, Roxb., (Asam, *Tuntuni*). A very common weed, and green in every part, with the exception of a crescent-shaped cloud or fillet of paler green, crossing the centre of the leaves.

A. spinosus, Linn. A very troublesome weed in gardens.

A. polygamus, Linn. (Asam, *Chumli*).

Spinacia tetrandra, Roxb., spinach, or more probably a species of it. It is held in considerable estimation by the natives, and is as palatable as the European kind.

Trigonella corniculata, Linn. This is not so much esteemed as the preceding.

T. Fœnum græcum, Linn. (Asam, *Metho*); Chenopodium album, Linn.; C. viride, Willdenow; Basella cordifolia, Hamilt; (*Poi Sag*); Hibiscus cannabinus, Linn. (Asam, *Mista*). The leaves are occasionally used as an acid greens.

Oxalis coreniculata, Linn. (Asam, *Singri tengá*). The leaves have a very pleasant acid flavour.

The tender leaves of the Urtica nivea, Linn., Crotularia juncea, and Papaver somniferum, are also frequently used.

Besides the above, there are various other plants used by the natives, too numerous to be mentioned here. The poorer classes, as we have already stated, being unable to procure from gardens the vegetable seasoning so requisite for their insipid diet, generally have recourse to the fields, to ponds, and thickets, whence they obtain a plentiful, though a very coarse supply.

IV. *Tenga*, or acids used in cookery. By far the greater part of these are produced by trees that grow with little care near villages, most of which have been noticed in the preceding pages.

Elœocarpus serratus; Dellenia speciosa; Spondias mangifera; Tamarindus indica; Zizyphus Jujuba, and most of the limes.

The greater part of European kitchen vegetables and salads thrive exceedingly well; as also most of the sweet pot herbs, such as thyme, marjoram, and mint; but the natives seem as yet to have acquired little or no relish for them.

In almost every civilized country plants cultivated for their grain are a principal object of the farmer's care, and this is especially the case in Asam, where these grains form almost the only sustenance of man. The kinds of grain which are cultivated in this province, may be ranked under the following heads.

I. Culmiferous plants.
II. Leguminous grains.
III. Oily seeds.

I. *Culmiferous plants.* Rice, Oryza sativa, Linn., is by far the principal grain, of which there are two great crops, the *Ahu* or sown, and the *Hali* or planted rice.

In some parts of the country the same land will produce annually both these crops, but this is not very general. The cultivation of the *Ahu dhan,* is mostly confined to deeply flooded lands, or to the sides of hills and undulating grounds which, from their nature, cannot be easily reduced to a level; whilst the *Hali dhan* is generally grown on those lands which can either be flooded from the adjacent streams, or be reduced to a dead level, and be made to retain a sufficient head of rain water. These lands are usually called *rupit,* and are esteemed of the highest value. Much of the land on which the *ahu* crop is raised might, by careful husbandry and more attention to levelling, draining, &c. than is now bestowed on these operations, be converted into *rupit* land. This will no doubt in some measure be effected when the increase of population renders it necessary for the inhabitants of the province to take up lands which require more labour, and are less conveniently watered.

The *Ahu* crop is sown in February, March, and April, according to the level of the lands on which it is sown; and the rice is reaped in June and July. The *Háli* crop is first sown in May and June, and transplanted in July, August, and September, and cut in November, December, and January.

The varieties of rice which compose these crops are very numerous, and seem to be selected according to the opinion the farmers have formed of them, more with reference to their adaptation for the different levels of ground, the kinds of soil, and the seasons of sowing, together with their productiveness, under these circumstances, than to their other qualities of size, the appearance of the grain, its flavour, or wholesomeness. So numerous indeed are these varieties, that we cannot even pretend to give a full enumeration of them: we shall therefore merely mention the principal kinds belonging to each class.*

Ahu dhán, or summer rice. The most common kinds are—

1. *Kechelepa;* 2. *Saphle;* 3. *Kikibila;* 4. *Shar jal;* 5. *Horcha jal;* 6. *Boge tora;* 7. *Sorai tuni;* 8. *Ahabini;* 9. *Chutrule;* 10. *Boga baugan jute;* 11. *Bor kuli baugan jute;* 12. *Horu ditto ditto ditto;* 13. *Dubri Singa;* 14. *Malbhog.*

Háli dhán, or transplanted winter rice—

1. *Khonka joha;* 2. *Maniki mudhori;* 3. *Toliki joha;* 4. *Khude joha;* 5. *Gedapura joha;*—

These are of a finer quality than the following—

6. *Mainigiri;* 7. *Tengiri;* 8. *Luciguminі;* 9. *Boka;* 10. *Maguri;* 11. *Haldiarang;* 12. *Hato mal;* 13. *Kola phua;* 14. *Moliti;* 15. *Kanai maluk;* 16. *Oká;* 17. *Hanjul;* 18. *Lolioti;* 19. *Bor huldá.*

* As far as sixty different kinds have been collected, and they are probably much more numerous.

Báo dhán; this crop is produced at all times of the year.

1. *Gotha*; 2. *Hanjul*; 3. *Megheri*; 4. *Kekua*; 5. *Khagori.*

Wheat, Triticun æstivum, Linn.; barley, Hordeum vulgare, Linn.; and millet, Sefaria italica, Beauv., are very little used, and the cultivation of them is necessarily very small.

Maize, Zea Mays, Linn., is very generally cultivated, but no where as an extensive crop.

Leguminous Plants.

The most common in Asam is the Phaseolus Max, Roxb., (Asam, *Mati-máh*); it is sown on high land, in a loose soil, which seldom requires more than a single ploughing. The seed is sown broad-cast in September and October, and it is reaped about the end of December.

Phaseolus Mungo, Linn., (Asam, *Mug-máh*). This plant is a considerable object of the farmer's culture. It requires a strong, rich, dry soil: during the rains it is sometimes cultivated, but the greatest quantity is raised, like the former, during the cold season, on high lands. The ground is slightly ploughed, and after the first shower of rain the grain is sown, and harrowed in, by dragging some bushes over it. It needs no further care; the dews and mists, which are copious at this season, furnish all the moisture it requires; and in from seventy-five to ninety days it is ready to cut. The ripe grain is well tasted, is esteemed wholesome, and affords much alimentary matter: it is much used in food by the natives.

Lathyrus sativus, Linn., (Asam, *Kolá-máh*), is sown on a strong rich soil, about the close of the rains; and the harvest is three or four months after. The seeds, when the plant is suffered to remain till they are ripe, are used as a wholesome aliment by the natives.

Pisum sativum, Linn., (Asam, *Borkolá-máh*), like the other leguminous plants, is raised on high rich land, as a winter crop.

Ervum hirsutum, Linn., (Asam, *Nohu-máh*).

Cicer arietinum, Linn., chick pea.

Ervum Lens, Linn., (Asam, *Másur*), Lentil; cultivated to a considerable extent.

Cajanus indicus, Spreng.*

Of the plants which produce *oil*, by far the most common is the Sinapis dichotoma, Roxb. (Asam, *Sarsu*), which is extensively cultivated during the cold season for its seed, from which the natives express an oil, used by them for various purposes, chiefly for anointing the body.

Sinapis ramosa, Roxb.: this also is cultivated during the cold season, the seed time being in October, and the harvest in February. The seed, and the oil yielded by expression, are useful ingredients in the diet of the natives.

Sesamum indicum, Linn., (Asam, *Til*): both the black and white varieties are grown, but in small quantities, and principally on the hills amongst the cotton.

Papaver somniferum, Linn.

Ricinus communis, Linn., the castor oil plant.

The natives extract little or no oil from the seeds of these plants.

* This has been already noticed.

SECTION III.—ZOOLOGY.

General observations—Quadrupeds—Birds—Reptiles—Fishes—Insects.

Abounding as Asam does in extensive tracts of wild and uncultivated wastes, it is, as may be conjectured, the rendezvous of a countless multitude of animated beings, which live and move upon its surface. Of these, myriads swarm upon the land; others, still more incalculable, give animation to the numerous streams and rivulets with which the country abounds; while unnumbered hosts take their "pastime in the ambient air." The native zoology must therefore present a vast field for observation, and so remarkable is it for the variety, splendour, and singularity of its forms, that it is difficult to say in which department it is most interesting. Flourishing beneath a genial clime, and nourished by dense vapours and frequent showers, in a soil naturally humid, vegetation here attains a luxuriance inconceivably magnificent. Animal life equally partakes in this exuberance, and exhibits, under every form, the most singular shapes, and the most brilliant combinations of colours.

The zoology of Asam has been partially investigated by Dr. McClelland, one of the most eminent naturalists in India, whose researches, it is hoped, will before long be given to the public.

It is to his list, inserted in the *Quarterly Journal* for July, 1837, that we are indebted for the greater part of the names in our collection.

To enter in this place on the natural economy of each animal, viewed in reference to its peculiarities, would be impracticable; a bare list is all we can propose to lay before the reader.

In the following arrangement, we shall endeavour, as much as possible, to follow up the general plan, as adopted, in the London Encyclopædia, (vide Art. Zoology). On the

Classification of Quadrupeds, we trust we shall be excused, in deviating from this plan, whilst we follow an easier and more recent arrangement.*

Class I.—Mammalia.

ORDER I.—QUADRUMANA.

FAMILY.—SIMIADÆ.

Gen. *Simia.*

Simia Hylobates, *Harlan,* (Asam, *Hulluk*). These live in considerable herds; and although exceedingly noisy, it is difficult to procure a view of them, their activity in springing from tree to tree being very great. In the dry season, when water is scarce, and they are under the necessity of leaving the woods to procure drink, they are readily caught, as nothing can be more awkward than their gait, which is always erect. Their colour is uniformly black.

Simia Moloch of *Audibert.* This is of a grey colour; in other respects it very much resembles the former.

Simia Cyrocephalus, Stridentatus of *McClelland.*

Gen. *Cercopithecus.*

Simia rubra, of *Linnæus.*

Simia Entellus, of *Audibert.*

FAMILY.—LEMURIEÆ, Lemurs.

Gen. *Lemur.*

Lemur tardi-gradus, *Linn.*† (Asam, *Lajjatá bánor*—the bashful monkey).

* Vide Dr. Lardner's Cabinet Cyclopædia—"Natural History; Classification of Quadrupeds," by W. Swainson.

† For a description of this curious little animal, see Lardner's Cabinet Cyclopædia, "Animals in Menageries, by Swainson," p. 34.

It is a native of the Garrow hills, and may also be found in great abundance throughout the forests of Asam. It feeds chiefly on small *buds*, insects, and grasshoppers, which it takes at night.

Family.—Vespertilionidæ, Bats.

Gen. *Pteropinæ.*
Pteropus asamensis, *McClelland.*
Pteropus rubicollis ?

Gen. *Vespertilionidæ.*
Vespertilio noctula ; Great Bat.
Vespertilio pipistrellus, of *Gmelin ;* Pepistrelle.
Vespertilio borbustellus ; Barbastelle.

Gen. *Plecotis.*
Plecotus auritus, of *Geoffry ;* Long-eared Bat.

Nyctinomus murinus of *Gray.*

ORDER II.—FERÆ.

Family.—Felidæ.

Gen. *Felis.*

Felis Tigris, Linn. Tiger. Very abundant; and notwithstanding the great numbers that are annually killed for the sake of the Government reward, they do not appear to be at all diminished.

Felis Leopardus *of Smith.*

Felis Wiedii, *Sching.*

Felis domestica, the common Cat. These are numerous, but in general are merely tolerated.

Hyæna vulgaris, *Linn.* ?

Gen. *Canis.*

Canis vulpes; the Fox.

Canis familiaris; the common Dog.

Canis bengalensis, *Pennant.* The breed of this animal is very numerous, and every village swarms with half-starved curs. They eat all manner of carcases and impurities, and are not reckoned the property of any individual. The natives never enter into any sort of familiarity with them, nor are the children often seen caressing or tormenting them, but they are tolerated, and one or two, according to the wealth of the family, are permitted to eat the scraps. In return they sleep in the yard, and make a noise when any stranger approaches them, especially at night. The bitches are few in number, and being weaker, are generally more starved than the dogs, no one interesting himself in their quarrels; but they are so prolific that the number of dogs always exceeds that of the houses which give them shelter, and a large proportion have no resource but to live like jackals upon whatever comes in their way; and numbers are hanging about the villages in the utmost misery. Their nature, however, is very different from the suspicious temper of the jackal, and the least attention shewn to one of these dogs is repaid with gratitude.

Canis aureus, Jackal. Though commonly met with, seem particularly to abound in Upper Asam. In general they are a large and well fed race.

FAMILY.—MUSTELIDÆ. Weasels.

Gen. *Viverinæ.*

Viverra mongos, *Gray,* the Ichneumon.

Gen. *Mustelinæ.*

Mustela vulgaris, *Linn.,* the common Weasel.

Mustela Furo, a species of Ferret.

Mephite asamensis, of *McClelland.* A species of Pole-cat.

Lutra vulgaris, of *Ray.* The Otter; very common.

Family.—Ursinæ. Bears.

Ursus ferox, *Cuvier*. These are numerous, and in some places accidents caused by them are unfortunately frequent.

Arctonix collaris, of *Cuvier*.* In habit this singular little animal may be compared to a bear, furnished with the snout, eyes, and tail of a hog. From the number and form of the toes, and the disposition of the teeth, this genus would appear to belong to the *Carnivora*, to the extreme of which, and in close connection with the bears, it is referred by its plantigrade motion, its strong and curved claws, and its little inclination for flesh. Like the bears, moreover, when much irritated, it supports itself on its hind feet, and exhibits in its arms and claws, weapons equally to be dreaded with its teeth. In its flat and tubercular molar tooth, its preference for vegetables and fruits, and its snout apparently destined for digging, it deviates considerably from the bears.

Family.—Sorecidæ.

Gen. *Erenaceus*.

Erinaceus europœus, *Linn*. The common Hedgehog.

Gen. *Mygale*.

Sorex moschatus, *Cuv*. The common Musk Rat.

Gen. *Talpa*.

Talpa europœa of *Linn*., probably a variety of the Mole.

ORDER III.—UNGULATA. Hoofed Quadrupeds.

Tribe I.—Pachydermes.

Gen. *Elephas*.

Elephas indicus, *Cuv*.

Wild elephants are plentiful. They generally move in large

* See Livraison 51 éme Histoire Naturelle des Mammiferes.

herds, and are very destructive to the crops, and not unfrequently to human life also.

The Asam elephants are commonly supposed to be less hardy than those of Chittagong, chiefly from the circumstance of many of them having died when newly caught, and exported from the country. This prejudice against them will, however, wear off as they become better known. In point of courage they cannot be surpassed, though in appearance probably they are not so handsome as those exported from Chittagong, having in general smaller heads, and a blown-out appearance about the belly, solely attributable to the nature of their food.

From seven hundred to a thousand elephants are exported from Asam every year, but the speculation is very precarious. About twice as many as are exported are generally killed in training; and if to this sum we add the great number of these animals annually killed by the hill tribes for their tusks, we may form some faint idea of the vast multitude that usually roam in the forests.

Gen. *Rhinoceros.*

Rhinoceros Indicus, *Cuv.*

This animal inhabits the densest parts of the forests, and is generally found to frequent swampy places. The old ones are frequently killed for their skin or their horn. The skin is valuable, the best shields in the country being made of it, and a great degree of sanctity is attached to the horn. The horn is not a process of the bones of the nose, but united to them by a concave surface so as to admit of being detached by laceration or a severe blow. The rhinoceros makes no use of its horn as a weapon of offence, but for this purpose invariably makes use of its teeth.

Tribe II.—Anoplotheres.

Gen. *Sus.*

Sus scropha, *Linn.*

The wild hog is very abundant. A small black species, bearing a great resemblance to the well known China pigs, is domesticated by the hill tribes.

Tribe III.—Edentates.

Gen. *Dasypus ?*

Dasypus, *Linn.* a species of Ārmadillo.

Gen. *Manis.*

Manis brachyura, of *Hardwicke ;* the Pangolin.

Gen. *Echidna.*

Echidna hystrix, *Cuv.* Porcupine.

Tribe IV.—Ruminantes.

1. Family.—Bovidæ, Oxen.

Gen. *Bos.*

Bos taurus, the common Ox. Cows are of very inferior quality, and, as in most parts of Bengal, are generally in a wretched condition.

Gen. *Bubálus.*

Bos bubalus ; Buffaloe. Plentiful ; wild ones abound in all parts of Asam, and perhaps of all the animals that frequent the jungles, these are among the most formidable, the solitary excommunicated males being most ferocious. On a representation made by the local authorities, rewards have been of late offered by Government for their extermination. Besides this incentive to kill them, vast numbers are slaughtered by the hill tribes for their flesh, which by them is considered a dainty they have not always the means of possessing. Numbers too are killed for their horns, and probably still more are domesticated. Unfortunately however their numbers are not much decreased.

We have besides these the Bos of the Naga and Duphla hills. Bos sylheticus, of *Duvancel,* or B. Garceus, of *Smith,* and one or two other varieties.

2. Family.—Antelopidæ, Antelope.

Gen. *Antelope.*

Two or three species are found in the plains of Asam.

Gen. *Nemorhœdus.*

Capra Nemorhœdus; the Goral, or great Antelope. It is a mountainous animal, singularly active and lively; in size it resembles the common goat. The deer-like conformation of its structure is not only characterized by a robuster form, but the head assumes a caprine shape, and the wild dark eye of the true antelope gives place to the yellow or light hazel pupil. The skull is solid and heavy, but the horns retain a round or falcated character. The legs and character of the hair, which is coarse and often shaggy, belong to the goats. It inhabits, in numerous herds, the adjacent mountains.

Gen. *Capra.*

Capra hircus; the common Goat. Great numbers are kept in all parts of the country. The hill goat is generally a large, fine looking animal. That of the Khassia hills is usually clothed with long, white, rather coarse hair, whilst the Naga goat differs from it in the beautiful streaks with which its body is marked.

Gen. *Ovis.*

Ovis aries; Sheep.

Sheep are all imported from Bengal or Butan. Those from Butan are superior by far.

3. Family.—Cervidæ, Stags.

Gen. *Alces.*
Cervus alces, *Linn.*

Gen. *Dama*
Cervus dama; the Fallow Deer.

Gen. *Cervus.*
Cervus elephas; the Stag.
Cervus procinus, of *Pennant,*
Cervus pumilio; *Griff.* Synop.

4. Family.—Moschidæ.

Gen. *Moschus.*
Moschus moschiferus, *Linn.* the Musk Deer. These inhabit the adjacent country of Thibet. They differ from the other ruminants in the want of horns, and in the long canine teeth of the upper jaw, which spring from the mouth of the male, and ultimately become very long.

Tribe V.—Solipedes.

Equus.

There are no horses indigenous to the country. A number of ponies are imported from Butan; these are in general superior animals, strong, rather handsome, and fit for almost any work.

A few mules are also occasionally brought down by the Butias.

ORDER.—GLIRES.

I. Glires Proper, *with clavicles.*
1. *Rats and mice.*

Gen. *Arvicola.*
Arvicola amphibia of Lacipede; the Water Rat.

Gen. *Mus*.

Mus messorius ?

Mus musculus, *Cuv*. The common Mouse.

Mus rattus, *Cuv*. The common Rat. Both these exceedingly numerous.

2. *Squirrels*.

Sciurus vulgaris; the common Squirrel.

Sciurus giganteus, of *M'Clelland*.

Sciurus caudatus, *Ibid*.

Sciurus asamica, *Ibid*.

Sciurus dubius, *Ibid*.

II. Clavicles rudimentary, or none.

Gen. *Lepus*.

Lepus timidus, *Linn*.

Lepus *(Lagomys, Cuv.)* Hispidus, of *J. T. Pearson*.

Class II.—Aves.

ORDER I.—OCCIPITRES. Rapacious.

Division 1.—Diurni. Acie in obliquum.

Family.—Vultures.

Vultur fuvus; the common Vulture. There is besides a red headed variety.

Family.—Falcones.

Gen. *Falco*.

Falco communis, of *Bechstein*.

Falco interstinctus, of *M'Clelland*.

Family.—Aquilæ.

Gen. *Haliactus*.

Falco procella, *M'Clelland*.

Gen. *Pandion.*

Falco pondicerianus, of *Latham.*

Gen. *Harpyia.*

Harpyia rufitinctus, *M'Clelland.*

Gen. *Morphus.*

Morphus humeralis, *M'Clelland.*

Family.—Milvi.

Gen. *Milvus.*

Falco milvus, *Linn.*

Division II.—Nocturn, striges. Acie direct.

Gen. *Otus.*

Otus vulgaris; the long-eared Owl.
Otus brachyatus; the short-eared Owl.

Gen. *Strix.*

Strix flummea, of *Savigny.*
Strix alco, *Linn.*
Strix ascalaphus, *Savig.*

Nearly allied to this genus is a new and unique species, Bathyrynchus, brevirostris, *M'Clelland.* "It approaches the Strigidæ (owls) by the general form of the head, while the plumage approaches that of Swainson's Scotophilus perlatus.

"Specific character, brown, beneath yellowish brown, with a black auricular disk under each eye, the anterior feathers of which have white tips, wings short."

ORDER II.—PASSERES.

The common character of this order is purely negative, for it embraces all those birds which are neither swimmers, waders, climbers, rapacious, nor gallinaceous.

Family.—Lanii.

Group I.

Gen. *Lanius.*

Lanius excubitor, Linn, Butcher bird; *rare.*
Lanius collurio, of *Gmelin.*
Colurio atricapilla, *M'Clelland.*
Colurio erythronotus, *Gould.*
Lanius indicus, *M'Clelland.*
Irena puella, *Horsf.*
Glareola fluvialis, *M'Clelland.*

Gen. *Graucalus.*

Graucalus maculosus, *M'Clelland.*
Graucalus ruficapilla, *Ibid.*
Graucalus monticolus, *Ibid.*

Group—Muscicapæ.

Gen. *Muscicapa.*

Muscicapa princeps, *Gould.*
Muscicapa brevirostris, *Gould.*
Muscicapa asamensis, *M'Clelland.*
Muscicapa elegans, *Ibid.*
Muscicapa capitalis, *Ibid.*
Muscicapa melanops, *Gould.*

Platyrhynchus albicollis, *Vieil.*
Eurylaimus cyaneus, *M'Clelland.*
Eurylaimus dalhousiæ, *Royle.*
Lamprotormis spilopterus, *Gould.*

Gen. *Edolius.*

Lanius longicauda, *M'Clelland.*
Lanius galeatus, *Ibid.*

Lanius nigerrimus, *M'Clelland.*
Muscicapa indica, *Ibid.*

Gen. *Turdus.*
Turdus musicus.
Turdus merula, *Linn.*
Turdus longicauda, *M'Clelland.*

Group.——

Gen. *Oriolus.*
Oriolus galbula, *Linn.*
Oriolus melanocephalus, *Lath.*
Pastor trailii, *Gould.*
Pastor fuscus, *Temminck ?*

Gen. *Cinclus.*
Cinclus cinerus, *M'Clelland.*

Gen. *Philedon.*
Philedon gularis, *M'Clelland.*
Philedon lunaris, *Ibid.*
Philedon asamensis, *Ibid.*

Gen. *Gracula.*
Gracula ruficapilla ?
Paradisaca heistis, *Gmel.*
Gracula cantoriana, *M'Clelland.*

FAMILY.—ROSTRO-GRACILI.

Gen. *Saxicola.*
Saxicola elegans, *M'Clelland.*

Gen. *Sylvia.*
Sylvia asamica, *M'Clelland.*
Sylvia variegata, *Ibid.*

Gen. *Curruca.*
Motacilla arundinacea, *Gmel.*

Gen. *Troglodytes.*
Troglodytes armillata, *M'Clelland.*
Troglodytes ornatus, *Ibid.*

Gen. *Regulus.*
Regulus cinericapillus, *M'Clelland.*

Gen. *Motacilla.*
Motacilla cineria, *Linn.*
Motacilla alba, *Ibid.* Pied Wagtail.

Gen. *Budytes.*
Motacilla flava, Yellow Wagtail.

Gen. *Anthus.*
Anthus pratensis, *Gmel.*
Anthus arboreus, of *Bechstein.*

Family.—Rostro in caput profundissime fisso.

Group.—Hirundines.

Gen. *Apus.*
Hirundo atricollis, *M'Clelland.*

Gen. *Hirundo.*
Hirundo rustica, *Cuv.* Swallow.
Hirundo brevirostris, *M'Clelland.*
Hirundo brevicaudatus, *Ibid.*

Gen. *Caprimulgus.*
Caprimulgus grandis. Great Goat-sucker.

Family.—Rostro plerumque forma coni.

Group I.

Gen. *Alauda.*
Alauda arvensis. Skylark.
Alauda asamica, *M'Clelland.*
Timalia pileata, (?) *Horsf.*

Group II.—*Pari.*

Gen. *Parus.*

Parus Major, *Linn.*

Parus Palustris; var. *Linn.*

Gen. *Les moustaches.*

Parus biarmicus, *Cuv.*

Mystacinus falconarius, *M'Clelland.*

Gen. *Emberiza.*

Emberiza miliaria, *Linn.*

Emberiza nigricephala, *M'Clelland.*

Emberiza subfuscus, *M'Clelland.*

Group III.—*Fringillæ.*

Gen. *Ploceus.*

Ploceus Griffithii, *M'Clelland.*

Gen. *Pyrgita.*

Fringilla domestica. The common House-sparrow.

Pyrgita flavicollis, —— ?

Gen. *Linaria.*

Fringilla cannabina, *Linn.* The Linnet.

Group IV.—*Loxiæ*

Gen. *Coccothraustes.*

Loxia coccothraustes, *Linn.*

Gen. *Loxia.*

Loxia curvirostra, Crossbill.

FAMILY.—AVES GRANDIORES.

Group I.—*Corvi.*

Gen. *Corvus.*

Corvus corax, *Linn.* Raven.

Corvus corone, *Linn.* Crow.

Corvus frugiligus, *Linn.*
Corvus monedula.
Corvus cinereus, *M'Clelland.*

Gen. *Pica.*
Pica vagabunda, *Lath.*

Gen. *Garrulus.*
Corvus glandarius, *Cuv.* Jay.

Gen. ———
Kitta venatorius, *Hardw.*

Group II.—*Coraciæ.*

Gen. *Coracias.*
Coracias Themminckii, *Vail.*

Gen. *Eulabes.*
Gracula religiosa, *Linn.*

Group III.—*Paradiseæ.*

Gracula œnoptera, *M'Clelland.*

FAMILY.—ROSTRO TENUI.

Group I.—*Upupa.*

Gen. *Upupa.*
Upupa epops, *Linn.*
Upupa asamica, *M'Clelland.*

Group II.—*Scandentes.*

Gen. *Nectarina.*
Nectarina coccus, *M'Clelland.*
Nectarina viridis, *Ibid.*
Nectarina asamica, *Ibid.*
Nectarina gulares, *Ibid.*

Gen. *Cinnyris.*

Cinnyris labecula, *M'Clelland.*
Cinnyris metallica, *Ibid.*
Cinnyris asamensis, *Ibid.*

FAMILY.—DIGITIS JUNCTIS.

Group I.—*Meropes.*

Gen. *Merops.*

Merops asamensis, *M'Clelland.*

Group II.—*Alcedines.*

Alcedo ispida, —— ?
Alcedo asamensis, *M'Clelland.*
Alcedo rudis, *Lath.*
Alcedo indica, *M'Clelland.*
Alcedo minor, *Ibid.*

Group III.—*Buceros.*

Buceros rhinoceros, *Linn.*
Buceros homraix, *Hodgson.*
Buceros asamensis (malabaricus, *Lath.*), *M'Clelland.*

ORDER III.—SCANDENTES.

AVES RATIONE PEDUM HABITA SCANDENTES.

This order comprises birds which have the outward toe directed behind like the great toe, whence there results a firmer means of support, by which they climb the trunks of trees with peculiar facility.

Group.—*Pici.*

Gen. *Picus.*

Picus viridus.
Picus minor.

Picus major.
Picus orientalis, *M'Clelland.*
Picus occipitalis, *Gould.*
Picus calolophus, *M'Clelland.*

Gen. *Picoides.*
Picoides Grantii, *M'Clelland.*

Gen. *Yunix.*
Yunix torquilla, *Linn.*

Group.—Cuculi.

Gen. *Cuculus.*
Cuculus asamensis, *M'Clelland.*

Gen. *Centropus.*
Centropus (cuculus ?) Philippensis, *Cuv.*
Centropus *(cuculus ?)* Nigrorufus, *Cuv.*

Group.—Bucco.

Bucco cucullatus, *M'Clell.*
Bucco sylvicola, *M'Clell.*

Gen. *Trogon.*
Trogon asamensis, *M'Clell.*

Group.—Psittaci.

Of the parrot genus there are many species. The most common are—

Psittacus gingianus.
Psittaca torquata, of *Busson.*

The description which Wilson gives of the flight of the Carolina-parrot is probably applicable to many other species which have not, in their wild state, been noticed by an equally intelligent observer. "There is a remarkable contrast between their elegant manner of flight, and their lame and crawling gait among the branches. They fly very much like the wild pigeon, in close, compact bodies, and with great rapidity, making a loud and outrageous screaming. There flight is sometimes in a direct line, but most usually circuitous, making a great variety of elegant and serpentine meanders, as if for pleasure."

ORDER IV.—GALLINACEÆ.

Thus denominated from their relationship with the cock, who for his courage, and the favour of man, is entitled to stand at the head of an order which exhibits so many natural affinities.

Group I.

Gen. *Pavo.*

Pavo asamensis, *M'Clell.*

M'Clelland makes the following remarks on the Asam variety of peacock :—

Head and neck golden green, changing to blue; the same colour, but with less iridescence, covers the breast and sides, becoming dark grey on the vent, and yellowish white, transversely vermiculated on the thighs.

Between the shoulders the loose barbs of the nuchal plumage become more connected, and the feathers assume crescented extremities marked by more varied colours, a change which increases along the back. The primary quills are sepia brown, the secondaries plain greenish black. Upper wing coverts light grey and brownish black, alternating in narrow and equal transverse bands; the tail is composed of twenty feathers, which are grey, vermiculated above with brown. The crest is composed of thirty feathers, with naked shafts and crescented summits.

The female is uniformly light grey above, with dark olive vermiculations, the same as the wing coverts of the male.

It would appear from the foregoing description, compared with that of M. Temminck derived from two wild peacocks, one from Batavia and the other in a menagerie in London, that there must either be two varieties of wild peacocks, or some errors in the description of ornithologists.* M. Temminck is made to say of the superiority of the wild over the domestic peacock,† that it is in the richly assorted colours of the alar coverts that one of the principal differences consists. "The wild peacock has all the small coverts of the upper part of the wings as well as the subalar plumes of a deep and brilliant green. They are bordered by green, with reflections of gold; the small and middle coverts are deep blue, bordered with golden green. The great coverts are of a greenish and metallic black, &c."

These parts in the Asam wild peacock do not at all agree with this description. The secondary quills in M. Temminck's variety have their inner barbs bistre-red, whereas in the Asam peacocks they are brownish-black, the same as in the under surface of the outer barbs.

The length of the Asam peacock from the beak to the extremity of the tail covert is from six feet six inches to seven feet, and from the extremity of the beak to that of the tail three feet eight inches to four feet. Tarsi, from five to five and a half inches long.

Group.—Phasiani.

Gen. *Gallus.*

Phasianus gallus, *Linn.*

Gallus domestica, Domestic fowl.

Gallus sonnerati, of *Temminck.*

* There is on the coast of Arracan a species of peacock of the ordinary size, but of a general blue colour, in addition to which each feather on every part of the body is distinguished by a number of disks or moons.

† Griffith's Animal Kingdom, vol. viii. p. 188.

Gen. *Phasianus.*

Phasianus leucomelanos, *Lath.*

Phasianus colehicas, *Linn.* the Pheasant.

Group.—Perdices.

Gen. *Perdix.*

Perdix gularis, of *Buchanan.*

Perdix pictus, of *Shaw.*

Perdix cinereus, the Partridge.

Perdix coturnix, the Quail.

Group.—Columbæ.

Gen. *Columba.*

Columba palumbas, *Linn.* Ring-dove.

Columba turtur, *Lath.* Turtle-dove.

Columba occipitalis, *M'Clell.*

Gen. *Vinaga.*

Vinaga occularis, *M'Clell.*

Vinaga asamica, *Ibid.*

Columba longicauda, *Ibid.*

Columba olivaceo viridis, *Ibid.*

ORDER V.—GRALLÆ.

Family.—Rostro presso.

Group.—Charadrii.

Gen. *Œdicnemus.*

Œdicnemus crepitans.

Œdicnemus recurvirostris, *Cuv.**

* Since formed into a new genus by Hodgson.

Gen. *Charadrius.*

Charadrius asamensis, *M'Clell.*

Charadrius arenarius, *Ibid.*

Charadrius ventialis, *Wagler.*

FAMILY.—ROSTRO CULTRUM SESEFERENTE.

Group.—Grues.

Gen. *Grus.*

Grus arcuatus, *M'Clell.*

Grus cinerea.

Group.—Ardeæ.

Ardea antigone.

Ardea cinerea. The common Heron.

Ardea pollicaris, *M'Clell.*

Ardea Indica (var. A. cinnamonea, *Lath.)* *M'Clell.*

Ardea asamica? *M'Clell.*

Ardea vulgaris? *Ibid.*

Ardea varia? *Ibid.*

Ardea orientalis, of *Hardwicke.*

Group.—Ciconiæ.

Gen. *Ciconia.*

Ciconia cristata, *M'Clell.*

Ciconia nudifrons, *Ibid.*

A gigantic bird, very much resembling

Ciconia argala; the Adjutant.

Ciconia nigricorona, *M'Clell.*

Gen. *Mycteria.*

Mycteria asamica, *M'Clell.*

Gen. *Anastomus.*

Anastomus asamensis (Coromandelicus, Sonn). *M'Clell.*

Family.—Rostro longo.

Group.—Scolapaces.

Gen. *Ibis.*
Ibis Bengala, *Cuv.*

Gen. *Numenius.*
Numenius arquata, *Cuv.* Curlew.

Gen. *Scolopax.*
Scolopax major, *Cuv.* The great Snipe.
Scolopax gallinago, *Cuv.* Common Snipe.
Scolopax asamensis, *M'Clell.*
Scolopax rusticola, *Cuv.*

Gen. *Arenaria.*
Arenaria cinera, *M'Clell.*

Gen. *Totanus.*
Totanus asamica, *M'Clell.*
Totanus maculatus, *Ibid.*

Gen. *Recurvirostra.*
Recurvirostra asamica, *M'Clell.*

Family.—Digitis longissmus.

Group.—Parræ.

Gen. *Parra.*
Parra jacana, *Linn.*

Group.—Fulicæ.

Gen. *Gallinula.*
Fulica cinericollis, *M'Clell.*

Gen. *Porphyrio.*
Fulica porphyrio ?
Porphyrio ventralis, *M'Clell.*

ORDER VI.—PALMIPEDES-ANSERES.

FAMILY.—BRACHYPTERA.

Gen. *Pediceps.*
Colymbus mutuccensis, *M'Clell.*

FAMILY.—ALIS LONGISSIMUS.

Group.—Lari.

Gen. *Larus.*
Larus canus?
Larus glaucus?
Larus allenus, *M'Clell.*

Group.—Sternæ.

Gen. *Sterna, Terns.*
Sterna nigricorona, *M'Clell.*
Sterna brevirostris, *Hardw.*

FAMILY.—PEDIBUS PALMATIS.

Group.—Pelecani.

Gen. *Halicus.*
Halicus grandis, *M'Clell.*
Carbo javanica, *Horsf.*

Gen. *Pelicanus.*
Pelicanus philippensis.

Gen. *Plotus.*
Plotus Levaillantii, *Viel.*

FAMILY.—ROSTRO LAMINIS INSTRUCTO.

Group.—Anseres.

Gen. *Anser.*
Anas anser.

Group.—Anates.

Anas ferus ?
Anas indica, *M'Clell.*
Anas frontalis, *Ibid.*
Anas subfuscus, *Ibid.*
Anas clypeatus ?
Anas acuta ? Pintail.

Gen. *Millouins.*
Anas ferina.

Gen. *Tadorna.*
Anas boschos, *Linn.*
Anas creca, *Linn.*

Class III.—Reptilia.

ORDER.—TESTUDINES.

Of the genus testudo, tortoise, and emys, the fresh water turtle, there are many species, or more probably varieties.

Emys Asamica of Cantor. Near the Brahmaputra, both river turtles and land tortoises are much used in the diet of the natives; but in the interior they are used in a far smaller proportion, although according to the Hindu law both are pure.

ORDER.—LACERTACEÆ.

FAMILY.—CROCODILI.

In the Brahmaputra, as well as in the Ganges, there are two kinds of crocodile, each having a specific name.

Gen. *Les gavials.*

Lacerta gangetica. Snout slender and very much elongated, teeth equal.

Gen. *Crocodilus.*

Lacerta crocodilus. Snout oblong and depressed; teeth unequal.

FAMILY.—LACERTÆ.

Group.—Monitores.

Monitor indicus *(bengalensis)* var. *Daudin.*

Monitor bivittatus. *Kuhl.*

Measuring usually from six to eight feet in length, and in this respect surpassing the hitherto known monitors; which, according to the Rev. Dr. Buckland, (Bridw. Treat. vol. i. p. 217), do not exceed five feet. This fact may probably prove very interesting, as these gigantic modern monitors form a slight approximation to the Mosasaurus, "the monstrous monitor of the ancient deep."

FAMILY.—IGAUNACEÆ.

Igaunas, of different species and varieties, are numerous.

ORDER.—SERPENTES.

Serpents, as in most warm climates, are pretty numerous; but it is chiefly in high places, of small extent, which are every where surrounded by low lands, that accidents happen, as when the floods begin the reptiles are driven suddenly into one small space, and before they can find lurking places, often take shelter in the houses, where they are accidentally trodden on, and bite their assailants. In general, however, the number of persons stated to be annually bitten is very small, and very few indeed are known to die from the wounds, which is by the natives entirely attributed to the power of magic, or incantation. The bite is usually in a limb, and immediately on a person being bitten the magician is called; and, in the meantime, a ligature is tied very tight round the limb above the bite, and probably has a considerable effect in mitigating the symptoms.

Of the serpents proper, Serpentes propriæ, or serpents without venom, we have the Boa Constrictor—the great Boa—which is frequently from thirty to forty feet in length, and of a proportionate thickness.

Python poda Russell, (the Pedda Poda of Bengal) *Boye*.

Calamaria monticola.

Coronella albocincta.

Coluber porphyraceus.

,, quadrifasciatus.

,, curvirostris.

,, reticularis.

,, bipunctatus.

Psammophis cerasogaster.

Dipsas Indica.

Dipsas ferruginea.

Dipsas monticola.

Acrochordius dubius.

Cophias viridis, *Merr.*

The venomous serpents, Serpentes venemosi, are occasionally met with; among these we find the Cobra, and one or two species of Viperæ.

Trigonocephalus mucrosquamatus.

Bungarius sividus.

Naja larvata.

Elaps bungaroides, and a few others, which our scanty information prevents us from enumerating.

ORDER.—BATRACHI.

FAMILY.—RANÆ, Frogs.

Gen. *Rana*.
Rana temporaria.
Rana taurina.
Rana esculenta.

Gen. *Hyla*.
Rana arborea.
Rana tinctoria.

Gen. *Bufo*.
Rana bufo.
Rana bufo calamita.

Gen. *Pipa*.
Rana pipa.

Class IV.—Pisces.

ORDER I.—PLAGIOSTOMA.

FAMILY.—RAIÆ.

Raia, Spec. (Asam *Suchi*).

ORDER.—MALOCOPTERGYII ABDOMINALIS.

FAMILY.—CLUPEÆ.

Clupea Spec. (Asam *Gudira*).

FAMILY.—ESOCES.

Esox Sp. (Asam *Kokila)*.
Esox cancila, *Buch*.

FAMILY.—CYPRINIDEÆ.

1 SUB-FAMILY—PAEONOMINÆ, *M'Clell.*

The greater part of these are of economical importance. Their food consists chiefly of confervoid plants, and other productions of the vegetable kingdom.

1. Gen. *Cirrhinus.*

Cirrhinus macronotus, *M'Clell.* attains from two to three feet in length.

C. nandina, *Buch.*

C. culbasu, *Buch.*

C. rohita, *Buch.*

C. gonius, *Buch.*

Sub-Gen. *Labeo.*

Cyprinus curchius, *Buch.*

Cyp. cursis, *Buch.*

Cyp. dyocheilus, *M'Clell.* (Asam *Goriya*); it usually attains two feet and upwards in length.

2. Gen. *Barbus.*

Barbus hexastichus, *M'Clell.* (Asam, *Lobura*) ordinarily from one and a half to three feet.

B. progeneius, *M'Clell.*

B. macrocephalus, *Ibid* (Asam, *Barapetiya*); ordinary length from two to three and a half feet.

B. hexagonolepis, *M'Clell.* (Asam, *Bokar.*)

B. megalepis, *Hardw.*

B. deliciosus, *M'Clell.* ordinary size about ten inches in length.

B. rodactylus, *M'Clell.* Fins red and orange, usual size about five inches in length.

Sub-Gen. *Oreinus, M'Clell.*

Oreinus progastus, *M'Clell.* (Asam, *Adoi*).

Found in the rapids in Upper Asam, where it occasionally attains eighteen inches in length, but its flesh is believed to produce vertigo, and other alarming effects, on those who use it.

3. Gen. *Cyprinus Proprius.*

Cyprinus semiplotus, *M'Clell.* (Asam, *Senturi*). Found in the rapids of the Brahmaputra, in Upper Asam. Usual size 1 foot to 1½ in length.

C. catla, *Buch.* Ordinary size from 1½ to 3 feet in length; but occasionally it is found twice that size.*

4. Gen. *Gobio.*

Cyprinus mrigala, *Buch.* Ordinary length two feet.

Cyp. angra, *Buch.*

Cyp. Hamiltonii, *Gray, Hardw.* (Asam, *Lasim*). Habitat. Brahmaputra.

G. lissorhynchus, *M'Clelland* Usual length six to nine inches.

Gobio isurus, *M'Clell.*

Cyp. boga, *Buch.* Usual length about nine inches.

Gobio bicolor, *M'Clell.*

G. anisurus, *Ibid.*

G. malocostomus, *Ibid.* (Asam, *Nepura*). Length from six to twelve inches.

5. Gen. *Gonorhynchus.*

G. gobioides, *M'Clell.* (Asam, *Herila*). Length about a span.

G. rupiculus, *M'Clell.* Hab. Mishmie mountains. Length about two inches.

G. bimaculatus, *M'Clell.*

G. brachypterus, *M'Clell.*

* These are the only two species of this group that have as yet been found in India.

II. Sub-Family—Sarcoborinæ,* *M'Clell.*

1. Gen. *Systomus, M'Clell.*

S. immaculatus, *M'Clell.* Hab. Small streams with sandy bottoms in Asam, and probably occasionally in large rivers.

S. tetrarupagus, *M'Clell.* Hab. Brahmaputra, and ponds in Asam.

S. chrysopterus, *M'Clell.* Numerically of great importance, though its size is small.

S. pyropterus, *M'Clell.* Very numerous in ponds in Upper Asam; fins red.

2. Gen. *Abramis.*

It is doubtful whether any species exist in Asam.

3. Gen. *Perilampus, M'Clell.*

All the species of this group subsist chiefly on insects, which they seize by leaping above the surface.

Cyp. devario, *Buch.*

P. ostreographus, *M'Clell.* Sides marked with several blue streaks.

P. perseus, *M'Clell.* one blue streak on either side.

4. Gen. *Leuciscus.*

L. dystomus, *M'Clell.*

Cyp. rasobora, *Buch.*

Cyp. mola, *Buch.*

L. pellucidus, *M'Clell.*

L. branchiatus, *Ibid.*

L. margaroides, *Ibid.*—The scales of this species would afford abundant materials for the manufacture of mock pearl.

Cyp. morar, *Buch.* (Asam, *Chula*).

* From Σαρκοβορος, carnivorous.

5. Gen. *Opsarius, M'Clell.*

O. pholicephalus, *Ibid.*

O. leucerus, *Ibid.*

O. fasciatus ?

O. maculosus ?

O. brachialis, *M'Clell.*

Cyp. bendilisis, *Buch.*

O. gracilis, *M'Clell.* Cyp. goha, *Buch.*

O. megastomus, *Ibid.* Cyp. bola, *Buch.*

O. latipinnatus, *M'Clell.* (Asam, *Balisundari*).

III. Sub-Family—Apalopterinæ, *M'Clell.*

Gen. *Cobitis.*

a. Sub-Gen. *Cobitis propria.*

Cobitis oculata, *M'Clell.* C. gongota, *Buch.*

C. guntea, *Buch.*

C. ocellata, *M'Clell.* C. bilturia, *Buch.*

C. gibbosa, *M'Clell.* C. turio, *Buch.*

C. pavonacea, *M'Clell.*

C. monocera, *Ibid.*

C. chlorosoma, *Ibid.* Colour light green, clouded with a darker green

C. guttata, *Ibid.* Light green with dark blotches, eight rays in the dorsal.

C. phoxocheita, *M'Clell.* Hab. Mishmee mountains.

β. Sub-Gen. *Schistura, M'Clell.*

C. dario, *Buch.*

C. geta, *Ibid.*

S. aculeata, *M'Clell.*

S. subfusca, *Ibid.*

Variet. S. punctata, *M'Clell.* or C. corica, *Buch.*

S. zonata, *M'Clell.* Eleven dark green bars across the body, with light green zones between them.

Variet. S. rupecula, *M'Clell.*, thirteen rays round the body.
Hab. Stagnant pools in Upper Asam.

We proceed now to a slight notice of the insects.

Of the beautiful and sparkling genus *Cicindela*, several examples are found in Asam: the most remarkable is C. aurulenta.

Of the great genus *Carabus*, many specimens occur.

The nearly allied genus *Calosoma* (which though much less numerous than the preceding, is likewise widely spread over the old world and the new) presents us with a few species.

Of the great tribe of Water Beetles:—*Hydrocanthari*, of which the old genera *Dytiscus* and *Gyrinus* form the principal component portions, several examples occur.

In relation to the brachelytrous tribes (*Staphylinus*, Linn). the naturalist who knows how characteristic these insects are of temperate or somewhat northern countries, and how rare they become in continental India and other tropical situations, will be less sanguine in his expectations regarding the abundance of Asamese species. A few specimens are occasionally, though rarely, met with.

Asam presents a few varieties, if not species, of the Lamellicorn Beetles; their specific names, however, we have not the means of ascertaining.

Of the magnificent *Buprestidæ*, which form so gorgeous a feature in most entomological cabinets, we may name as a well known specific variety the *Ludius fulgens* of Latreille. *B. vittata* is another imposing species, no less common than the preceding, of considerable size, and great richness of aspect, being of the brightest golden green, with varied reflections of blue and flame colour.

Various *Hemipterous* insects are found throughout the province. Some of these are extremely annoying, from the almost constant stridulous sounds which they utter, especially a species of *Cicada*. These insects seem among the most cosmopolite of their class, being found in every part of the earth, with the exception probably of the arctic and antarctic regions. This insect forms the subject of Meleoger's beautiful invocation :—

> ...."O shrill-voiced insect! that with dew drops meet,
> Inebriate, dost in desert woodlands sing,
> Perched in the spray-top with indented feet,
> Thy dusky body's echoings, harp-like ring."

The quiet disposition of the females is a singular characteristic, of which we have long since been informed by Xenurchus, the Rhodian :—

> ...." Happy the Cicada's lives,
> Since they all have voiceless wives."

Of the Lantern Flies, or luminous insects, the *Fulgora laternaria* is very abundant. It is easily recognized by its long cylindrical snout, arched in an upward direction, its greenish reticulated elytra, and orange-yellow wings with black extremities. They are seen to glitter at night among the dark and leafy recesses of the forest trees, or flit with varied motions around their utmost branches, producing an effect so brilliant, and so singularly beautiful, as to seem almost the effect of magic.

Of *Hymenopterous* insects, including wasps and bees, there are many species; the *Neuropterous* order likewise affords a few beautiful examples.

The *Lepidopterous* insects, as may be inferred, are extremely numerous. Some of them are particularly large, their colours are wonderfully diversified, and lively to a surprising degree.

Of all the entomological productions of Asam, the most important are assuredly the silk-worms, the produce of the Muga moth, (Saturnia), the Eria-worm, (Phalæna Cunthia), and the Bombyx mori, which latter is indigenous to China.

In regard to the *Dipterous* order, it may be remarked that the low and marshy tracts so common in most parts of the country, are but too favourable to the multiplication of those numerous winged insects of the gnat kind, which pass their earlier stages in the water. Most of these are well known to be extremely troublesome, particularly on account of their stinging propensities, or more correctly speaking, the wounds which they inflict with their proboscis, while searching for their natural food—the blood of man and beast.

We here close our sketch of the Zoological productions of the country, and, with it, our remarks on its Natural Geography; entertaining the sanguine hope, that not many years will elapse, without numerous additions being made to our knowledge of a subject, at once so interesting and important.

The Tea-Plant.

Thea Viridis, Linn. *Camellia theifera*, Griff.*

Description of the tea plant—Its localities—Character of the soil—Comparison with the tea soils of China—The tea plant Botanically considered—Considered as an object of Agricultural produce—Account of manufacture—Names whereby the principal sorts of tea are known in China—Tea the favourite beverage of the adjacent hill tribes—Mode of manufacture by the Singphos and other tribes—Mode of preparing it for drink by the Butias—A very successful result anticipated from the general culture of the tea plant in Asam, were it only with the view of rendering it a staple article of trade with the adjacent hill tribes—Captain Turner's estimate of the value of tea consumed in Teshu Lumbu—Sketch of the History of the British trade—A cheering prospect opened up to British enterprise in Asam—Discovery of the tea plant—Tea Committee appointed—Mr. Gordon deputed to China—Captain Jenkins highly instrumental in bringing the tea plant to notice—Reports from Captain Jenkins and Lieut. Charlton—Deputation of scientific gentlemen to Asam—Appointment of Mr. Bruce—Asam tea manufactured and sent to England—Opinions of the sample sent—Mr. Bruce succeeds in manufacturing a small specimen of green tea—The importance and advantages of the discovery of the tea plant in Asam—Formation of the Asam Company—Their subsequent arrangements—Altered temper of the Singphos—Terms for the grant of lands to tea cultivators.

From the importance of the tea plant in the future advancement of the country, we have deemed it necessary to devote a separate section to a description of the plant, with a short account of its discovery, and the subsequent measures undertaken for its cultivation, terminating in the formation of the "Asam Company."

The ordinary height of the shrub is from five to eight feet, though it occasionally attains a far greater size. It is a polyandrous plant of the natural order *Ternstiomicæ*. The

* For Dr. Griffith's remarks on the genus to which the Tea plant belongs, see his "Report on the Tea plant of Asam."

flowers, which open early in spring, appear upon the plant about a month, are smaller in size, and much less elegant than those that render some species of the Camellia so attractive. They are about an inch in diameter, slightly odorous, and of a pure white colour; they proceed from the axils of the branches, and stand on short foot-stalks, at the most two or three together, but usually solitary. There are five or six imbricate sepals or leaves supporting the blossom, which fall off after the flower has expanded, and leave from six to nine petals surrounding a great number of yellow stamens, that are joined together in such a manner at their bases, as to form a sort of floral coronal. The seeds are inclosed in a smooth hard capsule, of a flattish triangular shape, which is interiorly divided into two, three, and even five cells, each containing a firm, white, and somewhat oily nut, about the size of a hazel-nut, of a bitterish and nauseous taste. They ripen in December and January, the stem is generally bushy, with numerous branches bearing a very dense foliage, and in its general appearance is not unlike a myrtle, though not so symmetrical as that plant. The wood is light coloured, close grained, of great comparative density, and when freshly cut or peeled, gives off a strong smell resembling that of the black currant bush. The leaves are alternate, on short, thick channelled foot-stalks, coriaceous, or leathery, but smooth and shining, of a dark green colour, and a longish elliptic form, with a blunt notched point, and serrated except at the base. It is needless to mention that these leaves are the valuable part of the plant. They are, however, a good deal affected by the site in which the plant is grown, whether under the thick umbrage of large trees, or in open spots exposed to the influence of the sun's rays, as well as by the nature of the soil in which the plant is found.

The tea shrub may be described as a very hardy evergreen, growing readily in the open air, from the equator to the 45th degree of latitude. The progress of research in the hilly tracts on this frontier, leads to the conclusion that the plant prevails far more generally amongst them, than is usually supposed; so much so, that it may be looked upon as one of the common plants of a large portion of Upper Asam. From this circumstance it is evident too that its cultivation may be extended with advantage, as the present existence of the plant proves that no obstacle, arising from peculiarity of climate or soil, can be fairly anticipated. The districts in which the finest tea is produced in China, lie between the 25th and 33rd degrees of latitude; and, in Asam, the ranges in which it has been discovered are between the 27th and 28th parallels, or almost centrically situated within those limits, which experience has proved the most favourable to the development of the plant.

Almost all the tea localities occur within very short distances of each other, and are very limited in extent; although some tracts are farther apart, and cover a larger extent of land than others. These localities may be characterized as presenting an excess of humidity, and are, in almost every instance, clothed with excessively dense tree jungle. The chief characteristic of the localities is their intersection by numerous ravines and hollows, the spaces between which often assume a conical shape. The presence of these, which are proofs of the lightness of the soil, Dr. M'Clelland seems to attribute to the action of the water collected on the foliage of the surrounding trees, and thence precipitated in heavy volumes. The plants, however, seem undoubtedly to thrive best near small rivers and pools of water, and in those places where, after heavy falls of rain, large quantities of water have accumulated, and in their struggle to get free, have cut out for themselves numerous small channels.

The prevailing characters of the soil are lightness and porousness; and its prevailing colour is yellow, or reddish yellow, which generally becomes more developed, as the depth increases, up to a certain point, when it passes into sand.

Dr. M'Clelland is of opinion, that the requisite quality of the soil, which is comparatively of rare occurrence, will account for the manner in which the plant is distributed in spots or distinct colonies, instead of being uniformly diffused with the common vegetation.

The component parts of the soil, he observes, consist of

Free water, ...	22½
Water of absorption, ...	3
Vegetable matter, ...	16
Oxide of Iron, ...	6
Alumina, ...	6½
Silex in the state of fine dusty sand, or coarse sharp sand, and dusty matter,.. ..	130
	184

Mr. Piddington, who has had an opportunity of comparing and analyzing the tea soils of Asam and those of China, gives the following result.

	Tea soil of Asam. Surface soil.	At 2½ feet deep.	Tea soil of China.
Water,	2·45	2·00	3·00
Vegetable matter,	1·00	·80	1·00
Carbonate of Iron,	7·40	6·70	9·90
Alumina,	3·50	5·45	9·10
Silex,	85·40	84·10	76·00
	99·75	99·05	99·00
Traces of phosphate and sulphate of lime and loss.	·25	·95	1·00
	100·00	100·00	100·00

"The two peculiarities in these soils," observes Mr. Piddington, "are the first, that they contain no carbonate of lime, and only traces of phosphate and sulphate, and the next that their iron is almost wholly in the state of carbonate of iron, a widely different compound from the simple oxides. They would be called poor yellow loams, and cotton, tobacco, or sugar-cane, would probably starve upon them; but we find that they suit the tea plant perfectly. It is a striking coincidence that we should find our tea soils and those of China, so exactly alike."

Botanically considered, the tea plant is a single species; the green and black, with all the diversities of each, being mere varieties produced by a difference in the culture, qualities of soil, age of the crop when taken up, and modes of preparation for the market.

Considered as an object of agricultural produce, the tea plant bears a close resemblance to the vine. Skill and care both in husbandry and preparation, are quite as necessary to the production of good tea, as of good wine.

The following account of the manufacture of tea, we gather from the reports of Mr. Bruce.

The leaves are gathered from one to four times during the year, according to the age of the tree; most commonly there are three periods of gathering. The leaves that are earliest gathered are of the most delicate colour and most aromatic flavour, with the least portion of either fibre or bitterness. The gathering is made as soon as the 15th of April, and in favourable seasons even earlier, when the delicate leaf buds appear, and the foliage is just opening, and is covered with a whitish down. The quantity obtained is small; but the quality is superior, and the finest sorts of tea are made from it. Leaves of the second gathering are of a dull green colour, and have less valuable qualities than the former. This picking is by the Chinese technically termed *urh chun*, or "second spring," as the first is *show chun*, or "first spring," and takes place about the first part of June, when the branches are covered with leaves, and produce the greatest quantity.

The third picking called *san chun*, or "third spring," is about a month after the last, when the shrubs are again searched; the leaves are then of a dark green, and the produce is made into the most common sorts of tea. A fourth gleaning is not a common practice, for the leaves are old, and fit only for the coarsest kinds. The usual mode of gathering is to cull the leaves by hand, and lay them loosely on bamboo trays or baskets.

The produce of a single plant varies so much, that it is difficult to estimate the average. As far as Mr. Bruce has been able to judge, he gives the following statement: "I think you will be pretty correct if you allow one tola of tea for each plant every year; for instance one tola for the first year after cutting and burning. Two *tolas* the second year, and so on until the sixth year, when the plant will be in its prime; one *purah* of land, (a natural tea *Barri*), after it has been cut down the first year, might produce one *tola* each plant, or 18 *seers*, 1 *pow*, and 9 *tolas*; the second year 36 *seers*, 2 *pows*, and 18 *tolas*; the third year 1 *maund*, 15 *seers*, and 7 *tolas*; the sixth year 2 *maunds*, 30 *seers*, and 14 *tolas*. One hundred *puras* would give 11,000 *seers*, which at 2 rupees per seer, would give rupees 22,000 per year, or 1833 rupees per month. But it should be borne in mind, that all soils are not alike; in some tracts it may be more, and in others less."

The weather is said to have great influence upon the quality of the leaves. If there is too much rain, they will become mildewed and broken, of a yellow colour, thin and sickly; if too little, they will be small in size, and the foliage not at all abundant. But if the rains fall equably, and after the showers a bright sun appears, the leaves will be numerous and flourishing, of a bright green colour and luxuriant texture, and the flavour superior. The quality of the leaf is further influenced by the age of the wood on which the leaves are borne, and by the degree of exposure to which they have been accustomed.

The leaves as soon as gathered, are put into wide shallow baskets placed in the air or wind, or sunshine, for a few hours, (the length of time they are exposed generally depending on the heat of the sun), or until they become somewhat soft. Then, while lying on the tray, they are gently rubbed and rolled. When the leaves have been rubbed sufficiently they are considered ready for firing. They are now placed on a flat cast-iron pan, over a stove heated with charcoal; and from a half to three-quarters of a pound is operated on at one time. These leaves are stirred quickly about with a kind of brush, and then quickly swept off the pan into baskets. The next process is that of rolling, which is effected by carefully rolling the leaves between men's hands, after which they are again put in larger quantities on the pan, and subjected anew to heat, but at this time to a lower degree than at first, and just sufficient to dry them effectually, without risk of scorching. This effected, the tea is placed on a table, and carefully picked over, every unsightly or imperfectly dried leaf that is detected being removed from the rest, in order that the sample may present a more even and a better appearance. With different and finer sorts of tea, a slight difference in manipulation is of necessity employed.

Here it may not be out of place to state, that the principal sorts of tea known in China, are distinguished according to the places in which they are produced; while others are distinguished according to the periods of gathering, the manner employed in curing, or other extrinsic circumstances.

Tea has hitherto been the favourite beverage of those hill tribes in whose vicinity the wild plant has been found. The Singphos have long known and drank the tea, but their mode of preparing it is very different from that we have already described. The young and tender leaves are first plucked and dried in the sun; by some they are exposed alternately to the night dews, and the heat of the sun for three successive days; whilst by others they are put into flat hot pans and turned about till quite dry. This done the leaves are placed in the hollow of a bamboo, and driven firmly down by means of a stick, the bamboo being at the same time held in the heat of a fire. When full, the ends of the bamboos are tied up with leaves, and then hung up in places where they may be exposed to the smoke of the fire. Thus prepared, the tea is said to keep good for years.

In other places, the natives have a different mode of manufacture. Holes are dug in the earth, the sides of which are lined with large leaves. The tea is then boiled, the decoction thrown away, and the leaves themselves are buried in the earth. This is done with the view of reducing the leaves to a state of fermentation; and when this has been effected, the leaves are put into hollow bamboos, and thus prepared are taken to market. When intended for use, the leaves are boiled and the infusion is drunk.

The Butias are said to be particularly attached to this beverage. Their supplies are, however, imported overland from Pekin. The liquor they drink is extremely unlike what we are used to under the same name. It is a compound of water, flour, butter, salt, and bohea tea, with some other astringent ingredients, all boiled, beat up, and intimately blended together.

From the well known fact of tea being the favourite drink of those tribes in whose vicinity it has been found, as well as from the immense quantity expended in the adjacent kingdom of Butan, it would appear far from chimerical to anticipate a very successful result from the general culture of the plant in Asam, were it merely with the view of rendering it a staple article of trade with the regions in which it is so extensively consumed, and where from the peculiar mode of preparing it for use, less skill in its culture would be necessary, than in those varieties intended for European markets.

Captain Turner estimated that the value of the tea consumed in the district of Teshu Lumbu alone, amounted to *seven lakhs of rupees* per annum; and considering that it is imported from Pekin by a land journey of eight months' duration, and then comparing the regions it is compelled to traverse, with the nature of the country that intervenes between Asam and Butan, and the time that caravans would respectively take in reaching the same place from Pekin and Gowhatti, it would seem very probable that were the tea trade carried on with Butan alone, it would tend in no small measure to promote the future welfare of the country.*

The history of commerce does not, perhaps, present a parallel to the extraordinary circumstances which have attended the introduction of tea into Great Britain.† This leaf was first imported into Europe by the Dutch East India Company, in the early part of the seventeenth century; but it was not until the year 1664, that a small quantity was carried to England, when the East India Company bought 2lbs. 2oz. of tea as a present for His Majesty. Yet from a period earlier than any to which the memories of any of the existing generation can reach, tea has been one of the principal necessaries of life among all classes of the British community. To provide a sufficient supply of this aliment, many thousand tons of the finest mercantile navy in the world are annually employed in trading with a people by whom all dealings with foreigners are merely tolerated; and from this recently acquired taste a very large and easily collected revenue is obtained by the state.

The first direct importation of tea by the Society of Merchants trading to the East Indies (afterwards the East

* Some tea of Asam manufacture which was lately shown to the members of a Mission of Kampo Butias, some of whom where from Lassa, was very much approved of by them. They said that a seer of tea at Lassa cost 10 Rupees or 12 Rupees, and as Asam tea could be given them at less than half that price, it is evident there is an opening in this direction for a most extensive trade in this article.

† Vide M'Culloch's Commercial Dictionary.

India Company) in 1669, was 150℔s.; and in 1833, the Honorable Company retained for home consumption alone, no less a quantity than 31,829, 620℔s.

If therefore with such a steadily increasing demand, a field can be pointed out within British territory, in which British capital and industry can produce a tea capable of competing with the produce of China, it is not saying too much when we venture to assert, that a more cheering prospect was never opened up to British enterprize, with a greater certainty of a rich reward.

In 1823 Mr. Robert Bruce first came into Asam* with a large assortment of goods for disposal. He was the first British merchant who had proceeded so far beyond our then Eastern frontier. The country was then known little more than by name, and was occupied by the Burmese. He visited Rungpore, then the capital, and there formed an acquaintance with a Singpho chief, and being addicted to botanical researches, he soon discovered that the tea plant was growing on the hills in a state of nature; he made a written engagement with the chief to furnish him with some plants for an equivalent. At the breaking out of the Burmese war in 1824, his brother, Mr. C. A. Bruce, was appointed to the command of a division of gun-boats, and ordered up to Sadiya. After the capital had fallen into our hands, the Singpho chief came down to pay his respects. Mr. Bruce took the opportunity to speak to him of the tea plant, when the chief produced his brother's agreement. A request for plants and seeds followed, which upon his return he sent down to the amount of several hundred plants, and a considerable quantity of the seed. Some of these were forwarded to Mr. David Scott, (at that time the Governor General's Agent), and the remainder planted in his own gardens. About that time also specimens were forwarded by Mr. Scott to the Superintendent of the Botanic Garden at Calcutta; they were pronounced

* See Dr. Leonard's letter to A. Rogers, Esq. 5th January.

of the same family, but not of the same species as the plant from which the Chinese took the leaf.

In 1832, Lord William Bentinck deputed Captain Jenkins to report upon the resources of the country. The subject of the tea plant was brought to his attention by Mr. Bruce, who furnished him with an official account of the localities where the plant grew, and the different modes of preparation employed by the natives.

Two years afterwards, the Government nominated a Committee* for effecting the introduction of the tea plant into the Company's territories, and Mr. Gordon was appointed Secretary to it. It is to be remembered, that at this period the existence of the real tea plant in Asam was questioned; but a strong opinion was entertained, that some parts of India were well calculated for its introduction and growth.

Mr. Gordon proceeded in June 1834, in the "Water Witch" to China, with instructions to obtain a supply of tea plants and seeds, and reaching Macao in July, went to the coast in company with the Reverend Mr. Gutslaff, in fulfilment of his instructions.

During his absence, inquiries were again instituted relative to the tea plant of Asam. In promoting this important object, Captain Jenkins, as in numerous other projects for improving the interests of Asam, gave his warm and decided support. To him, no less than to Mr. Bruce, is Great Britain indebted for the discovery of the indigenous tea plant of Asam; and the merit is so much the greater, for the spirited manner in which he has taken the necessary steps to promote the culture of the tea plant.

The Tea Committee soon received communications from Captain Jenkins and Lieut. Charlton, proving beyond all doubt that the tea shrub is indigenous in Asam. In forwarding these communications to Government, the Committee observe that, "it is with feelings of the highest

* See "Sketch of the Tea Plant, &c. of Asam."

possible satisfaction, that we are enabled to announce to his Lordship in Council, that the tea shrub is beyond all doubt indigenous in Upper Asam, being found there through an extent of country of one month's march, within the Honorable Company's territories, from Sudiya and Beesa to the Chinese frontier province of Yumian, where the shrub is cultivated for the sake of its leaf. We have no hesitation in declaring this discovery, which is due to the indefatigable researches of Captain Jenkins and Lieut. Charlton, to be by far the most important and valuable that has ever been made on matters connected with the agricultural or commercial resources of this empire." The Committee in consequence earnestly recommended to Government, at Captain Jenkins' suggestion, that in the first instance, and as early as practicable, one or more scientific gentlemen might be deputed into Upper Asam, for the purpose of collecting details on the spot, as preliminary information absolutely necessary, before ulterior measures could be successfully taken.

The Governor General entirely concurred in these views; and Dr. Wallich, who had offered his services, and Messrs. Assistant Surgeons M'Clelland and Griffiths, (selected, at Dr. Wallich's recommendation, for their scientific attainments, the latter then at *Tavoy*, the former in *Kumaon*,) were accordingly nominated, and directed to be at Sudiya by the 1st of November 1835. The Governor General subsequently sanctioned the selection of Mr. C. A. Bruce, for the charge of the tea-nurseries to be established in Upper Asam. At the suggestion of Captain Jenkins and the Tea Committee, Mr. Bruce, was shortly afterwards supplied with a few Chinese tea plants, and manufacturers brought round from China by Mr. Gordon, and at the end of 1837, was enabled to submit to the Tea Committee a consignment of 46 boxes of Asam tea.

In a letter dated the 20th March following, the Tea Committee observed, that "Owing to a deficiency in the original packing, and the great degree of dampness to which the boxes had been exposed during the passage from Asam, a considerable portion of the tea was either wholly spoiled or so much deteriorated, that no process could have restored, it to any thing like a fair quality; they had therefore rejected all that portion as unfit to be sent home, at least with the present supply, deeming it a matter of primary importance that the value of the first samples transmitted to Europe should not be diminished by any thing that might add to the many disadvantages under which they must necessarily arrive at a destination, where they would, in all probability, have to be subjected to the severe test of examination by the first tea inspectors in London.

"The Committee begged most particularly to urge on the consideration of Government, that not only were the plants from which the leaves were gathered, still in their original wild and uncultivated state, but the details of the various processes employed in preparing and transmitting the tea, must obviously have laboured under the many and serious difficulties and obstacles of a first attempt, but which may reasonably be 'expected will be diminished and progressively overcome, as further trials are made. Besides which, it ought to be borne in mind, that, strange as it may appear, it is by no means settled whether it is not actually the green sort that has been prepared in the fashion of black tea; a point, which can only be satisfactorily determined, when the green tea manufacturers are set at work in Asam."

Such were the unfavourable circumstances under which the first importation of BRITISH TEA, made its appearance in the English market. It was notwithstanding declared, in a very satisfactory manner, by the principal tea brokers in Great Britain, to be capable of competing with that of China, when more care shall be taken in the selection of leaves from plants better pruned, and when greater experience shall have perfected the mode of preparation.* The general opinion was

* See Dr. Leonard's letter to A. Rogers, Esq. 5th January 1839.

that the quality of the tea completely established the success of the experiment. It was described as "tea, good, middling, strong, high burnt, rather smoky, Pekoe kind, and if there was any deficiency in its character, it arose from want of care in the preparation, rather than from the quality of the plant."

In April, 1838, Mr. Bruce succeeded in manufacturing a small specimen of tea, which he thought he had prepared in the manner in which green tea must be made by the Chinese. Capt. Jenkins, in writing to Lord W. Bentinck, in the following month, states that he has been long of opinion that the tea plant we possess was of the green variety, from the great fragrance of the smell of the leaves. "I have now the great pleasure of informing your Lordship, that I consider the question put beyond all doubt, for within the last week I have had a specimen of tea manufactured as green tea, from Mr. Bruce, recording to some information which he has lately fallen upon. The tea has been fully acknowledged to be good green tea by every gentleman who has drank it, and it has been drank as excellent fresh green tea, by those who were led to suppose it came from Calcutta. I have therefore entire confidence now, that when the green tea China manufacturers, who are on the way up from Calcutta, commence operations, we shall be able to send home green tea of as good a quality as the black tea under dispatch."

He then justly, but forcibly, remarks, that he is apprehensive if the first dispatch be condemned, all our prospects will be at once lost; and expresses a hope that if his Lordship should have an opportunity, he would let it be known, that the attempts to manufacture have been made very rudely indeed, and that they still laboured under so many difficulties, only to be removed by a greater expenditure than the Government has thought fit to allow on the experiment, that no tea we can at present send home, can be a fair test of what may be done in time, with experience, and appropriate means.*

* See "Sketch of the Tea Plant, &c., of Asam."

The green tea manufacturers alluded to, have since arrived; and specimens of their manufacture have been forwarded to England, where they have been highly approved of.

The above facts all tend to prove, that we have it in our power, at no distant period, to take into our own hands a trade which China has heretofore monopolised; a trade which has cost England two very expensive, but useless embassies, and to continue which the merchants of Great Britain have been obliged to submit to innumerable restrictions, and insults, and occasional suspensions of trade. The immense wealth which has flowed for a century and a half from Great Britain and her colonies to a foreign country, will henceforth be distributed amongst British subjects, and a new source of lucrative employment be opened up to millions. The Chinese Government deeply sensible of the demoralizing effects of the trade in opium, are now seriously setting about the prevention of the importation of it, in which, if they succeed, the only form of payment for our teas will be in specie, as the quantity of British manufactures taken in return is scarcely worth notice. The growth of that necessary of life, therefore, in India, is an object so decidedly national, that it calls for the warmest support and encouragement from our government. Nor can it be for a moment doubted, that the call will be promptly responded to; for, with the incontrovertible evidence before us, of the excellent quality of the article to be supplied, the extent of the demand for it, and the certainty of a ready market, it almost ceases to deserve the name of *a speculation*, and becomes rather a prudent investment of capital, which at the same time that it offers to all concerned in it, the *certainty* of a fair profit, developes the vast resources of a territory hitherto unproductive, and will add another to the many fine examples of British mercantile enterprise, which, no less than the brilliant achievements of her Nelson and her Wellington, have placed Great

Britain in the eminent position she occupies in the rank of nations.*

Satisfied of the successful result of the Government experimental culture of the tea plant, and the favourable opinions of the principal tea brokers in Great Britain on the samples of tea sent to England, imperfect as the first attempts at manufacture were acknowledged to have been, it appeared advisable to take further and more decisive steps for extending the future cultivation of the tea plant.

The Honorable Court of Directors, the Board of Control, the Supreme Government of India, the Tea Committee at Calcutta, and all other parties most conversant with the subject, concurred in opinion that the cultivation of the plant, and the manufacture of tea in Asam, should become matter of private adventure. The Asam Company was accordingly formed in England in the month of February 1839, with a present capital of 500,000*l.* in 10,000 shares of 50*l.* each; 8,000 shares were set apart for allotment in England, and 2,000 for allotment in India. The Provisional Committee was authorised to open books to receive the names of parties desirous of becoming shareholders, to take such further steps as might be necessary for forming a direction, incorporating the Company, and limiting the liability of shareholders, and for carrying into effect generally the object contemplated by the Society.

Simultaneously with the formation of the Asam Company in England, an association, having the same objects in view, was formed in Calcutta. Subsequently, however, both the Companies agreed upon merging their interests, and forming one association under the name of the ASAM COMPANY, the management of which in India, should be vested in a Committee of Directors chosen by the Bengal Branch of the association.

After the agreement had been effected, Mr. J. Masters, a

* See Dr. Leonard's letter to A. Rogers, Esq. 5th January, 1839.

gentleman well known in Calcutta for his botanical and agricultural pursuits, was deputed to Asam, to take up tea tracts for the Company. After visiting Jaipur, and the tea tracts on the eastern districts, he established his head-quarters at Nazira, close to the old fort and capital of Ghergong, pending negotiations with the Government for the transfer of their experimental factories to the Asam Company.

Mr. Masters was subsequently joined by several assistants, and was shortly enabled to establish plantations at Sathseyah, Gabru-Parbut, and China-doe.

Since Lord Auckland's return from the North-west Provinces, the Asam Company have been enabled to bring their negotiations with the Government to a termination; and His Lordship has decided on transferring to the Company two-thirds of all the Government establishment and tea plantations, at the same time permitting Mr. Bruce to join the Company.

Agreeably to this decision, all the tea *Barris* between the Bari-Dihung and Tingri, and the high road from Jaipur to Sudiya, joining these two rivers, (a tract comprising nearly 70,000 British acres) were transferred to the Company. There are a number of tea tracts, but the population is exceedingly thin, and it can only be by a large importation of labourers, that the produce of the country can be increased to any extent.

The Company have established their chief factory at the junction of the Bari-Dihung and Tingri rivers. Since the jurisdiction of the territory known as the Muttack country has lapsed from the family of the Bar Senapati to the British Government, the Company have established another factory at Diburghur, the head-quarters of the civil functionaries in this division. The unsettled state of the Muttacks, however, will for some time prevent the resources of this fine district from being fully available to the public; for political considerations render it inexpedient, in the opinion of the local authorities, to permit strangers to settle in the more populated part of the country, amongst a people so jealous of their privileges and independence, and so little accustomed to the restraints of a regular Government.

The scattered tracts in the interior of this division have been reserved for the Government, and are at present managed under the immediate surveillance of Captain Veitch, the Political Agent of the Eastern districts of Asam.

It has already been stated, that in 1837 the quantity of tea manufactured in Asam, and sent down to Calcutta, amounted to forty-six boxes, from which number twelve were selected and sent to England. In 1838, forty-five chests of tea were dispatched; and last year, the export from Asam amounted to a hundred and twenty boxes. The export of the present year (1840), it is expected will amount to nearly five hundred chests of a *maund* each, of which about 200 will be the produce of the Government factories, and 300 the manufacture of the Asam Company.

From this large ratio of increase, and the rapid enlargement of the tea *Barris*, we may assume that the export of 1841, will fall little short of a thousand and five hundred chests of 80lbs each, or a total of 1,20,000lbs of tea.

One of the most favourable features in our tea prospects is, the altered temper of our Singpho subjects. Since the rule of the British Government has been fairly established over the Muttack country, and those intrigues put an end to, which originating in the mistaken policy and jealousy of the Bar Senapati and his numerous sons, kept the whole frontier in perpetual disturbance, the Singpho chiefs, always disunited among themselves, and willing to engage in any rencounter where there was a prospect of plunder, have either seen that the factions promoted by the chiefs of Muttack were fomented for their own sinister purposes, or they have felt the necessity of submitting to a power which has now so nearly approached to them, and whose strength they clearly perceive they cannot resist. They have in consequence shewn an inclination to abandon their old habits of lawlessness and rapine, and turn their attention to agriculture, now become necessary for their subsistence.

Captain Veitch judiciously availing himself of the impressions made upon them by their reverses and present wants, prevailed on one of the most influential of the Singpho chiefs, Ningroola, to become a superintendent and cultivator of tea in the extensive Baris near his own village, and the result has been very satisfactory. No less than thirty chests of tea, partly black, and partly green, are expected from the Ningroo plantations this first season, entirely the produce of Singpho industry.*

In conclusion, it may be necessary to state, that the Government of India have lately decided on the terms on which lands for cultivation of the tea plant and the collection of tea leaves, may be granted to the Asam Tea Company, or to any intending speculators.

These terms which are to hold for the next ten years, are as follows :—

Waste lands for the establishment of new tea cultivations, or for the cultivation of gram, or other purposes, for the labourers employed in the culture and manufacture of tea, are to be granted, at the discretion of the local officers of Government, on the terms determined on for the waste grants in other parts of Asam

Lands on which tea baries are indigenous, are not to be given in possession to any party, but individuals may be allowed to collect or purchase tea leaves, plants, and seeds, within certain defined boundaries, for ten years, free of any rent to the Government.

* By the latest accounts Capt. Veitch, was in negotiation with other chiefs, endeavouring to make similar engagements with them, and with every prospect of like success.

CHAPTER IV.

HISTORICAL GEOGRAPHY.

Ancient History obscure and fabulous—Hindoo territory of Kamroop—Earliest tradition concerning it—Ancient Kings of Kamroop—Pal family—Succeeded by another dynasty—Invasion of the Moosulmans—Anarchy—Rise of the Siba-bangsa—Their possession of Durang—The gradual downfall of the Kingdom—The Ahoms—Their traditions—Descendants of the Shyans—Traces of their origin—Change in the royal genealogies—Early History of their kings, lost in fable—Cheekapha the first king of note—Subsequent conquests of the Ahoms—Their progressive History—Insurrection of the Moomariyas—Civil Wars—Capt. Welsh deputed to Asam—Quells the disturbances—Returns to Calcutta—Civil feuds—Invasion of the Burmese—Interference of the British Government—War with the Burmans—British Government obtain possession of Asam.

The Ancient History of Asam, like that of most oriental nations, is involved in a great degree of obscurity. Though we have a few chronicles and other works of native composition to refer to, most of the occurrences mentioned in them, especially those relating to the more ancient history, are so intimately blended with what is fabulous and uncertain, that we are obliged to receive them with the greatest diffidence.

By far the greater portion of the country now known as Asam, was originally included in the ancient Hindoo territory of Kamroop; besides which it also included the whole of the modern divisions of Rungpoor, and Rangamati, a portion of the Mymansing district and Silhet, and in all probability also extended over Munipur, Jyntia, and Kachar. The earliest tradition concerning the history of Kamroop is, that it was given by Krishna to Norok, the son of Prithibi, (the Earth).

This Norok, although an infidel, (Osur), was for some time a favourite of the gods, who appointed him guardian of the temple of Kamakhya, (the giver of pleasure,) who naturally presided over Kamroop, the region of desire. This deity is by the Hindoos considered a female, and her temple situated near Gowhatti, the place where Norok resided, is still one of great celebrity.

Kamroop is said to have been divided into four Piths, or portions, each of which may naturally be expected to have had an appellation suited to its name, and tutelary deity. They are accordingly called Kam Pith, Ratno Pith, Sevarna Pith, and Choumar Pith. By the natives the country is considered as the principal seat of amorous delight, a sort of Paphian land; and a great indulgence in promiscuous pleasures is consequently considered as allowable.

Norok did not long merit the favour of Krishna. Being a great oppressor, and a worshipper of the rival god Sib, he was put to death, and was succeeded by his son Bhagadatta. At the time of the wars which are said to have placed Judisthir on the throne of India, this prince engaged in the great contest on the losing side, and followed the fortunes of Durjudhan. There seems a great probability that this is the same person with *Bhagrat* of Mr. Gladwin's translation of the Ayen Akberry, "who came to the assistance of Durjudhan, and gallantly fell in the war of the Mahabarat."

In this great war, Bhagadatta is said to have fallen by the hands of Arjun, brother of Judisthir; but, according to the Ayen Akberry, twenty-three princes of the same family continued to govern after his death. The authority of this work is however diminished by its supposing that these princes governed the whole of Bengal; which seems entirely without foundation. It is, however, very likely, and is said indeed to be mentioned in the Purans, that for some time the descendants of Bhagadatta retained the government of Kamroop.

This account does not agree with that given in the Jogini Tantro, which is considered as the highest authority concerning every thing relating to Kamroop. In it there is no mention of Bhagadatta; but it states that the god Sib prophesied, that after the infidel Norok, and at the commencement of the era of Saka, that is, about the end of the first century of our era, there would be Sudra kings of Kamroop. The first Raja mentioned is Debeswar, in whose time the worship of Kameswari, or Kamakhya, the knowledge of which had hitherto been confined to the learned, would be published even to the vulgar; and this would happen at the very begining of the era of Saka, or A.D. 76. The worship of the Linga, according to this prophecy, would begin in the 19th year of Saka. Some indefinite time, after that period, a Brahman, born of the Kerotya river, and named Nagasankar, would be king, and extend the doctrine. After him, but at what interval is not mentioned, would be a Raja, named Jolpeswar, who would still further encourage that worship, and who would build the celebrated temple of Jolpis, in Rungpoor (Bengal). Very considerable ruins are at no great distance from that place, but are ascribed to Prithu Raja, who may have been a person of the same family. This Prithu Raja, from the size of his capital, and the numerous works raised in the vicinity by various dependents and connexions of the court, it is supposed, must have governed a large extent of country, and for a considerable period of time.

It would not appear that during the dynasty of Adisur any part of Kamroop was comprehended in the Hindoo kingdom of Bengal. On the contrary, about that time, or not long after, the western parts of the kingdom seem to have been subject to a family of princes, the first of whom that has any traces left, was Dharma Pal. Whether or not from his name, we may suppose that he was one of the Pal family, which preceded the dynasty of Adisur, who in the wreck of this family may have saved a portion of their possessions, we have not the means to determine. From the works that are attributed to Dharma Pal, he would appear to have been a person of some power, and even the works attributed to relations and dependents of his family possess some degree of magnitude. A few copper grants still in existence would serve to prove, that Dharma Pal's rule extended up the valley as far as Tezpur.

With regard to the next dynasty, there is greater certainty, although as usual the chronology is attended with many difficulties. According to tradition, there was a Brahman whose name is unknown, but who had a servant that tended his cattle, no one knows where. Many complaints were lodged against him, and his master was called one day to come and see him asleep, while his cattle were permitted to destroy the crops of the neighbours. The Brahmin was advancing with a determination to bestow the merited punishment, when he observed the lines on the naked feet of his servant, and immediately, by his "profound skill in the most noble science of Samudrick Joytish," knew that the sleeper would become a prince. On this discovery the Brahman paid him all due respect, rendered it unnecessary for him to perform any low office, and showed him still more kindness by disclosing the certainty of his future greatness. The servant in return promised that when he became a prince the Brahmin, his master, should be his chief minister. Accordingly some time afterwards, it is not known how, he became king, and is said to have destroyed the last of the Pal family. It is however more probable, that on the death or dethronement of the last king, Kamroop had fallen into a state of anarchy favourable for an upstart, and was overrun by a bordering tribe.

The new Raja seems to have been much guided by his minister, the Brahman, assumed a Hindoo title, Nilodhoj, and placed himself under the tuition of the sacred order.

For this purpose a colony of Brahmans was introduced from Maithilo; and from thence we may perhaps infer the country of the minister. There is no trace of an earlier colony of Brahmans in Kamroop than this from Maithilo. The great merits of the prince were rewarded by the Brahmans, by elevating his tribe, called Khyen, to the dignity of pure Hindoos. The Raja having settled his government, built a city called Komatapur on a branch of the Singimari river, in the present district of Rungpoor. He and his successors then took the title of Komoteswar, or Lords of Komatu.

The second prince of this family was Chokrodhoj. During this dynasty the office of chief minister seems to have been hereditary, as well as the regal dignity.

Chokrodhoj was succeeded by Nilambor, the third and last prince of the family. His dominions are said to have extended over the greater part of Kamroop. The upper portion of his kingdom had, however, prior to this period, been invaded by a new race of conquerors; who poured in from the northern extremity of the valley, and not long after succeeded in gaining complete possession of the country. Their origin, and the progress of their conquests, we shall shortly have to notice.

Numerous public works, especially the construction of magnificent roads, and the erection of the fort at Ghoraghat, are attributed to Nilambor, who would seem to have governed this portion of the country with attention. The circumstances related concerning his overthrow, are accompanied with traits of the most savage barbarity.

Whether from a natural suspiciousness of temper, or from an uncommon accuracy of observing such circumstances, the Raja on entering his seraglio one day, is said to have observed traces which convinced him that a man had been there. He was immediately inflamed with jealousy and having placed some of his people on the look out, a young

Brahman, son of Sachi Patro the prime minister, was soon caught attempting to enter the royal apartments. He was taken before the king and privately put to death, and part of his body was prepared for food. His father having been invited to a grand entertainment given by the king, is said to have eaten of his son's body. After he had satiated himself with this monstrous food, the king shewed him his son's head, and informed him of the crime, and of what he had been eating. The minister is said to have acted with a presence of mind well suited for such an occasion. He said that his son had no doubt deserved any punishment: but as the king had made him eat such a horrid repast, he could no longer continue in his service, but would retire from the world, and dedicate himself to the duties of a religious mendicant. By this stratagem he was allowed to retire, and having assumed the habit of a Sunyasi, immediately left Kamroop. His first object was to procure revenge; and he proceeded without delay to Gour, where he laid before the Mahomedan king information which was followed by an attack on Nilambor. For some time, however, the invasion did not seem likely to terminate in success; for, after a seige of twelve years, the Mussulman had made no impression on the works of Komatapur. Although the length of the seige is very much exaggerated by tradition, its issue is likely to have long continued doubtful. The place is said to have been at length taken by stratagem, or rather by shameful treachery. The Mahomedan commander informed the king by message, that having lost all hopes of taking the place, he was desirous of making peace, and of leaving the country on the most friendly terms. This having been accepted, it was proposed that the ladies of the Mussulman chiefs should pay their respects to the queen. This also was received as a mark of polite attention, and a number of covered litters were admitted into the queen's apartments within the citadel. Instead of ladies these litters contained arms, and the bearers were soldiers, who immediately on gaining admission seized their weapons, and secured the person of the Raja.

After the overthrow of Nilambor, two brothers, named Chondon and Madon, established a short government of eight years, at a place about thirty miles north from Komatapur. Their power was not only transient, but seems to have extended to no great distance. It is more than probable, that the parts of Lower Kamroop which were not retained by the Mussulmans, had fallen into anarchy under the chiefs of the adjacent tribes. Among these tribes, by far the most powerful were the Kuchis, who had a number of chiefs at first independent, but who gradually united under the authority of one of themselves named Hajo. He seems to have been a person of great vigour, and is said to have reduced under his government the whole of Rungpoor, Ghoraghat excepted, together with a large portion of Asam, included in the government of Kamroop.

He is reported to have had two daughters, Hira and Jira. Hira before the rise of her family had been married to a certain Herya, who is said to have been of the impure tribe called Mech. To whom Jira was married is not known, but she had a son named Sisu, while her sister bore a son named Bisu. The latter succeeded to the whole power of his grandfather. As he was not contented with the instruction of the Kolitas, who seem to have been the original priesthood of his tribe, nor with the learning of the Brahmans of Maithilo, who had been formerly introduced, he procured some men of piety, Bardiks from Srihotta (Sylhet ?,) and gave them the title of Kamrupi Brahmans, and these form the second colony of the sacred order that settled here.

To this era, observes Buchanan, may probably be referred the composition, or, as the Hindoos would say, the publication of many or most of the books called Tantros ; which are supposed to have been communicated by the god Sib to his wife Parboti about 5,000 years ago. One of the most celebrated of these compositions is the Jogini Tantro, which mentions the Amows of Hira, and the government of her son; nor is there any doubt that Kamroop is usually considered as the grand source of this system of magic. The period between the time of Bisu, and of his great-grandson Prikit, seems to have been the only period when the learning of the Brahmins flourished in this province.

The doctrines contained in these works admit of many indulgences for new converts, and place no restrictions on the Brahmins from sharing in the pleasures of a most sensual people: they inculcate chiefly the worship of the female spirits, which was the original worship of the country, and which has now become very generally diffused among the Brahmins of Bengal, with whom these Tantros are in great repute.

It was now discovered that the Raja was not a son of the poor barbarian Herya; but that his mother, although descended from a Kuch, was not only of a celestial origin, but had been the peculiar favourite of the god Sib, who was the actual father of the prince. He then took the name of Biswa Sing, and bestowed on the son of his aunt Jira that of Siba Sing: this latter prince also claimed for his mother, the honour of the most intimate favour of the god whose name he bore. On this pretended descent, the Kuchis, or at least all of them that have adopted the Hindoo religion, and have relinquished their impure practices, now assume the title of Rajbangsi, or descendants of princes. All the descendants of Hira, still further elated by their supposed divine origin, assume the title of Deb, or lord, and all the reigning princes of the family claim the title of Naraiyan, which among the Hindoos is one of the names of the Supreme Deity.

Biswa Sing died A.D. 1528, leaving eighteen sons; the eldest of whom, Nur Naraiyan, succeeded to the throne. His reign is said to have been very prosperous. He patronised learning, and caused the 12th book of the Bhagabat, and the 18th chapter of the Bharat, together with the Ram Sarasevah to be drawn up under his immediate inspection. In 1565 he rebuilt the temple of Kamakhya, which had been pulled down by Kalapahar, a general of Soliman the governor of Bengal, who entered Asam some time between 1550 and 1560, and fearful were the ravages committed by him. He persecuted the Brahmins with great fury, destroyed numberless images, and the ruins of many splendid temples scattered throughout the Lower Provinces of Asam, are to this day pointed out, as the work of this terrific general. "He was by birth a Brahmin, but one of the princesses of Gour having become enamoured of him, he turned Mahomedan, and married her, and then became the most violent persecutor of the Hindoos, mentioned in history. Indeed so great was the terror excited by his persecutions, that according to the natives, at the sound of his kettle drum the arms and legs of the idols dropped off for many a coss around."*

It was during the reign of Biswa Sing, too, that the great *bund* road was constructed, called the *Goham Kamul Ali.* He died in 1584, after a reign of fifty-six years, in which he won the affections of all his people.

Prior to his death he had nominated his nephew Ragadeo Nara Naranjan to the succession; but soon after, himself having a son, Ragadeo was led to suspect that he would be deprived of his promised inheritance. Accordingly on the plea of proceeding on a sporting excursion, he is said to have left the royal palace, to which he never after returned. The old king, in order to appease his nephew, made over part of his possessions to him, A.D. 1581. The Dikrai formed his eastern boundary, while the Sankos flowed along the western extremity of his dominions. He is reputed to have founded

* Marshman's History of Bengal.

the city of Ghelabijai, in Kamroop: the present temple at Haju, which is said to have been built in 1583, is also ascribed to him.

On the death of Nara Naranjan, his son Lakhi Naranjan succeeded to the other portion of his father's kingdom which extended from the Sankos on the east, to the Karatuja on the west. From him are said to have descended the subsequent kings of Kuch Behar.

In 1593 Ragadeo dying, was succeeded in his possessions by his son Parikhit Naranjan.

When Abul Fazil composed the Ayen Akberry, the subdivision of the kingdom of Biswa Sing was not known at Dehli, although in all probability it had recently taken place. From prudential motives, perhaps, it had been carefully concealed; and the two branches of the family lived in an amity that was absolutely necessary for their safety. Abul Fazil says, that north from Bengal is the province of Kuch, the chief of which commands 1000 horse and 1,00,000 foot; which is probably an oriental exaggeration. Kamroop, which is also called Kamtah, makes a part of his dominion.

Soon after Parikhit's accession to the throne, he was engaged in hostilities with his neighbour and relative, Lakhi Naranjan. The latter fearing his own safety, is said to have asked the assistance of the Mahomedan governor of Dacca; who, on discovering the real state of affairs, became very urgent with Parikhit for tribute. The Raja being afraid, did not absolutely refuse to comply, but in order to procure favourable terms, was advised to undertake a journey to Agra, where he was kindly received, and procured an order from the king, directing the governor to take whatever tribute the Raja chose to offer. On returning to Dacca, the Raja, who is said to have been totally ignorant of human affairs, and of the immensity of the sum, offered 20,000,000 of rupees, and returned to his capital highly satisfied with his conduct. When his minister explained to him the nature of the promise he had made, the poor Raja was thrown into consternation, and again set out for Agra, taking his minister with him in order to avoid such mistakes.

Unfortunately he died by the way;* and the Musulmans in the meantime took possession of the country, in order to recover the money that had been promised. The minister proceeded to Court; where, after some trouble, he was appointed Kanango, or Register of the country, which was divided into four Sirkars.

The brother of Parikhit, Balit Naraiyan, was confirmed in his government of a portion of his brother's dominions, extending from the Dikrai on the east, to the Manah Nadi on the west; whilst on the unfortunate son of the Raja, Bijut Naraiyan, was conferred a large estate extending from the Manah Nadi on the east, to the Sankos on the west. This territory is still occupied by his descendants, the Rajas of Bijni.

On the death of Balit Naraiyan, which occurred in 1634, he was succeeded by his son Mohindra Naraiyan. He was a pacific prince, and employed his time in improving the condition of his subjects, and, among other good deeds, conferred large grants of rent-free lands on the Brahmins. He died A.D. 1653, after a reign of nineteen years. He was succeeded by his son Chandra Naraiyan, who in all general respects trod in the footsteps of his father. On his death, his son Surja Naraiyan succeeded to the throne A.D. 1671.

About the year 1682 his territories were invaded by Munjoor Khan, a general of the Emperor of Dehli, when he was himself taken prisoner, and conveyed to the presence of the Emperor. Sometime after, effecting his escape, he returned to his own dominions, but from a sense of shame, is said to have refused resuming the reins of government.

When he had been taken away prisoner, his brother Indra

* At Patna, A.D. 1606.

Naraiyan, then only five years of age, was placed on the throne. During his reign the country was distracted with internal convulsions; and the Ahom kings, taking advantage of these occurrences, made themselves masters of Choumarpith, and Kampith. Durrung alone was all this weak prince found it in his power to retain; and for this portion he was obliged to pay an annual tribute to the Ahom king.

On his death, which occurred in 1725, his son Adhitya Naraiyan succeeded to but a small portion of the territories of his ancestors. His boundaries were the Dhansiri on the east, and the Barnadi on the west: the great *bund* road, called the Gohain Kamul Ali, on the north, and the Brahmaputra on the south.

In 1728 his younger brother Mudh Naraiyan seized upon two-thirds of his already very insignificant kingdom, and proclaimed himself king of his newly acquired possessions. Four years after this occurrence, Adhitya Naraiyan died, and was succeeded by another brother, Dhaj Naraiyan, A.D. 1732. About this time the Ahom kings had become very powerful; and the Durrung family was obliged to acknowledge allegiance to them.

In 1744 Dhir Naraiyan, a son of Surja Naraiyan, usurped the throne of Mudh Naraiyan, but three years afterwards was constrained to give it up, and seek an asylum elsewhere.

Mudh Naraiyan died in the year 1778, and was succeeded by his son Mahat Naraiyan. Two years after, his brother Dalab Naraiyan shared the throne with him; and they continued to reign conjointly till 1783, when Dalab Naraiyan died.

Mahat Naraiyan also died soon after; and Hangsa Naraiyan, second son of Dalab, succeeded to the throne.

In 1787 the throne was usurped by Kriti Naraiyan, a son of Dhir Naraiyan; but he was not destined long to sway the sceptre, for in the same year he was deposed, and his brother Hangsa Naraiyan assumed the reins of government.

In 1789, however, Bishtu Naraiyan, the son of Kriti Naraiyan, obtained possession of the throne. A succession of internal commotions followed soon after, which eventually caused the downfall of this once extensive kingdom.

. We turn now to the origin of the Ahoms, a fierce and independent race, who, it is probable, entered the northern extremity of the valley about the beginning of the thirteenth century, and gradually extended their conquests till the whole country was brought under their subjection.

Like most eastern nations, willing to derive merit from the splendour of their original, where history is silent, they have made no scruples in having recourse to fable to supply the defect. The Ahoms seem particularly desirous of being thought descended from the gods: from them, therefore, we can glean no credible memorials relative to their real ancestry.

Their chronicles begin by informing us of a consultation held between Lengdun and Thenkham, kings of heaven, the result of which was the appointment of two brothers, Khunlung and Khanlai,* to be kings over the earth. Khuntun, the son of the moon, and Khunbun, son of the Sun, were at the same time appointed to the office of Gai Mantri, or prime ministers; twelve families of Phokuns and Burunas were also appointed to attend them, together with a body of eight hundred thousand men. These descending from heaven by means of a golden ladder, alighted on the hill Charai Karang, supposed to be one of the mountains of the Patkoi range. Here the brothers divided their ministers and subjects, and took possession of separate sections of the country. At the end of fourteen years, the brothers quarrelled. To put a final termination to their disputes, Khunlung, the more peaceable of the two, returned to heaven, leaving Khunlai in possession of undivided sovereignty

* According to some Khunlai and Khuntai.

below. From him the subsequent kings of Asam are said to have sprung. Such is the fabulous account given of their descent.

That the Ahoms, or original conquerors of Asam, were of eastern origin, and descended from the Shyans, there can be but little doubt; though the precise period of their emigration it is now impossible to ascertain. As we have already observed, it is probable they may have poured in about the beginning of the thirteenth century; in which case, the immediate cause of their emigration may be sought for in the breaking up of the Chinese empire by the Moguls, for at the epoch when Chukapha, the first Ahom king of whom we have any authentic record, had fixed himself in Asam, Kablai Khan had just established himself in China.

Connected with the origin of the Ahoms, is a singular fact that we may here allude to, namely, that no trace of Buddhism is to be found in their religion. This seems a remarkable deviation from the circumstance of the other Shyan families, the Shyans, Khamti, Laos, &c. whose literature is but a direct translation of Burmese Buddhism, as their alphabets are seen to be but mere modifications of the Burmese, or Pali. From this fact it may be argued, that the emigration of the Ahoms from their own country, Siam, had taken place prior to the introduction of the Buddhist religion into that quarter. But if this be true, where are we to find the means of reconciling this circumstance with the date of the first emigration.

For traces in proof of the Shyan origin of this people, we return again to their ancient traditions, and comparing them with the old Shyan chronicles discovered by Captain Pemberton during his residence in Munipur, we may meet with sufficient evidence to support the above supposition.

The territory of the Shyans,* under its ancient limits,

* Vide Pemberton's Report on the North-eastern Frontier.

was, and is still known as the kingdom of Pong, of which the city called Mogaung, or by the Shyans themselves, Mongmaorong, was the capital.

From Khubliai, the first king whose name is recorded in the Shyan chronicle, and whose reign is dated as far back as the eightieth year of the Christian era, to the time of Murgnow, A.D. 667, the names of twelve kings are given. To this period the Pong kings appear to have been so fully engaged in attempts to consolidate their power at home, as to have had but little leisure to extend their conquests to countries more remotely situated.

In the year 777 Murgnow died, leaving two sons, Sukampha and Samlongpha, or Chukampha and Chamlongpha, of whom the elder, Sukampha, succeeded to his father's throne; and in his reign we find the first traces of a connexion with the more western countries, many of which he is said to have brought under subjection to his authority.

Samlongpha was dispatched by his elder brother, at the head of a powerful force, to subdue first the countries to the eastward, including probably the country of Bhumo, which extended from the left bank of the Irawadi to the frontier of Yunan.

On his return from this expedition, which proved successful, he is said to have turned his arms towards the western country of the Basa king, which probably means Banga, the ancient capital of Kachar, where he met with like success. Returning thence he descended into the Munipur valley. The fact of this visit is also recorded in the ancient chronicles of Munipur, though the period assigned to it is earlier by thirty years than that given in the Shyan chronicles—a discrepancy in dates which it were equally vain and useless to attempt to reconcile.

From Munipur, Samlongpha turned his victorious arms upon Asam, which he also succeeded in placing under his brother's authority. He then dispatched messengers to Mongmaorong, to communicate the intelligence of his success to his brother, and to announce his intended return. The messengers, however, instilled the most serious suspicions into the mind of Sukampha, of the designs of his brother, representing him as determined to assume the sovereignty of the country on his return from Asam. A conspiracy was in consequence entered into, for the purpose of poisoning Samlongpha; who, however, was saved by his mother's having accidentally overheard the plot, of which she gave him timely notice by letter, and which led to his continuing in Asam. His wife and son were permitted to join him; and from this son, called Chownakhum, the subsequent princes of the Asam dynasty are said to be descended.

If this account may be depended upon, we are led to the reasonable conclusion, that the origin of the ancient sovereigns of Asam may be clearly traced to their eastern neighbours the Shyans. In all our researches, however, we meet with a great discrepancy in names, which we have no possible means of reconciling.

Since the conversion of the last dynasty to the Brahminical faith, we find a corresponding change in the royal genealogies which have been traced up to India; and the princes of Asam now claim a descent from the king of the gods.

From Indra to Chukapha we have a list of no less than forty-eight names, and nothing but a list. The history of these kings, if they ever did exist, has long since been lost in the shades of oblivion. This portion of our history then we gladly abandon, whether more or less, to conjecture, and turn to other events, in which we have the light of more modern history to illuminate our path.

Chukapha is said to have commenced his reign A.D. 1228. He soon after made conquests which had never been equalled at any preceding period; these were termed *Asama*, whence the Brahmins derive the etymology of the word Asam, "unequalled, unrivalled."

In 1628 he was succeeded by his son Chutuopha, who, bent on following up the conquests of his father, considerably extended the boundaries of his kingdom. He died in 1281, when his son Chubinpha succeeded to the throne. He was in his turn followed by his son Chukangpha, A.D. 1293. After a reign of thirty-nine years, his son Chukampha succeeded to the kingdom, which he continued to govern till 1364. The Ahoms who, as we have already stated, had been hitherto engaged in gradually extending the boundaries of their dominions, had now made considerable progress down the left bank of the Brahmaputra.

Chukampha was succeeded by his brother Chutupha; who, anxious to add to the conquests of his predecessors, turned his arms upon the Chutiyas, a tribe occupying the north bank of the river, as far down as Chardwar; and these he succeeded in bringing under his authority. The Chutiyas were probably, like the Ahoms, the descendants of a Shyan family; though the period of their emigration it is now in vain to look for. That they had occupied the north bank for a long period prior to this invasion, seems very probable. Certain monuments of their reign are still to be met with in that portion of the country.

The death of Chutupha, which occurred A.D. 1376, was followed by an interregnum of four years; after which the ministers installed Chukemthi, a brother of the late king. He was ruled by his wife, a cruel and tyrannical woman. At her instance he oppressed his subjects, and despoiled them of their property. His ministers seeing that all remonstrance was ineffectual, and being no longer able to endure his tyranny, laid a plot to assassinate him, in which they proved successful, A.D. 1389.

His death was followed by another interregnum of nine years; after which his son Chudangpha ascended the throne. After a reign of nine years, he was succeeded by his son Chiyangpha A.D. 1407. He reigned fifteen years, and in

1422 was succeeded by his son Chuphukpha. On his death, which occurred in 1439, his son Chusingpha succeeded to the throne. He died after a lengthened reign of forty-nine years.

His son Chuhangpha now succeeded to the throne. In 1493 he was killed by the spear of a commoner, who, it is said, had embezzled the government grain, for which the Raja fined him in the sum of a hundred rupees. A short time after the Raja had desired him to assist in repairing the raised bamboo floor on which the palace was built. In this the ruffian managed to secrete a spear, which, watching an opportunity, as the prince one day unsuspectingly came to the front door of his house, he plunged into his bosom.

The throne now fell into the hand of a ruthless tyrant, who, after a reign of four years, was put to death at the instigation of his ministers. His brother Chu-hum-mung now ascended the throne. His cognomens were Chu-hum-pha, and Sarga Naraiyan, he also bore the title of the Dihingiaja Raja from the locality of his birth. He is said to have made various conquests, but in what part of the country we are not informed. Very probably he was engaged in quelling insurrections, and reducing the refractory chiefs to obedience. He also succeeded in gaining possession of a small portion of Kamroop, which about this time had fallen into anarchy. After a reign of forty-two years, he was assassinated by a common man-servant, who was instigated to the deed by the heir apparent.

On the death of Sarga Naraiyan, A.D. 1539, Chukhenmung succeeded to the throne. He is said to have built the town and fort of Gargawn or Ghergong. He reigned thirteen years, and was succeeded by his son Chukampha. Nothing remarkable is recorded of him, except that he enjoyed the throne fifty-nine years in comparative peace and comfort.

In 1611 he was succeeded by Chuchengpha, a hotheaded youth, who no sooner felt himself established in the supreme power, than he proceeded to execute that vengeance upon those who had offended him, which he had not previously the power to inflict. He called to mind many frivolous circumstances that occurred during his boyhood, and perpetrated acts of the grossest injustice and tyranny, on those who had given him the slightest offence. At length feeling the pangs of conscience, he professed his inability further to preside over state affairs, alleging as the reason the influence exercised over his actions by those malignant influences of the destroying spirit which had been sent from heaven to control the government of his body. Acting upon this conviction, and with a view to cast out the spirit within him, he erected a temple on the banks of the river Dikhu. This temple, known by the name of Maheswar, he consecrated to Mahadeb (Siba), and instituted the worship of that deity by appointing Brahmins to his service, and endowing the temple with a suitable munificence, and the requisite establishment. From this date, Brahmins are said to have taken the lead in the religious institutions of the country, and the Hindoo creed was established as the religion of the realm.

Chuchengpha reigned thirty-eight years, and in 1649 was succeeded by his son Churumpha. This prince grievously oppressed his people, and after a reign of three years was dethroned by his ministers, who installed his brother Chuchingpha. He however was not destined long to sway the sceptre. He was a weak and imbecile prince, entirely under the control of his wife: after a short reign of two years, A.D. 1654, he was deposed and cast into prison.

His son Chutumla was then intrusted with the reins of government: and soon after his accession to the throne he adopted the Hindoo faith, and introduced Brahmins into his court. He then assumed the Hindoo name of Jaiyadhajia Sing.

At the latter end of his reign, the valley was invaded by Mir Jumla, the Subadar of Bengal. It will be observed that, about fifty years prior to this period, the Mussulmans had obtained possession of the lower part of Kamroop. The usual desire of encroachment, however, induced them to proceed higher up, and to invade the territories of the northern conquerors. The people they were now about to contend with, were far different from those they had hitherto met on the field. They were fierce in their independence, and would not brook submission to a foreign power: they were moreover "invigorated" by a nourishing diet and strong drink; and their princes still retained their energy of mind, and had not then sunk under the enervating and increasing ceremonies of the Hindoo doctrines.

Having placed his stores and provisions in his boats, to move up the Brahmaputra, Mir Jumla crossed that river at Rangamati, and marched his army by land.* The march was tedious, and on its progress the army was greatly annoyed by the Asamese. This, added to the fatigue of dragging the boats, greatly affected the troops: but as Mir Jumla shared every privation with them, and often walked on foot the whole day, there was no murmuring in his camp. The Subadar at length reached the capital, Ghergong; which, after a severe conflict, he succeeded in taking, and the Raja was obliged to take refuge in the mountains.

Mir Jumla, elated at his success, wrote to the Emperor Aurungzebe, boasting that he had opened the road to China, and that he would the next year plant the Mahomedan flag on the walls of Pekin.

But a sad change was now at hand. The rains of 1662 set in with great violence. The Raja boldly issued from his place of concealment in the mountains, and cut off the provisions of the Moguls. To add to their distresses, a pestilence also broke out in their camp, which carried off many; whether they returned or remained, they were equally ex-

* See Marshman's History of Bengal.

posed to death. In this miserable state they passed the rains: but no sooner was the country dry, than, according to the Mussulman historians, they took courage, and bravely repelled the enemy. The Raja is said to have solicited peace, which Mir Jumla was happy to grant; for he was himself attacked by disease, and his troops were mutinous. The same accounts state, that the Asamese were obliged to give twenty thousand tolas of gold, a hundred thousand of silver, and forty elephants; and the Raja gave up his daughter to be married to one of the Mahomedan princes, and agreed to pay an annual tribute. The native annals, on the contrary, inform us that Mir Jumla's army was entirely defeated, and he was obliged to give up the whole of zillah Kamroop to the Asamese, which was from that time placed under the management of a great Asamese officer, the Bar Phukan, and formed a government equal to about a third part of the whole kingdom.

Jaiyadhajia Sing died A.D. 1663, after a reign of nine years, and was succeeded by Chupungmung, alias Chakradhajia Sing. He reigned seven years, and leaving no male issue, his brother Sanyatpha, known also by the name of Adayaditya Sing, ascended the throne. There came to his court a *Bairagi*, (religious mendicant), who is said to have been skilled in occult sciences, and possessed of supernatural powers. The Raja ordered all his subjects to consider this individual as their spiritual guide; but the injunction greatly incensed the ministers, who immediately invited the younger brother of the king to accept the throne. This ill-fated prince was assassinated after a reign of two years, A.D. 1672.

The ministers then installed his younger brother Suklumpha. After a reign of two years he was secretly poisoned, at the instigation of the Bar Baruwa, who installed Suhung, the young prince of Samaguriya. The Bar Baruwa continued to assume a great degree of authority, which the queen maintained was an usurpation of her lord's prerogative. At her instigation therefore the king laid a plot for destroying him. His intentions, however, were secretly conveyed to the Bar Baruwa, who lost no time in proceeding to the royal residence. There he found the king and his royal consort promenading the gardens; the former he dispatched with his own hands, while his myrmidons assassinated the queen and the members of their council. Thus fell this young king, after a reign of one month and fifteen days.

The self-constituted Bar Baruwa next raised Teenkungiya to the supreme dignity; but he was not permitted to usurp his arbitrary power much longer. The officers of Gowhatti, with a band of armed men, proceeded to the metropolis, and soon succeeded in securing the Bar Baruwa. Him they beheaded; and they ordered the newly raised Raja to be strangled, after a reign of twenty days.

On the destruction of his predecessor, the lords of the ascendant raised Dehingiya Chuhungpha, or Chujinpha, to the throne. It was once intimated to him by his queen, that these individuals were usurping the powers which ought alone to attach to his prerogative. His pride being thereby aroused, he determined upon assassinating them. His prime minister, the Bura Gohain, however, being secretly informed of his intentions, ordered the unfortunate Raja's eyes to be plucked out. The agonized king in despair, and burning with indignation, put an end to his own existence, after a reign of little more than two years, A.D. 1677.

He was succeeded by Chudinpha, the son-in-law of the Bura Gohain, by whom he was installed. This minister however, not long after, laid a plot for his life. He was assassinated in 1679, after a reign of two years.

In the same year Chulekpha, more commonly known as the Lora Raja, the stripling king, was raised to the throne by the Bar Phukan, who himself assumed the office of regent. He practised deeds of the most barbarous tyranny, without regard even to the sacred person of royalty. This caused

Gadhadhar Sing, a near relative, with a few others, to conspire his destruction. Having assassinated him, they proceeded to seize the person of the prince, whom they abused and degraded; when Gadhadhar, who had previously received homage as his successor, discharged a javelin at him as the *coup de grace*, in payment of a debt he had contracted with him when they played together as boys: and thus terminated his career after a reign of sixteen months.

On his death, A.D. 1681, Ghadhadhar Sing, surnamed Chupatpha, ascended the throne. He died in 1695, after a reign of fourteen years.

He was succeeded by his son Chukungpha, alias Rudru Sing. In 1699, this prince is said to have founded the fort and city of Rungpoor, where he also caused an extensive tank to be dug, which still bears his name. In the same year he erected a theatre,* for the exhibition of sports denominated *Tulatuli*. In the following year he visited Gowhatti, and died on the side of the river directly opposite the town, on which spot his son afterwards erected a temple in honour of Siba, called Rudreshwar.

Rudru Sing was without doubt the greatest of all the Asamese princes; he reduced the whole valley to order, and received the submission of all the hill tribes. He also established an extensive trade with Thibet, which of late years has dwindled down to a mere nothing.

Rudru Sing reigned nineteen years, and was succeeded by his son Chutunpha (Siba Sing). He ordered a new rent roll of the revenues of the country to be drawn up, in which was included the settlement of the Durrung country; whence might be inferred that the Durrung family had acknowledged allegiance to their powerful neighbours the Ahoms. He died in 1744, after a reign of thirty years. On his death his brother Churenpha, alias Prumutta Sing, was raised to the throne. He reigned seven years, and was succeeded by his brother Churenpha, or Rajeswar Sing. He was afterwards married to the daughter of Juya Sing, the ruling prince of Manipur; he died A.D. 1769.

Chunguapha, surnamed Lakhmi Sing, next ascended the throne. He was brother to the late king, and youngest son of Rudru Sing. The first act of note which distinguished the reign of this prince, was the expulsion of the three sons of Rujirhwar Sing from Court. They were banished to the usual place of exile appropriated to the outcasts of the royal family, called Runwur Gaon, in Kamroop, and were there placed under the custody of the usual officers. Not long after his accession to the throne the Moamariahs, headed by their prelate, rose up in rebellion against him. The priest mustering a body of 12,000 men, (his own disciples), led them to the capital. He availed himself of a *ruse de guerre* by causing the Bar Jona Gohain, the eldest brother of the reigning prince,* to be taken away from his retreat at Kamroop, and carried along with his force; and on their approach to the capital he was placed in front of the troops. An army was sent out on the part of the Raja to oppose their progress. The Deka Phukan, their leader, and son-in-law to the Bar Baruwa, on meeting the opponents, and seeing that the Bar Jona Gohain was at their head, dreaded the consequence of the impious act of shedding the blood of royalty. Instead therefore of withstanding the advance of the insurgents, he and his comrades paid homage to the prince, and allowed them to pass unmolested. The Moamariahs soon obtained possession of the citadel; the Bar Baruwa, who it is said had originally incensed the rebellious priest, was put to death, together with every individual member of his family, and the Raja was deposed and placed in confinement. About five months afterwards the adherents of the king raised an insurrection;

* He was disqualified for the succession by being marked with the small-pox. His son is now residing at Benares, a pensioner on the British government.

the Moamariah priest and his partizans were taken by stratagem and put to death, and the deposed king, Lukhmi Sing, was again placed on the *ghuddi*. He died in 1780, eleven years after his first accession to the throne.

Chuhitpungpha, alias Gourinath Sing, succeeded his father Lukhmi Sing at the age of fourteen. Four years after his instalment the Moamariahs again collected the scattered members of their fraternity, and made their appearance in large numbers, to the amount of about 10,000. The Raja hearing of this demonstration of their force, sent a body of 9,000 men to oppose them. A severe battle ensued, in which great numbers fell on both sides. The insurgents at length prevailed, and the Raja's people were dispersed.

Another expedition was soon after detached against them, at the head of which were a number of the leading members of the state. The banks of the Gouri Sagur tank formed the point at which it was determined to await the attack of the insurgents. Elated by their late success the Moamariahs flew to the assault with the greatest precipitation. They had, however, miscalculated their power; for, after a most arduous and severe struggle, in which the field was disputed for three days, and an immense loss sustained on both sides, the rebels were compelled to give way, and leave the royalists in possession of the field.

The Moamariahs though discomfited were not subdued: they again collected their resources, and took up a strong and well fortified position on the banks of the Joy Sagur. Here they were followed up by the Raja's people, and it is said another arduous battle was fought, which, like the former, also lasted for three days. In this, however, the Moamariahs prevailed, and Gourinath with his courtiers was obliged to effect his escape to Gowhatti. The Moamariahs, elated with their success, installed a successor of their own choice in the person of Bharota Sing.

Nine months elapsed after this event, during which time the Raja and the members of his government were assiduously employed in retrieving their affairs and re-collecting the scattered portions of their army.

At the end of that period, A.D. 1788, an overwhelming force was sent from Gowhatti against the Moamariahs: the contest is said to have lasted a number of days, and after many reverses the Raja's people were obliged to retreat. The Raja perceiving the failure of all his resources, at length sent to Mr. Raush* at Gowalpara, to procure the assistance of the British government.

The history further proceeds to say, that seven hundred Burkundaze Sepahees were sent by Mr. Raush, with whom the Raja proceeded to Nowgong, from thence he sent the Burkundazes to the relief of the Bura Gohain at Jorehaut. At a plain about a couple of miles to the north of Jorehaut another action was fought, in which the Burkundazes were cut up to a man.

A short time after the veteran Raja of Manipur arrived at Nowgong, according to the invitation of Raja Gourinath, with 500 cavalry and 4,000 infantry, and with this force he proceeded to Jorehaut, where he met the Moamariahs. The Manipuris were however repulsed with a loss of 1,500 men.† The Raja of Manipur was in consequence compelled to retreat with the remnant of his force, and Raja Gourinath was again constrained to take his departure for Gowhatti.

New disasters however awaited him. About this time Bistu Naraiyan, the king of Durrung, was deposed, and a relation, Kissen Naraiyan, seized upon the throne. Elated at his success he determined to add the pergunnahs of Kamroop to his possessions. He took into his employ a band of Bengali Bur-

* A merchant who had the farm of the Bengal salt in Asam.

† It is said they were entrapped amongst concealed pitfalls, their horses fell, and the riders were cut up.

kundazes, with whose assistance he made an attack on Gowhatti.

Gourinath being thus pressed on all sides, and as he himself expressed it, "representing a laden boat in the act of sinking," again applied to Mr. Raush, who in his behalf wrote to Messrs. Colvin, Bazette and Co. Calcutta, whilst the Raja sent a deputation composed of Bistu Naraiyan, Raja of Durrung, and three other influential men, to solicit the assistance of the British government. The result was, that at the close of 1792 a detachment was sent to his assistance, under the command of Captain T. Welsh.

The grounds on which the British government interfered in the domestic quarrels of the Asamese were, that large bodies of Hindoostanee Sepoys and Fakeers, subjects of the Company, were represented by Gourinath to have taken part in the civil wars, and were devastating the province. It was conceived by Lord Cornwallis, that it was incumbent on the British to restrain their own subjects, and it was to eject these ruthless mercenaries that Captain Welsh was deputed to Asam. The person who had hired these burkundazes was Kissen Naraiyan, whom Gourinath and his agents, through Mr. Raush, represented as a rebel. Sometime before Captain Welsh came to Asam the government, at the requisition of Gourinath, endeavoured to stop these armed bands from passing into the province; but they found their way round by the Butan Doars by force or fraud, and it was only when the government found they could not prevent their getting into Asam, that they determined to drive them out.

Captain Welsh left Gowalpara for Gowhatti on the 16th November 1792. Three days after he was met by the Raja of Asam, who with a few of his attendants was making his escape from Gowhatti. From him he learnt that the Moamari chief was in possession of the southern bank of Gowhatti, and that Kissen Naraiyan and his rabble had located themselves on the opposite bank. On the morning of the 29th, Captain Welsh took possession of the southern bank of the river, having completely surprised the Moamariah chief, and on the morning of the 6th December proceeded to the opposite bank, and succeeded in completely routing Kissen Naraiyan from his strong post. Eventually he succeeded in bringing him under an engagement to pay to the Asam Raja an annual tribute of fifty-eight thousand rupees. In lieu of men furnished him from—

	Rupees.
Durrung, ...	50,000
In lieu of men furnished from Chutiya,..	2,000
Ditto ditto Chardwar, ...	3,000
In lieu of customs on the trade between Durrung and Butan, ...	3,000
	58,000

Having thus satisfactorily settled the affairs of the Raja as it respected the Durrung family, Capt. Welsh next proceeded to quell the insurrections of the Moamariahs.

After Capt. Welsh had arrived at Gowhatti and made himself acquainted with the state of affairs, he found the Raja a blood-thirsty tyrant, and his intellect so totally destroyed by excesses, that he was perfectly incapable of restoring the kingdom to tranquillity, or of governing it when its affairs were restored to order.

He found that Kissen Naraiyan had been driven by injustice to rebellion, and that by our intermeddling so far we had been taking a measure the justice of which was very doubtful, unless we went further. Hereon he represented the state of affairs to Lord Cornwallis, and obtained that nobleman's full consent to convene the native chiefs and officers, and, in consultation with them, to take such steps as he found necessary, not only to restore order throughout the kingdom, but to secure good government to the people, and protection against their imbecile and barbarous Raja.

Capt. Welsh successfully put down the Moamariah insurrection, and made arrangements for the permanent retention of a brigade of British troops in Asam; for the payment of which the revenues of Lower Asam were pledged by the government, with the full consent of the Bura Gohain, and all the nobles.

But most unfortunately, just as Capt. Welsh had effected all his arrangements, the great statesman, and excellent man who had sent Capt. Welsh to Asam, and who had evinced the liveliest interest in the welfare of this kingdom, and constantly corresponded directly with Capt. Welsh on the measures to be adopted for its complete re-organization, returned to his native land, leaving the Government of Bengal to Sir John Shore.

With his government commenced a total change of measures towards Asam: and, on the weakest of all pretences—the non-interference system—the whole people of Asam were delivered over to the tender mercies of their fatuous, bloody-minded Raja, and again plunged into the miseries of anarchy. Nor would the Bengal government listen to any remonstrances of Capt. Welsh, who begged to be allowed a short period to prepare the people for his departure, and to leave a small force behind him. But he was ordered instantly to return to Bengal. The miseries this lamentable policy of the Bengal government inflicted upon Asam may not be dwelt upon. The British government were in a position to preserve order and good government to a then flourishing and populous kingdom; but their duty as the paramount power was neglected, and the result was the heaviest blow that British India has sustained—the drain of its finances, and the stoppage of all its internal improvements, caused by the Burmese war. Capt. Welsh returned to Calcutta in July 1794.

A few months after, Raja Gourinath was attacked with a bilious fever, of which he died, after a reign of nearly fifteen years.

On the death of the Raja, the Bura Gohain knowing that he possessed a powerful rival in authority in the person of the Bar Baruwa, and that the present was the time for securing the predominance of his interest, before the succession to the government was established, determined to seize the opportunity, before the announcement of the death of the Raja should enable the Bar Baruwa to consolidate his influence.

For this purpose, while yet the corpse was warm, he carried into effect a stratagem which soon brought his victim within his grasp. The Bar Baruwa was sent for in the name of the deceased Raja, under pretence of the latter wishing to make to him some particular communications before his death. He unsuspectingly complied with the summons, and the Bura Gohain lying in ambush for him, seized him as soon as he came within the precincts of the Raja's apartments, and caused him to be put to death.

Three days after the foregoing events, Komaleswar Sing was placed on the throne by Purnananda, the Bura Gohain. From this date this able but violent minister, the Bura Gohain, who as just described had given the first earnest of his disposition, and who was afterwards so notorious for his rigorous tyranny, assumed and reserved to himself all the substantial executive authority of the state, the Raja being in his hands a mere puppet of convenience.

Nothing remarkable is communicated during the reign of this king; he died without issue in 1809, and was succeeded by his brother Chundra Kanto Sing.

This prince, upon his accession, countenanced a conspiracy for the destruction of the Bura Gohain; who, on receiving private intimation of it, immediately summoned a state council, and proceeded to put all the conspirators to death. The Bar Phukan, who was implicated in the plot, fled from Asam, and proceeded to Rungpore, whence he took his departure for Calcutta. There, on the part of the Raja, he petitioned the English government for troops, which, acting upon their lately received notions of non-interference, were refused.

While at Calcutta, the Bar Phukan gained the friendship of an agent of the Burmese government, and accompanied him back to the court of Umeerapooru. Thence he came with 6,000 Burmese troops, to which were added about 8,000 of different tribes, which they collected on their way to Asam. With this force the Bar Phukan entered Asam, and proceeded to Jorehaut to the assistance of the Raja; but the Raja's enemies had made their escape to Gowhatti. Chunderkant, however, reimbursed the Burmese army for the trouble and expence of their expedition.

At the instigation of the Bura Gohain, the Bar Phukan was put to death; and the former immediately sent to the Bura Gohain and his adherents at Gowhatti, to inform them that he had dispatched their enemy, and invited them to join him.

The Bura Gohain however did not accede to this invitation. On the contrary, inheriting his father's resentment against the reigning Raja, he sent his younger brother to Chilmari to invite up Purunder Sing, (a prince of the royal family, and a great-grandson of Rajeswar Sing, who had resided sometime in obscurity), to become a competitor for the throne. Purunder Sing was prevented from coming up by the commands of his father Brajanath, who came up himself instead to Gowhatti. The Bura Gohain then accompanied him with his army to Jorehaut. The Raja with his troops fell back in consequence upon Rungpore. He was however soon after inveigled into a consent to visit Jorehaut, where he was deprived of his throne, and imprisoned; and Purunder Sing having been brought up from Chilmari was proclaimed Raja by the Bura Gohain, A.D. 1816. He succeeded in prejudice to his father Brajanath, who had been previously disqualified from the succession by the mutilation of one of his ears. On the third day after the Raja Chunderkant's deposal, he was visited by the Marangi Khowa Gohain; who, after the preliminary formula of vilification and abuse, superintended the slitting of his right ear.

The friends of the murdered Bur Phukan fled in fear of their lives to Ava, where "placing their heads under the golden soles of the royal feet," of his Burman Majesty, they informed him of the late proceedings in Asam. The consequence was, that Keeo Mingee was sent by that court at the head of an army of 30,000 men. The Burmese at first met with considerable opposition, but the Asamese were soon obliged to seek refuge in flight, and in 1818 Keeo Mingee, the Burmese general, reinstated Chunderkant on his throne. A short time after he returned to Ava, leaving 2,000 troops for the protection of the Raja. A portion of these troops was deputed by the Raja to apprehend Purunder; they accordingly proceeded on their expedition, and Purunder, who was then at Gowhatti, fearing that all resistance was vain, took to his boats and fled to Hadira Choke, leaving the Burmese in possession of Gowhatti. He was however constrained to proceed further down, and take refuge at Chilmari, in the British territories.

In September 1819, Purunder Sing, who had gone to Calcutta, addressed a letter to the British government, stating that he had been driven from his territories by the Burmese, and soliciting the protection and assistance of the Honorable Company, and offering to become tributary, and to pay the expence of the detachment that would be necessary to effect his restoration to the throne of his ancestors. This application was repeated in the following month, but met with a refusal.

Shortly after Mr. Scott, Commissioner of Cooch Bahar, reported to government that Purunder Sing was employed in collecting troops in the Butan territory for the purpose of invading Asam. He added, that the reigning Raja Chunderkant was supposed to be very desirous of getting rid of his allies, the Burmese, and was understood to be treating with the Bura Gohain, and other refugees of consequence, for their return, with a view to a combination of the whole means and strength of the country against the Burmese.

On the 30th April 1820, Mr. Scott made known to the British government that the Bur Phokun, who was an adherent of the interests of the Burmese party, had been murdered, as was supposed with the connivance of Raja Chunderkant; that the latter had in consequence retired from Jorehat to Gowhatti, and that it was generally believed an army from Ava would soon invade the country to avenge the death of the Bur Phokun, and to depose the reigning prince. The above communication was followed immediately by information that the Burmese had set up another Raja in Asam, and that it was supposed Chunderkant would shortly be compelled to flee the country.

In the month of September following, Chunderkant was expelled from Asam, and took refuge in the Choke opposite to Gowalpara. At the end of 1821, however, the cause of Chunderkant became again temporarily triumphant; he defeated the Burmese in several skirmishes, and advanced back to Asam nearly as far as Gowhatti. These successes, and the continued attempts of Purunder Sing and the Bura Gohain from the side of Butan and Bijnee to recover their lost dominion, drew forth a letter from the Burmese general, Mengee Maha Silwa (who had arrived some months before, to take the command of the troops in Asam), to the address of the Governor General. The object of the letter was apparently to request that assistance might not be afforded to Raja Chunderkant by any persons residing within the British dominions, and to suggest the expediency of his being surrendered, with all other refugees who might seek refuge, or had already taken shelter there; but the British government did not think it expedient to comply with the wishes of the general.

In the month of April, or May, 1822, the Burmese party received a considerable reinforcement, commanded by an officer of high rank from the court of Ameerapoora, named Mengee Maha Bandoola. Chunderkant soon gave way before the new force, and in June was reported to have sustained a decisive defeat at Mowghur, in an action in which he displayed great personal bravery, and was compelled once more to seek safety in flight.

The continuance of these disturbances in Asam, and dread excited by the excesses committed by the Burmese, had now reduced the natives to a most distressing situation; and several thousands of them were compelled to flee the country, and take refuge in the British territory.

The event of Chunderkant's defeat was followed by a representation of rather threatening character on the part of the Burmese officers to Lieutenant Davidson, the officer commanding the post of Gowalpara, stating that their army consisted of 18,000 fighting men, commanded by forty Rajas; that they had every wish to remain in friendship with the Company, and to respect cautiously the British territories, but that should protection be given to Raja Chunderkant, they had received positive orders to follow him wherever he might go, and to take him by force out of the Company's dominions. Instructions were accordingly issued to the officer commanding at Dacca, to detach such reinforcements as Mr. Scott might require, with directions that should the Burmese attempt to carry their threat into execution, they must be instantly repelled by force.

This effectually put a stop to the further progress of the Burmese on the side of Asam; but their encroachments on another point of our frontier, Kachar, led to the force assembled at Gowalpara being ordered to advance into Asam, and the declaration of war against the king of Ava on the 5th of March 1824.

Before however proceeding to follow the footsteps of the

British army in their conquest of Asam, it will be expedient to notice the state of our relations with Kachar.

From the year 1817 downwards, constant applications had been received from the ancient and legitimate Raja of Kachar, Govind Chunder Naraiyan, praying for the aid and intervention of the British government to settle his affairs, and to protect him against the subjugation with which he was menaced from the side of Manipur. In 1820, the above chief was entirely dispossessed by three brothers, adventurers from Manipur, named Chorjit, Manjit, and Gambheer Sing; who had themselves been expelled from their hereditary possessions by the Burmese, and had originally obtained a footing in Kachar by engaging in the Raja's service. Shortly after the expulsion of the legitimate ruler, a struggle for superiority ensued between the brothers; which, involving the country in much suffering, disturbed the peace of the frontier, and occasioned renewed appeals for the interference of the British power.

The receipt of an application from Chorjit Sing, in May 1823, offering to cede the sovereignty of Kachar to the British government, and stating his apprehension that designs were entertained against the country by the Burmese, induced the government to take the subject of his proposition into serious consideration.

It did not appear that Kachar had ever been subject or tributary to the government of Ava. It is true that Manjit when in possession of the Raj of Manipur, which he attained by the aid of the Burmese, and held as their feudatory, did invade, and for a time possess himself of Kachar: but he was speedily repulsed, and no traces appear of the Burmese having ever laid claim to that country, or to any right of interference in its affairs. At the same time there appeared several inducements for the British government to establish its direct authority, or at least a preponderating influence, in the territory of Kachar. These considerations were not deemed of sufficient strength on former occasions to lead our government to avail itself of the opportunities that presented themselves of effecting this object; nor did they indeed possess the weight that subsequent occurrences and further experience have given them. The position of Kachar, as naturally affording one of the easiest passes from Ava into the Company's territories, the recent progress of the Burmese arms, and their occupation of Asam, the force stationed in which country it would also contribute to keep in check, gave the possession of Kachar an importance which did not before belong to it. As the employment of British influence over that country was deemed of importance, and as that could be rendered effectual in no other way than by taking the country openly and decidedly under British protection, it was deemed expedient to extend to Kachar the protection of the government, on the usual conditions of political dependency.

Whilst arrangements and negotiations were in train for defining the terms of our connection with the chief, whom it was determined to reinstate in possession, and who was residing under British protection within the Honorable Company's territory, intelligence was received that the Burmese were preparing an army to invade and conquer Kachar. The Governor General's agent on the North-east frontier lost no time in addressing letters to the Burmese governor of Asam briefly apprising him of the nature of our views and measures in regard to the Raj of Kachar, and calling upon him to desist from any project of molesting that country.

It soon appeared that an army had been assembled in the Burmese *dependency* of Manipur, as well as in Asam, for the execution of the purpose of aggression now distinctly threatened.

Whilst occupying their threatening position in Kachar, the generals of the king of Ava had moreover planned the conquest of Jamtiya, another petty chieftainship situated similarly with Kachar in regard to the British frontier, but which having formerly been restored as a gift to the Raja's family by the British government, after a temporary convulsion, was more distinctly recognized as a dependency of Bengal. The Raja of Jamtiya in a letter addressed to him by the Burmese commanders, was called upon to acknowledge submission and allegiance to the king of Ava, and to repair forthwith to the Burman camp. A demonstration was further actually made against Jamtiya to enforce the above requisition, when the British troops frustrated the execution of this hostile and menacing encroachment: and simultaneously the advance of the Burmese force both from Manipur and Asam, led to the first collision with the British troops in Kachar, close to the frontier of Sylhet, at the entrance of the Bikrampore pass.

The Governor General in Council was, in consequence of these circumstances, induced to order the advance of the force previously assembled at Gowalpara into the territory of Asam, to dislodge the enemy from the commanding position which they occupied at the head of the Brahmaputra, and to pursue such other measures of offensive warfare as the honour, the interests, and the safety of the British government demanded recourse to.

In obedience to these instructions, Brigadier M'Morin, commanding the force, commenced moving from Gowalpara up the Berhampootur on the 13th March 1824.* On the 28th the force arrived at Gowhatti, where the Burmese had erected strong stockades, which were however evacuated on the approach of the British. The necessity of retreat had apparently exasperated them against their unfortunate subjects, and fellows in arms—the Asamese; the bodies of a great number of whom, barbarously mutilated, were found upon the road and in the stockade at Gowhatti.

* See Wilson's Burmese war; from which valuable work the subsequent paragraphs have been extracted.

Several of the tribes in the eastern portion of Asam, as the Khamtis and Singphos, availed themselves of the unsettled state of affairs to harass the Burmese; but their operations were equally directed against the unfortunate natives of Asam, numbers of whom were carried off by them as slaves.

The Asamese displayed the most favourable disposition towards the British; but their unwarlike character, scanty numbers, and reduced means, rendered their co-operation of no value; and the uncertainty of support, and doubt of the capability of the country to maintain a large advancing force, as well as inaccurate information of the state of the roads, induced the commanding officer to pause at Gowhatti, and at one time to abandon all thoughts of prosecuting the campaign further in the season, notwithstanding the fairest prospect offered of expelling the Burmese altogether from Asam, even by the partial advance of the British force.

Mr. Scott, the Political Agent, having crossed from Sylhet through Jamtiya, arrived at Nowgong, in advance of the Brigadier, on the 15th April, with a party of some strength. Leaving his escort under Capt. Horsburgh to occupy Nowgong, which the Burmese had deserted, he traced a retrograde route to Gowhatti, to communicate with the head quarters of the invading force. The Burmese had now retreated to their chief stockade at Moramukh; but finding that no steps were taken in pursuit of them, they in the end of April returned to Koliabar. Colonel Richards was now therefore detached from Gowhatti with five companies of the 23rd N. I. and the flotilla, and having joined the Commissioner's escort at Nowgong, he advanced to Koliabar. The Burmese now stockaded themselves at Hatbur, on the Kullung, at a short distance from its junction with the main stream; there they pursued their previous system of not waiting for an attack, but deserted it and returned to Ranglighur, a post at the distance of about eight hours' march. A small party however having returned to re-occupy the Hatbur stockade, were surprized by Lieut. Richardson, with a *resalla* of horse, and a company of infantry. The surprize was effectual: the enemy in attempting to escape, fell upon the horse, by whom a number were killed.

Whilst the main body of the detachment continued at Koliabar, a small party was left under Capt. Horsburgh in the stockade of Hatbur. The Burmese exhibited on this occasion the only proof of enterprize which they had yet displayed in the campaign in Asam; and advancing from their entrenchment at Ranglighur, they attempted to cut off Captain Horsburgh and his division. Their advance was, however, seasonably ascertained and arrested by the picquet, until the whole detachment could form. Upon Captain Horsburgh's approach with the infantry the Burmese fled; but the irregular horse, which had been sent to their rear, having intercepted the retreat of about two hundred, a great number of them were sabred on the spot, or drowned in crossing the Kullung.

After this repulse, they abandoned the Ranglighur stockade, and retrograded to Mara Mukh, where the chief force of the Burmese, now not exceeding one thousand men, was posted under the governor of Asam.

Brigadier M'Morin having died of cholera early in May, Colonel Richards succeeded to the command, and established his head-quarters at Koliabar; but finding the rains setting in, he deemed it necessary to retire to Gowhatti, in order to secure the receipt of supplies. The operations of the first campaign in Asam, were closed by a successful attack upon a stockade on the north bank of the Brahmaputra, by Capt. Wallace; the enemy had time to escape, but the stockade was destroyed. The general result of the operations was decidedly favourable; and the British authority was established over a considerable tract of country between Gowalpara and Gowhatti.

Upon the return of the British forces in Asam to their

cantonments in Gowhatti, Burmese parties re-occupied the station of Kaliabar, Raha, and Nowgong, levying heavy contributions on the people, and pillaging the country. They even carried their incursions into the neighbouring states, and devastated the frontier districts of the British ally and dependant, the Raja of Jamtiya. The renewal of operations in this quarter, therefore, commenced with their expulsion once more from these positions.

The force under Lieut. Colonel Richards, who had been continued in the command, consisted altogether of about three thousand men, a corps more than adequate for the purposes it was directed to effect; being fully equal, if not superior, to the aggregate of the Burmese troops in Asam, and infinitely superior in equipment and efficiency.

The numbers of the army, and the necessity of recourse to water carriage, preventing the forward movement of the whole body, Colonel Richards detached a body of troops for the purpose of putting a stop to the exactions and excesses of the Burmese. His arrangements were attended with complete success: the enemy were compelled to concentrate their forces at Jorehat, leaving the country open for the British advance.

At Jorehat, intestine division contributed to weaken the Burmese still further, and the chief known by the name of the Bura Raja, who had been considered as the head of the Burmese party in Asam, was killed by the adherents of Shan Phukan, a rival leader, although equally an officer in the Burmese service. Despairing, consequently, of defending the position at Jorehaut, the Burmese commanders, after setting fire to the entrenchment, fell back upon Rungpur, the capital.

The country being thus cleared of the enemy, Colonel Richards proceeded up the Brahmapootra, and on the 25th January, 1825, fixed his head-quarters at Gowrisagur, on the Dikko river, about eight miles from Rungpur. On the morning of the 27th the Burmese garrison of Rungpur made an attack upon the British advanced post, where the thickness of the jungle rendered it impossible to meet them with advantage; but so soon as they offered a sufficient front, a charge was made, which the Burmese did not wait to sustain; for after delivering their fire, they broke and fled, but were overtaken, and a considerable number put to the sword; the loss of the British was trifling.

On the 29th, Colonel Richards resumed his march towards Rungpur. The approaches to the capital had been fortified by the enemy, and on nearing the defences the assailants were saluted by a heavy fire, which brought down half the leading division, and caused a momentary check; but a couple of shells, and a round or two of grape having been thrown in, the column again advanced, and the stockade was escaladed and carried.

The result of these two engagements not only dispirited the Burmans, but gave renewed inveteracy to the divisions that prevailed amongst them. The two chiefs, the Sham and Bagli Phukan, were willing to stipulate for terms; but the more numerous party, headed by the subordinate chiefs, were resolutely bent on resistance, and threatened the advocates of pacific measures with extermination. The latter, however, so far prevailed, as to dispatch a messenger to the British commander to negotiate terms for the surrender of Rungpur; and, through his mediation, they were finally agreed upon. Such of the garrison as continued hostile were allowed to retire into the Burman territory, on their engaging to abstain from any act of aggression on their retreat, and those who were pacifically inclined, were suffered to remain unmolested;—their final destination to await the decision of the Governor General's Agent, but in the event of peace with Ava, they were not to be given up to that government.

Colonel Richards was induced to accede to these conditions from a conviction of the impossibility of preventing the escape of the garrison upon the capture of the fort, or of pursuing them in their flight. It was also to have been apprehended, if the evacuation of the province had been much longer delayed, that it might not have been cleared of the enemy during the campaign, as the want of carriage and supplies would have detained the army sometime at Rungpur, and might have delayed its movements till the season was too advanced to admit of its progress far beyond the capital. By the occupation of Rungpur on the terms granted, much time was saved, as well as some loss of lives avoided; and the object of the campaign—the expulsion of the Burmese from Asam, without the fear of their renewing their irruptions with any success, was peaceably and promptly secured.

The persons who surrendered themselves upon these stipulations, were the Sham Phukan and about seven hundred of the garrison: the rest, about nine thousand of both sexes and all ages, including two thousand fighting men, withdrew to the frontiers, but many dropped off on the retreat, and established themselves in Asam.

The surrender of Rungpur, and the dispersion of the Burmans, terminated the regular campaign on the north-eastern frontier; but the state of anarchy into which Asam had fallen, and the lawless conduct of the Singphos, and other wild tribes inhabiting its eastern portion, continued to demand the active interference of British detachments throughout the remainder of the season. The Burmese also appeared in some force in May at Bisa Gam, a Singpho village on the right bank of the Nao Dihing, where they erected a stockade: they also advanced to Duffa Gam, a similar village, a few miles inland from the same river, about ten miles to the north of the former, where they entrenched themselves. The force at these posts consisted of about 1,000 men, of whom six hundred were Burmese, the rest Singphos, under the command of the governor of Mogaum. From these stations they were dislodged in the middle of June, by a party of troops under Lieutenants Neufville and Kerr, after a march of great exertion and fatigue.

At Bisa Gam the stockades were five in number, and were carried at the point of the bayonet. The enemy at first formed in front of the stockades, as if determined to offer a resolute resistance; but they retreated precipitately upon the charge of the British detachment, who, following them as quickly as the preservation of order, and the nature of the ground would permit, drove them out of each stockade in rapid succession without firing a shot. On quitting the last entrenchment, the Burmese fled towards their own frontier; but their retreat was pursued by a party under Ensign Bogle, and so closely were they pressed, that they were obliged to abandon several hundred Asamese, whom they were carrying off as slaves.

After this defeat no occasion offered for the further prosecution of hostilities against the Burmese in Asam. On the conclusion of the war with Ava, the Burmese government in a treaty concluded on the 24th February 1827, engaged to abstain from all interference with the province, and Asam has ever since continued in the undisturbed possession of the British authorities.

That the results of the war, as it respects Asam at least, have not failed to prove highly beneficial, will be evident from a consideration of the present state of the country. Distracted hitherto by incessant feuds, and overrun by hostile armies, or predatory bands, large tracts once inhabited by a happy and numerous population, had been converted into extensive and unwholesome jungles, and ceased not only to be the haunts of man, but had become hostile to human life. Under its new masters Asam has experienced a tranquillity and security not known for ages, and will again no doubt assume that character of plenty and prosperity which it once wore, and which tradition, and the remains of roads and towns still found in it, indicate it once enjoyed.

CHAPTER V.

POLITICAL GEOGRAPHY.

Ancient form of Government—Officers of State—Detached Viceroys—Military Stations—Ceremony of Enthronement—Ancient Laws and Institutions—Criminal Laws—Civil Laws—Laws of legitimacy relative to Property—Revenue System—Feudal Customs—Revenue Administration, subsequent to the occupation of the Country by the British Government—The present Civil Courts—Criminal Courts—Police—Military Establishments.

The political constitution of Asam may be viewed in a twofold light,—as it existed under the ancient Asamese administration, and as it exists at present.

The ancient form of government was a peculiar species of monarchy, wherein the plan according to which the power of the sovereign was exercised in the administration of public affairs, differed considerably from that of most monarchical governments. The king was nominally placed at the head of the constitution. Immediately under him in rank were three great councillors of state, called Gohains, who by law had no authority to issue orders, but whose duty it was to give advice to the king. With them he was expected to consult on the affairs of government; nor was he permitted to issue any orders without their approval, or enter into any negotiations without first consulting them. Neither indeed was the king himself considered legally enthroned, unless these great officers concurred in confirming his nomination to the throne.

Some Asamese historians account for this division of power by saying, that the original conquerors consisted of three families,* who united their forces for the invasion of the valley, and, after gaining possession of it, agreed upon a tripartite division of the power of the government.

This does not exactly coincide with the pretensions to the divine origin of the royal family; but as the authority of the Bura and Bar Gohains had from time immemorial descended in the same families, until the period of the Burmese invasion, it seems probable that this tradition is founded on fact. The divine origin of the royal family was most likely not thought of until the Rajas had become powerful, and had embraced Hinduism; when the Brahmins, in gratitude to their munificent patrons invented for them a genealogy accordant with their sacred books.

Though these dignified offices in the council of state were in the hereditary possession of three great families, the king was allowed the liberty of appointing to the office any member of these families he thought fit; and it was likewise acknowledged to be his prerogative to change them whenever he might deem it necessary to do so.

The individuals holding these offices always lived at court. The officer styled the Bura Gohain was the highest in rank, and next to him was the Bar Gohain. The Barpatru Gohain was created subsequently to the two former. He is said to have descended from an illegitimate son of one of the kings. To each of these officers was assigned a certain number of men, over whom no officer of government was allowed to possess any jurisdiction; they were amenable only to their immediate masters.

Next in rank to the three great councillors, was the Bar Buruwa, or chief secretary. He ought more properly to have been termed the prime minister, for to him the whole executive power, civil and military, was entrusted; and to his court

* There were originally only two great councillors.

there was an appeal in all cases, except where the servants of the great Gohains were concerned. He was allowed an assignment of a hundred men, besides the fees on all commissions, and on all cases that came before his court.

The inferior officers of state at the capital were as follow: there were six individuals styled Choruwa Phukans. Each of these possessed a separate title; and the whole formed the council of the Bar Buruwa, although each also had his own separate duties assigned him. They were—1st. the Nauboichá Phukan, who had an allotment of a thousand men, with whom he manned the royal boats; 2nd. Bhitaruyal Phukan; 3rd. the Na Phukan; 4th. the Dehingiya Phukan; 5th. the Deka Phukan; and 6th. the Neng Phukan. The duty of these officers seems generally to have been that of purveyors; they were employed in procuring whatever the king wanted. Each of them was allowed an assignment of thirty *gotes* of pykes; which, (that is their personal pykes, and the pykes allotted to them for their respective public services,) composed a *khol*, called after the respective title of each Phukan.

There were besides the above several Phukans of inferior grade; and as the government extended, and the affairs of the state seemed to need them, their numbers were from time to time increased. The more important among them were, the Parbatiya Phukan, a Brahmin, whose duty it was to manage the affairs of the chief of the queens. He was allowed a secretary, or Baruwa. The Raidingiya Phukan managed the affairs of the second queen; he was likewise allowed a secretary. The Khongiya Phukan performed the like duties for the mother of the king. The Jolbhari Phukan had charge of all the servants (1000), employed by the king in the Hindu temples. The Tambuli Phukan had care of the king's gardens; in which the beetlenut was the chief article of cultivation. The Noasalya Phukan was allowed a thousand men for building and repairing the royal boats. The Choladara Phukan had charge of all the king's effects. The

Chiring Phukan was master of the ceremonies, and had the superintendence of the Deodhings, the priests of the old religion. The Deulya Phukan superintended the repairs of the Hindu temples. The Khargariya Phukan superintended the manufacture of gunpowder. The Nek Phukan and the Dihinya Phukan had charge of the king's messengers.

Baruwa, seems to have been the title next in dignity to Phukan. The Baruwas were the Bhundari Baruwa, or the private treasurer. He was allowed an assistant, called the Kayastha Bhundain. The Dulya Baruwa in charge of the Raja's palanquins and bearers. The Chaudangiya Baruwa superintended the public executions. The Dola-kakuriya Baruwà was chief of the footmen. The Thanikar Baruwa, superintendent of artificers. The Sonadar Dolaya, mint master and chief jeweller. The Majumdar Baruwa, private secretary, he was allowed four Chang-kagotis, or assistants. The Bej Baruwa, physician to the royal family. The Changmari Baruwa, superintendent of the royal table. The Hati Baruwa, master of the elephants. The Ghora Baruwa, master of horse. The Heluidhari Baruwa, in charge of the arsenal; and the Debigha Baruwa, in charge of the private chapel.

There were twelve Rajkhuwas, who were placed under the immediate orders of the Bar Baruwa. These were officers of considerable importance, each being supposed to command three thousand men. They usually attended the courts of justice, and were employed as umpires to settle disputes, as well as to superintend any public work for the king.

Besides these, there were also other officers attendant on the king, called Katakis, Kakutis, and Dolois. The Katakis seem to have been employed chiefly as agents for the king in his negotiations with foreign states, and the independent hill tribes. The Kakatis were writers, and the Dolois were expounders of the Jytish shasters, whose duty it was by means of those shasters, to ascertain the lucky and unlucky days.

Among the detached viceroys, the principal was the Bar Phukan, who was governor of Kamrup. Before the conquest of this division by the Ahoms, this officer seems to have governed only the western end of the island lying between the Brahamaputra and Kullung rivers; and even this jurisdiction would seem to have been curtailed by the power of the great military forces stationed in that quarter. In the management of the affairs of Kamrup, the Bar Phukan was not permitted to do any thing of importance without the advice and consent of his council, which consisted of six Phukans. 1st. The Pani Phukan, who commanded six thousand pykes; these were constantly employed in cultivating land, in fishing, and in various manufactures on account of the king. Under the Pani Phukan an accountant was employed, called the Tekla Bura Majumdar. 2nd. The Deka Phukan, who commanded four thousand pykes. He was placed under the immediate direction of the Pani Phukan; and his men were employed in the same manner as those of his superior. 3rd. The Dihinggiya Phukan. 4th. The Nek Phukan; these were the immediate assistants of the Bar Phukan. The other two were called Chotiya Phukans, and were subordinate to the two former. Twelve Raj-khowas were also in attendance at the Bar Phukan's court. The collector of revenue was styled the Bajai Baruwa; he was under the orders and inspection of the governor of the province, but could not be dismissed from his office without the orders of the king.

The other viceroy, and next in importance to the Bar Phukan, was the Sadiya Khowa Gohain. To him was confided the north-eastern extremity of the kingdom.

The following governments were established as military stations to protect the frontier:—

The Morungikhowa Gohain governed a small district, called

Morung, on the west bank of the Dhansiri river. He had a thousand men under his command, and to him was intrusted the protection of the frontier from the incursions of the Khamtis.

The Holal Gohain governed another small territory, including the east end of the island between the Brahmaputra and the Kullung rivers. He also managed about a fourth part of the territory of Chardwar, collected the royal revenues, and administered justice. His force, stationed at Kaliabar, and in Noaduwar, was intended to act as a check on the conduct of the Butias, Meris, and Duflas, when these mountaineers came down to levy black mail on the districts of Choudwar, Noadwar, and Chardwar.

The Kojali Mukhiya Gohain commanded a thousand men, and his residence was at the Kajalichoki, at the junction of the Kullung and Brahmapootra, and towards the west end of the island alluded to above. The object of his force seems to have been to guard against the encroachments of the Kacharis and Jaintiyas. Though surrounded by the territory placed under the governor of Kamrup, he was entirely independent of that officer.

The coronation, or rather enthronement of the king, used to be performed with much ceremony. As a short account of it might not prove uninteresting, we proceed to give the following:—

After all the diversified arrangements necessary for such an important occasion had been finished, on the day appointed for the ceremony the Raja, mounted on a male elephant, and accompanied by his first or principal queen, styled the Bor Kuwanri, sitting on a female, proceeded to plant a tree (Ficus religiosa), on the hill Chorai Korang, where his ancestor Kuntai first appeared on earth. By the way he took up the young tree, and paid the proprietor whatever price he chose to demand. In performing this ceremony his tutelary deity in the shape of an image called Chung, was suspended round his neck; he was girt with the sword *Kyandang*, which was given to his ancestor on his leaving the celestial courts; he carried in his turban the feathers of the sacred bird Deokukura; and he was accompanied by all the principal officers of his kingdom, by a great part of the army, and by a vast multitude of people.

Having planted the tree, the Raja and his followers descended to three sheds erected for the occasion at the base of the hill; which were respectively termed the Patghur, Holonghur, and Hingorighur. The Raja and his queen first entered the Patghur, where some water was poured on them by the presiding priest, from a shell called *Dakhinabarto sangko*, the mouth of which is turned the contrary way to that of the shell in common use by the Hindus, in order, it is said, to attract the notice of the gods.

The two royal persons next entered the Holonghur, and took their seat on a stage made of bamboos, under which was placed one of each species of animal that could be procured: such as a man, an elephant, a horse, a cow, a deer, a hog, a fowl, a duck, an insect, a snake, a fish, &c. The water from *nine tirthas*, or holy places, in which certain sacred plants had previously been steeped, was then poured over the king and queen, and fell on the animals.

The royal persons having been bathed, the Raja replaced the feathers on his turban, and advanced with his queen to the Hingorighur, having in his hand the sword *Kyandang*, and with this, before he entered, he killed a buffaloe. The original custom was to kill a man, a criminal being selected for the purpose; but since the time of Rudra Sing, a buffaloe was substituted. The Raja then entered the Hingorighur, and ascended a throne of gold, consisting of seven stages; when, having taken his seat, the queen and the three chief councillors of state made him several presents of gold and jewels, and laid their hands on the four feet of the throne.

These nobles then walked seven times round the sovereign, when the principal ceremonies were supposed to be concluded. New money was coined by the orders of the king, and presents were made by him to the chief-priest, and to the Brahmin, who was his spiritual guide. Gratuities were also given to all the principal officers, and to religious mendicants; and several days' provisions were distributed to the multitude, who had assembled to witness the ceremonies. At the close of the day a splendid entertainment was got up for all the Asamese of high rank, at which the Raja and his queen presided. For the following successive days, till the expiration of a month, all the tributary rajas, landlords, and inferior officers were introduced to present their offerings to the king.

We turn now to the ancient laws and institutions of the country, and respecting these we may venture to assert, that, in all probability, there scarcely ever was any nation so distinguished for sanguinary laws, as the ancient Asamese. The penalties exacted seem not to have been so much from a just and cool discernment of the limits of defence, prevention, and reparation, as from the impulse of a keen resentment. Hence we find it was frequently from a strong sympathy with that resentment that the individual in authority judged, and condemned. A great injury committed could be expiated only by a great injury repaid. Severity and retaliation were consequently the two main principles that characterized the whole of their penal code. The cruel mutilations practised by them, were shocking to the highest degree. Besides pecuniary mulcts, the other punishments enacted were—whipping, branding, the pillory, amputation of limbs, mutilation of the nose, ears, and lips, plucking out the eyes, tearing off the hair, grinding the offender between wooden cylinders, sawing him asunder, application of red hot iron to different parts of his body, together with numerous other modes of punishment still more repugnant to humanity, and far too abominable to be mentioned, planned evidently by hearts, which

> ...."Neither bended knees, pure hands lift up,
> Sad sighs, deep groans, nor silver-shedding tears"

could penetrate.

Whatever the injury which the innocent man sustained, a similar injury, by way of punishment, was imposed upon the guilty. Whatever the member, or part of his body, with which the offender committed the crime, upon that part was the chastisement inflicted; and this spirit of retaliation was carried to a most extraordinary degree.

Rebels were never excused, though for other offences pardons were occasionally purchased. Capital punishment extended to the whole family of the rebel, to parents, brothers, sisters, wives, and children. Among the sentences of death, hanging was considered the most honorable.

With respect to the civil laws, it is almost needless to remark, that the sources of acquisition, by occupancy, by labour, by contract, by donation, by descent, which are recognized in all states of society, were recognized also in Asam; and that the privilege existed of alienating property for a valuable consideration, or of transferring it by purchase and sale.

The laws by which contracts and sales were regulated, were, for the most part, the same as those recognized in Hindusthan, and so amply laid down in the Institutes of Munoo. But there is another species of transactions which claims some share of our attention—that occasioned by the death of the owner.

The laws of legitimacy relative to property and rank are so various and complex in different parts of India, that we trust a slight notice of these laws, as they existed in Asam, will not be considered out of place.

Among a rude people, persons who belong to the same

family, are in general understood to enjoy a community of goods. And among the Asamese, we find it was the usual arrangement, that the different members of a family should live together, and possess the property in common. The father was, in consequence, looked upon rather as the head of a number of partners, than as the sole proprietor. On the event of his death, there was no transfer of property, but a continued possession; the copartnership being deprived only of one of its members.

During the father's life time, the property was held jointly in his name: when he died, and a separation happened to take place in the family, which was not unfrequently the case among the lower classes, the property was divided between the sons in equal shares. Should the property have consisted in landed estates, these lands were divided off into long strips either in the length or the breadth of the estate under division, as might be agreed upon either by the sharers themselves, or by arbitrators appointed for the purpose. The youngest son was allowed the first choice of the shares, and so on in succession to the eldest. The reason of giving the youngest brother the preference, might have been to secure the younger children against any schemes to appropriate the better shares, which the intelligence of the elders might contrive. Or this law might have originated in the idea, that the elder brothers were better able to provide for themselves.

Among the richer families it was the usual custom to hold the land in joint partnership; the brothers keeping a manager between them, and dividing the profits at the end of the year. As this, however, was not practised among the lower classes, the consequent minute subdivision of land could not but have acted in a highly prejudicial degree upon the progress of agriculture.

It is, however, particularly to be noted, that daughters were debarred from any share in the inheritance of their fathers. The woman indeed was so restricted in the means of acquiring property, that she was almost excluded from its rights. The exception consisted merely in certain presents; those given in the bridal processions, or given as tokens of affection, or those received from a father, a mother, or a brother. In these consisted the only property she could lay claim to. The widow was acknowledged by law to be entitled to a maintenance from her sons during her life time, or until she should marry again. Among the lower classes, however, the brother of the deceased had the power of sending back the widow to her parents, at the same time that he might claim back all the presents made to her either by her late husband, or his relations at the time of their marriage.

The idea of a joint interest in all the members of a family to the property of the whole, had originally an effect even upon the power of donation. Individuals were not at liberty to alienate by gift any part of the common stock. This rule was, however, not unfrequently violated by the parent during the minority of his sons.

With respect to the ancient revenue system, it must be remarked, that it was a fixed principle with the Asam government, that the land and the subject were alike the property of the state.

It seems to have been no uncommon principle, in a rude state of society, to vest the sovereign, as the representative of the society, with that property in the land which belongs to the society: and it was parcelled out by the sovereign to individuals, with all those powers of ownership which are regarded as most favourable to the extraction from the land of those benefits which it is calculated to yield. Thus we find in many of the rude parts of Africa the property of the land is understood to reside in the sovereign. It is in the shape of a donation from him that individuals are allowed to cultivate the land; and when the son, as is generally the case, succeeds to the father, it is only by a prolongation of the royal bounty, which in some places at least is not obtained without a formal solicitation.* In Java, "it was well understood that the sovereign was the lord of the soil,†" and it is to be presumed the same principle existed in all that part of the eastern islands, which in point of manners and civilization resembled Java. In China, likewise, it is a well known fact, that the property of the soil is vested in the emperor.

In Asam, however, as we have already stated, not only the land, but the subject also was the property of the state; and all males, except slaves, and those appropriated to religious institutions or granted to priests, were obliged to render service to the Raja, for the support and maintenance of himself, his officers, and the kingdom.

These individuals were denominated *pykes*, and were usually divided into clans or squads, under the general name of *khels* or *mels*. One division of these *khels* was devoted entirely to the service of the Gohains, or members of the supreme council; another division rendered its offices to the members of the royal family, and was placed under the immediate control of certain subordinate Phukans; whilst the third, and by far the largest division, contributed to the support of the Raja's household, and the officers of his personal train, as well as performed all the necessary services of the state.

Amongst these clans, all the inhabitants from sixteen years old and upwards, were enlisted under the general denomination of *pykes*. But in process of time many were separated from their respective *khels*, and attached to grants of land, devoted either to the service of the gods, (Deobutter), to religious purposes, (Dhurmutter), or to the maintenance of priests, (Brahmutter).

Other *pykes* were likewise detached from the *khels* and formed into *choumuahs*, which were charges taken from the

* Modern Universal History, vol. xvii. p. 322.

† Sir Stamford Raffles' Minutes on Java.

jurisdiction of the *kheldars*, for some particular offices to be formed for the royal household; hence there were *choumuahs* of silk weavers, gold gatherers, oil-makers, fishermen, and farmers, who all contributed their respective shares to the royal household, and filled it with the fat of the land.

The *pykes* by being separated from the *khels*, lost none of the privileges they previously possessed; but, on the contrary, acquired certain immunities, as exemptions from police and custom officers, which were of considerable importance to them.

As a remuneration for his services to the state, each *pyke* was entitled to two *puras* of the best description of rice land, *(roopit)*, rent free, or an equivalent proportion of inferior lands. In the event, however, of his services not being required, each *pyke* was liable to a capitation tax of two or three rupees.

These *pykes* had their regularly appointed officers over hundreds, and over thousands; and the whole *pyke* population was under as rigid discipline as a regular army, and, when occasion required it, were obliged every man to take the field. It is to be supposed, that from such an arrangement alone could have been effected the enormous public works so frequent throughout Asam; for the *pyke* on duty cost the government nothing, the other *pykes* of his *gote** being obliged to contribute every thing for his subsistence, whilst the sovereign had only to point out the work to be done.

All lands occupied by the *pykes*, at the great survey of the country in Rudra Sing's reign, were registered as *Pykar* lands, and were inalienable from the *pykes;* but at the same time were not hereditary.

* A minor division of the *pyke* population: three or four *pykes* formed what was called a *gote;* and, whilst one of the members of the *gote* was employed on service, the others were engaged in cultivating the lands allotted to them.

The principle adopted by the state was, that as every ryot, beyond a certain age was liable to personal service, or to a commutation thereof in money, he was on his part entitled to a certain quantity of land for his maintenance. It was therefore regulated, that each ryot, on coming of age, should, on demanding it of the *kheldar*, be invested with his set portion. If it so happened that in the village to which the individual belonged, there was no *putit* (fallow) land, his share was made up by curtailing a portion of the lands that had been by any way acquired by others in excess of the legal portion. In process of time, and in periods of tranquillity, as the village population increased, even portions of the legal share had to be abandoned, in some villages whatever might be the quantity of wastes in other villages. This practice, as might have been expected, subsequently led to many oppressions; the heads of *khels*, and villages, arbitrarily depriving *pykes* of lands in favour of others, under pretence of these adjustments.

From such an arrangement as the *pyke* system presented, it is but natural to suppose that there must have been in the people a great want of that energy which is the natural consequence of a full and inalienable possession on the one hand, and that stimulus to exertion and enterprize on the other, which the want of land would necessarily force upon them. Under the operation of such customs also, the land would continue to be infinitely divided in such parts as contained the best sites for the cultivation of rice, and the population concentrated in particular spots, whilst large tracts of somewhat inferior land would remain untouched. So far therefore from the ryots of Asam considering themselves as the possessors of the soils, the idea is perfectly novel to them; though at the same time the attachment of the Asamese to the soil their forefathers have occupied, is as strong as in any country, and instead of being a migratory race, as they have been erroneously supposed to be, they are the very reverse.

In addition to their quota of pyke lands, the *pykes* were allowed lands for their houses and villages, (Bari and Buri lands), which were not liable to taxation, nor to distribution to *pykes*, but were considered hereditary. How these lands were originally allotted does not appear from any records that have come down to us. It is known, that from one and a half to two *puras* of land, for homesteads, were granted to the *pykes* attached to temples; and it may be presumed, that something like this portion was originally allotted for the use of the reserved royal *pykes*. From the circumstance, however, of these lands not being noticed in the great general survey of the country, it appears sufficiently evident that the Raja laid no claims to them whatsoever.

All lands in excess to the allotted portions of the *pykes*, or surplus lands, were rented out at a low rate to any individual offering to cultivate them. Whether these lands were originally under the management of the *kheldars* or not, we have not the means of deciding; subsequently, however, they became separated, and a distinct set of officers were appointed to superintend the farming of them.

It is to be supposed that when the distribution of the people into *khels* was first instituted, it was done with reference to local divisions of the land: hence we find most of the existing *tangonis* or districts, in the Sibpur division of Upper Asam, corresponding with some of the ancient *khels*. But however this might have been originally, in later times the *khels* appear to have had no particular assigned locations; but to have been indiscriminately mixed up together, and scattered throughout the whole country. The *pykes* to avoid service, taxation, or oppressive offices, or for other reasons not known, constantly left their *khels*, and retired to distant parts of the province. There appears to have been no prohibition to this removal; but the retired (bhagonia) *pykes* were pursued by the officers of their own *khels*, and wherever they settled the officers of the village in which they resided were obliged to account for their revenue to their respective *kheldars*. The civil wars which had unsettled the kingdom for many years previous to the inroad of the Burmese, followed by the cruel devastation of these invaders, contributed in no small degree to the dispersion of the greater part of the *pykes*. The consequence was, that even in certain small villages there were families of from twenty to thirty different *khels*, all living together; but nevertheless amenable to their own respective *khel* officers. Some of the *khels* were in this manner scattered throughout the province; and it may be imagined how difficult it was to know where they had retired to, what a legion of officers would likewise be necessary to collect the revenues, and how easy were the modes of evading the claims of the state.

Another source of fraudulent evasion of the *pyke* tax, grew out of the exemption of slaves and bondsmen from service to the state.*

The great officers mostly possessed estates which had originally been granted from wastes, and which were cultivated by their slaves and servants; but these were exempt from taxation. Ryots to save themselves from service constantly took refuge on these estates, and passed themselves off as slaves, but the frequent consequence was, that their offspring in the second or third generation were considered as actual slaves.

The original revenues drawn from the *pykes* was, as we have already stated, by their personal service; but in process

* The slaves were persons taken in war, or bought of the hill tribes, or the descendants of slaves. The son of a *pyke* could not by law become a slave, nevertheless under circumstances of great distress male children were frequently sold: but the custom of the province gives freedom to any one who can trace back his descent to a *pyke* without the intervention of a slave female, for the children of a *pyke* by a slave mother were also slaves.

The bondsmen were either hill-men or liberated slaves, for a *pyke* could not be alienated from the government.

of time, as money became more an object to the state than servitude, a land tax began gradually to be introduced.

On the occupation of the country by the British government, the *pyke* system was still in a great measure prevalent in Upper Asam. But in Kamroop there was a land taxation according to local divisions called *Purganas*, an arrangement which had long existed previous to the Asamese Rajas getting possession of Kamroop, and was probably introduced by the Mahomedans. So far this agreed apparently with the arrangements which formerly prevailed in Bengal. The *Purganas* were managed by *Chowdries*, whose leases were annually renewed, after a summary comparison of their statements of the assets of the *Purgana* with former settlements.

The *Chowdries* were liable to dismissal for misdemeanor; but their successors were mostly, if not always, elected from members of the same family, and, from existing *sunnuds*, most of the *Purganas* appear to have been held hereditarily.

In addition to certain independent *talooks* and separated *choumuas*, there were nominally sixty-three *Purganas* in Kamroop; but instead of forming integral lots, they were in some instances scattered in small ill-defined portions throughout the division; and occasionally some portions were found situated in Durrung, whilst other portions of the same *Purgana* were on the remote western frontier of Kamroop. This division of the *Purganas* necessarily caused much embarrassment. Besides this, there were a vast number of religious institutions, Dewals, and Shustars, with lands, and *pykes* attached to them, placed under independent authorities, together with numerous grants of rent-free lands to Brahmins, which added not a little to the general confusion.

The land tax at the same time was not a simple tax upon the land, but was divided into *gaodhan*, or a poll tax, which the ryot paid as a *pyke; katani matti jumma,* or the tax upon the ryot's cultivation in excess to his allotted portion as a *pyke;* and *choroodhan,* a tax upon hearths.

The land tax was rendered still more difficult of adjustment, by being regulated in amount by the kinds of land under cultivation, as *rupit*, *faringalli*, and *boutulla*, &c.: and where the lands were annually inundated by the river, and cultivation consequently unsettled, the taxes were levied upon the ploughs, and not upon the lands.

Further to perplex the revenue arrangements of Kamroop, a large proportion of the inhabitants, such as fishermen, gold-washers, workers in brass, and almost all other tradesmen, were taxed not by the lands in their occupation, but as *pykes*.

The revenue system of Durrung was still different. In this division of the province was seated a branch of the family of the Rajas of Kuch Behar, commonly called the Durrung Rajas. This family had at one time the entire government of Durrung and the northern division of Kamroop, as independent princes; but were at length compelled to pay allegiance to the Ahom Rajas. In this state of dependence, however, they were permitted the management of the whole of the Durrung division, and were invested with civil and criminal jurisdiction in all minor cases; and the lands which had been cultivated by their own slaves and servants were allowed them for their support. Personal or *pyke* service was, however, exacted of all the ryots cultivating the remaining portion of the lands of this division.

Similar arrangements in most respects were made with the family of the Chalgari Baruwas, and with several minor Rajas, who apparently had military and political charge of the different frontiers.

On most of the frontier divisions certain complex arrangements were entered into with the tribes inhabiting the neighbouring hills. In some parts, as on the northern frontier of Kamroop, the Butias held large tracts of country, called Duwars, on the payment of a very small annual tribute. On the northern frontier of Durrung a tribute was paid for the occupation of the Duwars for eight months in the year; for the remaining four months, they were under the jurisdiction of the Asam Rajas. Again, on the northern frontier, from Durrung to the Dihong river, the Duflas, Abors, and Miris exacted a portion of the rents of all the ryots. And on the south bank, the Nagas and Mikirs were entitled to hold certain lands and *bhils*, (pieces of water); rent-free, and to be furnished with various contributions of fish, cloth, &c.

We turn now to the administration of the country since it has been placed under British authority.

From the first invasion of Asam, on the commencement of the war with the Burmese, almost up to the present date, the establishments for the administration of the country have been in a state of transition. Whilst the British troops were proceeding to the occupation of the country, the management of its civil affairs, with the general direction of the operations of the troops, was entrusted to Mr. David Scott, with the title of Governor-General's Agent on the north-east frontier. And as the forces advanced in the conquest of Upper Asam, the commandant of the troops, Colonel Richards, was connected with Mr. Scott* in a commission for the administration of the country.

On the conclusion of the treaty of Yandaboo, and the separation of Asam from Ava, the troops were gradually withdrawn from the province, and with them, Colonel Cooper, who had been appointed as Joint-Commissioner, and who for a short time had the management of Upper Asam, whilst Mr. Scott conducted the duties of Lower Asam. Upper Asam was then† placed under the charge of Captain Neufville, who also commanded the corps embodied for the defence of that part of the province, entitled the Asam Light Infantry. A short time previous to this period, at the urgent and repeated requisition of Mr. Scott for European assistants,

* April 1825. † Early in 1828.

Captain (the late Colonel) Adam White, was appointed to assist in Lower Asam.

Hitherto the affairs of the province had been conducted on much the same system as had previously prevailed before the conquest. The officers in charge of Lower and Upper Asam exercised a general superintendence, and more especially devoted their attention to fiscal business; whilst the criminal and civil duties were performed by councils of the Asamese gentry, under the name of *Punchayets*, of which there were two or three in each division of the province; appeals lying from the court of one *Punchayet* to that of the next superior court, and finally to the court of the Commissioner.

In judicial cases, the executive officers, Captains White and Neufville, were both Magistrates and Judges, trying the accused with the assistance of a *Punchayet*, but referring all heinous offences, accompanied with their opinions, to Mr. Scott for his final judgment.

The revenue affairs were carried on just in the same manner as they had existed before the conquest. It is, however, to be observed, that from long continued civil wars, and the occupation of the country by the Burmese, the native systems, perplexing as they were, from their novelty and intricacy, had fallen into almost inextricable confusion: yet only two officers were allowed for the management of these systems. They therefore had no alternative but to carry on the old arrangements by native management, in the best manner they could: and in experienced and unassisted as they were, it is not surprising that affairs rather retrograded than improved.

At this time, and for a long period afterwards, the intentions of the British government respecting Asam had not been decided on. There was no wish to retain the province from the native princes, but their inability to defend it was so apparent, as to leave no alternative. It was at length considered necessary to retain military occupation of the country, and to keep under British management such a portion of the province, as would pay for the maintenance of the required body of troops. But what portion should be retained, and what restored, or to whom the restoration should be made, was for a length of time undetermined. Whilst these questions therefore were unsettled, Mr. Scott was very justly averse from any alteration of the Asamese accustomed mode of managing the country. He was desirous likewise of continuing the natives of the province in all their former offices, that when the British government should determine what portion of the territories were to be made over to the management of a native prince, the transfer might be readily effected, and the prince himself find the same system of administration to which he had been accustomed.

In Upper Asam, until the appointment of Captain Neufville in 1828, the revenue collected was very small indeed; and that which was collected was never accounted for. In Lower Asam, notwithstanding Mr. Scott's great ability, and wonderful assiduity in the performance of his public duties, the state of affairs was not much better; and in fact no improvement could have been expected, while Mr. Scott was not only the controlling authority for all Upper as well as Lower Asam, but all the eastern frontier, including Manipur and Kachar on the east, and the Sikkim country on the west, was under his management as the Agent to the Governor-General. He was at the same time also Commissioner of NE. Rungpore and Kuch-Behar, and Judge of circuit and appeal in the zillah of Sylhet.

The appointment of Captain White in 1827, relieved Mr. Scott of the executive duties of Magistrate and Collector in Lower Asam, and some greater degree of justice was done to the people. The duties of all Lower Asam were, however, so overwhelming, that no leisure was left to Capt. White to suggest any improvements.

Captain Neufville died in August 1830, and was succeeded in Upper Asam by Captain White, to whom was also given the command of the Asam Light Infantry. In Lower Asam, Capt. White was succeeded by Lieut. James Matthie, who had been in charge of Upper Asam after Capt. Neufville's death, till the appointment of Captain White.

The chief measures suggested by Mr. Scott, during his residence in the province, were a census of all the slaves in Lower Asam, followed by a summary investigation into the rights of the owners to hold in slavery those whom they claimed as slaves. This investigation, as might have been expected, was attended with much discontent and distress among the proprietors of slaves; but under its operation no less than 12,000 individuals were released from hopeless bondage.

Mr. Scott also prepared the way for all the subsequent revenue arrangements, by taking an account of all the assets of the country, and making settlements on a sound basis, and with a near approach to a correct ascertainment of the number of cultivators, and quantity of cultivated lands. Mr. Scott likewise commenced a systematic survey of the country, with a view of settling it by Mouzas, and introducing a regular taxation on the lands only; but this indefatigable officer died before the Government had determined what arrangements should eventually be adopted for the province.

Mr. Scott died in August 1831, partly from over-exertion in the performance of the heavy duties entrusted to him without adequate assistance, and partly from delaying too long to retire for relaxation. He was greatly lamented by the Asamese, and generally by all the natives on the frontier; to whom he had ingratiated himself by a long course of kindness and affability.

Mr. Scott was succeeded by Mr. T. C. Robertson.

The want of assistants was now forcibly brought to the notice of the Government; and, in consequence, several officers were soon after appointed for the administration of the province.

Mr. Scott had previous to his death been rather favourable to the restoration of Raja Purunder Sing to that portion of the territories of his ancestors which the British government might deem advisable to transfer to native management. This measure was recommended by Mr. Robertson; and accordingly, in the beginning of 1832, Raja Purunder Sing was put in possession of the whole of Upper Asam, the Muttuck territory and Sadiya excepted.* By the treaty entered into with him, his relations with the British government were placed upon the same footing as those of other protected princes; the entire civil administration being left in his hands, and his territory secured from the attack of hostile states, on condition of his paying a tribute of 50,000 Rupees per annum to the British government.

In 1835-36, Purunder Sing fell off in his payments, and urged on the Government the reduction of a large portion of the tribute, alleging a very great falling off in his revenues. On examination, his assertion was found to be correct; and further inquiries led to the conclusion, that in a very short period he would be found totally incapable of paying up so much as one-half of the original stipulation. Moreover, it appeared that the diminution of the revenues was in a great measure owing to his own avaricious habits, and to the general system of corruption which he apparently encouraged. As these circumstances were deemed incompatible with the equitable administration of the country, his territories were resumed in October 1838, and placed on the same footing as the other districts in the province.

Mr. Robertson was succeeded in the offices of Governor General's Agent and Commissioner of Revenue, by Captain F. Jenkins, 23d January 1834.

The province of Asam since it has been entirely under the management of British officers, has been divided into six districts—Kamroop, Durrung, Nowgong, Sibpur, Lukimpur, and Muttuck, or Sadiya.

* See Local Geography, Muttuck and Sadiya division.

These divisions are further sub-divided into purganas, mehals, or mouzahs respectively, placed under the fiscal management of Chowdris, Patgiris, or Takuriahs, each of whom pays in the revenue of his division direct to the Collector. The powers of these officers resemble, in some measure, those conferred on the Tuhseldars of the Western provinces; but no exact definitions of their powers, nor any rules for the mutual guidance of the village officers and the ryots, have yet been drawn up.

To each of the revenue officers is attached a Putwari, or clerk, who keeps the accounts of the mehal, and over as many mouzahs, or villages, as yield an aggregate revenue of about 500 rupees. There is a Takuriah, or mandal, subordinate to the Chowdri aided by a Gong-kagoti, or village accountant. Each Takuriah has also one Tekla, or peon, attached to him; and the Chowdri has six, eight, or ten peons, according to the size of his division, who assist him in the discharge of his duties.

The aggregate remuneration paid to the mofussil officers, amounts to 14¼ per cent. in cash, and lands worth to Government about 3½ per cent. more—total 17¾, or to about 18 per cent. on the amount of their collections.

	In Cash.	*In Lands.*
Chowdri or other manager, ...	7 per cent.	1 pura for every 100 rupees.
Putwari, ...	1 ditto.	½ do. as above.
Takuriah, or head village officer,	4 ditto.	6 puras in all.
Kagoti, or village accountant, ..	2¼ ditto.	4 ditto ditto.
Teklas, or peons, ...		4 ditto ditto.
	14¼ per cent.	

The European revenue officers to each district are a Collector, (the assistant in charge of the district), and a junior or sub-assistant. The Collector has the same powers as a Collector in the regulation provinces; and a portion of those powers, such as the hearing and deciding of summary suits, he can depute to his assistants, with the sanction of the Commissioner.

The Collector periodically revises the settlements of the purganas and mouzahs of his district, subject to the instructions of the Commissioner, and the approval of the Board of Revenue and Government. The settlements having received the sanction of Government, the Collector is held responsible for the collection of the revenue.

In adverting to the subject of the administration of justice, it may be necessary to state what courts of civil justice are established in the several districts, their powers, and the rules by which they are regulated.

Besides the court of the Commissioner, there are three civil courts in each district—the Assistant Commissioner's, the Sudder Ameen's, and the Moonsiff's.

The Commissioner's court may not properly be called the court of a district, as it extends its jurisdiction throughout the province. It has, under the present rules, no jurisdiction in original suits, and only an appellate jurisdiction in ordinary and special appeals from the decision of the Assistant Commissioner.

The court of the Assistant Commissioner, which is equivalent to that of a zillah or city judge in Bengal, has power to try all suits, without any limitation regarding the amount involved in them. The Assistant, to whom all petitions of plaint are in the first instance presented, is to retain on his own file suits for property, moveable or immoveable, of a value exceeding one thousand rupees, but may refer suits for smaller amounts to the Sudder Ameen or Moonsiff.

The court of the Sudder Ameen has power to try all original suits not involving a larger amount of property than one thousand rupees, and also all cases of appeal from the decision of the Moonsiff.

The court of the Moonsiff has power to try and decide all suits not exceeding in value the sum of one hundred rupees.

The rules of practice, by which these courts are guided, are contained in a short code drawn up for Asam; and when these rules are not sufficiently explicit, the officers are to be guided by the general spirit of the Regulations, obtaining in the regulation provinces, as well as by a due conformity to the local customs.

In the administration of criminal justice, the functionaries employed are Senior Assistants, Junior Assistants, Sub-assistants, and Sudder Ameens.

The rules for the guidance of Assistants acting in the capacity of Magistrate, in the examination of criminal matters, are contained in a code similar to the civil code just adverted to. The punishments to be inflicted for various kinds of delinquencies are regulated by the general spirit of the Regulations.

The police of Asam is managed by darogahs, thannadars, and peons, stationed throughout the districts; and these are assisted by the officers of the revenue department.

The present military establishments of the province consist of a Local Regiment of Light Infantry, a Local Company of Artillery, and two Regiments of Sebundies.

The Asam Light Infantry consists of ten companies of ninety men each, or a total of 900 men. Forty of these are mounted on ponies, and employed as a troop of cavalry. The men of the corps are principally Hindusthanis and Gurkhas, with a few Manipuries, and natives of the province.

The head-quarters of this corps are at present at Sibpur, with detachments stationed at Saikwah, Dibrughur, and Jaipur.

The Local Artillery, which is at present under formation, will consist chiefly of Hindusthanies, with a complement of 100 men. The head quarters are at Dibrughur.

The 1st Asam Sebundy corps is composed principally of Rabus, Kacharis, and other natives of the Gowalpara and Kamrup districts. It consists of eight companies of 80 men each. The head-quarters are at Gowhatti, and upon it devolve all the duties of Lower Asam and Gowalpara. The second in command is stationed at Tezpur, and one of the officers doing duty at Gowalpara.

The 2nd Asam Sebundy corps was lately raised for the duties of the Muttuck and Sudiya district. It is composed principally of men from Lower Asam, similar to those of the 1st Sebundy Regiment of the natives of Muttuck Doaniwas, Asamese, who from having been carried into slavery by the hill tribes, or from living with them, have been thrown out of the pale of Hinduism.

The head-quarters of this regiment are at Rungpore; it also occupies the outposts on the Muttuck frontier. It consists of a complement of six companies of 100 men each.

It is fairly assumed that these forces, distributed as they are, will prove quite sufficient for all the detail duties of the province and surrounding country, for preserving internal tranquillity, and for effectually checking any hostile inroads of the numerous wild and independent tribes which surround the whole valley of Asam.

CHAPTER VI.

PRODUCTIVE INDUSTRY.

The Industry of Asam in an unimproved state—Agriculture—Amount of waste lands—Irreclaimable waste—Condition of labourers—Implements of Agriculture — Cattle — Irrigation—Imperfect drainage—Embankments—Objects of culture—Grain—Materials of manufacture—Vegetable luxuries—Metals and Minerals—Manufactures—Cotton—Silks—Dyeing stuffs—Mechanics of common life—Fishing—Commerce—Articles of Export—Articles of Import—Trade with the adjoining Hill Tribes—Estimate of total value of Trade—Capable of very great extension—Lines of communication between Asam and Bengal—Route to Butan—Route to Thibet—Route to Burma and China.

The industry of Asam, is in a very unimproved state. This may be attributable no doubt to her long barbarism, her constant internal discords, the prevalence of slavery, and the present thin population scattered over large tracts of territory. These tracts, however, being in many parts of great natural fertility, yield a large amount of bulky and useful commodities, which can be exchanged for the more delicate productions and finer manufactures of other countries.

Among the branches of industry, agriculture claims our first attention.

We have already had occasion to remark that the valley, supplied as it is with copious moisture from the mountain ranges which surround it on either side, is completely exempted from that arid character so common to the plains of India. It maintains a rough plenty, with little aid from human art. The only disadvantage of the soil is, that the combined influence of heat and moisture produces often a rank fertility, which renders a great degree of labour necessary to fit it for the production of the finer kinds of grain.

The amount of waste lands in Asam may be estimated at considerably more than one-half the extent of its area. These wastes are fully as rich as any of the lands now under cultivation. The scantiness of the population, combined with political causes, among which the ancient feudal customs, and the consequent minute division of land among the peasantry, were probably the most important, have alone prevented them from being turned to profitable account.

The extent of unimprovable wastes is comparatively very small indeed; for even the hills, which have in most cases a gentle slope, are not only for the most part free of rock, but generally covered with a fine rich soil, and capable of producing very profitable crops.

Although the Asamese have always been an agricultural people, nothing can be more imperfect than the instruments, or the skill with which they conduct that important art. The cultivators, either from insecurity through an imperfect police, or from mere custom, live in large villages, having each a small spot on the tillage of which they occupy themselves, in conjunction with the labours of the loom, and with other employments. Holding their lands by no certain tenure, they never think of expending capital in their improvement; in fact, but a very small proportion of the farmers can be supposed to have the means of doing so. They are for the most part a poor and oppressed people; the tax-gatherers, and the *Chowdris,* who are the nominal proprietors of the land, not unfrequently levy from the tenants a sum averaging as much as one-fourth the amount paid into government; and in addition to this, they have frequent other opportunities of extorting money from them.

The *Ryots*, or cultivators, in general, therefore, obtain but a bare maintenance from their labours, and it is in vain to look amongst them for a bold, happy, and independent yeomanry. A very few indeed are able to pay their rents before the harvest; but the greater proportion are obliged to borrow money, and in most cases with an exorbitant usury, upon the credit of the crop, and repay it after harvest. Thus the great body of the cultivators are, in fact, mere servants of the merchant, who engages to pay their rent for them, whilst they in turn agree to surrender all the produce of their land to him; from whom also they receive what is necessary for the maintenance of their families, till the harvest. If the produce be more than the debts, the farmer keeps the surplus. If it be less, which is not unfrequently the case, the remainder is written as debt in his name, and he engages to pay it out of the produce of the next year. If, on the other hand, he should be very unfortunate in his harvest, the poor cultivator's little all is sold by the merchant, and with his family he is turned out upon the cold unfeeling world, to beg his bread, or to perish. More frequently, however, the poor people are so oppressed by the exorbitant demands of the *Chowdris*, that they are obliged to resign their lands, and seek an asylum elsewhere, to which they are often allured by promises of better treatment.

Such is the state of the labourer: and under such circumstances how deplorable must be the state of agriculture! The hands of the labourer are said to be the mine out of which the wealth of a nation comes. "What is the prince of territories unbounded, or the lord of countless looms, without the help of his fellowman? The land is but a wilderness; the factory, but a hideous wall! The labourer is the true foundation of the great social building, and unless he have from his earnings what will support a wife with the average number of children, in the necessaries and decent comforts of life, independently to the end of his days, the labourer's condition is not what it ought to be. If that be so, however interested parties may proclaim a thriving state, and king's speeches may re-echo it, the fabric of society will totter, for its best timbers are rotten."

The implements of agriculture are to the highest degree rude. The *plough,* like that of Bengal, is the most simple instrument imaginable. It consists of a crooked piece of wood, sharpened at one end, and covered with a plate of iron, which forms the plough-share. A wooden handle, about a foot long, is fixed to the other end crossways, and in the middle is a long straight piece of wood, (sometimes a bamboo is used instead,) which goes between the bullocks, and falls on the middle of the yoke, to which it hangs by means of a peg, and is tied by a string. The *yoke* is usually a neat instrument, and lies over the neck of two bullocks, just before the hump; it has two pegs descending on the side of each bullock's neck, by means of which it is tied with a cord under the throat. There is only one man or boy to each plough, who with one hand holds the plough, and with the other guides the animals, by pulling them this or that way by the tail, and driving them forward with a stick.

This imperfect instrument, drawn by a couple of feeble animals, serves merely to scratch the ground to the depth of about four inches, and is incapable of bringing up fresh earth to mingle with that previously cropped; while the useless and hurtful vegetation is so far from being eradicated, that where burning precedes not, which helps for a short time to smooth the surface, the grasses and shrubs which have bid defiance to the plough, cover a large proportion of the surface. When the farmer can afford it, several ploughs are used in succession, all to deepen the same furrow; a second ploughing of the same sort is then performed across the first; and not unfrequently a third and fourth, in different directions, before so much as an appearance of mould is obtained for the seed.

The instrument employed as a harrow, is in many places literally nothing more than the branch of a tree; in other places, a thing resembling a ladder made of bamboo, about eighteen feet in length, is used, drawn by two bullocks, and guided by two men, who stand upon the instrument to increase its weight.

The cattle used in husbandry are oxen and buffaloes. During the dry season, there is almost a total failure of herbage for the support of cattle; many are in consequence annually lost by famine, and the remainder are reduced to the most deplorable state of emaciation and weakness. Hay is a commodity which it would not always be convenient to make; but various kinds of pulse and millet might be produced at all seasons, and would afford the most important relief to the cattle, when the pasture grounds are bare. The straw of the rice, which is now almost entirely wasted, might also be stacked up, and served out to the cattle in seasons of scarcity. But the natives, so remarkably indifferent to their own wants, can scarcely be expected to make any provision for the wants of their beasts.

Irrigation is practised to a very small extent, though the means of watering the crops are as abundant and convenient as in most parts of India. The streams are numerous, and frequently run in shallow beds; and springs are generally met with near the surface. There are besides in many parts of the country extensive tanks, and *jheels* (lakes), that might be turned to a very useful account. The rice crops, generally speaking, are not irrigated; but in some parts of the valley, where the means present themselves, the rice is flooded from the hill streams. Occasionally small fields of rice, situated near *jheels*, are irrigated by bailing up the water into small gutters prepared to carry it off.

The only cultivation in which watering is constantly had recourse to, is that of the poppy. The mode of irrigating this crop is by means of a small wicker basket tied to the end of a bamboo handle, used by one man, with which he bails up the water from small reservoirs made for the purpose.

The *Kacharis* along the northern frontier in Chatgari, and Chutia, and about the Butan Duwars, exhibit an exception to the general neglect of irrigation. They are in the habit of extensively irrigating their rice fields from the small streams which intersect these districts; and as no better rice crops are obtained elsewhere in the valley, a good deal of the fertility, the cause of this superiority, may be ascribed to the irrigation bestowed on the fields.

Generally speaking, no manure is used for any of the great crops; the stubble, and frequently the grass and weeds which overrun the fields, are burnt off, and the ashes serve in a small measure to answer the purpose.

The agriculture of Asam seems to suffer most from the imperfection of drainage. Those waters which traverse the valley, and are the chief source of its fertility, often overspread the country in a manner extremely destructive. There are in many parts extensive swamps and morasses that act in a still more prejudicial degree; for while during the rains they inundate the adjacent country, at the beginning of the dry season, when acted upon by the heat of the sun, the vegetable matter with which they are usually covered begins to decay, and they form the hot-beds of disease and malaria. In some places these fens are drained in the course of the extension of cultivation, and when once brought under culture, they may be considered as permanently reclaimed; for, unlike the marshes of Europe, they never return to their former useless state if kept under cultivation.

There is no general system of embankments in Lower Asam, though partial embankments to guard against the inundations of particular streams at particular places are not uncommon. These are most frequently met with on either bank of the *Kullung*, though there can be no doubt, much valuable land that is now covered by reeds, or abandoned owing to the periodical floods, might be recovered by adopting a general system of *bunds*. But it should be remarked, that nearly every stream in Upper Asam was anciently *bunded*, and the recovery of these embankments is now a great source of solicitude to the authorities.

Inundations are no doubt very beneficial to some tracts, which are so elevated that the inundation spreads over them very gradually. But on the whole there can be no hesitation in saying, that *bunds* would be far more advantageous to the country, than abandoning the lands to nature and the gradual operations of silting. Whenever the inundations move violently, they never have the effect of raising the land, but, on the contrary, do infinite mischief by carrying off all the loam, and leaving a sandy deposit. In some places, especially in the vicinity of the great river, where the inundations move slowly, and by depositing a fine soil tend gradually to raise the level, yet the operation is so exceedingly slow that ages may pass away before the land will be culturable, while, in the mean time, the unrestrained currents are often making particular sets, and in one season destroy the work of years. Were embankments raised, these lands might, on the contrary, be rendered abundantly productive, and not being liable to the effects of currents across their surface, would be permanently protected.

The products of agriculture may be divided into three classes;—food for man, which is almost exclusively grain; materials of manufacture; and vegetable luxuries—chiefly substances of a stimulant and exhilarating quality.

Rice, considered as the staff of life, takes the lead among the objects of cultivation. Of this article there are generally speaking two great crops,—the *aeu*, or sown; and the *hali*, or planted rice.

The first crop is sown early in the year, the first ploughings commencing about the middle of February; the ground is frequently ploughed a second or a third time before the seed is cast, the farmer availing himself of the first fall of rain to weed his ground; this done he casts his seed, and the harrow which we have already described is then drawn over it. The field is now carefully watched during the day, and the individuals on guard are usually armed with bows and clay balls, with which they scare away the crows and other depredators of that sort. Should no rain fall during the four or five days which succeed the operation of sowing, and the sun be very hot, the seed is sometimes destroyed; and the ploughing and sowing are repeated.

When the rice has reached the height of about six inches, a piece of wood with spikes driven through it is drawn over the ground, in order to prevent the rice growing too rank, as well as to loosen the earth, and destroy the weeds.

The corn being nearly ripe, the farmer erects a stage of bamboos in the field, sufficiently high to be a refuge from wild beasts, covers it with thatch, and places a man there to watch, especially during the night. When a buffalo or a wild hog comes into the field, the keeper takes a wisp of lighted straw in his hand; and shaking it, and making a loud noise, he approaches the animal, which is thus speedily driven away.

Harvest usually commences about the end of June, or beginning of July; four months after seed time. The sickle resembles that used in England. When reaped, the corn is bound up in sheaves, which are sometimes left two or three days on the ground to dry, but never raised in mows; at other times it is carried home on the day it is cut. The sheaves are generally conveyed on men's heads, or are attached to the ends of bamboos, and suspended on their shoulders. Bullocks are seldom used for carriage.

The poor, after the harvest, are usually permitted to glean the fields.

When brought home, the rice is by some piled up in round stacks, while others immediately separate it from the husk with bullocks. In performing this operation, two or more bullocks are tied together, side by side, and driven round upon a quantity of sheaves spread upon the ground. By this means about ten maunds or more will be trodden out every hour: not unfrequently men are employed in treading it down. It is a common practice to "muzzle the ox that treadeth out the corn," until the upper sheaves have been reduced to mere straw. The rice is then cleaned from the husk by means of large hand fans; one person letting the grain fall from his hands, while another winnows it. It is next deposited in granaries, or sent to the corn merchants.

In May and June the farmer sows other lands, for his second and principal harvest: as it is meant to be transplanted, a great quantity of rice is sown in a small space. About the end of July, or the beginning of August, when the plant begins to shoot up, the farmer ploughs his fields, which are now well saturated with water, and to these he transplants the rice which he sowed in June. The lands are usually so embanked, as to retain a sufficient head of rain water; should there be a deficiency of rain after the transplanting, the farmer is often obliged to water his fields.

In December or January he reaps the crop. It is after the reaping of this harvest that the great festival of the harvest-home is celebrated.

Wheat, barley, and millet, as we have already had occasion to mention, are very little used; and the cultivation of them necessarily very small.

Maize is generally cultivated in small patches about the houses of the farmers; but no where is it raised as an extensive crop.

The leguminous plants, as well as the vegetables commonly cultivated, have been noticed at large while treating of these plants, in our article on the Botany of the country.

Immense as is the demand for human food, provision must also be made for clothing and other necessaries, and a proportion of the land employed in raising the materials of manufacture.

For information respecting the various plants cultivated for these purposes, and their mode of treatment, we beg again to refer the reader to the article on Botany.

Although the Asamese in general devote their soil exclusively to purposes of utility, yet like all other nations, they seek to procure some vegetables possessing peculiar properties agreeable to the taste, and exhilarating to the spirits. For this purpose they employ opium, tobacco, the beetle leaf, and the fruit of the beetlenut palm. A few spices are also occasionally cultivated.

Among articles of luxurious consumption, sugar may be mentioned; but the natives seldom carry the manufacture of the cane to a further extent than the state of *gur*, or treacle.

The mill used in this work is of the most simple and clumsy construction. The trunk of a tree, about seven cubits long, is put into the earth to the depth of about four feet, leaving five feet above ground; and at the top a cup is excavated about a foot deep, and perforated near the bottom to let out the liquor. Into this excavation falls another trunk of a tree like a pestle, which passes through a hollow piece of wood resembling a hopper, in which is placed the cane, cut into small pieces. From this pestle is suspended a lever, to which four or five bullocks are fastened to draw it round, and thus bruise the cane. A board is hung to the lever, and stones put on it, to preserve the balance. Sometimes a man sits on this board for this purpose, and goes round with the machine. To prevent the lever from sinking down, it is tied to the top of the trunk which is fastened in the ground. A pan is placed beneath the machine to receive the juice, which is afterwards boiled once into molasses, and in this state is used by the natives.

The mineral wealth of Asam, though in all probability abundant, is very imperfectly known. The beds of limestone and coal are of very great extent; and if worked, there is every reason to suppose they will lead to very important results in the advancement of the country. The natives, however, are yet ignorant of their value.

Iron may be found in great abundance about the foot of the mountain ranges, along the southern extremity of the valley. Though it is reasonable to suppose the people in the vicinity at one time engaged extensively in its manufacture, yet of late it has been all but abandoned. Unacquainted with the proper process of smelting it, the manufacturers are unable to contend with the iron of the Khassia hills, usually brought down to their markets.

The gold dust found in the sands of most of the mountain streams is of a very superior quality, but owing to the labour necessary in collecting it, very few individuals are found willing to engage in the occupation.

Brine springs are frequent about the low ranges of the Naga hills, and some of these are still worked by the natives. But the salt imported from Bengal being cheaper, is fast driving the native salt from the market.

The manufactures of Asam are, generally speaking, of a rude character, and for the most part adapted merely for its home consumption. The staple is cotton and silk stuffs, with which the people are universally clothed.

The cotton plant is grown extensively by the adjacent hill tribes. Women of all castes prepare the cotton thread for the weaver, spinning the thread on a very fine piece of bamboo, with a ball of clay at one end; this they turn round with the left hand, and supply the cotton with the right. The thread is then wound upon a stick, and sold to the merchants, or weavers. For the coarser thread, the women make use of a wheel very similar to that of the English spinster, though upon a smaller construction. The cloths generally worn by the natives are made in almost every village, and such being their destination, little pains are taken to render them fine. The muslin and calico used by the more affluent, are imported from Bengal. The loom, like that used in Bengal, is in substance the same as the English, though much more simple and imperfect. The frame is laid almost on the ground, in which a hole is cut to receive the feet of the weaver while at work.

The muga silk, a texture peculiar to the country, affords the dress, which above all others is considered rich and valuable. It was the prescribed attire of all the high officers of government, and is still worn by every one who makes any pretensions to opulence. Yet this manufacture, like most others, is carried on without capital, without division of labour, by single individuals, each of whom spins, weaves, and dyes his own web. Some of the fabrics produced are notwithstanding very creditable indeed.

The silks of Asam, denominated by the natives the eria and the muga, are respectively the produce of the *phalæna cynthia* and *saturnia*. The former, as we have already had occasion to state, is reared entirely within doors, and is fed principally on the leaves of the Ricinus communis. The duration of its life varies according to seasons; in summer it is shorter, and the produce both greater and better. At this season, from its birth to the time it begins its cocoon, twenty to twenty-four days expire; in fifteen more the moth is produced, the eggs are laid in three days, and in five they are hatched: making the total duration of a breed forty-three days. In winter it lives nearly two months; the number of breeds in the year are reckoned at seven.

For the purpose of breeding, the natives select cocoons from those which begin to be formed in the largest numbers on the same day; those that contain males are distinguished by a more pointed end. On the second or third day after the cocoons have begun to be formed, they are put in a closed basket, and hung up in the house, out of reach of rats or insects. Twenty-four hours after the moths have been produced the females (known only by the larger body) are tied to long reeds or canes, from twenty to twenty-five to each, and these are hung up in the house. The eggs that have been laid during the first three days are alone kept; they are tied in a piece of cloth, and suspended to the roof till a few begin to hatch; these eggs are white, and about the size of a turnip seed. When a few of the worms are hatched, the cloths are put on small bamboo platters hung up in the house, and here they are fed with tender leaves. After the second moulting they are removed to feed on bunches of leaves suspended a little above the ground and upon the ground a mat is laid to receive them when they fall. When they have ceased feeding, they are placed in baskets filled with dry leaves, amongst which they form their cocoons.

In four days the cocoons are said to be complete. After a selection has been made for the next breed, the remainder are exposed to the sun for two or three days to destroy the vitality of the chrysalis.*

The cocoons are next put over a slow fire in a solution of potash, whereby the drawing of the silk is rendered easy: they are then removed, and the water gently squeezed out. This done, they are taken one by one, and the silk placed within the thumb of the left hand, whilst the right is employed in drawing out the silk. Any inequalities that might exist are reduced by rubbing them down between the thumb and finger: this mode is also adopted for joining on new cocoons. The thread is allowed to accumulate in small quantities of about a quarter of a seer: these are afterwards exposed to the sun, or near a fire till dry, when they are wound up into skeins, and the silk is then ready for the weaver.

* The hill tribes settled in the plains are very fond of eating the chrysalis; they perforate the cocoons the third day to get them; they do the same with the muga, and sell few cocoons imperforated.

It is difficult to ascertain the quantity of eria procurable from an acre of land. No person can give information as to the extent of his plantation, or even the quantity of eria thread he usually gets in a year, beyond the circumstance that he has enough for the use of his family. Every ryot has a few plants round his house or farm hedges, which would almost amount to the twentieth part of an acre; so that for this to afford clothing for a family, the produce must be very large indeed.

The muga moth, (saturnia), is usually reared on trees in the open air, and the tending of the worms is attended with much care.

There are generally five breeds of muga worms in the year, distinguished by the natives according to the month in which they generally occur.

1. Jaruwa, in January and February.
2. Jeituwa, in May and June.
3. Aharuwa, June and July.
4. Bhodia, in August and September.
5. Kholia, in October and November.

The first and last are the best crops, as to quality and quantity. Were the Asamese acquainted with the process of retarding the hatching of the eggs, as is practised in China in regard to the mulberry silk worm, it is probable they would find it more advantageous to have only two or three crops during the year, instead of five; for the aharuwa and bhodia crops yield but a small quantity of silk, and that of a very inferior quality.

The same rule is followed in the selection of cocoons to breed from with the muga, as with the eria. They are put into a closed basket suspended from the roof; the day after they are hatched the female moths are taken out, and tied to small wisps of thatching grass, taken always from that part of the house immediately over the hearth; its darkened colour being thought more acceptable to the moth.

These wisps are then hung on a string tied across the house, to protect them from rats and lizards: they are taken out morning and evening, and exposed to the rays of the sun. The eggs laid during the first three days, are the only ones considered worth keeping. Ten days after the laying of the eggs, when a few of them are hatched, the wisps of straw to which the moths had been fastened are hung to the trees on which it is intended the caterpillars should feed; and these soon find their way to the leaves. Care must be taken that there be no ants about the trees, for their bite usually proves fatal to the worms in their early stages. Previous to placing the worms on the trees, the natives generally rub the trunk with molasses, and tie fish and other things to it to attract the ants; when accumulated in great numbers they destroy them with fire. The ground about the trees must also be kept free from underwood, which renders it easier to find the worms should they happen to fall off.

To prevent the worms coming to the ground, fresh plantain leaves are tied round the trunk, over the slippery surface of which they cannot crawl.

During the day the worms require to be constantly watched, crows and other birds being so fond of them, that they lie in wait for them in the neighbouring trees. Bats, owls, and rats are very destructive at nights. A number of caterpillars are also destroyed in the more advanced stages by the sting of wasps, and by the ichneumon insect, which deposits its eggs in their body.

The worms thrive best in dry weather; but a very hot sunny day proves fatal to many at the time of moulting. At these periods rain is considered very favourable; thunder-storms do not injure them as they do the mulberry worm. Continual heavy rains (which by the way seldom occur) are hurtful by throwing them off the trees; showers, however heavy, cause no great damage; the worms generally taking shelter under the leaves with perfect safety. The worms during their moulting remain, on the branches; but when about beginning to spin, they come down the trunk; and the plantain leaves preventing their going further down, they are then collected in baskets, which are afterwards put under branches of dry leaves suspended from the roof of the house: they crawl up into these, and there form their cocoons.

The total duration of a breed varies from sixty to seventy days. The period is thus divided:

Four moultings, ...	20
From fourth moulting to beginning of cocoon, ...	10
In the cocoon, ...	20
As a moth, ...	6
Hatching of the eggs, ...	10
Total	66 days.

The chrysalis not being easily killed by exposure to the sun, a number of cocoons are placed on bamboo stages, and covered over with leaves, whilst below them a quantity of dry grass is set on fire, which in a short time helps to kill them. The cocoons are then boiled for about an hour in a solution of potash, when they are taken out and laid in folds of cloth; hence they are taken as required. The floss is removed with the hand, and the cocoons are thrown into hot water.

The instrument used for winding off the silk is the coarsest imaginable. "A thick bamboo, about three feet long, is split in two, and the pieces driven equally into the ground two feet apart: over the interior projection of one of the knots is laid a stick, to which is fixed, a little on one side, a round piece of plank, about a foot in diameter; the rotatory motion is given by jerking this axle, on which the thread rolls itself, in front of the vessel holding the cocoons; a stick is placed horizontally for the thread to travel upon. Two persons are employed; one attends the cocoons, the other jerks the axle with the right hand, and with the same hand directs the thread up the left fore-arm, so that it is twisted in coming down again towards the hand; the left hand directs the thread over the axle." Fifty cocoons is the smallest number they can wind off in one thread, though twenty is the usual number; this is no doubt to be attributed to the coarseness of the instrument used. When nearly a quarter of a seer of the silk has accumulated on the axle, it is dried in the sun, and made into skeins of one or two rupees weight.

Fifty thousand cocoons, the produce of an acre of muga trees, which yield upwards of twelve seers of silk, are considered by the Asamese a good annual return. It is no doubt a very profitable one; for the value of twelve seers of silk is usually about sixty rupees. The labour and expense of making and keeping up a plantation of these trees is very trifling indeed.

The following is a list of the Cloths made in Asam, of the Muga and Eria Silks.

Names of cloth.	Size in cubits.	Weight.	Price of Thread.	Cost of weaving.	Total.	Remarks.
		Seer Chs.	Rs. A. P.	Rs. A. P.	Rs. A. P.	
Muga.						
Suria, ...	7 by 1½	6	1 14	3	2 1	Used as Dhoties.
Ditto, ...	16 by 2	1	5	8	5 8	
Mekla, ..	5 by 1¾	4	1 4	2	1 6	Petticoats.
Rhia, ...	12 by 1¼	8	2 8	4	2 12	Scarfs.
Gamsha, ..	8 by 1	2	10	1	11	Worn as turbans or round the waist.
Jotha Borkapur, ..	12 by 2½	1	2	6	2 6	Made of the floss of the cocoons, and worn as covering during the winter.
Eria.						
Borkapur,	16 by 3	1 8	3	8	3 8	Worn in winter, and used as blankets, also made into coats.
Meklas, ..	5 by 2	6	12	2	14	Used only by the poorer classes.
Rhia, ...	10 by 1½	8	1	2	1 2	
Gamsha, ..	8 by ½	4	8	2	10	

The mulberry worm is also raised in the province, but it is very scarce, and none is found in the wild state. From the circumstance of the use of the silk being formerly confined to the members of the royal family, and the grandees of the country, and the rearing of the worm to one particular caste, the *Jugis*. It is to be inferred that the worm was introduced about the time that Hinduism was gaining ground in the province.

The management of the worms is in most respects the same as it is in Bengal. They are reared within doors, and require a great deal of care and attention. A separate hut is used, which is filled with bamboo stages, with a passage left all round, between them and the outer wall: these huts are usually built north and south, with a single door opening to the east.

The moths are made to deposit their eggs on pieces of cloth; these are generally packed up with the household clothing, and when the time of hatching approaches, (December), they are taken out and exposed to the air. When hatched, the worms are fed for the first three or four days on the tender leaves of the mulberry, cut up and placed in new earthen pots, and afterwards on a bamboo tray. After the first moulting, the caterpillars are removed to the stages already mentioned. When about beginning to spin, they are put on bamboo trays filled up with pieces of matting fixed perpendicularly, about two inches apart; these in the first afternoon, are exposed for half an hour to the rays of the sun, and afterwards hung up in the house.

Previous to winding off the silk, the cocoons are exposed to the sun for three or four days, and then boiled over a slow fire. The instrument on which the silk is wound, is composed of three pieces of bamboo, one placed perpendicularly, whilst the other two are tied horizontally across it. This is held with the right hand, while the left directs the thread over the cross bars, taking care whilst doing this to make it rub against the fore-arm, in order to twist it; a second person attends to the fire, and the putting on new cocoons. When a sufficient quantity for a skein has thus accumulated, it is taken off the cross bars. The price of the silk varies from eight to ten rupees a seer; but is not readily procurable.*

The dyes chiefly used by the natives are *lac*, *munjit*, and *indigo*.

The lac after having been exposed to the sun for a short time, to render it brittle, is ground and sieved very fine. This powder is then thrown into a basin of water, and allowed to stand for twelve hours, the thread is then steeped in it with a few leaves of a tree called by the Asamese *leteku*.† When the thread has absorbed a sufficient quantity of this solution, it is taken out and dried in the sun; the same process is repeated twice. To give it a higher colour, the thread is again dyed with *munjit*,‡ which is reduced to a powder and thrown into a bowl of water, where it is allowed to stand forty-eight hours; the thread is then put in and boiled together with the leaves of a tree called *hoh;* this done the thread is dried in the sun, and ready for use.

The preparation of indigo is a very simple process.§

In the mechanics of common life, we find the Asamese are very deficient.

Blacksmiths are by no means numerous, there seldom being more than one or two families of this occupation in the most populous villages, while generally six or eight villages possess but one Vulcan between them. They are, as may be expected, very unskilful workmen. A blacksmith is in general, what is vulgarly termed "a jack of all trades;" he makes the *kodals*, or spades, hoes, axes, ploughshares, cooking utensils, and in fact all iron instruments, and is a carpenter besides.

* For these remarks on the silk and silkworms of Asam, I am indebted to Mr. Hugon's Observations in the Journal of the Asiatic Society.

† Pirardia sapida.

‡ The roots and stems of Rubea munjista.

§ Vide Botany plants used for dyeing

Braziers though not wealthy, are seemingly in what may be termed easy circumstances, and are not destitute of knowledge. They make no less than fifty various articles of brass, copper, and mixed metal; some of which, however, are of a coarse and clumsy manufacture.

Potters are comparatively very few, though their employments are numerous and varied. They are unacquainted with the use of the lathe, and make all their wares by means of the hand. They are commonly speaking very poor, and have a *furnace* between five or six families.

The distillers make two or three kinds of arrack, in producing which the principal ingredients are rice, molasses, and water. They place equal quantities of rice and molasses, and sometimes a few spices, into a jar containing double the measure of water; the mouth of the jar is closed with clay, to prevent the entrance of the external air; in this state it continues from five to ten days, according to the heat of the weather. When it has fermented, the liquor is carried to the still, which, like every other article of native mechanism, is extremely simple, and not the less clumsy. The liquor is poured into an earthen pan, and placed over the fire, whilst another pan answers the purpose of a cover, the crevices being closed with clay. In the cover two incisions are made, in which are inserted two bamboo pipes, which communicate with two other pans placed beneath, and into which the spirituous vapour is conducted. These two pans rest on a board placed on a larger earthen vessel, containing water, which a person is employed in throwing on the pans in order to condense the spirit.

Confectioners are not numerous; they are found chiefly in the larger towns, and were probably introduced from Bengal. They make and vend numerous sorts of sweetmeats, composed chiefly of sugar, molasses, and flour. Children are often permitted to indulge their taste for sweetmeats to the injury of their health; and their parents, with tastes little less crude, likewise devour immense quantities of them at their weddings and other festivals.

There are neither shoemakers nor washermen. The Asamese till lately were unaccustomed to the use of shoes. A few are now imported from Bengal, but very few Asamese purchase them. The native women generally wash their own clothes, and the more respectable employ their slaves to do it for them. They are unacquainted with the use of soap, but use the ashes of the plantain-tree instead.

Fish forming by the far the greater part of the animal food consumed in the country, fishing is a pursuit carried on by the natives with exemplary industry. During five months of the year, when the rivers are much swollen, fish are very scarce; for they have then such an extensive range, that they are not easily taken: but as the inundation subsides, and when the fish are confined within narrow bounds, they are easily secured by various simple means which the natives employ.

The most simple method when a pond, ditch, or marsh, has become nearly dry, and the fish of a large space have been collected into a small pool, is to divide it by dams of mud, and then having thrown the water from each successively, to catch the fish as they are left dry.

A few simple traps are frequently used. One is a basket, with a hole in the bottom, called *polo*. In shallow water the fisher puts the mouth of the basket on the mud, and then passing his arm through a hole in the bottom, gropes for the fish which he may have secured. Another, *jokai*, is a basket of an irregular three-sided form, open at one end; to this basket is attached a bamboo shaft, which serves as a handle. The fisher places the bottom flat on the mud, treads among the weeds before the opening, and thus drives the fish into the trap, then suddenly raising the handle, he brings the opening above the surface of the water. These methods can be practised only in very muddy places, covered with aquatic plants, and are commonly employed by the poorest classes to catch fish for their own use.

Nets are used only by the professional fishermen. The most simple net in the country is the *dainijal,* which is stretched between two bamboos that meet behind at an acute angle, where it is held by the fisherman. The net is of a triangular form, so as to apply to the bamboos; but is much bagged behind. The fisherman walking up to the middle in water, pushes the points of the bamboos along the bottom for a little way, and then raises them up to secure whatever fish may have come into his net. The length of the bamboos used for these nets, varies from twelve to fifteen feet.

A net of the same form, but enlarged so as to have bamboos about nineteen cubits long, is frequently used in a canoe. Two men manage the canoe, which is kept broadside on the stream, while a third lowers the points of the bamboos, which are fixed at right angles to the gunwale, and then occasionally raises them to secure the fish.

The same kind of net, called by the natives *jaujal,* but still more enlarged, is fixed on the steep side of some river, and is raised by a complicated machinery of bamboos. A frame of four strong bamboos supports the net, which is placed with its descending edge towards the river; this frame also supports two sloping bamboos, on which a man walks, who has one end of a long rope round his middle, while the other end passes over a bamboo, (for they have no pulley), and raises the net when the man walks down, and lowers it into the water when he walks up the sloping bamboos. Two men are employed at this net.

The fishermen use also another kind of net somewhat of a similar nature, and which would appear better fitted for the large machine already described. This net is called *parangani.* It is of a square form, a good deal bagged in the centre. Its angles are fastened to the ends of two bamboo bars, that cross each other at right angles in the centre, which is suspended from the end of a bamboo lever, the other end of which rests against the bank where the fisher sits. He lowers and raises his net by means of a rope that is fastened to the far end of the lever. This net is used chiefly by poor farmers and labourers.

The casting net is very much used by the fishermen; they are of various sizes, and are commonly thrown from the shoulder, either from the shore or from a boat. In these nets the mesh is usually small, and the sinkers are often merely earthen rings baked by the potters; but iron rings are also used for the purpose. Fishermen use also seines of several sizes, and different names.

In pursuance of the object now before us, we may remark that the most correct view at least of the commercial resources of Asam, will be conveyed to the reader by a detail of its exports and imports; which, therefore, we proceed at once to give.

Lac seems to be by far the principal article of export. It is for the most part taken out of the country in its natural state, or what is commonly termed stick-lac. It is the produce of a small insect, called the Coccus ficus. The substance is of a reddish colour, and incrusts the small twigs of the trees on which the insect feeds.*

* Dr. John who has minutely analyzed stick-lac, gives as its composition.—

Resin insoluble in ether, ...	66·66
Laccin, ...	16·66
Cochinellin, ...	3·75
Extractive, ...	2·50
Cochinell coverings of insects, ...	2·08
Waxy tallow, ...	1·66
Laccic acid, ...	0·62
Yellow extract, ...	0·41
Salt of potash, lime, iron, and earthy matter,	1·66
Loss,... ...	4·0
	1000

Notwithstanding

The quantity of stick-lac annually exported, may be fairly computed at about 20,000 maunds. Its value in the province varies from five to nine rupees a maund.

A considerable factory for the preparation of shell-lac, and lac dye, has lately been established at Gowhatti, by an enterprizing merchant, Mr. Becher. It is hoped the result of this attempt to introduce these manufactures amongst the Asamese will be attended with profit to the speculator, and much benefit to the Asamese producers; which latter may with certainty be expected from the competition now established, and the liberality of English merchants, compared with that of those with whom the natives have hitherto dealt.

The article next in importance is Cotton. This is raised chiefly by the hill tribes, who bring it down to the plains, and sell it to the petty traders who frequent the *hauts* (markets).

There is no article which shows in a manner more remarkable than this, the capacity of extended production possessed by Asam. In 1809, the total amount of cotton exported did not exceed 7,000 maunds. In the following years, ending with 1837-38, the average amount of cotton sold at the Garrow *hauts* alone, was about 50,000 maunds, and the total number of collections 35,000 rupees; but since the reduction of the duty to eight annas per maund, in 1838-39, the increase of collections was 1,400 rupees, and the increase of cotton sold amounted to upwards of 4,000 maunds, which shews that at present the total quantity of cotton sold by the Garrows alone, is little less than 60,000 maunds.

Notwithstanding the seeming accuracy of the detail of the above mentioned analysis, it would appear that further experiments are still required to determine the nature of lac; for Unverborden has, since these analyses were published, stated the results of his examination: 1st, laccin; 2nd, red colouring matter, (cochinellin); 3rd, resin soluble in alcohol, but not in ether; 4th, resinous looking matter, slightly soluble in cold alcohol; 5th, crystallizable resin; 6th, uncrystallizable resin, soluble in alcohol and ether, but not in naptha; 7th, wax; 8th, fat of coccus not saponified, and some oleic and margaric acids.

It is to be presumed, that this ratio of increase will be progressive, and that it will be attended with very valuable results, no less in enriching and humanizing the Garrow population, than in increased security along the frontier Mehals, and in extended traffic throughout N. E. Rungpore.

The amount of cotton exported from Asam, there is no means of knowing, as it was never subject to duty, but it is large, and evidently increasing; the Asam cotton fetches generally a higher price than that of the Garrow hills, and the cotton of the Muttack country bears a value nearly double that of the former.

The next article, if rated according to its importance, is *Mustard Seed.* Besides the vast quantity consumed in the country for the manufacture of oil, by far the greater proportion of the seed raised is exported. We have no means of ascertaining the actual quantity exported; but we may safely venture to state, that mustard seed forms about one-fifth part of the whole exports of the country.

Little *Eria* is exported to Bengal; but large quantities are sold in barter to all the hill tribes, especially the Bootiahs.

The *Muga* Silk, both in its raw state and the manufactured stuffs, forms a considerable article of export. The returns of the Hydra custom chokey at Goalpara in 1809, show the total quantity of the raw material to have been about 65 maunds, while the average quantity of manufactured silk was 75 maunds. In 1835, the quantity of raw material exported amounted to 225 maunds. These returns comprise only that exported by water. The total quantity of muga that leaves the province now, may be fairly computed at about four hundred maunds;* for it forms no inconsiderable portion of the traffic with Sylhet, (across the hills), the Khassias, Bhutias, and other hill tribes.

Although within the last few years, the production of the

* Estimating the value of the silk at 5 rupees a seer, 400 maunds will yield 80,000 rupees.

silk has been greater from the more settled state of the country; yet strange to say, the price of the article has risen upwards of twenty per cent. The competition is now so great that the traders pay for it in advance, not as with other products to get it at a lower rate, but merely to secure their getting it.

The *Eria* silk is of a fine strong fibre, and very soft and silky; but hitherto all attempts to reel it have failed, and until this is effected, it is to be feared little will be done to render it of value as a merchantable commodity.

To promote the discovery of an efficient method of bringing the cocoons of the Eri silk worm into use, as an article of commercial value, Capt. Jenkins has very liberally placed the sum of 500 rupees at the disposal of the Agricultural Society of India, to which the Society has added a similar amount; and a schedule of prizes to the extent of 1,000 rupees is now before the public, for the purpose of encouraging the discovery.*

Ivory still continues to be exported in pretty large quantities. It is no doubt a very profitable article of commerce. The average quantity exported in 1809 was about 6,500

* "The Agricultural and Horticultural Society, in conjunction with Capt. Jenkins, the Governor-General's Agent in Asam, beg to call the attention of the public to the following notification:—

"1st. To any person who may succeed in discovering an effectual and cheap solvent for the adhesive material which attaches to the cocoons of the Eri silk worm, so that the silk can be made useful to commercial purposes,

"The Society's gold medal, and 200 rupees.

"2nd. For the best and most economical mode of preparing floss, and also the manufacturing of a thread from the floss of the Eri cocoons.

"The Society's gold medal, and 200 rupees.

3rd. "For the best and most economical method of bleaching cloth, manufactured from the Eri cocoon, so as to take permanent, and fugitive dyes well—

"The Society's gold medal, and 200 rupees."—*Agricultural and Horticultural Society's Transactions.*

maunds, and it is very probable that the amount is now at least doubled.

Gold bullion to a large amount is annually exported from Asam; but this is rather an unprofitable branch of commerce, which will probably in a great measure cease, when the trade has assumed a more rational basis.

Of the minor articles, it is not necessary to speak at large. They consist of *rice, paddy, wax, black pepper, long pepper, manjit,* (Indian madder,) *ao-tenga* (fruit of the Dellenia speciosa,) *beetlenuts, ratans,* and these to no very large amount.

We turn now to the imports, which are principally conveyed from Bengal. By far the most important article is *Salt.* In 1809, the quantity imported was no less than 35,000 maunds, which at 5½ rupees amounted to 1,92,500 rupees. We have not the means of forming an exact estimate of the quantity now imported; but we feel no hesitation in saying that it must be more than 50,000 maunds.

The other articles compared with that already mentioned, are of very inferior importance and value; they consist of copper, iron, European cutlery and glass-ware, muslins, calicoes, satin, English woollens, *taffetas,* a small quantity of jewels, pearls, corals, and stone beads, shells, spices, fine pulse, and sugar.

Of the trade with the adjoining hill tribes, which at present is comparatively very inconsiderable, it is not necessary to say much.

The trade with Butan was formerly conducted through the instrumentality of the Wazir Baruwa, who resided at Simliyabari, about a day's journey north from the residence of the Raja of Durrung. He levied no duties, but received presents, and was the only broker employed by the Butias and Asamese in their mutual exchange, or purchase of goods. In 1809, the trade between Butan and Asam was said to amount to two lakhs of rupees, (2,00,000 Rs.) per annum, even when the latter country was in a most unsettled state.

The exports from Asam were lac, munjit, (madder), silks—muga and eria, and dried fish. The Butias imported woollen cloths, gold dust, salt, musk, ponies, the celebrated Thibet chowries, (tails of the Thibet *yak*), Chinese silks, and musk. As the state of affairs in Asam became more distracted, this trade necessarily declined; but under all these disadvantages, the Khumpa Butias, or Lassa merchants, just prior to the last Burmese invasion, brought down gold which alone amounted to upwards of 70,000 rupees. This gold was brought principally for the purpose of purchasing muga silks. So severely has the trade suffered from the occupation of the country by the Burmese, that in 1833 only two Butia merchants came down from the hills; when Capt. Rutherfôrd, who then had charge of the district of Durrung, succeeded in obtaining their consent to the re-establishment of the annual fair at Chatgari. It is probable that if again resumed, this trade will flourish to an extent it never before attained, and be the means of widely disseminating British manufactures through the vast regions of Thibet and Butan.

The Mishmis, a tribe occupying the hills to the north of Sudiya, are in the habit of frequenting the markets at that place. They bring with them a few Lama swords and spears, *mishmi tita (?)* and a considerable quantity of vegetable poison, used in poisoning arrows, and *gertheana*, much esteemed by the natives for its peculiar, and rather pleasant smell. They also bring a little musk, a few musk deer skins, and some ivory, which they obtain from the Lama country. These they exchange for glass beads, of which they are very fond, cloths, salt, and money, to which last they begin to attach great value. When a sufficient sum of money is procured they lay it out in purchasing buffaloes, and the country cattle.

The Abors and Miris bring down pepper, ginger, manjit, (madder), and wax, which they exchange for the produce of the plains.

The only valuable article of trade with the Singphos is ivory, which they bring down in considerable quantities.

The Nagas occasionally frequent the markets at Nagura and Kacharihath, and other spots along the borders, where they barter their cotton and ginger for a few minor articles. They also manufacture and sell a little salt, the produce of the brine springs in the vicinity of their hills. This seems to be the only intercourse held with them by the inhabitants of the low lands, who rarely ever venture to visit their haunts on the hills.

The intercourse with the Khassias and Garrows has always been more intimate and friendly; and since our occupation of the country of the former, the trade has increased very considerably, and no doubt it will ultimately be the means of greatly ameliorating their condition. We have already noticed the extensive trade carried on with the Garrows in cotton. The Khassias import a great quantity of iron, potatoes, and honey, which they exchange for cloths and silks, the manufactures of the country.

We shall not here attempt to offer an estimate of the total value of the trade with the hill tribes, as we have no means of doing so with any degree of confidence.

In 1808-9, when the country was still suffering from the effects of long internal dissension, and its inhabitants were living in a most unsettled and precarious state of society, the exports and imports to and from Bengal, amounted to rupees 3,59,200. This trade has since been greatly augmented; and its value may now be estimated at between five and six lakhs of rupees.

We trust we have been able to furnish, within the short compass of these few pages, a pretty correct and comprehensive view of the commerce of Asam. The reader will perceive that the trade of the country has only begun to expand; but as European intercourse increases, and communications are renewed with the numerous tribes surrounding it, it will no doubt be capable of still greater extension.

At present, almost the whole of the commerce of Asam is engrossed by the Kaiyahs, a very enterprising class of men, resident in the principal towns. They are emigrants from Marwar, and seem to have been induced to settle in Asam for the sake of trading merely. They employ a number of petty agents, who stroll about the frontier wherever there is a chance of gaining a single rupee, bartering salt and other necessaries for lac, gold dust, ivory, and in short all the productions of the valley. They are generally wealthy, and live in a state of comfort and elegance far superior to the aborigines.

The intercourse between Asam and Bengal is almost entirely maintained by water. There is a free communication between the Brahmaputra and the Ganges, and boats of the largest size pass, by different inosculations out of the one into the other, throughout the year.

The overland routes are two; one by Moorshedabad, Malda, Dinagepore, Rungpore, Bugwah, and Gowalparah; this is the line of the Calcutta dawk, but it is almost impassable during the rains: and the other road is viâ Dacca, Jumalpore, Singimari, and Gowalparah; in the rains this route is almost as bad as the former.

It was not until a few years ago, that any attempt was made to explore and ascertain the nature of the tract which separated southern Kachar from central Asam, when a route extending from the Bikrampur Pass in Kachar to Raha Choki on the Kallung in Asam, (which had before been frequently visited by parties of Manipuris under Gambhir Sing), was visited by Captains Jenkins and Fisher.*

The first portion of the route, or that extending from Kartigora on the north bank of the Surma or Barak river, to the summit of the central ridge at the Dowsing Pass,

* Vide Pemberton's Report on the Eastern Frontier.

about 4,000 feet above the Kachar plain, is about forty-one miles long, and passes for the greater portion of the distance up the rocky bed of the Jatinga Nulla, on the southern side of the dividing range; from thence it descends on the northern face by a succession of declivities, round and between which flow several small streams, to the valley of the Jamun and Kossili rivers, which unite not far from Raha Choki. This latter portion of the route occupies about twelve marches, and may be estimated at 110 miles in length. Scarcely an inhabitant is seen along the whole line of the road and there are but a very few scattered villages occupied by the hill Kacharis and Kookis in that portion of the tract between the summit of the range and the confluence of the Kossili and Dyung rivers, a distance of about fifty miles. Following the course of the former stream, the banks are found to be better inhabited, and the villages on the right bank are represented as being surrounded by extensive tracts of cultivation, consisting principally of rice and cotton; the ground up the southern bank of the Jamuna is covered with dense forests of timber, bamboos, and close underwood; and the whole tract, except during the cold season of the year, is very unhealthy.

The next line of route, west of the one just noticed, passes from Sylhet, a little to the eastward of north, across the eastern boundary of the Khassia hills, through the territory of the Jaintiya Raja to Raha Choki on the Kallung. The whole distance is 130 miles, which is easily accomplished in thirteen marches, and an express messenger has been known to effect it in eight days.

The most western, and by far the best known of these routes, which unite the provinces of Kachar and Sylhet with Asam, is that which leads from the town of Sylhet viâ Chirrapunji to Gowhatti; the total distance is 126 miles, or fourteen marches, of which ten lie among the Khassia hills, two in the Asam plains between Ranigong and Gowhatti, and two between Pandua and Sylhet. By this route almost all communication is carried on between Sylhet and Asam, and the other two routes are but rarely frequented, from the want of adequate population, and supplies on that which leads from the Bikrampur Pass, and on the other from the objections almost invariably urged by the Raja of Jaintiah against its being used by foreigners.

There are numerous passes into Butan along the frontier, some of which lead direct to the capital; these passes are called Duwars, the principal of which are Bijniduwar, Bingaduwar, Nowduwar and Charduwar.

Thibet is open to travellers on foot from the extreme east of Asam. The route runs across the Himalya mountains, parallel with the course of the Brahmaputra. The journey from Sadiya, the most advanced British post on this frontier, to Bhaloo, the first town met with in Thibet, is performed by pilgrims in about sixteen days. The following are the towns in the line of march, in succession: Sadiya, Kudgin, Luckquee, Galoom, Namanoo, Dullee, Omono, Hullee, Sumlay, Hamay, Kumday, Rheeshah, and Bhaloo. About four days' journey beyond Bhaloo, stands the city of Rasheemah, containing fine stone buildings, a large population, and a government purely Chinese. This route is a very arduous task; the rugged nature of the snowy country is of itself nearly insurmountable, and the hostility shown by the tribes on the road to all ingress of strangers, is no less difficult to encounter.

There is an open road from Upper Asam into Burma, and thence into China, by which a considerable trade in Chinese and Burmese manufactures was at one time carried on. The Burmese in their invasions of Asam generally entered it by this route. The line of trade, after leaving Sadiya, passes by Bisa, across the Patkoye range of mountains, and through the valley of Hukung to the town of Munkung, situated on a navigable branch of the Irawatti, called Namyang.

Merchants proceeding from Munkung to Ava, at once descend the Irawatti to the capital, while those to China ascend the Irawatti for many miles to a place called Katemow, where they disembark their goods, and thence convey them on mules over a range of mountainous country, inhabited by Shyans, (subject to Ava), into the Chinese province of Yeman.

The intercourse between China and Asam by this route is extremely tedious, and can only be followed by a trading people who traffic as they go along. A knowledge of the extreme navigable branches of the Brahmaputra has pointed out a much shorter and more convenient path, and this was travelled over by Lieut. Wilcox. Tracking the Moadihing, which enters the Lohit, the great eastern branch of the Brahmaputra, a few miles above Sadiya, Lieut. Wilcox was able to proceed by water conveyance to within nine days march of Munlung on the Irawatti, and this journey he accomplished without any serious difficulty, or any inconvenience more than what arose from the jungly state of the country.

On the acquisition of the province by the British government a variety of coins were found current in Asam; they were the Rajmohri, or the coin of the Asam Rajas; the Naraini, or Kuchbehar rupee; the Company's sicca rupee; the Deba Mohri of Butan; and the Arcot rupee. The Rajmohri and the Naraini rupees had the most extensive currency; the former in Upper, and the latter in Lower Asam. The Rajmohri was of the same value as the old Sonat rupee; but the silver was of somewhat superior quality; in ordinary transactions it was taken at par with the latter coinage. The Asamese had, besides the usual fractional parts of the rupee—half and quarter, two annas and even one anna pieces, and these in sufficient quantities to be able to dispense with a copper coinage, which latter was till lately unknown in Asam; cowris, or small shells, passed current in petty transactions. In more extensive commercial dealings, coins were seldom used; the whole trade of the country consisted almost entirely in a barter of Bengal salt, for silk, lac, cotton, and other products of the country.

Besides the silver coinage, there was a plentiful supply of gold mohurs of good intrinsic value. The price they are now valued at, varies from twelve to fourteen Company's Rupees a piece. Gold did, and to the present day continues to pass current in small uncoined round balls, usually weighing one tola.

The first Asam Raja known to have coined money, was Surganarian. His coins, as well as most of those of his successors, were inscribed with Bengali characters.

The following is a list of the Asam coins in the collection of Messrs. Marsden and Prinsep. Most of them are also in Captain Wemyss's collection; those marked with an asterisk in his only.

Asam Alra.

Surganarian,. . ..	1570.
Chakradhaj, ...	*1575, 1576, 1585. (Ahom characters).
Gadadhar Sing,. .	1603.
Rudra Sing, ...	1616, 18, 19,* 22,* 26,* 27,* 30, 31.
Sib Sing, ...	1637, 41, 43, 47,* 52, 61 ,63,* 65,* 66.*
Sib Sing's Queens.	
Phulesnari, ..	1647.
Pramathisnari,	1649*, 52.
Ambika Devi,. .	1650, 54, 58, 60.
Surbeswari, ..	1661*, 63, 66.
Pramatha Sing, ..	1660, 62, *63, *66, 68,* 69,* 70, 72, 73. (Some of these in Ahom characters).
Rajeswar Sing, ..	1674, 76, 78, 79, 81, 82, 84, 85,* 88, 90, (In Ahom, Bengali, and Persian characters; the one dated 1685, in Captain Wemyss's collection, is inscribed with Nagri characters).

Ramakant Sing, ..	1691, (Rajeswar's elder brother, raised to the throne by the Moamariahs.)
Lakmi Sing, ...	1692,* 93,* 94,* 95, 96, 97,* 99.
Gowrinath Sing,	1707,* 08,* 09,* 10, 11.*
Pretenders :—	
Bharata Sing, ..	1715, 16, 18.*
Surbananda Sing,	1715,* 16.
Kamaleswar Sing,	1720.
Brijanath Sing ..	1739, 40. (father of Purunder Sing,)
Chandrakant Sing,	1741.

The Naraini rupee was coined in Kuch Bahar, and the coins of all the reigning princes are still extant. The regulated exchange of this coin is 100 Nar. Rs. 68=Furruckabad Rs. 100 Fur. Rs.=147 Nar. Rs.

The Debamohri is a coin very similiar to the foregoing, but of inferior quality, the half rupee being equal to five or six annas of Company's money.

Shortly after the conquest of the country, the accounts of Lower Asam were kept in Sicca as well as Naraini rupees; but subsequently in Siccas only. In Durrung, the Collector's accounts were kept partly in Rajmohri, partly in Naraini, and partly in Sicca rupees, to the confusion of all payers, and to the great gain of the Treasurers and Podars.

To abate the inconveniencies experienced by the currency of the local coins, they were prohibited from being re-issued, and were remitted to the Calcutta mint. In 1835 the new Sonat Rupee was introduced into the province, and the accounts were again disturbed. In 1836-37, however, the Company's Rupees were introduced, and now form the common currency.

Under the operation of the double change of currency, which has occurred since 1834, the import of coin for the public service has been Rupees 21,04,016 (inclusive of Rs. 1,00,000 on account of the Asam Company), and the export has been Rs. 24,17,723, consisting of Narainis, Debmohris, Rajmohris, Arcots, Siccas, and Sonat Rupees.

We have no means of judging of the exports and imports of coin by private traders, nor can we form any opinion of the amount of currency in the province. It however appears amply sufficient for all the purposes of the inhabitants, both revenue and commercial.

The current coins in the province at present are the Company's Rupees, and the half and quarter Rupee. Cowries have of late been greatly superseded by the Company's pice and pie pieces.

Very few transactions take place with other parts of India by bills of exchange, there being no regular bankers or shroffs in the province. Drafts on the General Treasury at Calcutta, are procurable at all the treasuries in the province at a premium of one per cent. The remittances of the Marwari merchants are believed to be made almost solely in produce, and perhaps to some extent in gold bullion.

Of the countries bordering on Asam, the only one, Butan excepted, which had a mint was the little kingdom of Jaintia, before its occupation by the British Government. The Jaintia coin was called the Kuttra rupee; but so debased, that it was valued at little more than three or four annas. Captain Wemyss has a silver coin in his collection said to be a Garrow one; it bears no inscription.

CHAPTER VII.

CIVIL AND SOCIAL STATE.

Population—Ahoms—Asamese language—Physical appearance of the people—Traits in the Character of the Ancient Asamese—Compared with their present Condition—Religion—Traces of their primitive Worship—Introduction of Hinduism—Site of Sacred Buildings—Principal Temples—Various Castes of Hindus—Mussulmans—Manners and Customs—Amusements—Music—Musical Instruments—Dancing—Festivals—Diet—Houses—Furniture—Dress—Condition of the Women—Marriage and Funeral Ceremonies—The Fine Arts—Literature—Education—Slavery.

The total population of Asam is computed at about 8,00,000. About a sixth part of this number may probably consist of Mahomedans, whilst the remainder is composed of various sects of Hindoos, and other castes common to the Frontier. A large mass of the population consists of tribes who originally descended from the hills in the neighbourhood, such as Rabhas, Kacharies, Chuteyas, Mikirs, and Lalongs. The very scanty information we at present possess, does not admit of our forming any minute classification of them.

A very small portion indeed of the Ahoms, the race of the last conquerors of the valley, is now to be met with, and these, through the many revolutions which the country has undergone, still remain unmixed, and retain unaltered their ancient habits and institutions. They have, however, so far adopted the customs of the Hindus, as to relinquish the use of beef. Their language, which is a branch of the Tai, is now nearly extinct, being cultivated only by their priests, the Deodhaings, as the ancient language of their religion. Their common or colloquial dialect is that usually known as the Asamese.

As the Ahoms were once the rulers of Asam, it is somewhat surprising that more traces of their language are not to be found in the present dialect of the Asamese, which, with the exception of a very few words of Tai origin, seems to have been originally derived from the Sungskrit, and in most cases possesses a close affinity to the Bengali. A greater portion of the words in common use seem identical, and are distinguished only by a slight difference in pronunciation. The most important of these are, the substitution of *s* in Asamese for the Bengali *ch*, and a guttural *h* for the Bengali *s* and *sh*. The form of three or four letters has also undergone a slight variation. The grammatical peculiarities of the two languages are considerably unlike, though there is scarcely any difference in their syntactical construction.*

The people present several peculiarities of external form, which it may be necessary to notice.

The Asamese have frequently been described as a degenerate and weakly race, and in these respects inferior even to their effeminate neighbours the Bengalis; but as a general description, it does not accord with the true state of the case. Though certainly inferior to the people of the Western Provinces, yet in most points they seem as much removed above those of Bengal. In complexion they are a shade or two lighter coloured than the Bengalis. Their persons are in general short, robust, and active, when they choose to be so; but devoid of that grace and flexibility so peculiar to the Hindu. Their face flat, with high cheek bones, presents a physiognomy resembling the Chinese, and suggesting no idea of beauty. Their hair is abundant, black, lank, and coarse; but

* For further particulars, the author begs to refer the reader to his "*Grammar of the Asamese Language.*"

the beard is scanty, and usually plucked out, which gives the men an effeminate appearance.

But though these peculiarities are general, we must not omit to mention, that there are a few particular exceptions, whose forms more properly belong to that variety termed by Blumenbach, the *Caucasian*, and which includes also the inhabitants of Europe. But even from them they are distinguished by a peculiar delicacy, and exility of shape, suggesting the idea of a refined, and even effeminate people. These exceptions are, however, to be met with only in the higher rank of life.

The women in general form a striking contrast to the men; there is a great deal more of feminine beauty in them than is commonly met with in the women of Bengal, with a form and feature somewhat approaching the European. In most parts of the country the women of rank go about in public, quite divested of that artificial modesty, practised to such an extensive degree by native ladies in the other parts of India.

Though the Asamese have been said to borrow the outward forms of life from the Chinese and Hindus, they are not schooled into that mechanical routine of observance, which is so firmly established in those countries. Much greater freedom prevails in the intercourse of society; they are quick, lively, and stirring, and in general appear to be an intelligent people.

In the *Alumgrinamah* of Mahomed Cazim, which has been translated by Henry Vansittart, Esq. and presented to us in several publications, is a short description of the inhabitants of Asam, which we shall here transcribe, in as much as it will in some measure tend to shew a few traits in their character as they then existed. It is to be remembered, however, that the descriptions of the chronicler can only be attributed to the Ahoms, and the population of Upper Asam; not to the Hindu race of Kamrup. We are told that the country, at least in many places, is well inhabited, and in an excellent state of tillage; that "it presents on every side charming prospects of ploughed fields, harvests, gardens, and groves." Hence we might infer, that the Asamese were a highly industrious and agricultural people.

The Mussulman, however, who finds no excellence where he finds not his faith, discovers no qualities but evil in the minds of the Asamese. "They do not adopt," he says, "any mode of worship practised either by the heathens or Mahomedans, nor do they concur in any of the known sects which prevail amongst mankind. They are a base and unprincipled nation, and have no fixed religion. They follow no rule, but that of their own inclination; and make the approbation of their own vicious minds the test of the propriety of their actions. Their strength and courage are apparent in their looks, but their ferocious manners, and brutal tempers, are also betrayed by their physiognomy. They are superior to most nations in corporal force, and hardy exertions. They are enterprising, savage, fond of war, vindictive, treacherous, and deceitful. The virtues of compassion, kindness, friendship, sincerity, truth, honour, good faith, shame, and purity of morals, have been left out of their composition. The seeds of tenderness and humanity have not been sown in the field of their frames." Yet he speaks in lofty terms of the royal magnificence of their courts. "The Rajahs of this country have always raised the crest of pride and vain-glory, and displayed an ostentatious appearance of grandeur, and a numerous train of attendants and servants." And he expresses himself with mingled horror and admiration of the prowess and superiority of the Asamese in war. "They have not bowed the head of submission and obedience, nor have they paid tribute to the most powerful monarch; but they have curbed the ambition, and checked the conquests, of the most victorious princes of Hindusthan. The solution of the difficulties attending a war against them, has baffled the penetration of heroes, who have been styled conquerors of the world."

If the above description may be depended upon, we are led to believe that the natives at that early period were in external form at least a far superior race to what they are at present, and that in the midst of the convulsions that overturned their empire, combined with the superstitions, the tedious formalities, and the bondage of the Brahminical faith, they have fallen into a lamentable state of degeneracy.

In considering any tribe or family of mankind, our view would be eminently imperfect were religion omitted; but where the greater portion of the population is composed of Hindus, the omission would be impracticable, inasmuch as it is his religion, and nothing else, that renders the Hindu what he is.

The religion of the Hindus is a theme that has from time to time occupied the attention of many of the most distinguished *literati* of the world. It is a subject the importance of which is at least equalled, if not surpassed, by the obscurity which surrounds it. For, notwithstanding the labours of the talented individuals by whom we have been admitted into the Hindu Pantheon, we still grope about the huge structure in comparative darkness, amidst myriads of gods and goddesses, whose forms and attributes we can discern but dimly. It would therefore be nothing short of presumption in us, to make any remarks on this extensive and complicated subject.

There appears to have existed among all ancient nations some faint idea of the one true God, (whether preserved by tradition, or which is equally probable, created by the efforts of unsophisticated reason,) with the primitive worship of whom we find an extraordinary form of superstition, denominated the worship of aërial beings, under the general name of spirits, by which it was probably superseded, more particularly among a rude and barbarous people. This may easily be accounted for, from the proneness of mankind to superstitious fears respecting invisible existence. These spirits it is reasonable to suppose, were soon after divided into two great classes—good and evil spirits. These appear to have been the first gods worshipped by the ancient inhabitants, and probably continued till their conversion to the Brahminical faith. Traces of this strange system are, however, still discoverable among the lower classes, and the wilder mountain tribes, who are still free from the shackles of Hinduism.

On the introduction of the Brahmins into the country, followed the promulgation of the Hindu faith, which, with its numerous forms and gaudy ceremonies, were well calculated to attract the attention of a wild and uncivilized people. They soon imbibed the tenets of the new faith, whilst the priests acquired and maintained an authority, more exalted, more commanding, and extensive, than they had been able to engross in any other part of India. Numerous temples and holy edifices soon rose into existence, more numerous than are generally met with in any province of equal extent. Almost every grove and secluded valley, and wild and lofty mountain summit, had some religious or superstitious notions connected with it, and frequently presented to the eye, some picturesque shrine or antique temple. The greater number of these temples are now in ruins, the remaining offspring of the piety of former days.

The Brahmins seem in general to have exhibited a remarkable taste and judgment in selecting the site of their sacred buildings. Sometimes they are situated in the midst of the wildest scenery, surrounded by woods and forests, and almost concealed from observation by thick groves, within the dark gorge of the mountain, or on its rugged summit, and at the sources of streams, where sites of seclusion, beauty, and sublimity excite alternately the fervour and the awe of superstitious devotion.

One of the most remarkable temples in Asam, is the shrine of Kamakhya, the goddess of love, situated on the summit of a hill, about two miles to the west of Gowhatty. This fane is one of great celebrity, and is frequented by a vast number of pilgrims from all parts of India. It owes its celebrity neither to its structure nor situation; but to the image itself. Yet the site is not uninteresting, nor is it devoid of beauty. To the south it is shut in by a cluster of hills, and to the north flows the sacred Brahmaputra, which bathes the extreme points of the hill. Within these bounds, is the sanctuary of the goddess; but her sway is not confined to these precincts. The whole of the province of Kamrup, as its name implies, was in ancient times a sort of *Idalian* grove, a privileged region for mirth, and dance, and revelry, and all manner of licentiousness.

Some of the formulas used at the festival in honour of this goddess, relate to things which can never become the subject of description. Here the most abominable rites are practised, and the most licentious scenes exhibited, which it is hardly possible to suppose the human mind, even when sunk to the very lowest depths of depravity, could be capable of devising.

During the daily ceremonies of worship performed before the image, the spectators are very few, and these feel no interest whatever in the mummery going forward. Were it not for those who come to pay a visit of ceremony to the image, and to present their offerings, the temple would be as little crowded on festival, as on common days; but as soon as the well-known sound of the drum is heard, calling the people to the midnight orgies, the dance and the song, whole multitudes assemble, and the crowd becomes dense. The women employed to dance and sing on these occasions, are those consecrated to the temple, of whom it is reputed there are no less than five hundred. Their presence, together with their filthy songs, and more obscene dances, form the chief attractions. A song is scarcely tolerated which does not contain the most marked allusions to unchastity; while those which are so abominable, that no person could repeat them out of the temple, receive in general the loudest plaudits. All this is done in the very face of the idol, nor does the thought, "Thou God seest me," ever produce the slightest pause in these midnight revels. But, we decline blotting these pages with any further allusion to such unutterable abominations.

Another temple, of no less consequence than the one we have just noticed, is that situated at Haju, a village in Kamrup, about six miles from the northern bank of the Brahmaputra. The great object of veneration is an image called "Mahamuni," in a temple on the summit of a hill about 300 feet high. Thousands of votaries of every rank and condition are here annually congregated together, and towards this shrine a tide of costly offerings from every point of the compass is constantly setting in. It is visited not only by pilgrims of the Brahminical faith, who proceed to it from all parts of India, but Budhists likewise contend that it was the presence of their great prophet and legislator, which conferred its holy fragrance and mysterious virtue on the spot. But whatever was the original cause of its sanctity, no orthodox Hindu now doubts the efficacy of its atmosphere in removing sin. The pious Budhist too, imbued with the same faith, leaves his home in the distant regions of China and Thibet, and crossing the pathless tracts of the snowy Himalayas, burdened with the load of his offences, hastens to make obeisance at the shrine of his country's deity, and departs in joy and gladness, lightened of his load.

Besides the temples, another place distinguished for its peculiar sanctity, is the supposed source of the Brahmaputra, or that large circular basin termed the Brahmakhund. The shastras of the Hindu religion have taught, that the performance of religious rites at this sacred place is an act of peculiar merit, productive of great spiritual benefit. Accordingly, numerous pilgrims annually resort thither. Of these, some reside there for a time in the hope of imbibing a sort of odour of sanctity, which shall shed its influence over all the actions of their remaining life. Others, who have devoted the prime of their days to Mammon, retire thither when the lamp of life begins to burn low, that they may thus make sure of heaven after death.

As the Asamese have been led to adopt the creed of the Hindus, it is not at all surprising to find amongst them that *distribution into castes*, which forms the most prominent feature in Hindu society.

In all half-civilized communities, aristocratic distinctions are carried to an extreme height; but by no means is the distinction between man and man rendered so broad, and so monstrous, as by this institution.

Very few traces of the four original castes are met with, though the people are divided by an infinite number of distinctions.

The priesthood, beyond all comparison, hold the first place in point of dignity, and, clothed with the terrors of religion, are regarded by the other classes with deep veneration.

A number of the Rarhi Brahmins of Bengal have emigrated into the country, and to them were formerly committed the spiritual guidance of the king and principal officers of the Court. Those usually known as the Asamese Brahmins, are Baidicks of the ancient kingdom of Kamrup, and were probably introduced by Biswas Sing; but having penetrated into the upper parts of Asam, they no longer intermarried with the families in Bengal. A great number of these are said to be learned in Hindu science. A very small portion are Saktis; they are chiefly of the sect of Vishnu. They have a few academies, or *choubaris*, where the Ratnamala, Byakuran, law, and metaphysics are taught. Some few pretend to a knowledge of astrology and magic. The chief study, however, of the spiritual guides, is the Shri Bhagabut. The persons who instruct the worshippers of Vishnu, that is, most of those who have adopted the Hindu creed, are called

Mahajons, and live in *chatras*. They have generally a large number of men entirely devoted to their service. Their office is hereditary in certain families. The Brahmins, who are elevated to this high dignity, are said to avoid all worldly pleasures, and bind themselves by an oath of celibacy.

These men seem to give themselves more trouble than usual, in the instruction of their followers. They not only teach them a form of prayer, but usually assembling forty or fifty of their scholars, they instruct them in their duty, and read some books, which were composed by their great doctors, and which seem to consist chiefly of extracts from the Bhagabut, translated into the vernacular.

The chief *chatras* are as follow :—In the district of Kamrup, at Baropeta, Pat Bousi, Biha Kuchi, Bhowanipur, Plasbari, and Shrihati. In Asam Proper—Annihati, Dakhynpat, Kurabasi, Gormurchotra, Dihingya, Noraya, Sologuri, Samguri, Koyamariya, and Mahari.

In the district of Sudiya, the worshippers of Vishnu are not numerous enough to have procured religious guides that are of any importance.

Some of the Baidiks have become Barna, and in consequence, have degraded themselves in the eyes of their brethren. They instruct the impure tribes, which is considered a great degradation, to which none of the Baidiks of Bengal have submitted.

There is also a class of Brahmins, usually known as Muno Singha Brahmins. They are usually employed in low offices, totally unconnected with religion.

The Koch or Kuchis, are a numerous tribe. Amongst them, may also be classed the Rajbungsis; for it seems very probable that they have both sprung from the same stock, or if they had at one time been distinct sects, the former having abandoned their impure practices, have been since admitted to a communion. In fact, there is reason to suppose, that, until very lately, the different tribes of Kamrup permitted intermarriage. Thus it must be observed, that Koch Haju, the valiant chief who is said to have expelled the Mussulmans from the northern parts of Rungpore, married his daughter to the Mech Herya, and from this marriage, with the fabulous assistance of the god Sib, are sprung the principal chiefs of the Rajbungsis.

Their principal worship is paid to a god named Rishi, and to his wife Jago, though some pretend to say, they worship Sib and Parboti. Every year, at the end of the rainy season, a grand sacrifice to these deities is made by the whole tribe, and occasionally sacrifices are offered in cases of distress. The blood of the sacrifice is left for the deity, while the votaries eat the meat. The people worship no images. They call on the name of their gods, and clap their hands during the ceremony of worship.

As soon as the Koch became noted in tradition or history, we find that they had adopted a priesthood, called Kolita or Kolta. These possessed some learning, and long continued to be the only spiritual guides of the Koch, and in fact in some places still retain by far the chief authority over that sect. It is not therefore surprising, that in the Allumghar Nama, already alluded to, the people of the country are said to be "Asamians," and "Koltanians," the former the temporal lords, the latter the spiritual guides; when probably the Kolitas were far more powerful than they are at present. What tenets the Kolitas, while independent of the Brahmins, possessed, we have now no means of learning; but that they were not orthodox, there can be little doubt. The power of the Kolitas received a severe blow by the introduction of the Brahmins by their prince, whose example they were under the necessity of following, and of receiving instruction from the sacred order. These persons have now entirely adopted the Hindu worship and customs, and are contented with being considered as pure Sudras, an honour that is not usually conceded to them.

The Kolitas and most of their followers, have taken the part of Krishna, and assume the title of *bhokot,* that is worshippers or disciples, as being alone those who follow the true God. They have of late been very successful in converting many of the Kacharis, Mikirs, and other ignorant tribes of mountaineers.

The Mech are a small tribe, but appear at one time to have been a far more numerous people than they are at present. A large proportion of their number have assumed the title of Rajbungsi. It is to be presumed, that this innovation took place when Biswas Sing, the son of a Mech's wife, became the sovereign of Kamrup, and being ashamed of his barbarous ancestors, discovered that he was the son of a god.

The Nodigals or, Domes, are, on the whole, the most numerous tribe in Asam. That they originally emigrated from Bengal, there can be little doubt. Their original employment is that of fishermen. They seem to observe all the rules of purity, in eating and drinking, with a greater strictness than even the Brahmins of Bengal; notwithstanding this, they have not procured a Brahmin for a spiritual guide, but follow the instructions of the Kolitas.

It is difficult to ascertain the number of the true Kaiasths that are in the province; because since the Kolitas lost their importance, especially in the more civilized parts, they have assumed the title of Kaiasths. The number of the pure scribes of Bengal it is presumed must be very small indeed, and these are mostly of the division called Uttar Rarhi.

There are a good many Keyots, or as some please to call themselves, Kaibartas. They are divided into several classes, the two principal are called the Haluya Keyots, and the Jaluya Keyots. The former class are chiefly cultivators of the ground; these retain the worship of Krishna. The Jaluya Keyots are fishermen, and without having relinquished their name or profession, have in many points followed the tenets of Mahomed; yet they keep themselves distinct as a caste, and will not mix with the Moslems.

The Haris, or potters, are a very small sect.

The Sonars, or goldsmiths, though probably more diffused, are proportionately very few.

The art of the washerman not having been practised as a trade, the Dhobas are mostly from Bengal. They amount to but a few families.

The Moriyas are generally employed as braziers. They are looked upon as a very impure tribe. They are by no means scrupulous in their food. They eat beef and pork, and are in general very much addicted to the use of spirituous liquors. They bury their dead.

In Asam there seems to have been little or no distinction of castes from profession, and each caste, or rather tribe, practised all the arts which are known in the country. They were farmers, traders, blacksmiths, goldsmiths, carpenters, extractors of oil, potters, weavers, dyers, &c.; but they had not the art of shaving, or washing, or bleaching, of working in leather, or of making sweetmeats, butter, or ghee. All these arts seem to have been unknown, and now are entirely followed by strangers, while the old arts are still practised indifferently by all.

Mussulmans, as we have already shown, form a large proportion of the inhabitants of Asam. But these are generally held in very low estimation; like most of the Hindus, they are by no means rigidly observant of high caste principles. In fact, a far greater latitude and toleration exists among the inhabitants of Asam in general, than is usually observed in other parts of India.

By the manners of a nation, are understood the peculiar mode in which the ordinary business of human life is carried on. The business itself is every where essentially the same. In all nations men eat and drink, they meet, converse, transact business, and sport together. But the manner in which these and other things are performed, is as different as the nations are numerous into which the race is divided.

The manners of the Asamese resemble, in most respects, those of the generality of Hindus, whose creed they have adopted, and whose daily avocations consist so much in religious services, that the delineation of their religion is a delineation of the principal branch of their manners.

Much of that gentleness and urbanity of manner which reign to a greater or less degree in the whole intercourse of native society, and which in the superficial observer would produce a high conception of their benevolence and amiability, would, on a more minute inspection, present a much less favourable picture.

The species of polity under which the national character is formed is perhaps to a great degree the cause of this peculiarity of behaviour. When the mind is free, and may vent its passions with little fear, the nation, while ignorant and rude, is also fierce and impetuous. Where political slavery prevails, and any departure from the most perfect obsequiousness is followed with the most direful consequences, an insinuating and fawning behaviour is the interest, and thence becomes the habit, of the people. Hence arises that outward politeness observable in the natives of Asam. It is entirely prompted by self-interest, which forms the basis of the native character, and is cherished without regard to any feelings of honour and dignity. These feelings in fact are entirely broken down by the influence of that despotism which was not only the principle of their government, but an original, irreversible, and fundamental principle in the very frame of society. With the same causes are connected other leading features in the character of the natives. They are remarkably prone to flattery; which appears to be the most prevailing mode of address from the weak to the strong, while men are still ignorant and unreflecting. In their form of government, where the generality of men were excluded from the pursuits of ambition, and checked at least in any public or lively amusements, selfishness turned almost entirely into avarice. This passion is indulged with an almost total disregard of the principles of honour or honesty; the grossest breaches of which are so common, as to cause no surprize, and scarcely any indignation even in those who suffer by them. In the same light do they regard that deliberate and systematic violation of truth, which seems but too firmly rooted in their character. Speaking of the inhabitants of Hindusthan in general, to whom the Asamese bear too great a resemblance, Sir John Shore remarks: "It is the business of all, from the ryot to the dewan, to conceal and deceive; the simplest matters of fact are designedly covered with a veil, which no human understanding can penetrate." This extends even to a form of guilt, from which the religious, or rather the superstitious, habits of the people might have been expected to secure them. Perjury, the most deliberate and complete, marks almost every deposition made before a court of justice. "But such is the corrupt state even of their erroneous religion, that if the most binding form on the conscience of men could be known and established, there would be few consciences to be bound by it."*

On a close inspection too much disappears of the mildness and quietude, which are so conspicuous on the surface of the native character. Deadly feuds reign in the interior of villages; and between those who have no motive to be on ceremony or on terms of courtesy with each other, violent wordy altercations often take place, seldom, however, proceeding to blows. The following picture, applicable also to the natives of Asam, if not finely, is at least clearly drawn:— "The timidity of the Hindu may in general prevent his fighting, boxing, or shedding of blood; but it by no means restrains him from scolding, and upbraiding his neighbours. In

* Sir William Jones.

this respect, they are the most litigious and quarrelsome of all men. Have two persons a misunderstanding? Let them meet in the street, and they will upbraid each other for an hour together, with every foul epithet of abuse, which their imagination can suggest, or their language supply. A few natives, (women in particular), engaged in one of these bickerings, display a furious gesticulation; a volubility of words, and coarseness of expression, which leave the eloquence of Billingsgate far behind."*

After all, however, the Asamese possess some good qualities.

Their habits of life are pre-eminently domestic. Respect for old age is carried to a great height; and when parents are no longer capable of labour, they are supported by their children, and are seldom allowed to become a burden on the public. They have also in general a very tender regard for their offspring, and are affectionate and kind to their relations. They are also hospitable to people of their own caste, but to no others.

The modes in which various nations contrive to fill up the intervals of business, are among the most curious portions of their manners, since it is here their character, left entirely to itself, manifests its natural bias unequivocally. The amusements of the Asamese are few, and these are, for the most part, of an innocent nature.

Children may frequently be seen playing with earthen balls, and with *kouries*, small shells, which pass for money. Bigger boys are seen amusing themselves in different kinds of inferior gaming, throwing *kouries*, &c.; in boyish imitations of idolatrous ceremonies; with kites; leaping; wrestling; in a play in which two sides are formed, bounds fixed, and each side endeavours to make incursions into the boundary of the other without being caught; in hide and seek, and the like.

* Tennant's Indian Recreations, vol. i. p. 123.

A fondness for those surprising feats of bodily agility, and dexterity which form the art of the tumbler and the juggler, as well as a taste for buffoonery, are occasionally indulged in, and may be considered as a part of the character of a rude people.

Story-telling, which entirely harmonizes with the tone of the native mind, is also a favourite diversion. The recitations of the bards, which in general consist of the wildest fictions, afford an entertainment of the same description; and to these may be added, music and dancing.

Many of the native melodies possess a plaintive, touching simplicity, and others, on the contrary, a peculiar wild originality no less pleasing.

The musical instruments are in general rude, and consist of drums of a great variety of shapes and dimensions, of cymbals, tabors, horns, and trumpets, used usually during the festivals, whilst in attendance on religious ceremonies, and on occasions of great rejoicings. The violin, though rude and usually composed of an excavated gourd, is, when played by a master hand, one of the most pleasing instruments the natives possess.

Their dancing, to say the least, is very rude, and utterly void of that graceful and measured step, so much admired in the dancing girls of Hindusthan. "No perfumes, nor elegant and attractive attire ornament their figures," nor are their heads decked with "sweet-scented flowers, intwined with exquisite art, about their beautiful hair."

The Asamese have two principal festivals, called *Bihu*. The first festival of the year is termed the Baisak Bihu, and is celebrated in the first three days of Baisak. On this occasion people devote the whole of the first day to mutual visits and compliments, as Europeans do the first day of the year. The cause of their rejoicing is two-fold: first, that the month of Choitro, every day of which is considered unlucky, has expired; second, that it is succeeded by a month of which every day is fortunate. The cows are then worshipped with peculiar honours. They are first sprinkled with holy water, like the horses in the Circusian Games, or bathed in the sacred stream of the Brahmaputra; the devotees next prostrate themselves before them, their horns are painted with various colours, and their necks are decked with garlands of flowers and strings of fruit. The consecrated animals are then driven in a body through the villages, by crowds of people who make a discordant noise upon various musical instruments. During the remainder of the day the cows are permitted to stray wherever they please, and seek a pasture in every field without restraint. On the two following days of the festival, large groups of people parade about, attended by numbers of dancing girls, who pause from time to time to exhibit their wanton movements, and charm the audience with their lascivious songs.

The other Bihu, or festival known as the Magh Bihu, is celebrated about the end of the month of Pous, or the beginning of Magh. It is equivalent to the Harvest-Home, the festival occurring after the inning of the winter harvest. It occupies two days, both of which are devoted to feasting and merriment.

The month of Phalgoon, is one of peculiar liveliness, as it ushers in the Spring saturnalia. During this festival groups of men and children are continually patrolling the streets, throwing a crimson powder at each other, or ejecting a solution of it from syringes, so that the garments and visages of all are one mass of crimson. At night fall, the last day of the festival concludes with the burning of the *Holi*, the crimson powder used at this festival, when large fires are lit, into which various combustible substances are thrown, and around which groups of children are seen dancing and screaming like so many little infernals.

The other festival we shall here allude to, as one of the most important, is the *Durga puja*, celebrated in the month of Ashin, in honour of the ten-armed goddess. We shall not attempt to enter upon any description of this festival, since it is well known to all who are in any degree conversant with the customs of the Hindus.* Innumerable bloody sacrifices are offered at this festival, when the multitude, rich and poor, daub their bodies all over with the mud formed with the blood which has collected when the animals were slain, and dance like furies on the spot. On the three last days of the festival, dancing and singing are kept up at the houses where the images of the goddess have been set up. On the afternoon of the last day, the images are brought out, placed on a stage, and carried to the river. Each idol is here placed on the centre of two canoes lashed together, and filled with people, among whom are a number of dancers, musicians, singers, &c., who chaunt the praises of the goddess.

The river on this occasion presents a scene of peculiar animation, and the banks are crowded with spectators, rich and poor, old and young, who come from many miles round, arrayed in their gayest costumes. Whilst the images are rowed up and down the stream to the melody of songs and music, the vast number of boats accompanying the procession are engaged in racing. The boats or canoes are most gaudily painted, each containing a complement of from twelve to twenty men, according to its size. The emulation of the native gentry, and that of the crew, is to the greatest degree exciting, and the whole scene is one that baffles description.

In regard to diet, the natives practice abstemiousness to a very great degree, and not merely from feelings of duty, but in a great measure from actual necessity. It is surprising, how the poor are able to support life with their scanty earnings. The wages of a day-labourer do not much

* See Ward on the Hindus, vol. ii. p. 83.

exceed two rupees a month. To enable us to form some idea how these people are able to maintain their families on so small a sum, it is necessary to consider, that their fire-wood herbs, fruits, &c. cost them nothing; they lie on a mat laid on the ground; the wife spins thread for her own, and her husband's clothes; and the children go naked. A man with a wife and two children, usually consumes two maunds of rice in the month, the price of which is one rupee. The other rupee procures him salt, a little oil, and one or two other prime necessaries; though a great many obtain only from day to day a little boiled rice, a few chillies, and boiled herbs, and instead of salt they use the potash procured from the plaintain tree; the step above this is a little oil.

Game is often procurable, especially during the rains, when the poor have frequent opportunities of indulging in the luxury "of a haunch of venison, or steaks of the wild hog, or buffaloe," and most of the inhabitants have sense enough to enjoy them.

Milk is very little used by the mass of the people.

It is only during the dry season that fish are plentiful in the markets, and those in easy circumstances then procure abundance; but during the floods the middle ranks are badly supplied. The lower classes are seldom able to purchase at any season, but it is during the floods they have their principal supply. Every rice field then swarms with small miserable fish, which are caught in baskets, and what is not immediately used, is dried in the sun and preserved.

The green vegetables used in the diet of the natives, consist more of the kinds called *hak*, that is of leaves and tender stems, than of the kind called *torkari*, which includes fruits and roots. The poorer classes usually content themselves with such vegetables as grow wild, or with the leaves of crops that are commonly cultivated for other purposes, such as mustard, and the tender leaves of the poppy, &c., which cost them nothing.

Tobacco is pretty plentiful, and most of the natives indulge themselves in the luxury of inhaling its fumes.

The use of opium is in some instances carried to an excessive degree; not only the men, but the women also are remarkably addicted to it.

The juice of the poppy is usually collected on slips of cloth, about three inches broad, which, when fully saturated and dried, are tied up into little bundles, and called *kani*. In using it, from about two to four and sometimes six inches square of the cloth are infused in water, which is drunk at a draught. The cloth is kept, and afterwards chewed like tobacco, till all its virtues are extracted; some however prefer smoking it. They first boil some betle leaves, amounting to about 100 or 150; and then parching them, add to these about three or four drams of opium: the whole being mixed in the hot vessel is formed into small balls. Two or three of these balls are placed in a *chillum* of tobacco and lighted, and the amateur proceeds to inhale four or five whiffs, when he lies down and resigns himself to his dreams. The debility, both moral and physical, attendant on the excitement caused by the abuse of opium is terrible: the appetite is soon destroyed, and every fibre in the body trembles, all the nerves become affected, and the muscles get rigid. Notwithstanding, those habituated to it, seem miserable until the hour arrives for taking their daily dose. This can scarcely be wondered at. Habits of inebriety, even from ordinary stimulants, are not often overcome, and the visions of beauty and splendour which opium superadds, renders it all but impossible to relinquish the habitual indulgence which has once been created. They know that the indulgence shortens life, and that the opium eater dies of old age in his youth. But the knowledge has no effect, and all remonstrance is unavailing. When one expostulates, the opium eater answers with impatience at his ignorance, and with the cold and haughty pity of one who has the secret of happiness of which the other knows nothing. Though almost constantly intoxicated, they are seldom disabled from performing their work. When completely under its influence, their features are flushed, their eyes have an unnatural brilliancy, and the general expression of their countenance is horribly wild. They seem to be in a constant dream or giddiness, and appear, by a strange efficacy, to expel tedious thoughts of labour and fatigue, and sometimes for days together deceive the body of its reasonable rest. If deprived of a single dose, they soon get feeble and stupid, and their constitution is speedily exhausted.

The use of the betle nut and the leaf is usually carried to an excessive degree, and many have their mouths literally crammed with it.

Intoxication by means of spirituous liquors is not very general. The natives are ignorant of the use of the palm wine; but they distil a considerable quantity of grain, and the poorer classes, who alone make free use of the liquor, can consequently afford to indulge themselves at a very moderate rate.

The simplicity of the houses, dress, and furniture of the natives, corresponds with that of their diet. Their houses are built principally of bamboo and reeds, and thatched with grass. The floor is usually plastered with cow-dung; and although this act proceeds from a spirit of religion, it is of use in keeping out insects. The furniture, which is almost nothing in the houses of the poor, is in the highest degree scanty and simple even in those of the rich. Mats or carpets for the floor, on which they are accustomed both to sit and lie, with a few earthern and other vessels for the preparation of their food, form the inventory in general of their household goods.

Their vestments resemble those of Hindus in other parts of India; they are suited to the climate, and composed of the manufactures of the country.

All classes wear the *jhapis*, or hats, common to the country, and made of the leaves of the Corypha Talliera, Roxb.;

in appearance they very much resemble those worn by the Chinese.

The condition of the women is one of the most remarkable circumstances in the manners of the natives. Among rude people the women are generally degraded; among civilized people they are exalted: and the history of every uncultivated nation, uniformly represents the women as in a state of abject slavery, from which they slowly emerge as civilization advances. A state of dependence more humiliating than that to which the weaker sex is here subject, cannot easily be conceived. Like most women of India, they are denied even the least portion of education, and are excluded from every social circle. They are even accounted unworthy to partake of religious rites, except in conjunction with their husbands, and hence that remarkable proof of barbarity—the wife held unworthy to eat with her husband, is also prevalent. The women in fact, are in all respects held in extreme degradation.

Notwithstanding marriage is considered a religious duty, and in most cases is viewed as an indispensible part of life, so that very few that can afford it, neglect at an early age to fulfil this sacred obligation. Early marriages are common, though in the lower classes many young women do not succeed in getting husbands till the age of twenty. To these premature marriages, we are undoubtedly to attribute the general appearance of old age in the persons of the women, before they have reached even the meridian of life.

In no respect are the native manners more deficient, than in filial and conjugal fidelity. The natives feel indeed a very strong attachment to their children, but they are exceedingly neglectful of early discipline; and the children having none of the moral advantages of the offspring of Christian parents, ripen fast in iniquity, and among the rest, in disobedience to parents.

The women, to say the least, are notoriously corrupt, and totally devoid of delicacy; their language is often gross and disgusting. Their terms of abuse and reproach are indelicate to the utmost degree. We will not disgust the reader by mentioning any of them; but we may safely aver, that it is not possible for language to express, or the imagination to conceive, more indecent or grosser images.

Morality is at a very low ebb. If the vices of lying, deceit, dishonesty, and impurity in all its forms, can degrade a people, then the Asamese have sunk to the utmost depths of human depravity. Whole pages might be written on this painful subject, till the reader was perfectly nauseated with the picture of their disgusting vices.

The funeral ceremonies are nearly the same as in Bengal, only the mourning *(Shradho)*, is not by one half so expensive. The ceremony to a poor man will cost only from two to five rupees.

In Asam the fine arts have made little or no progress; with regard to them, therefore a slight sketch will suffice.

Of the arts which at an early stage of society acquire the greatest excellence, the first is that of preparing brilliant trinkets for ornamenting the person. The natives cut precious stones, polish them to a high degree of brilliancy, and set them in gold and silver with an extraordinary neatness; and when we come to compare the extreme imperfection, the scantiness and rudeness of the tools by which the artists in general perform their task, with the simplicity of the process, the neatness, and in some cases the celerity of the execution, we cannot but acknowledge that the degree of delicacy which the artizans have acquired in their several professions, challenges a high admiration.

The workers in gold and silver usually finish their work with a great degree of neatness, and the same may be said of the workers in ivory, who have carried their art, comparatively, to a high state of perfection. But of all the artists it may be said, that their style and taste are very wretched. They possess a wonderful aptitude for imitating the arts and inventions of the Europeans, as soon as the method has been pointed out to them. They are in general correct workmen, but possess merely the glimmerings of genius.

With respect to the sculpture, painting, and music of the natives, hardly by any panegyrist can it be pretended that they are in a state beyond that in which they usually appear in the most early stages of society. The remains of temples, and other public buildings, which are so often met with in various parts of the country, testify that the Asamese had once made considerable progress in sculpture. Their productions, however, are not merely void of attraction, they are unnatural, and not unfrequently offensive and disgusting.

In the sister art of painting, the natives can scarcely be said to have made any progress.

It is anomalous, and not a little surprising, that the music of the Asamese should be so devoid of all excellence. As music is in its origin the imitation of the tones of passion, and is most naturally employed for the expression of passion in rude ages, when the power of expressing it by articulate language is the most imperfect, simple melodies, and these often highly expressive and affecting, are natural to uncultivated tribes. Yet in general, the music of the natives is unpleasing, and void both of expression and art. Dr. Tennant's observations on the music of the Hindus in general, would apply with equal accuracy to that of the natives of this country. "If we are to judge," says he, "merely from the number of instruments and the frequency with which they apply them, the natives might be regarded as considerable proficients in music; yet has the testimoney of all strangers deemed it equally imperfect as the other arts. Their musical instruments are rude, noisy, and inartificial; and in temples, those employed for the purposes of religion are managed apparently on the same principle; for in their idea, the most pleasant and harmonious is that which makes the most noise."

The literature of Asam rests, like its social state, almost entirely upon its religion. To almost all the books which it owns, as valuable or classical, a divine origin is ascribed. These are in general found amongst the Hindus in other parts of India, and were introduced into Asam by the Brahmins; in this branch, the natives themselves possessing no share of genuine merit. They have a few historical works; but like those of most oriental nations they are so made up of wild and extravagant legends, that it is difficult even to form a conjecture of the worth of their narrations, through the mist of fable in which they are enveloped.

The state of education may in general terms be described as deplorable in the extreme. Unlike the provinces of Bengal, where every village has its teacher supported by general contribution, never till lately was a provincial school known in Asam. In some places there are a few Brahmins who teach the arts of reading and writing; but even this elementary knowledge is by no means extensively diffused. All instruction is unattainable to the labouring poor, whose own necessities require the assistance of the children as soon as their tender limbs are capable of the smallest labour. With the higher classes, and those that can afford to pay for a teacher, education usually ends at ten years of age, and never reaches further than reading, writing, (a scarcely legible hand), and the simplest rules of arithmetic.

Females are not included within the pale of education; every ray of mental improvement is carefully kept from the sex. As they are always confined to domestic duties, and excluded from the society of the other sex, the people see no necessity for their education. A woman's duties are comprised in "pleasing her husband, and cherishing her children."*

* To this there are a few exceptions. In the higher ranks of life, and among families of some importance, the females are frequently taught to read and write.

But we may here remark, that where the blessings of education are held out to the natives, they usually avail themselves of it with great avidity.

Towards the close of the year 1835, a school was established at Gowhatti, under the patronage of the General Committee of Public Education. The gradual yet continued increase of its numbers, shews, that the institution has achieved one great stride towards its right position in the country. The natives begin to appreciate the advantages to be derived from it; they are willing to give it a trial; and it is presumed will quickly draw the desired conclusion for themselves. We would therefore confidently anticipate that this institution, in the course of a few years, will become an important Provincial College, and be the means of disseminating knowledge in the neighbouring districts.

In connection with the Gowhatti Seminary, there are at present three branch schools, supported by local funds. Besides these institutions, there are in Kamrup no less than twenty Mofussil vernacular schools, supported by Government, and placed under the management of the Collector. In the districts of Durrung and Nowgong, there are a few schools placed on a similar footing; but the number of pupils that usually attend them is very small, and the general standard of proficiency very low. This however can be attributed to no other cause than a want of proper superintendence, for it cannot be expected that the Collectors, in addition to the multifarious duties that devolve upon them, can pay that attention to the schools which they demand.

At Jaipur, in the Sibpur division, is a flourishing school, under the superintendence of the American Baptist Missionaries, located at that station. One of their number, who has lately taken up his residence on the hills occupied by the Namsangiya Nagas, has just opened a small school for the instruction of that wild tribe, which it is hoped will eventually be the means of reclaiming that people from their present ignorant and barbarous condition.

Slavery exists to a very considerable extent; and most of the domestics, both male and female, are either slaves, or bondsmen, who for a few rupees have been enthralled by mortgaging their bodies, and for the want of means of accumulating the original sum, increased by exorbitant usury, continue in bondage for life. The unfortunate subjects of this disgraceful system are bought and sold, and even mortgaged like any other article of property. In the event of their death, their hard masters seize upon their descendants or their nearest relations, whom they keep in bondage, and so from generation to generation. The persons and labour of these slaves are laid claim to, from their forefathers having been purchased by the forefathers of their masters, and on this account not only are they themselves held as slaves, but also their children and posterity to the end of the chapter. The females among them are permitted to marry, but have no right to go away with their husbands, and when they beget children, these children become the property of their master, and neither the parents nor other relations have any claim to them. The males also by marriage increase their masters' stock, and render their partners slaves with themselves. A great number of slaves are disposed of to the neighbouring states, where they are in general devoted to the most menial and degrading offices.

These poor creatures feel that they are the property of their masters, who have the power to do as they like with them, and it is their duty to submit to all. It is also their impression that any appeal to a public authority will not redeem them from thraldom, while on the contrary this will only bring upon them the displeasure of their masters and their connections.

In Asam most of the higher classes keep slaves, it being difficult to procure servants, especially of the female sex.

The number of slaves and bondsmen in Kamrup alone, where the population is estimated at 300,000, amounts to upwards of 20,000.

The free men-servants, *bhundaris*, who are almost the only domestics besides slaves, are usually paid twelve annas to one rupee a month; their food and raiment are allowed them besides. *Bhundaris* properly signifies a storekeeper; but such servants are usually employed in all manner of work.

A map has been removed from this book for preservation purposes and placed in a secure area.
When requesting the map at the service desk, please present the book or request the map by classification number.

CHAPTER VIII.

LOCAL GEOGRAPHY.

SECTION I.*—KAMRUP, OR LOWER ASAM.

Boundaries—Area—Population—Revenue—Civil Officers—Former Divisions—Present Divisions—Duwars—Deshes—Choumuwas—Shusters—Temples—Nakhiraz Lands—Police Thanahs—Gowhatti—Its ancient splendour—Principal rivers in the Division.

In the historical sketch of the province, we had occasion to state, that the district of Kamrup once gave its name to an extensive Hindu kingdom, which besides including that division of Asam which still retains the name, extended also over a large portion of Bengal, and the adjoining states.

That portion of Asam now commonly known as Kamrup, or Lower Asam, is bounded on the west by the district of Gowalpara; on the north by Butan; on the east (north of the Brahmaputra) by the Barnaddi, which divides it from Durrung, and (south of the Brahmaputra), by the district of Nowgong; and on the south by the Khassia hills.

The total area of this division is estimated at 2,520 square miles. The quantity of land under cultivation amounts to about 788 square miles; the culturable lands may be averaged at 1,532 square miles; and 200 square miles consist of hills, irreclaimable wastes, and water.

* It has already been remarked that the province of Asam, since it was placed under British rule, has been divided into six districts; viz. Kamrup, Durrung, Nowgong, Sibpur, Lakimpur, and Muttuk, or Sadiya.

In surveying the field which the Local Geography of Asam opens, it will be expedient to offer a few remarks on each of the afore-mentioned districts in succession.

From a census lately taken, the population is supposed to consist of 2,71,944 souls.*

The net revenue now drawn from this division, amounts to upwards of Company's rupees 2,40,000 annually.

The officers employed in conducting the civil duties of the district, are at present, a Senior Assistant to the Commissioner, a Junior Assistant, a Deputy Collector, a Sudder Ameen, and five Munsiffs.

Long antecedent to the conquest of this division by the Asamese, Kamrup had been assimilated, in regard to revenue management, to what may be supposed to have been the original arrangements that obtained in the provinces of Bengal. Kamrup was originally divided into seventeen Purgunas, under the fiscal management of as many Choudris; some of these Purgunas were again subdivided into Taluks, and all still further subdivided into Mouzas and villages. The number of these divisions had constantly been increasing, so that on the British acquisition of the province, it amounted to forty-one.

These divisions were for some time preserved; but as a number of the Purgunas had detached portions scattered all over the district, the inconveniences arising from this arrangement, as well as the impracticability of fixing the responsibility of each Choudri, became so apparent, as to render a new organization desirable. Accordingly in 1834, Captain A. Bogle, (then the Collector of the division), sub-

* *Census of the District of Kamrup.*

Divisions.	Total Souls.	Males.	Females	Mahomedans.	Hindus.	Kacharis and other tribes.	Slaves.	Bondsmen.
North bank of the Brahmaputra, ...	1,93,212	1,08,536	84,666	17,284	1,49,411	26,517	14,204	2,641
South bank of Do.	78,732	42,666	36,076	6,206	52,197	20,329	2,160	1,143
Total, ...	2,71,944	1,51,202	1,20,742	23,490	2,01,608	46,846	16,364	7,9[illegible]3

mitted a plan for newly dividing the district, which met with the approval of Government.

Having abolished the boundaries of the former local divisions, excepting those on the left or south bank of the Brahmaputra, which were not intermixed with each other, and having thrown all the Purgunas, as it were *en masse*, he proceeded to parcel them out again into new Purgunas. In effecting these divisions he was guided principally by natural boundaries, such as rivers and other features, presenting good lines of demarcation, as well as by a desire to disturb the old Mouzas as little as possible, and to allot to each of the old Choudris a convenient tract of country in the immediate neighbourhood of his own house. All the former Choudris who were worthy of trust, thus obtained charges sufficiently large to satisfy them, and yet to be perfectly manageable. The old names of Purgunas were given to those divisions, chiefly composed of the Mouzas of the old Purgunas; and where new ones were formed the most respectable resident Asamese was appointed Choudri.

Under these new arrangements the whole district was divided into seventy independent fiscal divisions.*

The Duwars are similar to the Ghauts in many parts of India. They are lands adjacent to the passes into the hills, and were during the latter reigns of the Asam dynasty assigned to hill chieftains, on the condition that the hill men, who resorted to the plains for the purpose of bartering their products at certain appointed *hauts*, or market places, were kept under restraint, and the peace of the frontier preserved.

The Deshes were apparently held on the same tenures as were the Duwars; but the managing men, who were usually styled Rajas, approached more nearly to the state of tributary princes, paying more or less tribute according to the strength of the paramount government. These Rajas

* See the Table at the end of this section.

possessed every sort of jurisdiction in their own territories, except the power of inflicting very severe or capital punishment; and in case of war, they were expected to take the field at the head of their Pykes.

When the assessment of a private estate exceeds one hundred rupees per annum, the proprietor pays his revenue direct to the Collector, on the principle of the Huzzuri Malguzars of the Hindusthan provinces, and the estate is entered as a separate Mehal in the Collector's books, and called a Choumuwa. When the sum is less than 100 rupees, and more than fifty, it does not form a separate Mehal, but is included in the Choudri's collection, the proprietor, however, having the option of paying the revenue either to the Choudri, or into the treasury direct.

Besides these divisions, there are in Kamrup alone three-hundred and eighty-one Shusters, or endowments, partaking both of a charitable and religious character, and having Dhurmooter lands* and people attached. The Shusters are scattered throughout the district, and from six to a dozen are sometimes found in each Purguna. Over them the Choudri has no controul. They are nearly all managed by an officer called the Shusteria Buruwa, who collects the revenue from them, and pays it into the treasury.

There are also in this district thirty-seven Dewals, or temples, having Deobuter lands and people appertaining to them. A small portion of these lands is to be found in nearly every Mouza in the district. Each temple is under a separate manager, who realizes the tax upon them, and also pays it into the treasury, independently of the Choudri.

Thus although the Collector designed to make each Purguna a compact and independent charge, it has been found in practice incompatible with existing claims to place all the

* Dhurmooter lands signify lands given for religious purposes, and Deobuter for the purposes of the gods.

estates of a Purguna under the management of the Choudri, and as the exemption from this officer's authority has always been considered a high privilege, it perhaps would not have been desirable, if practicable, to reduce all the wealthier families to the same level of subserviency, inasmuch as the distinction of Huzzuri Malguzars preserves a superior rank among the population, and maintains a constant stimulus to the ryots to advance themselves to this envied position, by increasing the extent of their cultivation, and thus gradually creating larger farms, and raising up a body of men of larger capital and superior intelligence.

The total quantity of Nakhiraj or privileged lands, which are assessed at a low rate, amounts to nearly one-half of the cultivated area of the district; besides including an immense extent of garden and other lands of great value. Adverting to the circumstances under which the British Government conquered the province from the Burmese, who had held it for seven or eight years previously, and had annihilated every thing in the shape of rent-free tenures, there could have been no just reasons offered, why all the lands should not have been alike fully assessed. Every right or privilege given under the former Rajas of Asam, was extinguished by the Burmese invasion; and the British Government, it may be supposed, is in no way pledged to revive them. The people have attained peaceable possession of their lands, which they had in many instances entirely lost, and they could consequently have had no reason to complain, were they required to pay a full cess for them; nor, on the other hand, could they have reasonably expected that the species of policy observed by the British Government, with regard to Bengal and other ceded districts, should have been followed in Asam, inasmuch as there is a wide difference between the acquisitions of an infant power, gained by treaties and negotiations, and the conquests of a great empire made at the point of the bayonet.

The district of Kamrup is divided into seven Police Thanahs, each Thanah having a certain number of Purgunas under its jurisdiction.* There is no village Police; but the heads of villages, Thakurias and Choudris, are required, if necessary, to assist in apprehending all offenders, and making them over to the Police authorities.

The chief town in Kamrup is Gowhatti, or, as it is called in the ancient books of the Hindus, Pragjoitishpur. It is the residence of the Commissioner, and of the Civil Authorities in charge of the district. It is situated on the left bank of the Brahmaputra, at the eastern extremity of the division, and occupies a plain of 2½ square miles in extent. This plain is bounded on the interior by a chain of pretty hills, stretching from NE. to SW. in form of a semicircle; with its two promontories resting upon the river; while the river itself taking a bend concentric with the hills, cuts it out in the form of a crescent. The town is situated in the centre of this crescent, and extends the whole length of the space between its horns.†

During the splendour of the Asam dynasty, Gowhatti was one of the largest cities in the kingdom. It occupied within its fortifications a vast extent of country on both banks of the great stream; the hills on either side forming a spacious amphitheatre, equally well fortified by nature and by art. It was the capital of all Lower Asam, and the residence of the Viceroy, or Bar Phukan. The entrances into the city were by guarded passes, or chowkies, of which there were five on either bank of the river. Those on the southern bank, were the Luttasil or Pani Chouki, the Joiduwar, the Dharum-duwar, Duwar Guria, and the Pandu Chouki. Those on the northern side, were the Kanai-barsi-bowa Chouki, the Hillar Chouki, Hindurigopa, Pat-duwar, and

* See the Table at the end of this section.

† M'Cosh's Topograhpy of Asam.

the Korai, or Pani Chouki. The ruins of the gateways of some of these passes are still to be seen, and the remains of the extensive fortifications may to this day be traced for miles, in the mounds and ditches, that now serve only to mark the extent of the ancient citadel. Beside these relics, but a small portion of its former grandeur now remains. Its brick, its mortar, and earthenware, constitute in some places a large proportion of the soil. Numerous carved stones and beautifully finished slabs, the remains of once noble temples, are constantly found beneath the surface of the ground; its numerous spacious tanks, the works of tens of thousands, the pride of its princes, and the wonder of the present day, are now choked up with weeds and jungle, or altogether effaced by a false, though luxuriant soil, that floats on the stagnant waters concealed beneath.

In the centre of the river, opposite the station, stands a little rocky island, called Umananda. According to the Hindu legends, this island was formed by the god Sib of the dust with which he had marked his forehead. It presents a very picturesque object, clothed as it is with trees, and crowned with temples.

A reference to the map of this division, will shew, that it is intersected by numerous streams, which doubtless contribute considerably to render the soil exceedingly fertile. Many of these are navigable for the greater part of the year, and thus afford the means of carrying on an inland trade with considerable advantage. We can merely notice a few of the more important streams.

Proceeding from the westward, and confining ourselves at present to the rivers on the north bank of the Brahmaputra, the first that deserves our notice is the Monass. This river takes its rise in the Butan hills, and after receiving several small tributary streams, falls into the Brahmaputra, opposite the station of Gowalpara. During the rainy season, a considerable quantity of gold dust is washed down with the sands of this stream. The communication it opens with most of the inland streams in this division, renders this river one of considerable importance.

The next is the Chaulkhowa. This river flows east and west, and may be considered as the great drain of all the minor streams in north Kamrup. Its most important tributaries are the Pugla Monass; the Soroo Monass, which empties itself into this remarkable stream about a mile above Burpeta; the Pohomara, a very winding stream; the Kaldia; the Noa-nadi; and the Borolia, a very winding but deep stream, which passing through the Baidya-ghor, receives the waters of the Nunai, prior to emptying itself into the Chaulkhowa. The Raorowah forms one of the principal outlets of the Chaulkhowa into the Bramaputra; it is navigable for the greater part of the year. The main channel of the Chaulkhowa, however, empties itself into the Monass, a little above the junction of that stream with the Brahmaputra.

The only other rivers meriting notice are the Lakhitora and the Barnadi. These taking their rise in the Butan hills, and flowing in a southerly direction, empty themselves into the channel of the Brahmaputra. They are both navigable for boats of considerable size during the rains, and for the common canoes of the country, throughout the year. The Barnadi forms the boundary between north Kamrup and the division of Durrung.

The rivers in southern Kamrup are the Diboroo or Sonapur, which takes its rise in the Khasia hills, in the district of Kyrung, and passing through Desh Dumuria, empties itself into the Kullung about four miles above the junction of that river with the Brahmaputra. The Bata Nadi or Barnadi, which also takes its rise in the Khassia hills, and after a long and winding course falls into the Koosi in Purguna Choianni. The Koolsi or Kulohi, which after washing the base of the Nungklow range, takes a northerly direction and passes through Pantam, then winding its course westward, and re-

ceiving the waters of numerous minor streams, passes through Purguna Chumuria, and empties itself into the Brahmaputra, about eight miles above the Nagarbera hills. It is a rapid stream, and from its impetuous course, frequently cuts out new channels for itself; the last, or most western, is the Singara Nadi. It rises in the Khassia hills, and flowing in a north-westerly direction through Lukhiduwar and Purguna Chumuria, falls into the Brahmaputra immediately above Nagarbera.

TABLE

Of the Purgunas of Kamrup, and the number connected with each Police Thanah.

South Bank of the Brahmaputra.	Thanah Gowhatti.	Desh Dumuria.
		„ Panbarri.
		„ Beltulla.
		Purguna Ramsah.
	Thanah Chumuria.	Purguna Nagarbera.
		„ Bekali.
		„ Chumuria.
		„ Barunti.
		„ Choiani.
		„ Dakhin Sorubangsa.
		Duwar Lakhi.
		„ Boko.
		„ Bungong.
		„ Bogie.
		„ Chorigong.
		„ Pantan.
		„ Burduwar.
		„ Bholagong.
		„ Mourapur.
		Desh Rani.
Eastern Div. of N. Bank of the Brahmaputra.	Thanah Byderghor.	Purguna Betunah.
		„ Paschim Kachari Mehal.
		„ Kaoor Baha.
		„ Dumduma.
		„ Hochung.
		„ Panduri.
		„ Burigong.
		„ Jhargong.
		„ Ghoramara.
	Thanah Komulpur in Purguna Purbpar.	Purguna Purbpar.
		„ Madur Tulla.
		„ Bar Bangsa.
		„ Sinduri Gopa
		„ Ramdia.
		„ Hazoo.
		„ Satti Durrung.
		„ Oottur sorubangsa.
		„ Silah.
Centre Division of North Bank of the Brahmaputra.	Thanah Norbari in Purguna Khatta.	Purguna Uper Burbhag.
		„ Purb Bunbhag.
		„ Paschim Do.
		„ Batasgila.
		„ Khatta.
		„ Bahajani.
		„ Chandkuchi.
		„ Pokawa.
		„ New Dehur.
		„ Dhurmpur.
		„ Bar Khettree.
	Thanah Bujali in Purguna Purb Bujali.	Purguna Namburbhag.
		„ Nowamati.
		„ Manickpur.
		„ Utter Bujali.
		„ Dakhin ditto.
		„ Purb ditto.
		„ Suria.
		„ Panbari.
		„ Paka.
		„ Soroukhettree.
		„ Kuchojar Murmela
Western Division of North Bank.	Thanah Buwanipur.	Purguna Rupasi.
		„ Buguribari.
		„ Buwanipur.
		„ Dumka.
		„ Chokaboose.
		„ Burpetah.
		„ Chongah.
		„ Kholabanda.
		„ Hustinapur.
		Talook Sila.

SECTION II.—DURRUNG.

Boundaries—Area—Population—Revenue—Civil Officers—Divisions—Police Thanahs—Desh Durrung—Chatgari—Kullung Duwar—Buriguma Duwar—Kariapara Duwar—Population of Chatgari—Kacharis—Their Manners and Customs—Chutia—Its inhabitants—Charduwar—Tezpur—Important Ruins—Naoduwar.

Central Asam contains the two divisions of Durrung and Nowgong. The former is situated on the north bank of the Brahmaputra, which forms its southern boundary; on the north it is bounded by a continuous range of mountains, inhabited by Butias, Akas, and Duflas; on the west by the Barnadi, which separates it from Kamrup; and on the east by the Kobhi Jan, which divides it from the Lakimpur district.

The total area of this district is estimated at,..	1911½	square	miles.
Lands under cultivation, ...	232	"	"
Culturable lands,..	1556	"	"
Irreclaimable wastes and water,.. ..	123½	"	"

The population is said to consist of about 80,000 souls.

The revenue drawn from this division amounts to Company's rupees 1,09,213 per annum.

The officers conducting the duties of the district, are a Junior Assistant to the Commissioner, in charge, a Sub-Assistant, a Sudder Ameen, and two Munsiffs.

The district is divided into five grand divisions, viz., Desh Durrung, Chatgari, Chutia, Charduwar, and Nauduwar. These are, for fiscal management, further subdivided into villages, of which two, three, or more, constitute a Mouza or Mehal, placed under the direction of a Patgiri, who is endowed with the same powers as a Chowdri in Kamrup.

There are three Police Thanahs in the district. The one in Desh Durrung extends its jurisdiction over the three divisions of Durrung, Chutia, and Chatgari, with a dependant Pharee in the latter division. A second is at Tezpur, in the division of Charduwar; its jurisdiction is confined to this division. The third Thanah is at Bishnath, in the Nauduwar division, to which its jurisdiction is confined.

DESH DURRUNG.

Desh Durrung.—This is the largest, and by far the most important division. It is situated on the extreme western portion of the district, and contains an area of 490 square miles.

It was formerly under the jurisdiction of a family of independent princes, who at one time governed the whole of Lower Asam, but are now commonly known as the Durrung Rajas. On their subjection to the Raja of Asam, all the lands which had previously been cultivated by their own slaves and servants, were allowed them for their support. These lands like those granted for religious purposes, are now designated *Nakhiraz,* and pay only half the ordinary rent to Government.

Desh Durrung is, for fiscal management, subdivided into seventy Mouzas or Mehals. The fisheries in this division yield an annual revenue of about 700 rupees.

The rivers of note in this division are the Kulohi, which falls into the Barnadi; the Noa-nadi; the Mangaldie; and the Mora Dhansiri. The three latter take their rise in the Butan hills, and fall into the Brahmaputra. The Mora Dhunsiri forms the boundary between Desh Durrung and Chutiya. They are navigable to the canoes of the country for the greater part of the year.

CHATGARI.

Chatgari.—A frontier district, is situated to the north of Desh Durrung, and contains an area of 52 square miles.

During the reign of the Asam dynasty, it was under the management of a family of noblemen, whose members were called the Chatgari Baruwas, and to whom the district had apparently been assigned, on the conditions of their colonizing it, and preserving the peace of the frontier.

A number of years ago the tract of country between Chatgari and the hills, is said to have been granted to the Raja of Butan, to afford his subjects the means of cultivating rice and other necessaries, which were not procurable on their native mountains. In consideration of this grant, the Butias were to pay to the Asam Government an annual tribute of articles manufactured or produced on their mountains, with a further stipulation, that this district should come under the jurisdiction of the Asam Raja during the months of Asur, Shraban, Bhadur, and Assin, or from the 15th of June to the 15th of October.

This tract is divided into three passes, or Duwars, designated the Kullung Duwar, the Buriguma Duwar, and the Kariapara Duwar. To the two first of these Duwars a civil officer is appointed by the Deb Raja of Butan, who is invested with civil and criminal authority in his own respective division. He receives no stipulated salary, but is allowed a very liberal commission, with the additional license of appropriating all fines to his own private use. The revenue of these Duwars is realized in kind, and although a fixed rate is put upon every house, yet a most liberal remission is usually allowed for accidents of bad seasons.

The *Kullung Duwar* is said to contain about eight or nine thousand puras of land, of which only a third part is under cultivation. It pays a revenue in kind equivalent, to 6000 rupees, of which 390 rupees are paid to the British Government.

The *Buriguma Duwar* contains about 6000 puras, of which near 4000 are under cultivation. The revenue raised from this Duwar is equivalent to 1900 rupees, from which sum about 200 rupees accrue to the British Government.

The misrule in these Duwars, in consequence of the long continued civil wars in Butan having led to constant disturbances on the frontier, and to collisions with the British Police, and having occasioned the tribute due from the Duwars to fall heavily into arrears, they have both been attached, until some arrangement can be effected with the Butia Government for the better management of the Duwars generally, and the punctual payment of our demands. The attachment of these territories was hastened by the very atrocious murder of Gumbhir Wazir, a Kachari, and the chief of the Kullung Duwar, by a party of Butias. Gumbhir was a man of very considerable influence over all the men of his own race, and he was further accused of being more obedient to the British authorities than to the Government of Butan. But probably, the chief cause of the death of the Wazir was the comparatively great wealth he had amassed, and which it was supposed he was on the eve of conveying across the frontier into the British territories. He was most barbarously murdered by the party, who were visitors at his house, and of whose intentions he apparently had not the least suspicion. All his wealth that was portable was carried off by his murderers, together with a son and daughter; the latter has since been ransomed by some of her relatives, but the former, whose hands were mutilated, is still under confinement in the hills, and every application from the British authorities has hitherto failed to procure his release.

The *Kuriapara Duwar* is by far the most extensive and valuable division. It contains an area of about 15,000 puras, of which about 11,000 are cultivated. Unlike the two former, this Duwar is held by the Towung Raja, a chieftain immediately dependent upon Lassa.* The Duwar is divided into seven subdivisions, placed under the management of seven respective Rajas, who are invested with the same authority as the Zinkaffs of the other Duwars. For the better management of the Duwar, there are also Sunzattis, officers whose duty it is to realize the revenue, which is estimated at upwards of 8000 rupees. The portion that accrues to the British Government scarcely exceeds 350 rupees.

The total number of Mehals in the Chatgari division amounts to sixteen.

The population of Chatgari consists chiefly of Kacharis, a laborious and hardy race, and possessed of considerable physical strength. Their superiority to the Asamese is in a great measure attributable to their style of living. They are not trammelled by the prejudices and useless observances of the Hindus, and live freely and fully on animal food, and drink as much spirits as they can afford. They are not so cleanly in their habits as the Hindus are; but seem better versed in domestic economy, taking especial care to have abundance of provisions. They are in general neat in their architecture, although their poultry and all their live stock rest under the same roof with themselves.

In stature they are about the ordinary height, with exceedingly well proportioned limbs. They are active and industrious, and their services are generally in great request. Their women have a masculine appearance, pretty fair in complexion, with broad features, and countenances somewhat forbidding. They share with the men in all the usual occupations of the field.

The Kacharis are naturally of a quiet disposition, and even their Bacchanalian feasts are seldom ruffled by serious quar-

* This Duwar has also of late been attached by the British Government, on account of the barbarous murder of Modhoo Saikia, a *Patgiri* of Charduwar.

rels. It is only extreme poverty, or severe oppression, that induces them to the commission of crime. Adultery is looked upon as a very serious offence, and the adulterer becomes an outcast, unless he can pay a heavy fine; no blame is attached to the adultress.

At the celebration of the marriage ceremonies, a large party is usually assembled; some dance, whilst others play on certain musical instruments, and all contribute to their mutual conviviality. The whole company bear witness to the mutual consent of the happy couple to their union, and a sacrifice, consisting chiefly of fowls, is offered to propitiate the favour of either the good or the evil spirit, whichever may best suit the occasion; the whole party then dance promiscuously round the sacrifice, and the ceremony is concluded. A feast follows, and copious libations are drunk to the honour of Bacchus.

Cases of separation are not unfrequent, and both husband and wife may marry again, if they have parted from each other with mutual consent. When the parties have mutually agreed on a divorce, their friends are informed of it, and in their presence the husband and wife each take hold of either end of a *pawn* leaf, (leaf of the betle vine,) and tear it into two pieces. This ceremony renders the marriage null and void, and the by-standers are witnesses to the divorce.

The Kacharis burn their dead; but funeral is attended with no further ceremonies. They have so far adopted the customs of the Hindus, as to abstain from the use of beef. They believe in the existence of one Supreme Being; but they suppose that the affairs of nations and individuals are under the superintendence of two divine agents, a good and an evil spirit; the favour of the one may be obtained, and the wrath of the other appeased by the sacrifice of a fowl. In such sacrifices consist all their religious ceremonies.

The principal productions of Chatgari are rice, lac, and mustard seed.

The only mart of any note is held at the village of Silputa, which was established during the Asam dynasty, and was in former days a place of considerable importance.

There are no public works of utility, with the exception of a high *bund* road running north and south, constructed about fifty years ago by the Baruwa in charge of the division.

CHUTIA.

Chutia.—This district is bounded on the west by Desh Durrung, and on the east by the Rotass river, which divides it from Charduwar. It contains an area of 125½ square miles; but the population is so exceedingly small, that extensive tracts of culturable lands are at present lying waste. It is divided into five Mehals, which collectively pay an annual revenue of about 5160 rupees.

The greater part of Chutia consists of a plain of diluvial land, much above the level of the inundations of the great river. A large portion of the district is in consequence ill adapted to rice cultivation, the only branch of agriculture now practised by the inhabitants; but hereafter, as the more valuable products are introduced into the province, these comparatively high lands, which are so well suited to the growth of sugar-cane, the mulberry plant, &c. will no doubt become of considerable value.

There seems every reason to suppose that the Chutias, from whom the division takes its name, were originally descended from a race of Shyans, who in all probability emigrated into the province a short time prior to the invasion of the Ahoms, by whom they were subsequently defeated, and the principal families removed to this division. The greater portion of the present inhabitants of Chutia are Kacharis. They carry on a small traffic with the Butias, bartering dried fish, liquor, and opium, for rock salt and blankets.

The principal rivers in Chutia are the Jia Dhansiri and the Rotass; which take their rise in the Butan mountains, and passing through the division, fall into the Brahmaputra. They are navigable to small boats throughout the year.

CHARDUWAR.

Charduwar.—This division is situated to the east of Chutia, and extends as far as the Barelli Nuddi. It occupies an area of 712 square miles, the surface presenting a peculiar undulating appearance, not common to the other divisions of the district. This division takes its name from the circumstance of there being four passes from it to the adjacent mountains.

The mountain tribes on its northern frontier, the Butias, Akas, and Duphlas, levy a black mail on the ryots, and for this purpose usually come down in large parties in the month of February. This system, besides the opportunities it affords the hill tribes of practising treachery, if inclined to make any aggressions, cannot but be extremely detrimental in putting a most effectual check to agricultural improvement, and speculations of every kind.

For fiscal management, Charduwar is divided into eighteen Mehals.

There is a fair held annually at Dymara, the only one of any importance in this division. Here a small traffic is carried on with the Butias, who bring down rock salt, blankets, some gold, and a few ponies, which they barter for rice, tobacco, and dried fish.

Extensive forests of *Ficus elastica* exist in this division, and a trade in caoutchouc has already commenced, which promises to be one of considerable value to the province.

TEZPUR.

Tezpur,—The residence of the civil authorities in charge of the district, is situated at the eastern extremity of this division. It stands on a high plain on the banks of the Mora Barelli, and about a mile from the junction of this river with the Brahmaputra. The Sudder station was formerly in Desh Durrung, on the east bank of the Mangaldie river, and close to its confluence with the Brahmaputra. But as this was far from being a centrical situation, and at a considerable distance from the divisions of Charduwar and Noiduwar, in which the Duphlas were at the time extremely troublesome, the head-quarters of the district were in 1835 removed to Tezpur; chiefly to allow the officers in charge to watch over the proceedings of these restless predatory tribes, and give confidence to the ryots, who were fast deserting the eastern divisions. The removal of the head-quarters has been attended with the best effects; the depredations of the Duphlas have been put a stop to, and arrangements have lately been entered into with all the hill chiefs, by which they are no longer to levy a black mail from house to house, but to receive fixed payments direct from the officers of Government appointed to meet them, and to adjust their annual demands on the Duwars.

The most important ruins in Charduwar are found in the vicinity of Tezpur. A very interesting account is given of them by Captain Westmacott, in the 40th No. of the *Asiatic Society's Journal*, from which we make the following extracts.

"The first temple I examined appeared to have faced the north, and to have been provided with a portico supported on three columns of sixteen sides; each shaft, not including the plinth and pedestal, which stand four feet above the ground, measured eight feet high, and five and a half in girth, and was wrought from a single block of fine granite. The shafts have sculptured capitals, while the surbases take the form of an octagon, and the plinths are circular at top, and spread into four feet, making a sort of cross that measured four and three quarter feet each way. These gigantic stones, with the fragments of a fourth, each hewn from a single block fourteen feet long, and cut into five irregular sides, of which the total shewed a circumference of eight feet, seem to have formed the entablature of the entrance porch, which I judged to have been fifty-six feet long. The frieze has three tiers of carving in basso relievo, representing scrolls of flowers. The apertures in which iron rivets were introduced can be distinctly traced, and it is evident that no cement was employed to unite the materials. The other members were too much shattered and dispersed, to enable me to conjecture the form of the temple. From a great portion of the surrounding works being in an unfinished state, it affords the presumption, that the architect must have met some unlooked-for interruption; and that this, and the other buildings were overthrown at the same period by some hostile power opposed to the propagation of Hinduism, assisted perhaps subsequently by a convulsion of nature. Had time been the sole instrument of overthrowing these structures, it is but fair to suppose from the great solidity of the materials, that the ruin would have been less complete, and that the fragments would have lain in a narrower compass. The destruction of the temples at this place is ascribed by some to Kalapahar, an apostate Brahmin of Kanouj, at whose door the Asamese lay all the sacrilege and mischief that has been consummated in the province.

"From their massive proportions, and the carving and ornaments being so much worn by time and exposure, the fanes are evidently the work of a remote era: I sought in vain for an inscription, and neither the priests of the district, nor the ancient families whom I consulted, could assist my researches, or point, with any approximation to accuracy, to the date of their origin.

"Unconnected with the first temple, and retired some yards deeper in the wood, or rather grove of trees which was in likelihood planted by the priests who ministered at the temples, I found the ruins of six or seven other enormous structures of granite, broken into thousands of fragments, and dispersed over the ground in the same extraordinary manner as those already described. Altars of gigantic proportions were among the most remarkable objects; one of these measuring upwards of six feet each way, and eighteen inches thick, was elevated from seven to eight feet above the level of the plain, and approached on each side by layers of stone disposed in the nature of steps. It was hewn from a single block of granite; underneath was a sort of cavern; the top had holes for iron links, and a receptacle to receive flowers and water to bedew the Nandi, or sacred bull of Siva, who was placed, my informants imagined, on the brink of the reservoir. Six or eight other altars, one of them making a square of forty-six feet and eighteen inches thick, are to be seen in other parts of the ruins, and several square blocks, each measuring from twenty to thirty feet, concave in the centre, and sculptured in imitation of circlets of flowers, must have formed the Bedi, or altar-piece of Siva, as there is a seat for the Linga, or symbol of the deity, in the middle of each.

"The ruins are partly encompassed by walls, which extend in so many directions that it is scarcely possible to guess at the purpose of the architect. The walls have their foundations laid very deep in the earth; they are in an unfinished state, and were evidently constructed at a period long subsequent to the temples; they are built of massive blocks of cut stone, sometimes disposed in a double row, and exhibit a good deal of carving. The stones are of various shapes, and rise three or four feet from the ground, and were all intended to be united with bands of iron. The entrance of the principal enclosure appears to have been from the south, where lie some pedestals, and three or four wedge-shaped stones, about five feet long and three broad, of a flattened pentagonal shape, intended I presume to have formed the voussoirs of an arch; and the middle of the key-stone is decorated with a handsome diadem or plumed tiara.

"A little to the north of the wood, buried in a forest of reeds, I discovered a very interesting fragment; this was a solid mass of granite, of a much finer grain than the kind used in the temples, measuring ten and half feet in length, two and three quarter in breadth, and two feet in depth. On this were sculptured in very high relief, eighteen figures of gods, partially mutilated, but generally in a good state of preservation.

"Near the images are nine square pedestals of large dimensions, with three carved feet, which must have been intended to give support to as many columns; of these several have almost disappeared in the earth, and it is likely others are lost altogether. It shews at all events, the design of the temple must have been projected on a large scale. The pedestals do not appear to have been moved from the spot where they were originally carved, and they are so little impaired by time and exposure to the elements, that I feel assured they are of modern date compared with the buildings in the plantations, and on the adjacent plains; they were indeed as fresh to look at, as if but recently executed by the mason's chisel. Vast fragments of the epistylium and frieze, carved with beaded drapery, also lie half-buried in the soil.

"In the south-west angle of the Pura* plains, there is another curious remnant of sculpture, also wrought from a

* In the south-east angle of Charduwar, a chain of granite hills, rising from 200 to 500 feet above sea level, and clothed with grass and forest trees, sweeps outwards in a crescent form, from the Bhairavi to the Brahmaputra. The inhabitants assert these hills were originally called Agnighar, the place or fort of fire, from their constantly sending forth flames; they add, that Krishna mounted on his *garura*, (a creature half-bird half-man, corresponding with the eagle of the Grecian Jupiter,) brought

single mass of granite, upwards of ten feet long and two and a half thick at the middle; it appears to have formed the side of a gate, and has a band of carving three inches broad on each side, shewing in relief, elephants, tigers, deer, rams, cattle, and swans, encircled by scrolls of flowers.

"No quarries were discovered, to indicate that the stones were disembowelled from the hills; but quantities of chips were seen in places; and once I came upon pillars and altars in an unfinished state, shaped from blocks of granite, on the surface of the earth; and there seems no question that all the material employed on the fabrics, was similarly procured from the masses of rock that cover the hills in great abundance. Once or twice only I fell in with well burnt bricks; they were smooth and thin, of rather a large size, but not badly shaped. Great part of these extensive ruins are buried or have sunk into the earth, and they cover altogether about four or five acres of land.

"I have been thus particular in noticing them, because there are not, so far as I know, any architectural remains in Asam, that can challenge a comparison with them for durability of material, and magnitude of design; and it is certain, from the prodigious number of ruinous and deserted temples, all of which appear to have been dedicated to Siva, being within the circuit of a few miles of Pura, (I discovered twelve or fifteen in as many days on the hills and highlands at their feet,) that this spot must have been the capital of a sovereign prince, or a principal seat of the Hindu religion, and enjoyed a large share of prosperity at some remote period.

---

brought hither a supply of water and quenched the fires, and that in commemoration of the event, the name of the hills was changed to *Pura*, (signifying burnt,) which name they still retain. Though it is possible this obscure tradition might be connected in some way with the existence of volcanoes at a former period, yet the most active scrutiny of the spot can discover no traces of subterranean fire, to bear out the supposition.

"The inhabitants of Charduwar assert, that Raja Banh, the founder of Pura, was a demi-god, sixth in direct descent from Brahma; they add, that his dominions were situated on the banks of the Nermada river; that he journeyed into Kamrup, Charduwar, and other parts of Asam, and was the first person who introduced the worship of Mahadeb into this quarter of India. The extensive walls which encompass the temples at Pura, are said to have made part of a fort or city founded by him, called Lohitpur, Sonitpur, or Tezpur, signifying the city of blood, in commemoration of a battle stated to have been fought there between Krishna and the Raja."

Since the foregoing was published, a *phulli* of three copper plates connected by a copper ring, to which was attached the royal seal, has been found in the ruins of the temples near Tezpur. The characters on these plates were quite distinct, but so ancient, that it could be read only by a reference to the key published by Mr. Prinsep, in the *Journal of the Asiatic Society*. The grant was found to be one of Dharmapal's, to a temple of brick still existing, but in a ruinous condition. This circumstance would serve to shew, that the probable æra of some of the temples may date as far back as A.D. 1027, when, in all probability, the whole valley was filled with a Hindu population.

NOIDUWAR.

Noiduwar.—The fifth and last division of the Durrung district is Noiduwar, situated on its extreme eastern frontier. It has the Duphla mountains on the north; the Bareli river on the west; the Brahmaputra on the south; and the Kobijan on the east; which latter river divides this district from the Lakimpur division. It occupies an area of five hundred and thirty-two miles, and is divided into seventeen Mehals.

Bishnath, formerly the head quarters of the Asam Light Infantry, is situated in this division. It stands on a bold rocky point, which, jutting out into the river a short distance above, and as suddenly retiring below to the north, forms a considerable promontory of upwards of a mile in breadth.* This promontory is again divided by a small nullah to the eastward, formed partly by the inundations during the rainy season, and partly by a small stream called the Burigong Nudi, which flows from the Duphla hills. To the back of the station the lands are considerably high, and rise in steppes to the foot of the hills; they are admirably adapted for the growth of wheat, sugar-cane, and potatoes.

The Bareli Nudi, which forms the boundary between Charduwar and Noiduwar, abounds with gold dust of superior quality. This river takes its rise in the Aka hills, and after a very winding course, empties itself into the Brahmaputra, a few miles above Tezpur.

* M'Leod's Medical Topography of Bishnath.

SECTION III.—NOWGONG.

Boundaries—Area—Population—Revenue Settlements—Present rates of Assessment—Fiscal Divisions—Civil Officers—Principal Rivers.

The district of Nowgong comprises that portion of Central Asam, situated on the left or south bank of the Brahmaputra, and bounded on the east by the Dhansiri river; on the west and south-west by the Brahmaputra, the Kullung and Desh Dumuria in Kamrup; on the south by the Jaintia and Kachar hills; and on the north by the Brahmaputra.

The whole area is 3870 square miles; about 1710 constitute the hilly country known as the Mikir hills; of the remaining 2160 square miles, about 300 are under cultivation; 1710 are culturable, and 150 consist of unreclaimable wastes and water.

The population is estimated at 90,000. Nowgong was separated from the Kamrup or Lower Asam division in 1832-33, and was then first placed under distinct European management. No regular settlement, however, was made till 1833-34; previous to which the ancient Pyke tax, or *khelwari* system, still prevailed.

During the existence of this system, the total revenue of the district was estimated at 45,666 rupees. The details fluctuated much by desertions and other causes, attributed by the civil authorities to the retention of that system, and in consequence the actual collections were far less than the demands; so that on Captain Rutherford's assuming charge in 1833-34, the collections were only 35,000 rupees, and the recorded arrears against the whole division amounted to rupees 1,24,000. He introduced a new system called the *mouzawarri* settlement, by which the Mehals were assessed according to the number of *mouzas*, or villages contained in each. From that period to the present date, many minor alterations have been introduced in the modes and rates of assessment, all tending to the ultimate abolition of the personal taxes, and the commutation of them to a taxation on all lands under cultivation.

With very little exception, this system has now been introduced throughout the division. The rates of assessments in the more settled and most thickly populated parts of the district, Nowgong, Koliabur, and the Mikur Mehals are 1 rupee and 4 annas on *rupit* or *hali* rice lands, and 14 annas on all other cultivated lands. In the less settled and newly acquired districts of Jamuna Mukh and Dantipar, the rates are one rupee on *rupit* lands, and 14 annas on all others.

The only exception to an assessment upon the actual quantity of land cultivated is, where the tax is levied on the ploughs, as is the case in some of the Chaporis, and other deeply inundated lands, where the cultivation is uncertain, and the lands constantly shifting; there the cultivators are subject to a tax of from two to three rupees a plough.

Under the above system of assessment, the net revenue of the division in 1838-39, had increased to Rs. 91,579 : 7 : 9; the whole of this amount was collected, with the exception of rupees 302 : 4 : 7; and this deficiency is attributed rather to erroneous statements than to any defalcation of the revenue, or the failure of the *ryots* to pay the full government demand. In 1839-40, the net revenue of the district amounted to rupees 10,3,925 : 2 : 5; the increase being chiefly occasioned by the extension of a regular tax on Mehals, hitherto taxed by the number of ploughs and bullocks possessed by the *ryots*.

The original subdivisions of the district were four,—Nowgong, Raha, Jamuna Mukh, and Desh Morung. These were afterwards found to be inconveniently large; this circumstance, together with further additions to the territories in that quarter, made it necessary to effect new divisions. These at present amount to nine.

Morung, containing	5	Mouzas.
Koliabur, ...	12	,,
Chapori Mehals,..	26	,,
Nowgong, ...	29	,,
Mikir Mehals, ...	9	,,
Mikir Hills,..	7	,,
Jamuna Mukh.	30	,,
Raha, ...	48	,,
Dantipar, ...	8	,,
Total, ...	174	Mouzas.

Morung is the most eastern division of the district. On the first occupation of the province by the British troops, Morung was almost entirely deserted; but the population has of late years greatly increased, and numerous Pykes, who fled from the oppressive rule of Raja Purunder Sing, have located themselves in this division. Morung is interspersed with numerous small hills, covered with wild and luxuriant vegetation; the soil is good, and the lands are not subject to periodical inundations. There is a fair of some little importance held here, frequented chiefly by the Latoo Nagas. This division contains an area of 352 square miles.

Koliabur is situated to the west of Desh Morung. It contains an area of sixty-eight square miles, and is for the most part under cultivation. A great number of Ahom families are located in this division, who in a great measure retain their ancient customs and institutions. Brahmins are likewise very numerous.

The *Chapori Mehals*, are certain lands that extend along the left bank of the Brahmaputra, from Koliabur to the mouth of the Kullung, and are more or less subject to inundations;

some are perfect *churs*, surrounded in the rains by deep channels of the river, whilst others appear permanently attached to the main land. The cultivation on these Chaporis was formerly confined to *ahu* rice and opium; the former always a very uncertain crop. These lands are now, however, fast rising in importance, chiefly from the introduction of the cold weather crops, sursoo, (mustard seed), and sugar-cane. To the first crop these lands are throughout very suitable, and many parts of the higher grounds yield valuable returns of sugar-cane. A large portion of these Chaporis seems admirably adapted to the growth of indigo. Collectively, they contain an area of 296 square miles.

Nowgong contains an area of 84⅗ square miles, and is inferior to no part of Asam in the state of its agriculture and the denseness of its population. The trade of Nowgong is in a great measure limited to agricultural and farm products. These consist of muga silk, rice, treacle, fowls, kids, fruit, betlenuts and betle-leaves, which are for the most part exported to Gowhatti and the neighbourhood. The two latter articles are exported in considerable quantities. Nowgong, the sudder station, is situated in this division, it stands on the banks of the Kullung, and on the whole has a very pretty appearance.

The *Mikir Mehals* comprise a narrow tract of land in the immediate vicinity of the Mikir hills, exceedingly fertile, and for the most part cultivated by the Mikirs. These Mehals contain 46½ square miles.

Mikir Hills.—That division of the Nowgong district known as the Mikir hills, occupies a tract of hilly country covering an area of 1710 square miles. These hills are inhabited by a fine athletic and industrious race of people, called Mikirs. Living as they do in a rude state of society, and possessing no written language, it is no easy matter to trace their origin. They have a tradition, that their ancestors originally came from the Jaintia hills; which might be assumed to be correct, from the circumstance of their having a few Jaintia words in their language. It is, however, more probable that they originally occupied the hills east of Jaintia, between the Kopili and Dyung rivers, previous to those hills being overrun by the Kachari tribes.

The manners and customs of these people are in all general respects, similar to those of their hill neighbours. They are free from the invidious distinctions of caste, and are entirely uncontaminated by the superstitions of the Brahmins. They have no prejudices with regard to food. One peculiarity however is worth noticing, they neither eat the flesh of the cow nor drink her milk. Whether this prejudice originally sprung from Brahminic influence or not, they themselves are not aware; it would however in some measure serve to shew their connexion with the Indo-Chinese nations.

The Mikirs rear a number of pigs and fowls; which are not kept for daily use, as their means could not admit of it, but are used chiefly in their ceremonies of worship, in which a feast with a good supply of liquor forms an important part. Their food consists chiefly of rice, with a few vegetables found about their hills. The use of tobacco is a luxury they are not much accustomed to. The betle-leaf is used very extensively.

Their dress is similar to that worn by the Asamese; that of the men consists of a *dhoti*, and the women wear broad blue *meklas*, or petticoats. Each house has a small patch of indigo adjoining it, which serves all the purposes of the family. The people usually live in detached villages, and though they occasionally build on some of the high peaks, their *chans*, or houses, are more frequently situated on the lower hills, or on the declivities of the higher ones. The houses of the Mikirs are much more comfortable than those belonging to the people on the plains. They are usually raised from fifteen to twenty feet above the ground, and the flooring, which is made of bamboos, is from forty to fifty feet long. These houses have no partitions, and the family all huddle together; in the centre a quantity of earth is placed, which serves as a fire place.

The occupation of the Mikirs consists chiefly of agriculture, in which cotton forms a principal article; rice is also very generally cultivated. These articles are usually grown on the slopes of the hills, the Mikirs seldom availing themselves of the valleys. They have notwithstanding an abundance of grain, and in times of scarcity, occasionally have the means of supplying the people of the plains. This must chiefly be attributed to the more industrious habits of the Mikirs, who from their hard and scanty soil, are able to procure a sufficiency to meet their own wants, and even to spare a portion of their hard earnings to others.

Their implements of husbandry are a small *kodal*, (the native hoe,) and a *daw*, used in felling trees. They use no ploughs, and keep no oxen.

They make a few cotton cloths themselves, and import a few from the Garos. These latter, called *selu*, are usually striped and used for throwing over the shoulders.

Their liquor is usually prepared by themselves. A certain quantity of rice is steeped in water for some time, and when sufficiently saturated, the water is squeezed out, the rice dried, pounded, and made into cakes, which are placed in the smoke of a fire for eight or ten days, at the end of which time the cakes are again put into water, and there allowed to stand for a day or two, when the liquor is drawn off.

The Mikirs carry on a small trade with the natives of the plains, bartering their cotton and *eria* thread, for salt and various little articles of luxury, in which they are beginning to indulge.

The women are not solely employed in domestic occupations; robust and hardy, they engage in more masculine pursuits. They share in the labours of the field, and as occasion may require, accompany the men to the markets in the plains, and share their burdens.

The Mikirs are not in the habit of marrying young. After making his choice, the man deputes a few of his friends to the parents of the young lady, to ask their consent to his marriage. These friends take with them a number of *bongs* (calabashes) of liquor, as a present to the parents of the lady. Should the young man's overtures prove acceptable, a day is fixed on for the solemnization of the union. On the day appointed, the bridegroom, attended by a number of his friends, proceeds to the house of the bride, where her friends are assembled; the bride and bridegroom are then asked if they are willing to have each other, if the replies be given in the affirmative, they are pronounced man and wife. A feast follows, which consists chiefly of fowls and pigs, and large potations of liquor. The young couple after Marriage remain in the house of the bride; should they have a family, or at least after the expiration of two years, the husband builds for himself, and removes his wife to his own house.

Polygamy is not allowed. After the death of the husband the widow may marry again, but not to an eldest son.

Their funeral like their marriage ceremonies are very similar to those of the Khassias, of whom we shall give a brief account in a subsequent chapter.

On the subject of their religion very little can be said. They believe in the existence of one Supreme Being, whom they call *Hempatin;* of an hereafter they know little or nothing, and live without hope in the world.

Besides the unmixed Mikir communities that occupy these hills, numerous families are scattered all over the south bank of Lower Asam. They seldom remain above three or four years in one place, and are always changing their locations. The hills to the east of Gowhatti, are mostly occupied by Mikir families. They employ themselves in cultivating the fields in the vicinity of the hills, and the women usually bring in to the station large quantities of wood for fuel.

The entire population of the Mikirs, may be estimated at about 20,000 souls.

Jamuna Mukh, or Dharumpur, includes that portion of the Nowgong district bordering on the Kopili, Jamuna, and Dyung rivers, and having the Mikir hills on the north, and the hills of Kachar on the south.

The present division, including the Hozai, covers an area of 580¾ square miles. The Hozai was a grant of Dhurmuter, or Nankar land, given during the reign of the last Raja of Kachar to a member of Tuliram's family, for the performance of certain religious services. It is at present farmed by Tuliram's nephew, Durgochurn, on a settlement liable to periodical revision.

Dharumpur, together with the adjoining territories of Tuliram Senapati, was at one time included in the possessions of the Raja of Kachar.* It was then divided into twelve districts, placed under the management of as many chiefs.

The whole of this tract of country is remarkably fertile, producing rich crops of rice, mustard seed, and sugar cane; while the hilly parts yield an abundance of cotton, which forms a staple article of export. The products of northern Kachar, are said to form a very large portion of the trade of Asam.

Raha.—This division is situated to the west of Nowgong, and contains an area of 582 square miles.

The population of this division is composed principally of Lalongs, who it is said, originally emigrated from the Jaintia hills. They are a simple and industrious class, and have for

* Vide Chapter on the Hill Tribes, Section X. Kachar.

the most part renounced their ancient institutions, and adopted the religion of the Hindus.

Raha, during the period of the Asam dynasty was a kind of fief, subject to the Bor Buruwa. It paid to the state little more than a nominal tribute, which consisted of buffaloes' horns, ivory, and the cotton of the *simul* tree. The other resources of the division were divided among the resident, or temporary functionaries, who received supplies, and made exactions according to their wants and power. This province was unfortunately one of the principal scenes of the diabolical cruelty of the Burmese, and was by them rendered almost desolate. Under the present administration, however, it begins to wear a very prosperous aspect. The soil is exceedingly rich, and admirably adapted for the growth of grain of every description. It is intersected by numerous navigable streams, and possesses excellent facilities for the purposes of trade.

Some years back, the trade of this division was entirely in the hands of a few Seiks, who had emigrated from the Punjab, to seek fresh channels of profitable traffic in this remote corner of India. They have now, however, dwindled down to but a few families, owing perhaps to the superior industry, fair dealing, and more extensive capital of the Kyahs or Murwari merchants, who now in a great measure monopolize the trade of Asam. They have still a small monastery at Doobri, in the Gowalpara district, and the few Seiks in the province, contribute to its support.

Dantipar.—That portion of Jaintia annexed to this district, and known as Dantipar, is bounded by the Barpani river to the east; Purgana Dumuria in Kamrup to the west; the Kullung river to the north; and the higher or Khassia range of hills to the south. The lower range inhabited by Lalongs and Mikirs, is, and always has been, under the management of the chief of the plains.

Dantipar covers an area of 150 square miles, and is subdivided into eight Mehals, each varying in extent from six to twenty square miles, and with two exceptions, extending from the hills to the Kullung.

Each of these Mehals was in former times under the management of a distinct Raja, or chief, appointed by the Raja of Jaintia. Latterly, however, the sway of the Raja has been merely nominal; the Nutting Khassias gaining the ascendancy and levying black mail on the inhabitants.

The population of Dantipar may be divided as follows :—

Asamese, ...	2,000
Mikirs,..	1,600
Lalongs,..	5,000
Total,	8,600

The products of the division consist principally of cotton, rice, eria silk, and a little pulse; it however enjoys admirable facilities for more extended cultivations. The numberless rivulets that intersect the division, offer considerable facilities for irrigating the lands; and the people in general avail themselves of these advantages.

One-half of the division is covered with a dense forest, in which are timber trees of various kinds. When the country shall have enjoyed more quiet than has hitherto fallen to its lot, and the security of property is established, which may speedily be expected under its present administration, boat-building is likely to be carried on to some extent, which must contribute considerably to the general prosperity of the district.

The officers conducting the duties of the district are, a Principal Assistant to the Commissioner, a Junior Assistant, a Sub-Assistant, a Sudder Ameen, and a Moonsiff.

There are four Police Thanahs in this district. The Nowgong Thanah includes within its jurisdiction, the divisions of Nowgong, Koliabar, the Mikir Mehals, the Chapori Mehals, and part of Raha. The second, situated at Jagi, exercises its jurisdiction over the remaining portion of Raha and Dantipar. The third situated at Dharumpur, exercises its jurisdiction over that division. The fourth Thanah is situated in Kachar.

The most important rivers in the district of Nowgong are the following :—The Kullung, which issuing from the Brahmaputra immediately opposite Bishnath, takes a winding course and empties itself again into the great river a few miles above Gowhatti. It is navigable to small boats throughout the year. The Letheri also, a branch of the Brahmaputra, takes its rise opposite Tezpur, and falls into it again near the village of Kauhagi. The Sonai takes its rise at the same place, and running parallel with the Kullung, empties itself at the mouth of that river.

The Kullung is, in its course through the district, fed by numerous small streams. Proceeding eastward, the first we meet with is the Killing, which takes its rise in the Jaintia hills, and falls into the Kullung near the town of Jagi. The Barpani rising in the same hills, after taking a short northerly course, falls into the Dimal below Chopper Mukh, which latter taking a westerly direction, empties itself into the Killing. The Kopili issuing also from the Jaintia hills, falls into the Kullung at Raha; another branch taking a westerly direction from Chopper Mukh, falls into the Barpani. It is navigable at all seasons of the year. The Dyung rises in the Kachar hills, and falls into the Kopili about two miles below Boraghat; it is navigable to the foot of the hills. The Jamuna takes its rise in the low Naga hills, and flowing past the villages of Mohung and Dubka, falls into the Kopili at Jamuna Mukh. It is navigable as far as the village of Silpata. Lime and coal of very excellent quality are found in some parts of this stream. The Kari Dipholu rises near Kazirunga in Morung, and falls into the Kullung at Sonari-chopri. It is one of the principal feeders of that river.

The only other river of importance is the Dhansiri, which forms the eastern boundary of the district. It takes its rise in the Naga hills, flows in a northerly direction, and after receiving the waters of the Dooyung, empties itself into the Brahmaputra immediately above the Bogiduwar Chopri. Lime and coal have been found along the banks of this stream.

SECTION IV.—SIBPUR.

Boundaries—Area—Physical Aspect—Former condition of the District—Population—Vegetable and Mineral Productions—Civil Officers—Fiscal Divisions—Revenue—Police Thanahs—Principal Rivers.

The division of Upper Asam comprises the present districts of Sibpur, Lakimpur, and Sadiya or Muttuck. The two former were formed into separate divisions, on the resumption of the territories of Rajah Purunder Sing.

Sibpur, situated on the left bank of the Brahmaputra, extends from the Dhansiri on the west to the Namsung river on the east; on the south, it is bounded by a continuous range of high mountains, inhabited by various tribes of Nagas; and on the north by the Brahmaputra and Buri Dihing rivers.

It contains an area of about 5,440 square miles.

The physical aspect of the district is very nearly the same throughout, and the inhabitants are, generally speaking, less mixed than is the case in any of the other districts.

All that portion of the country east of the Dessai, is one dead flat, with the exception of a small belt of land close under the Naga range, which rises a little above the general level, and in some parts, presents an undulating character. This flat consists, for the most part, of a whitish retentive loam, exceedingly well calculated for the growth of rice, which is throughout the district almost the only crop now raised. By far the greater portion of this extensive plain is more or less liable to heavy inundations, either, from the copious floods of the great river itself, or from those of the smaller streams which intersect it. Owing to the liability of these periodical inundations, all the rivers in this division have heretofore been guarded by embankments, which served alike as *bunds*, and the high roads of the country. These river embankments were crossed by high raised path-ways, which were again joined by smaller *bunds* graduating down; and connecting the Mouzas, villages, and fields, at once formed most commodious means of communication, and afforded opportunities for retaining or keeping out the inundations throughout the division. Of late years, however, these embankments have been greatly neglected, and heavy inundations, the effects of the bad condition of the *bunds*, have led to the abandonment of large tracts of valuable land.

West of the Dessai, although the surface soil is much the same as that of the foregoing portion of the district, the general aspect of the country is much diversified by the higher level here attained by the subsoil, while a stiff retentive clay, abounding in iron nodules, reposes on the surface, which furrowed by numerous ravines or water courses, presents in some parts so broken an appearance, that the culturable lands are divided in a singular manner into innumerable small sunken patches. The Tea localities are very numerous in this division.

Of the state of the district antecedent to the conquest of the Ahoms, we know nothing. It was in all probability filled by an abundant Hindu population, from whom the bulk of the present inhabitants have descended.

The Ahoms were for many generations confined to the tract east of the Dihing; as their power increased, their conquests were extended beyond that river, on the left bank of which they afterwards founded their first capital, Huluguri-nugur. About half way between Jaipur and Dihing Mukh, extensive remains of the fortifications of the Nuggur are still to be seen.

On the further advance of their arms, the Ahoms removed the seat of government to Ghergaon on the banks of the Dikho, which continued to be the principal residence of the princes, till the prosperity of the Ahom dynasty began to fade. The royal palace at Ghergaon was surrounded by a brick wall, about two miles in circumference; but the whole town and its suburbs, appear to have extended over many square miles of country. The ruins of gateways, built chiefly of masonry, are still to be seen within the fortified circumvallations, which surrounded the town. It may be observed, that one of the gateways is composed principally of large blocks of stone, bearing marks of iron crampings, which evidently shew that they once belonged to far more ancient edifices. From this evidence alone, were there no other, it might safely be presumed, that long antecedent to the conquests of the Ahoms, the country had been possessed by a race of inhabitants far advanced in some of the arts of civilized life.

Ghergaon was for certain reasons subsequently abandoned; and Rungpur, situated lower down the river and on its left bank, was fixed upon as the capital. In the troubled reign of Gourinath, Rungpur was abandoned for Jorehat; but even here the Raja was not safe, and he fled for refuge to Gowhatti. On Gourinath's restoration, Jorehat again became the seat of government, and continued so till the conquest of the country by the British troops.

Rungpur was then the first position chosen as the head-quarters of Upper Asam; but this place was shortly after abandoned by Captain Neufville for Jorehat, which place was also, in later years, the residence of Raja Purunder Sing. Since the resumption of this district from that prince, the residence of the civil authorities has been fixed at Sibpur, immediately opposite Rungpur; this place being on the whole considered a more centrical position.

The population of the Sibpur district may on a rough calculation be estimated at about 200,000 souls. Owing to the circumstance of the seat of government having been for a number of years situated in the district, it is to be expected that in it were located all the principal families of the country, and with very few exceptions, all the Ahoms of rank.

The inhabitants are mostly Hindus; but, as may be imagined, there has been so much intermixture with the race of the conquerors, that both are greatly assimilated in appearance. The only pure Ahoms are those on the banks of the Disang.

The cultivators are in general, a well-made race; but long continued oppression has had its baneful effects in making them sullen and obstinate, has driven them to inordinate excesses in the use of opium, and deprived them of much of their physical strength. Notwithstanding these disadvantages, they are generally in pretty comfortable circumstances.

Amongst the population, there is also a large proportion of Mahomedans, who being for the most part artizans and petty traders, as well as cultivators, possess amongst them a considerable share of wealth.

Rice forms the principal article of cultivation in the district. The muga and eria silks are abundantly manufactured, as well as cotton cloths, the cotton being imported from the Naga hills. The mineral products consist of salt, coal, petroleum, iron and gold dust. Though these articles exist in large quantities, as we have already had occasion to mention, a very small proportion has hitherto been obtainable. Almost all the streams are in a greater or less degree auriferous. The coal, which is of the very finest quality, has hitherto remained untouched; and the iron mines are scarcely ever worked.

The officers conducting the civil duties of the division, are a Principal Assistant to the Commissioner, two Sub-Assistants, a Sudder Ameen, and two Moonsiffs.

For fiscal management, the district is divided into 50 Tongonis, which are farther subdivided into Mouzas, the total number of the latter being 131. Besides these, there are 8 plough Mehals, or Mehals subject to a plough tax.

The net revenue of the division amounts (in 1839-40) to rupees 70,135: 10: 5.* The rates at which the lands are assess-

		Rs.	As.	Ps.
* 50 Tangonis, ...	65,462 3 0			
8 Plough Mehals,	3,149 3 8	68,611	6	8
Syrat duties,... ...	800 0 0			
Fisheries, ...	724 3 9	1,524	3	9
	Total, ...	70,135	10	5

N. B.—The Syrat duties are collected at the Naga market, called Paniphat.

ed, are one rupee each poora for *rupit*, rice lands, and eight annas a poora for all other cultivated lands. In the plough mchals the taxes are two rupees per plough, and one rupee for each spade. The révenue derived from the fisheries is obtained by a poll tax of one rupee on each fisherman.

The Police Thanahs in this district are three, situated at the towns of Sibpur, Jorehat, and Jaipur.

The principal rivers in the district are the Kakadargah Nudi; the Dessai, on which stands the town of Jorehat; the Dikho, which washes the ancient fortresses of Ghergong and Rungpur; the Namdisang river; and the Buri Dihing, on the left bank of which stands the little town of Jaipur. These are for the most part navigable to the ordinary boats of the country, while during the rains the three latter admit of the passage of boats of considerable size.

SECTION V.—LAKIMPUR.

Boundaries—Fiscal Divisions—Population—Early History—Civil Officers—Police—Revenue—Trade.

The district of Lakimpur is bounded on the east by the Dihing river; on the west by the Kobijan, which separates it from Naiduwar in the Durrung district; on the north by continuous ranges of mountains, the easternmost being inhabited by Abor tribes, those next by Miris, and from thence to the western boundary by Duphla tribes. On the south, it is bounded by that branch of the Brahmaputra, known as the Lohit.

The greatest length of this district from east to west may be estimated at 125 miles, its breadth varies from 10 to 20 miles. It is nearly bisected from north to south by the Subansiri river; the eastern half is divided into what may be termed the Mehals of Seesee, Domajee, Burdolonee, and Dowkwakhana; and the western into those of Lakimpur, Banskotta, Choiduwar, and Miri Mehal.

This division has suffered more of the calamities which the later events in the history of Asam have brought upon the province, than any other portion of it. It now presents little more than a miserable picture of depopulated villages, and orchards and plantations run to waste, or covered with dense jungles.

The population is exceedingly scanty, scarcely amounting to 30,000 souls, and the entire cultivation does not exceed 18,800 acres.

The early history of this division is very obscure, and involved in many fabulous traditions. The first accounts we have, that bear any semblance of truth, record the invasion and possession of the country by the Baro Bhuions, who are reported to have found it in a flourishing state. The vanquished inhabitants were in all probability Hindus, as the event is laid subsequently to the dynasty of the Pals.

All the traditions we have met with, agree in the fact, that the Baro Bhuions were leaders of colonists, who during the convulsions that disturbed the western provinces of India, were obliged to leave their troubled homes, and seek an asylum elsewhere. These soldiers of fortune are said to have been primarily subdued by their opponents; but shortly after to have recovered the country. To these twelve Bhuions are attributed some of the large tanks still to be seen about Banskatta and Lakimpur.

The dynasty of these chiefs was subsequently subdued by the Chutias, a branch of the great Shyan family, who in all probability emigrated into the province a short time prior to the invasion of the Ahoms.

The chief seat of the Chutias, when they were in the ascendant, appears to have been about Lakimpur and the banks of the Subansiri. They held all the country on the north of the Brahmaputra, probably as far down as Bishnath. On the arrival of the Ahoms, the Chutias sustained a long struggle with them, but were finally subdued. On their defeat, the greater portion of the people, or more probably the families of the most influential chiefs, were removed to the present district of Chutia in the Durrung division, whence it derived its name. Many of the inhabitants of Lakimpur still call themselves Chutias; but having now embraced Hinduism, and, as far as we have learnt, lost all traces of their original language, there is no longer any mark of distinction between them and the rest of the inhabitants.

Though this portion of the country had passed into the hands of the conquerors, it seems still to have retained its former prosperity. It, however, received its first great shock in the reign of Gourinath Sing. When this imbecile prince was driven out of his capital, and obliged to seek refuge in Lower Asam, the whole of this division was left a prey to the devastations of the Moamarias. The Khamtis, likewise, availing themselves of the commotions that troubled the province, followed on the track of the Moamarias, and laid waste and utterly depopulated this once flourishing district. The partial return of quiet effected by the great Bura Gohain had scarcely restored order, when the troubles brought on the province by the Burmese invasion, laid waste the whole province, and exposed this division in particular, to the wanton cruelties of these ruthless barbarians.

Left to their own resources, the people determined on opposing the excesses of their invaders, and having placed themselves under the direction of a leader, (How Burra,) they made a gallant stand against the invading armies near Lakimpur. They were however defeated with great loss, and the enemy, with redoubled fury, vented retribution on the miserable inhabitants.

The misfortunes to which this division was subject, did not cease with the expulsion of the Burmese. For years after the conquest of the country by the British troops, no officers could be spared for the management of this district, and it suffered considerably under native agency. During the first period of the British administration, the inordinate exactions of these agents conduced in no small degree to the emigration of a number of the inhabitants. Oppressions from the same causes contributed to the like effects during the administration of Raja Purunder Sing. The insufficiency of population likewise exposed this district to the aggressions of the adjacent hill tribes; and of late years, the exactions of the Duphlas and Miris have contributed largely to the desertion of a great portion of the inhabitants.

On the resumption of Upper Asam by the British government, this district was for the first time brought under European superintendence, and under the able management of Captain Vetch, it is hoped the foundation has been laid for future peace and prosperity.

In addition to Captain Vetch, the Principal Assistant to the Commissioner, and Political Agent for Upper Asam, the other officers connected with the civil duties of the district are, a Sub-assistant, a Sudder Ameen, and a Moonsiff.

The Police Thanah of this district is situated at Lakimpur; dependent on it are two Pharis, situated the one at Dowkwahkana, the other at Gourpur, in Mehal Choiduwar.

The rates of assessment in this district are the same as those adopted in the Sibpur district. The revenue at present amounts to Rupees 14,131 : 12 : 0.

The only river of importance in the division is the Subansiri; which, rising in the Himalaya range, empties itself into the Brahmaputra near the Majali Island. Gold dust is found in great abundance in the sands of this stream.

The staple commodities are rice and mustard seed, the muga silk and manjit; wax and honey are brought from the bordering hills. Salt forms almost the only article of import.

SECTION VI.—SADYIA.

Boundaries—Area—Moamarias—their History—Muttuk Country—Trade —Inhabitants—Sadiya—Civil Officers—Police—Revenue.

The Sadiya division is situated at the eastern extremity of the valley, and is bounded on the north-east and south by continuous ranges of mountains inhabited by Abors, Khamtis, Mishmis, Singphos, and Nagas; on the west it is divided from the Lakimpur and Sibpur districts by the Dihong, the Brahmaputra, the Buri Dihing, and the Namsing rivers.

The total area of the district is computed at 7073 square miles. This includes that division known as the Muttuk, or Moamaria country, which contains an area of 1218 square miles.

Moamaria, or Mora, is the designation of a particular sect of the Asamese population, who are noted in the latter days of Asam history. They also bear the appellation of Muttuks, a name given them originally by the Khamtis. This sect is divided into two distinct clans, the Moamarias, so called from their being a distinct sect from the generality of the Asamese, and the Morans, signifying inhabitants of the jungles.

The Moamarias are confined to no particular territory, but are scattered over the whole valley, and are found as far west as Gowalpara; the greater portion of the Morans seem to be located in that tract of country known at present as the Muttuk country.

About the time that the numerous tribes occupying the valley of Asam were converted to Hinduism, a division took place amongst them. A portion of the population dissenting from the general creed, followed the religious tenets of a certain Guru, or spiritual adviser, denouncing the supremacy of the Brahmins, and professing to worship only the incarnation of the deity, known to the Hindus as Vishnu. The residence of the first priest of this sect is said to have been on the Majuli island, on the banks of a small lake, now washed away by the Brahmaputra. The name of this lake, from the circumstance of its abounding in a description of small fish called *moa*, was termed in the usual style of Asamese phraseology "moa mora," whence arose the name of the sect, but which, from a spirit of contempt by those of the Brahminical faith, has since been changed to Moamaria.

Soon after the formation of this sect, the seat of the principal priest, the Moamaria Gosain, was removed to a place called Kutia Putta, a short distance to the west of Jorehat. The name of the first Gosain was Onirud, apparently a very popular personage, as disciples seem to have flocked to him from the various tribes of Kacharis, Ahoms, Kolitas, Kaists, Dūms, Haris, and others of the lowest classes.

Nothing particular is recorded of this sect until the reign of Lakhmi Sing, when having joined in the rebellion of this Raja's brother, a general massacre ensued, in which the Gosain and all his family were killed. This general massacre fell heavily on the Morans, who then formed a large portion of the Raja's army, and had the consequence of temporarily overthrowing his rule. To this indiscriminate slaughter may in a great measure be attributed the subsequent civil wars of Asam, which ultimately brought the country to its present degenerate and comparatively impoverished state.

Lakhmi Sing seems, shortly after, to have relented; and by way of pacifying the Moamarias, he appointed over them another Guru, in the person of the nephew of the late Gosain. As might indeed have been expected, this priest and his party retained all the vindictive feeling of their relatives towards the sovereigns of Asam. About the year 1793, these people rose up in arms against the reigning Raja, Gourinath Sing, and, after many bloody engagements with the royal troops, succeeded in driving him from his throne and kingdom, and in appointing a successor of their own choice, named Bharota Sing.

During this confusion, the setting up of Rajas seems to have been quite common in Upper Asam, as even the Dūms of the Moamaria sect set up at this time a Raja for themselves; this Raj was subsequently overthrown by the Khamtis. The Moran portion seem also to have set up for themselves, and appointed Surbananda Sing as their ruler, who took possession of Bengmara. But these lawless plunderers were not allowed long to enjoy the fruits of their conquests; they were speedily driven from their capital by some troops under the command of Captain Welsh, and were obliged to retreat to the district they have since inherited.

Under the firm government of the prime minister Purnanondo, the Moamarias received severe chastisement; and even those who escaped do not seem to have been able to establish themselves again as independent of their rightful sovereign, either during the remainder of Raja Gourinath's reign, or in those of his still weaker successors Kamaleswar and Chandrakant; although they made several attempts to do so, and once sent a person, called Ramnath Bar Buruwa, to treat with the Burmese monarch for assistance, but at that time without effect. Messengers were notwithstanding repeatedly sent to Burma, and parties of Burmese were twice brought into Asam. These Burmese were, however, always bribed or bought over through the influence and wealth of the prime minister, who in the end relaxed his severity towards the Moamarias, and subsequently gave the chief of Muttuk the title of Bar Senapati. He appears to have then remained obedient to his lawful sovereign, paying the revenue required from the portion of the sect over whom he was supposed to have authority.

But during the subsequent oppressive rule of the Burmese, the then Senapati availing himself of the confusion of the times, established himself in his father's position at Bengmara, and secured himself from the immediate controul of the Burmese government. On the arrival of the British forces in

Asam, he claimed their protection, and was found, with all the semblance of an independent prince, the ruler of a country containing upwards of 50,000 inhabitants.

It does not appear that the Senapati had formerly any particular boundary laid down or that any particular parts of the province were considered as his hereditary lands. But subsequent arrangements with the British authorities gave him a territory which, with the exception of the small district of Saikwa, opposite to Sadiya, had the Brahmaputra for its northern and western boundaries; the Buri Dihing on the south; and an imaginary line drawn south from Sadiya to the Buri Dihing on the east. The Bar Senapati was in return bound to abide by the following agreement:—That two-thirds of all the Pykes of Muttuk should be at the disposal of the British Government as troops and coolies, and that the remaining third be reserved for the use of the Senapati, and the officers and priests of the country. The criminal jurisdiction in all minor cases was to be entrusted to the Senapati; but all heinous offences were to be transferred to the political agent, or officer in charge of Sadiya. A census was summarily made of the Pykes, and the agreements solemnly ratified. The Pykes here alluded to were Moamarias, the Pykes of that division of the country; but for all other settlers the Senapati was expected to pay the full Pyke tax.

It shortly, however, became notorious, that the census of the Pykes as given by the Bar Senapati was very deficient, and that numerous *Bhagonia*, or runaway Pykes were concealed within his territories. Furthermore, the Pykes placed by him at the disposal of Government were very few, and the conduct of these in two or three instances was very suspicious. It was in consequence determined that in lieu of the Pyke militia supplied by him, as well as in payment of the taxes on the Pykes he had seduced, he should pay an annual tribute of 12,000 rupees. The Bar Senapati, however, strenuously opposed this, and claimed that the original agreement made with

Mr. Scott was a final and perpetual one; subsequently he offered to pay a tribute of 1800 rupees, to which terms the Government were pleased to accede during his life time.

The Bar Senapati died in November, 1839, leaving the management of the country to his second son, the Maju Gohain. The term of the engagement entered into with the British Government having now expired, it was considered expedient to form a new census of the people, and to exact the proportion of revenue as settled between Mr. Scott and the late Bar Senapati. The above terms proffered by Captain Vetch were insolently rejected by the sons of the Bar Senapati, and no motives could induce them to give the subject a second consideration. Captain Vetch in consequence assumed immediate management of the whole country, and this measure was subsequently sanctioned by the British Government; a portion of the revenue, amounting to one-third, is allowed for the subsistence of the Bar Senapati's family.

Although the Muttuk country is considerably interspered with jungle, it abounds in extensive grain flats, and is a rich depôt of grain, the greater part of the population being composed of those classes of people considered the best farmers in Asam, the cultivation is good, and the crops are of the same description as those raised in other parts of the province.

Cotton of an excellent quality is raised in great abundance in the upper section of the country inhabited by the Morans. The average quantity of cotton exported annually from this division amounts to nearly 7000 maunds, and being considered of a far superior quality to that grown in other parts of the valley, is consequently much higher priced. Whilst the common cotton sells from two to three rupees a maund, that of the Muttuk country fetches four rupees.

This tract of country also abounds with numerous tea localities.

Rice and cotton are the staple commodities, and with *gur* and elephant's teeth form the only exports. The imports, that find a ready sale, are salt, tobacco, betle-nuts, flints and steel, knives of Asamese manufacture, and brass, copper, and earthen pots.

The Moamarias being, as already stated, a sect of the Asamese population, they resemble those of the same classes in other parts of Asam. The Morans, however, are by no means that degenerate and weakly race that the Asamese in general are. They are rude and rough in their manners, robust in their persons, and hitherto not addicted to the use of opium.

The Muttuk country is for fiscal management divided into two Mehals, termed the Bhati Noukhel, or Lower Muttuk, and the Ujoni Noukhel, or Upper Muttuk; the former is subdivided into fifty-nine, the latter into seven zimbadars.

The other portion of the district, or that commonly known as Sadiya, is a spacious level plain, of a quadrangular form, in the midst of which is the town or village of Sadiya, from which the district takes its name. It is situated on the Kundil Nulla, two miles inland from the Brahmaputra, and thirteen miles east from the point of confluence of this stream with the great Dihong. The plain is intersected by numerous streams, the principal of which is the Brahmaputra, which from its flowing, as it were, into the axis of the main channel, retains the name of the great river.

The quantity of cultivation within this tract is very small. The village of Sadiya does not extend more than six miles between the post and the Dikrang river. Beyond Sadiya, and on the north of the Brahmaputra, the tract is one uninterrupted jungle to the foot of the hills, and on its southern side, a few scattered hamlets form mere specks in the widely-spread wilderness. The mountain scenery about Sadiya, it is said, would form a noble subject for a panorama, though the distance of the hills is rather too great for the larger features required in a detached picture.

The whole of this district is placed under the management of the Political Agent, aided by a Junior Assistant to the Commissioner.

There is one Police Thanah in the district, with two dependent Pharris.

The revenue is collected by a capitation tax of one rupee per head. It is, however, in contemplation to introduce a land tax, similar to that adopted in the Sibpur and Lakimpur districts.

The net jumma of the Muttuk country, amounts to Company's rupees 16,022, and that of the Sadiya division to Company's rupees 928, shewing at present an annual revenue of Company's rupees 16,950 for the whole district.

A SKETCH

OF

THE HILL TRIBES,

BORDERING ON

THE VALLEY OF ASAM.

A SKETCH OF THE HILL TRIBES,

BORDERING ON THE VALLEY OF ASAM.

As the numerous tribes that occupy the hills bordering on the valley of Asam must possess a prominent place in the statistics of the province, either from the trade they maintain with the inhabitants of the plains, the hostile incursions they occasionally make upon their unsuspecting neighbours, the treaties of tribute or alliance that unite their interests with the British Government or from various other important causes, we might be thought wanting in our duty, were we to close our sketch without a brief notice of them.

It seems almost vain to attempt to lift up the dark veil which conceals the origin of these tribes, to trace back their history, or to gain any information of the various revolutions by which they have been influenced; these subjects belong to times and circumstances, which are beyond the limits of certain knowledge. It would be the most cautious, and perhaps the most philosophical course, to abstain from any conjecture relative to their origin, or from any attempt to penetrate into the nature of causes, of which even the most distant results are but partially known to us. But the mind of man is so constituted, as in the impossibility of arriving at certain truth, to prefer a probable hypothesis to the alternative of acquiescing in absolute ignorance.

In the following pages, we shall aim at nothing more than, from known events, to discover what is the most probable opinion as to their antecedents.

The direct authority of history furnishes but a very imperfect insight into the origin and descent of these tribes. We must, therefore, depend on the reflected light which is obtained by the comparison of languages, by the analysis of civil and religious institutions and mythological fables, or by tracing clearly, marked affinities in the manners and customs of the different tribes.

Though the analysis of mythological systems may in most cases afford a strong evidence of a connexion between distant nations, and much information may be acquired by a diligent comparison of civil and religious institutions, the very scanty information we at present possess of these tribes, precludes the possibility of availing ourselves to any great extent of these sources of information.

Other indications of scarcely less importance may be drawn from the resemblance of habits and peculiar customs. But in this inquiry, caution and accuracy are peculiarly requisite. Those shades of character and manners, which have their origin in the general principle of human nature, or arise from circumstances and situations peculiar to all men, may be found to prevail more or less among tribes, which have had no intercourse. But if it happen, that we find clear coincidences in such peculiar habits and customs as are purely arbitrary and casual, we cannot suppose these instances to have been of separate production; but are in most cases compelled to acknowledge, that they evince a common origin or a connexion at some former period, between the tribes who continue to be marked by such traits. Illustrations of these remarks, we shall occasionally meet with in the following pages.

In addition to the above arguments, we derive a degree of evidence from the physical characters of the people. For although the latter are subject to great diversities, and very generally deviate more or less in the course of time, yet there will be found, for the most part, in the divided branches of the same stock, some considerable remains of the original type, some general characters which resemble, and may be regarded as, the stock on which the varieties have been engrafted. Generally speaking, the features of all the hill tribes bear a great resemblance to each other, and approach the broad form of the Mongolian. The eye is a very remarkable feature of the face; small, black, with long pointed corners, as though stretched and extended by artificial means. Below the eyes is the broadest part of the face, which in most of the tribes is rather flat, and narrows from the cheek bones to the chin, a character of countenance appearing first to take its rise among the Tartar tribes; but by far more strongly marked in the Chinese.

The most important aid, and which we can best avail ourselves of, in tracing the origin of these tribes, is the comparison of languages. When two nations ever so distantly separated, or however widely distinguished in all other points, are found to speak the same language, or to use dialects which, though differing in pronunciation and otherwise variously modified, can yet be traced to the same radicals or elements, so as to prove that an essential affinity existed in their primitive structure, it is certain that such nations have descended from the same stock. For history does not shew that languages have ever been communicated from one nation to another by intercourse, or even by conquest, unless when the vanquished people have remained long under subjection to their conquerors; nor indeed in that case, except in some rare examples, where colonization has been carried to such an extent, as to change the mass of the population. This argument is certainly liable to be abused. Many words may be introduced into the speech of any tribe by their immediate neighbours, if frequent communications subsist between them. A variety of terms may also be brought in with the adoption of a new religion, new laws, or a different state of manners from what before prevailed. But it must on the other hand be allowed, that it is possible to discover, by proper discrimination, what parts of the vocabulary are thus adventitious, and what are radical, elementary, or original.

We have not been able to procure vocabularies of all the languages spoken by the adjoining tribes; but as even a few, it is hoped, may not prove uninteresting, we venture to submit the following specimens, extracted from a paper published in the *Journal of the Asiatic Society*, and forwarded by the Rev. N. Brown. (see Table.)

It must be noted, that the words are spelled according to the romanized orthography. The vowels are sounded as follows:—

a	as in	America, woman.	*a*	as in	far, father.
e	„	men.	*e*	„	they.
i	„	pin.	*i*	„	police.
o	„	nor, not.	*o*	„	note.
u	„	put.	*u*	„	rule.
u	„	l'une (French.)			

The letter *h* is always used strictly as an aspirate, whether at the beginning of a syllable or following another consonant. Thus *th*, is sounded as in pries*th*ood, not as in *th*ink; *sh*, as in mis*h*ap, not as in *sh*ip; *ph*, as in u*ph*old, not as in *ph*ilosophy. The French nasal *n*, (as in *enfant*) is expressed by ṉ with a dash underneath.

English.	Bengali.	Asamese.	Khamti.	Siamese.	Aka.	Abor.	Mishmi.	Singpho.	Garo.	Manipur.
Air	báyu	botáh	lum	lóm	doú	ásar	arenga	mbóng	barówa	nungsit
Ant	pipiliká	poruá	mut	mót	tarak	táruk	aruang	kagin	shamalchak	kakcheng
Arrow	tir	kánr	lempün	luk son	apak	epúgh	mpü	pala	bra	tel
Bird	pakhyi	sorái	nok	nók	putáh	pettáng	tsa	wu	dúbring	úchek
Blood	rakta	tez	leüt	lüat	oyi	i	hærri	sai	kanchai	i
Boat	nouka	nau	heü	rüa	hulung	etkú	rrua	li	ring	hí
Bone	asthi	hár	núk	kra dúk	sala	álong	rubóh	nrang	gring	sarú
Buffaloe	mahish	moh	khwai	khwái	mendak	menzek	maji	nga	matma	iroi
Cat	birál	mekúri	miú	meau	ásá	kedári	nadzari	ngyau	menggo	haudong
Cow	goru	górú	nagö	ngoá	shye	sóu	matsokru	kansu	machú	samuk
Crow	kak	kauri	ká	ká	pák	pivág	tsakla	kokha	doka	kwak
Day	din	din	wan	wan	húmpáh	longe	kihingge	sini	saló	nungthil
Dog	kukkur	kúkúr	má	má	eki	ekki	neko	kwi	achak	hwi
Ear	karna	kán	hú	hú	nyárung	nórung	nakru	na	nachil	na
Earth	mátí	máti	lang nin	din		ámóng	tari	nyga	har	laipak
Egg	anda	kóni	khai	khai	pápúk	rokpi	mtiúmaie	wúdi	duchi	yerum
Elephant	hasti	háti	tsáng	chháng	háti	syite	datón	magwi	mongma	samú
Eye	chhakhyuh	sókú	tá	tá	nyek	ámig	malam	mi	mokron	mit
Father	pitá	bupai	po	po	ábba	bábu	naba	wa	afa	ipa
Fire	agni	júi	fai	fai	ummah	eme	naming	wan	wol	mai
[illegible]	[illegible]	[illegible]	[illegible]	[illegible]	[illegible]	[illegible]	[illegible]	[illegible]	[illegible]	[illegible]
Plantain	kalá	kolá	kue	klui	kepák	kopag	phaji	langó	tarik	laphoi
River	nodi	nói	me nam	me nam	subang	botte	tsalö	kha	chima	túrel
Road	rástá, bát	bát	tàng	táng	lamtau	lambe	nilam	lam	raina	lampí
Salt	laban	lun	kü	khia	álla	alo	plah	tsúm	karasam	thum
Skin	chamra, chhal	shál	nang	nang	sapen	asig	kua	phi	bigil	mawul (ipak
Sky	ákásh	ákáh	fá	fá	aúpa	taling	brra	mó	srigi	nongthaurai-lil
Snake	shánp	háp	ngú	ngú	tabuk	tabi	tabú	lapú	chapi	lil
Star	tárá	torá	náu	dáu	takar	tekar	kadang	sagan	asake	thawalbichak
Stone	prastar	hil	hin	hin	elung	eling	mpla	nlóng	rangta	nung
Sun	súrjya	beli	wan	tawan	dahani	arung	wanyi	tsan	salgra	númit
Tiger	bágh	bágh	se ü	süa	samnya	simioh	tamyah	sarong	macha	kai
Tooth	dauta	dant	khiú	fan	phi	ipang	lla	wa	waggam	ya
Tree	gáchh	gosh	tun	tón mai	sangná	sine	masang	phún	bolbiphang	úpal
Village	grám	gaun	mán	bán	nampum	dolung	mating	mareng	song	khúl
Water	jol, páni	pání	nam	nam	issi	asi	machi	ntsin	chi	ising
Yam	alu	álu	hó man	hoú man	———	engin	gí	nai	tajong	ha

Asamese,	63		1	1	7	1	1	5	0	0	0	0	0	0	0	3	1	0	0	0	0	1	1	3	0	1	0
Khamti,	1	1		92	1	1	5	8	8	3	10	3	3	1	0	1	0	0	0	0	0	0	0	0	5	1	3
Siamese,	1	1	92		0	0	3	6	8	3	10	1	3	1	0	1	0	0	0	0	0	0	0	0	5	1	3
Aka,	7	7	1	0		47	20	17	12	15	15	5	11	3	10	3	8	8	8	5	6	10	8	10	0	1	1
Abor,	0	1	1	0	47		20	11	10	18	11	6	15	6	11	5	8	6	8	8	8	10	10	18	0	1	1
Mishmi,	1	1	5	3	20	20		10	10	10	13	10	11	0	11	0	3	5	6	8	6	13	10	8	1	3	8
Burmese,	3	5	8	8	17	11	10		23	23	26	12	16	8	20	6	11	11	11	10	13	13	16	16	1	3	5
Karen,	0	0	8	8	12	10	10	23		17	21	8	15	10	15	8	12	4	12	8	12	12	10	15	2	6	3
Singpho,	1	0	3	3	15	18	10	23	17		70	16	25	10	18	11	11	13	15	13	25	13	20	18	5	5	3
Jili,	1	0	10	10	15	11	13	26	21	70		22	16	10	21	13	11	11	18	20	20	13	20	20	3	1	0
Garo,	3	0	3	1	5	6	10	12	8	16	28		10	5	6	5	8	5	8	13	11	5	5	5	3	6	1
Manipuri,	1	0	3	3	11	15	11	16	15	25	16	10		21	41	18	25	28	31	28	35	33	40	50	6	5	3
Songpu,	1	0	1	1	3	6	0	8	10	10	10	5	21		35	50	53	20	23	15	15	13	8	15	6	3	3
Kapwi,	1	0	0	0	10	11	11	20	15	18	21	6	41	35		30	33	20	35	30	40	45	38	40	5	5	1
Koreng,	3	3	1	1	3	5	0	6	8	11	13	5	18	50	30		41	18	21	20	20	—	10	15	3	5	1
Maram,	1	1	0	0	8	8	3	11	12	11	11	8	25	53	33	41		21	28	25	20	16	23	26	3	5	1
Champhung,	0	0	0	0	8	6	5	11	4	13	11	5	28	20	20	18	21		40	20	20	16	15	25	3	3	0
Luhuppa,	1	0	0	0	8	8	6	11	12	15	18	8	31	23	35	21	28	40		63	55	36	33	40	5	6	3
Northern Tangkhul,	1	0	0	0	5	8	8	10	8	13	20	13	28	15	30	20	25	20	63		85	30	31	31	3	3	6
Central ditto,	1	0	0	0	6	8	6	13	12	25	20	11	35	15	40	20	20	20	55	85		41	45	41	1	6	3
Southern ditto,	3	1	0	0	10	10	13	13	12	13	13	5	33	13	45	11	16	16	36	30	41		43	43	5	3	0
Khoibu,	1	1	0	0	8	10	10	16	10	20	20	5	40	8	38	10	23	15	33	31	45	43		78	3	3	1
Maring,	3	3	0	0	10	18	8	16	15	18	20	5	50	15	40	15	26	25	40	31	41	43	78		3	5	1
Anamese,	0	0	5	5	0	0	1	1	2	5	3	3	6	6	5	3	3	3	5	3	1	5	3	3		3	3
Japanese,	1	1	1	1	1	1	3	3	6	5	1	6	5	3	5	5	5	3	6	3	6	3	3	5	3		5
Corean,	0	0	3	3	1	1	8	5	3	3	0	1	3	3	1	1	1	0	3	6	3	0	1	1	3	5	

SECTION I.—THE BUTIAS.*

Butan—General Outline and Physical Aspect—Rivers—Geology—Government—Revenue—Productive Industry—Lines of communication between Asam and Butan—Civil and Social Sate of the People.

The tract of country commonly known as Butan, extends from the southern declivities of the great central ridge of the Himalaya mountains, to the foot of the inferior heights, which form a *talus* at their base, and constitute the natural northern boundary of the Asam valley. These limits are comprised between the parallels of 26° 30′ and 28° of north latitude. In length Butan extends from about 88° 45′ to 92° 25′ of east longitude, and is therefore about 220 geographical miles long, and ninety broad; which would give an area of *nineteen thousand eight hundred* square geographical miles, for that portion included within the mountains and subordinate ranges of hills.

By far the greater portion of the Butan territory presents a succession of the most lofty and rugged mountains on the surface of the globe; and this general character of extreme ruggedness is scarcely interrupted, save by a few geological basins between the retiring flanks of the ranges, which may appropriately be termed Alpine glens. These glens are surrounded by mountains, which rise from three to eight and nine thousand feet above them. The more lofty ones are clad in perpetual snow, while the less elevated ridges are frequently sprinkled by the storms which expend their fury principally on the more towering peaks.

The rivers of this Alpine region, as might have been anticipated from its physical structure and varying elevation, are numerous and rapid, and rush over highly inclined beds, which, for the most part, are strewed with huge boulders of

* These remarks form a brief abstract of Captain Pemberton's Report on Butan.

primitive and secondary rocks, with a force that renders all the larger streams perfectly unfordable. They almost all flow from the southern face of the mural rampart which supports the elevated plains of Thibet, and struggling through the defiles at the foot of the mountains, eventually pour their tributary streams into the mighty channel of the Brahmaputra. The most considerable of these streams is said to be the Monass, which empties itself into the great river opposite Gowalpara.

The bold and generally rugged character of the Butan mountains, when viewed from the plains, strongly impresses a traveller with the conviction, that they are composed principally of the primitive and secondary rocks.* Captain Pemberton remarks—"a very great similarity is perceptible between the descriptions of the rock found in Kumaon and those we observed in Butan, the similitude extending not only to the order of succession, but to the mineralogical character of the rocks."

The secular head of the government of Butan is generally known as an officer called the Deb Raja; while the spiritual supremacy is vested in another individual, known as the Dhurma Raja, who, like the principal Lama of Thibet, is supposed to be a perpetual incarnation of the Deity.

The Deb Raja is chosen from among the principal officers of the country, who are eligible to seats in a council, which will be subsequently noticed. He is by the established laws of the country, permitted to hold this distinguished rank for a period not exceeding three years. Both these rules are, however, frequently violated; and the conditions which the theory of the government enjoins, becomes a dead letter in practice, whenever any aspirant after regal honours

* These terms are employed in their generally received sense, and without reference to the recent views of Geologists, which would class granite and gneiss among the more recent formations.

possesses the power which might render their enforcement dangerous or inconvenient.

The Dhurma Raja, like his great prototype of Lassa, is supposed to be Budh himself, clothed in human form, who by successive transmigrations from one corporeal frame to another, escapes the ordinary lot of humanity. On the death or temporary withdrawal of the Dhurma from the sublunary scene of his existence, his office remains vacant for a twelvemonth, during which time the senior Gylong or priest regulates the religious observances of the country. The first appearance of the Dhurma Raja is supposed to be indicated by the refusal of his mother's milk, and an evident preference for that of the cow. He is also supposed to be capable of articulating a few words distinctly, and of conveying his meaning by certain intelligible signs. The intelligence of these miraculous manifestations of precocious intellect is conveyed to the court, and a deputation, composed of some of the principal priests, proceeds to the spot where the young Dhurma is said to have appeared, conveying with them all those articles which in his former state of existence he had been in the habit of using. These are spread before him, mingled with a number of others purposely made to resemble them, with the innocent intention of testing the infallibility of the re-nate god. As might have been anticipated, the infant always proves victorious in this contest of skill. The priests declare their conviction, that he is their former spiritual head, and he is conveyed with great ceremony to the palace of Poonakha, at which place all installations must be made, either in the rank of Dhurma or Deb, to give them validity. During the time that Captain Turner's mission was in Butan, it appears that both the secular and spiritual authority were united in the same person, which though apparently opposed to the institutions of the country, was nevertheless acknowledged.

Subordinate to these heads of the government, are two

councils; the one more immediately under the authority of the Dhurma Raja is composed of the twelve principal Gylongs or priests, from among those who habitually live in the palace, and to control and direct whom in their religious and literary pursuits, is the ostensible object of the council. It has, however, in imitation of its no less sagacious prototype in Europe, contrived at various times to exercise a very efficient control over less spiritual objects.

The council of which the Deb is the head, though he seldom presides at its deliberations, is composed of six principal members. The governors of the western and eastern divisions of Butan are also entitled to seats in this council whenever they visit the capital, and even when residing on their own jurisdictions their opinions are consulted on every occasion of importance. Each of these governors also presides over a distinct council. These are the principal officers by whom the machinery of government, such as it is, is kept in motion, aided also by a few subordinates.

The authority exercised by the more important officers in their several jurisdictions is absolute, extending even to the infliction of capital punishment, without the necessity of a reference to a higher authority. The punishment of the most heinous offences may be evaded by the payment of a fine, which for murder varies from 80 to 200 Deba rupees.

The form of government is in itself, if fairly administered, quite sufficient to produce far more favourable results to the people than are now perceptible. But as the removal of officers occupying the most responsible situations is so frequent, and they receive no fixed salaries, every successor endeavours to amass as much property as possible, during his tenure of office, which he is aware is likely to be but of short duration; and as the removal of the superior is generally attended by the dismissal of every subordinate under him, the incentive to industrious peculating exists in every grade, and the unfortunate cultivator is the victim of a system, which not only affords no protection to the weak against the injustice of the powerful, but systematically deprives industry of the rewards of its labour.

In Butan, on the death of any head of a family, however numerous his children, the whole of his property becomes escheated to the Deb or Dhurma, without the slightest reference to the wide-spreading distress which a sudden deprivation of the means of subsistence may entail on the afflicted survivors. No ingenuity could possibly have devised a system better calculated to strike at the root of national prosperity than this; and though the social ties are in Butan probably less powerful than in any other country on earth, save Thibet, where similar causes produce like results; still even here it is felt as a heavy infliction, and all desire of making provision for a family is destroyed by the certainty that even a favourite child cannot hope to reap the rewards of his father's industry. It must be sufficiently evident, that a government which is conducted on such principles, can do little more than preserve itself from total dissolution.

The revenue contributed by the population of the hills, is almost entirely confined to the payment of a certain proportion of the produce of the lands in grain, whether of wheat, barley, or rice; of a quota of goats, sheep, *ghee*, fowls, and cloths, all of which are paid by the cultivators to their respective chiefs, and by them transmitted to the superior officers.

The total amount of revenue drawn from every source can hardly be estimated at two lakhs of rupees per annum; of this sum but a very small portion can be fairly considered available for any public exigency. The little wealth which does exist, flows only through channels which terminate in the palaces and castles of the powerful chieftains of the country. The coin which circulates in the country, is almost entirely confined to a silver one called "*deba*," nominally of the value of the Company's half rupee.

The productive industry of the country is, as may be expected, on the most limited scale. In some spots, more favoured by nature than others, the Butias have exhibited considerable care in the mode of terracing their fields, and in availing themselves of the localities best adapted to purposes of husbandry; these, however, the geological structure and physical aspect of the country, limit to comparatively few spots. The articles cultivated are wheat, barley, buckwheat, hemp, and turnips. In the lower ranges, the mustard oil plant, *Cytisus cajan*, and maize, with some of the more hardy varieties of peas, are also grown. A few stunted sugar-canes, the castor-oil plant, some betle vines, with a few orange trees, are occasionally met with on the lower ranges. The mountains are generally covered with woods of oak and rhododendrons, or with forests of pine and fir.

The hoe and plough are the only instruments used in husbandry—and the whole system of agriculture, such as it is, has apparently been derived from the plains. A good deal of ingenuity has been occasionally displayed by the Butias in the mode of conveying water for the irrigation of their fields, and for domestic use. Pipes and troughs formed of the hollowed trunks of trees and bamboos, supported on cross sticks, sometimes extend for a distance of nearly two miles from the centre of the village to the fountain head of a stream in the side of some distant mountain.

The manufacturing industry of this people is at a very low ebb. It is almost entirely limited to the coarsest descriptions of dark coloured blankets; the coloured varieties seen amongst them being brought from Thibet; coarse cotton cloths are made by the villagers inhabiting the southern portion of the country. Butter, or *ghee*, which hardly suffices for home consumption, is as extensively prepared as the limited number of cattle will permit. Small circular bowls are neatly turned from a variety of wood peculiar to the mountains. *Daws*, or straight swords, about three feet in length, spear and arrow-heads, and large copper caldrons, are formed from the metals procured in the hills. Paper, which is manufactured from the plant known as the *Daphne pappifera*, is remarkable for its extreme toughness, and from not being liable to the ravages of insects. If more extensively made, it might become a very valuable article of export. Leather is very imperfectly tanned from the hide of the buffalo or bullock, and is principally used as soles for the snow-boots, worn by both men and women in the winter; another softer variety, manufactured from goat and sheep skins, is principally used in making the small leather pouches, which are suspended from the side of every man in the country, of whatever rank. Pottery is almost entirely confined to the manufacture of cooking utensils. The Butia women, by whom it is carried on, evince a good deal of manual dexterity in the operation.

The trade carried on by Butan is almost entirely confined to Bengal, Asam, and Thibet. The exports to the latter place very little more than is procurable from the Duwars subject to her authority in Bengal and Asam; and of these articles, the cotton cloths, silks, dried fish, and rice of Asam, constitute the principal portion.

The communication with Asam is principally carried on by that class of Thibetans, commonly called Kumpas. This designation of Kumpa appears to be applied to those Butias who live in tents or temporary booths, and are employed in traffic, and are constantly travelling from one province to another.

The principal lines of communication between Asam and Butan are through the Duwars, or passes into the mountains. Of these there are seven comprised within the limits of Asam, two border on the division of Durung, and five on that of Kamrup. They are known by the following names, reckoning from east to west:—

In Durrung, ...	Buri-guma Duwar. Kallang Duwar.
In North Kamrup,	Ghurkola Duwar. Baksha, or Banska Duwar. Chapaguri Duwar. Chapakamar Duwar. Bijni Duwar.

The principal difference existing in the tenures by which these Duwars are held, consists in the fact, that the first two are held alternately by the British and Butan governments during the year; the former retaining jurisdiction from July to November, and the latter for the remaining eight months. The five Duwars adjoining Kamrup are, on the contrary, held exclusively by the Butias, and the British government exercise, no control at any period of the year in their internal management.* No satisfactory account has ever been afforded of the origin of this difference in the nature of the tenures by which the Duwars were obtained originally from the Asam, and subsequently from the British government; and though great are the inconveniences attending the former arrangement, it has notwithstanding been deemed expedient to suffer the continuance of a prac-

* The Asam Government, it appears, always maintained their right to these Duwars, even down to the latest date of the Asam dynasty. Thus Butias coming down to the Duwars, were always attended by the Asam Katakis, who took care that they exacted from the ryots nothing more than their fixed dues. No Butia coming into one Duwar was allowed to pass to another without the previous sanction of the Katakis; and besides, there were always certain men living in the Duwars, who were allotted for Police duties; these were subject only to the orders of the Bur Phukan, and were entirely exempt from Butia exactions. The rights of the British Government were, however, lost sight of in the last days of anarchy, owing to the ignorance that prevailed relative to the former management of these Duwars.

tice, which had been sanctioned by years of uninterrupted toleration.

East of Buriguma, is another Duwar called Kuriapara, which is held on precisely the same terms as the former, by the Towung Raja, a chieftain immediately dependent upon Lassa.

These eight Duwars would, it is supposed, under British management, realize a revenue of between sixty and seventy thousand rupees per annum; but under the existing system, they are not supposed to yield more than between eight and nine thousand; and this sum is annually becoming less, from the unabated perseverance in a system, which ceases to demand, only when the power to give is totally exhausted.

Influenced as the character of every people necessarily is by the nature of the institutions under which they live, that of the Butias, observes Captain Pemberton, must stand low indeed in the social scale. Every element of deterioration is comprised in their government, both secular and spiritual. Their energies are paralyzed by the insecurity of property, their morals are degraded, and their numbers reduced by the unnatural system of polyandry, and the extensive prevalence of monastic institutions; alike unfavourable to the creation of domestic sources of happiness, a feeling of love for country, or a desire for improvement. Yet under all these disadvantages, some redeeming traits of character do occasionally appear, and prove them to be still connected with the more elevated of their species, by the links of a common sympathy.

It is impossible to form any thing like an accurate estimate of the population of Butan. It may, however, be assumed at about 1,452,000 souls, including the inhabitants both of the hills and low lands.

The population is divided into eight principal and a few minor classes; the latter appear to derive their designations from their trades and occupations. In addition to these several tribes, all of whom are of pure or mixed Mongolian races, there are a vast number of Bengalees and Asamese, the *helots* of the country, who have been carried off at various times from the plains by the Butias, in their several incursions, and who lead a life devoted to the most menial and degrading offices.

The language spoken by the Butias is said to be a dialect of the Thibetan, more or less blended with words and idioms from the languages of the countries on which they severally touch.

Their religion is a form of Buddhism. In their religious observances the most remarkable circumstance is the noise with which they are accompanied. The instruments used are clarionets, sometimes formed of silver and brass, but generally of wood with reed pipes, horns, shells, cymbals, drums, and gongs.

The garments of the people consist of a long loose robe, which wraps round the body, and is secured in its position by a leather belt round the waist. A legging of broad cloth is attached to a shoe, made generally of buffalo hide; no Butia ever travels during the winter without protecting his legs and feet against the effects of the snow by putting these boots on, which are secured by a garter tied under the knee. A cap made of fur or coarse woollen cloth completes the habiliment, and the only variation observable is, the substitution of a cloth for a woollen robe during the summer months of the year.

The food of the superior classes consists of the flesh of goats, swine, and cattle, and rice imported from the Duwars. The mode of preparing their food is most inartificial and rude, with little attention to cleanliness, and still less to the quality of the meat they consume. They are very fond of tea, and use it in large quantities. The diet of the great body of people is the most miserable it is possible to conceive; they are restricted to the refuse of wretched crops of unripe wheat and barley, and their food consists chiefly of cakes made from these grains, very imperfectly ground. All classes are very much addicted to the use of inebriating liquors.

The amusements of the Butias are almost entirely confined to archery and quoits; their character seldom appears to greater advantage, than when engaged in these exercises.

SECTION II.—THE AKAS AND KAPACHORS.

Extent of their Territories—Descent—Language—Their present Chief.

The Akas and Kapachors occupy the hills between the country of Butan and a portion of the Durung frontier.

Very little is known of these rude tribes, more than that they are a warlike and ferocious people. Of their forms of government, and their manners and customs, we are alike ignorant.

The Kapachors are said to be of the same stock as the Akas, from whom they differ in few respects. They were separated into a distinct clan, about sixty or seventy years ago.

The Akas speak a language nearly allied to that of the Abors, half the words being found nearly alike in both the languages. One-fifth of the words agree with the Mishmis, and a considerable number with the Burmese, Singpho, and Manipuri.

The present chief of these tribes, known as the Taghi Raja, was once arrested for murder on our borders, and confined for some time in the gaol at Gowhatti. He was imprudently released on a supposition that he would in future prove a friend, owing to the good treatment he had received, and that his good-will would be further gained by the undeserved lenity shewn to him. But, as might indeed have been expected, far from evincing a sense of gratitude for his release, he remembered only the insults and disgrace to which he had been subjected, and has ever since proved an inveterate foe, constantly causing great alarm to the inhabitants on the frontier and whenever an opportunity offers plundering them of their property.

SECTION III.—THE DUPHLAS.

Extent of their Territories—Levy Black Mail—Various Clans—Duphlas on the lower Ranges mostly refugees from the Plains—Those in the interior little known—Asamese Slaves—Dress and Appearance—Manjit.

The Duphlas inhabit all the low ranges of hills from Koriapara eastward to the Subanshiri. To the west, they appear to mix with the Butias and Akas, and eastward with the Miris. They border on the districts of Noiduwar and Choiduwar, and have long been in the custom of levying black mail on all the bordering Asamese Mehals. Of late years they have proved very troublesome neighbours.

The Duphlas are said to be divided into various tribes, and each small division of the country is placed under the management of a separate Gam or chief.

Duphlas occupying the lower ranges appear to be composed chiefly of refugees from the plains, and from the villages on the northern mountains. It is to the tribes inhabiting the higher ranges, that the black mail is rightly due; but those on the lower hills have of late been accustomed to intercept the tribute, and in their attempts to exact and appropriate it, have involved themselves in hostilities both with the British government and the upper Duphlas. For the last three years, they have, been blockaded by a line of military posts on our frontier; but they have nevertheless frequently succeeded in levying black mail, and in committing fearful depredations on the villagers. Their atrocities were so unchecked on the north bank in Upper Asam, during the time Raja Purunder Sing held that portion of the country, that nearly the whole population had been obliged to desert their villages. Lately, however, by the able conduct and perseverance of the authorities, as well as by opening communications with the chiefs of the interior hills, whose intercourse with the plains had been almost entirely cut off, and by an active co-operation with them, the chiefs of the lower ranges have been compelled to pay due submission to the British authorities, and to desist from any gross acts of violence.

The Asam government seem to have looked upon the Duphlas occupying the lower ranges as their subjects, and, as it would appear, often had occasion to punish them for their misdemeanors. During Raja Gourinath's reign, the Burra Gohain is said to have ordered or caused an invasion of their hills, and to have brought down several thousand prisoners. They were condemned to dig a canal on the north bank of the Brahmaputra, with the view of carrying off the water of some of the large morasses, which still exist near Kullunpoor. In effecting this arduous undertaking, and that also during an unhealthy season of the year, from the heat of the climate, together with the bad treatment the prisoners were subjected to, the greater portion of them are said to have perished.

Of the interior of the hills occupied by the Duphlas, we know but little. From the information given by a few Asamese slaves, who have made their escape from the hills, it would appear, that the villages are large and numerous, that the inhabitants keep large flocks of cattle, and have large supplies of grain. The hills are said to be thickly covered with forests, and during the winter months the falls of snow are very heavy.

The chiefs in general possess a great number of Asamese slaves who have been captured from the plains, and who are for the most part kept to tend their cattle or to cultivate their fields. The males are strictly prohibited from marrying the Duphla women; but their masters usually contrive to steal away Asamese girls for them.

The ordinary dress of the Duphlas is usually very scanty. The women wear a vast profusion of silver ornaments round the neck, and, like the Garrow ladies, they overload the lobes of the ear with huge rings, until they reach down to the shoulder.

Both males and females are very sparely built, and appear as though they were badly fed. Their countenances are in general ugly, and their appearance somewhat ferocious. They are however exceedingly timid in their intercourse with British officers.

Manjit, which forms a considerable article of the trade of the Duphlas, grows in great abundance on their hills, and is there of a very superior quality.

SECTION IV.—THE MIRIS.

Chief Seat—their Hills little known—Connection with the Abors—Manners and Customs—Language—Trade—Independent Miris—Intended Embassy to their Hills.

The chief seat of the Miris appears to be the low hills north of Banskotta and Lakimpur, from whence they have spread themselves out into the plains at the foot of the hills, and emigrated in large numbers throughout Upper Asam.

Captains Bedford and Wilcox are the only officers who have penetrated into their hills, endeavouring to trace the Dihong river, and the knowledge they were able to glean respecting this tribe was very trifling.

The Abors look upon the Miris as their dependents, and have generally exacted from them a heavy tribute; to escape which, the latter have removed in large numbers into the plains of Asam. The Abor chiefs have constantly demanded that they should all be sent back; but as no compliance has been made to these repeated demands, the Miris have gained confidence in the British authorities, and are emigrating in still greater numbers.

The Miris have some villages on the banks of the Dihong, of which Matgong is the principal. Till of late years, their territories were almost deserted on account of the ravages of their formidable neighbours the Abors. Their vicinity continues to act as a great drawback upon the Miris. The only cultivations seen in their territories, are on the banks of the great river.

The manners and customs of the Miris are wild and barbarous; but they have also many redeeming qualities. They are a laborious and highly industrious people, and seem partial to living on the skirts of the forests, clearing new ground which they cultivate for a year or two, and moving elsewhere when the soil is exhausted.

They are expert marksmen, and bows and arrows are their only weapons. Their arrows are usually poisoned, and the poison used is so fatal, that even a scratch from them is followed with certain death.

Their language is a dialect of that of the Abors, and appears in all essential points the same.

The Miris in the plains employ themselves chiefly in growing opium, and as they always cultivate new lands, their fields in general yield them large returns. They seldom use the drug themselves but they make a very large profit by bartering it to the Asamese for grain and other necessaries. They also cultivate cotton to a large extent, and engage in a manufacture of cotton rugs, peculiar to themselves. Manjit (Indian madder,) is found in great abundance on their hills, and forms a staple article of trade.

The Miris in general rear a great number of pigs and poultry, and live comparatively in a very expensive style.

The only tribes of Miris that we know of, as being at all powerful and independent, are those inhabiting the hills on the banks of the Subansiri; but more particularly along its eastern side. Their Gam, or chief, comes down to the plains annually to receive presents from the British government, as well as to collect black mail from both Asamese and Miris, the latter of whom acknowledge his supremacy. He and the attendants who usually come down with him, are for the most part large muscular men, and somewhat above the common stature of the generality of hill people. The tribes subordinate to this chief have always conducted themselves with great propriety towards the subjects of Asam. Their power appears to be considerable, as by their own accounts a large tract of mountainous country belongs to them, and though constantly at war with the Bor-Abors, they are able successfully to maintain their independence.

It was at one time understood, that a mission under Dr. Griffiths was to have visited the mountains of this chief;

but other avocations led to the postponement of the intended expedition. The Miris are by no means so jealous of British influence as most of the neighbouring tribes, and as a better acquaintance with them would lead to a free intercourse, and to the extension of the trade between them and the natives of the plains, and thus be of mutual advantage to both parties, it is hoped government will shortly avail themselves of such means as will best insure these advantages; and probably none would better answer the purpose than a friendly embassy.

SECTION V.—THE ABORS AND BOR-ABORS.

Extent of their Territories—Government—Cane Bridges—Villages—Dress—Food—Trade—Settlers in the Plains—Friendly Disposition—Supposed Fidelity.

These tribes occupy an extensive range of mountainous country, along the southern exposure of the great Himalaya chain, extending from the 94th to the 97th degree of east longitude, and bordering on Thibet and China.

It is difficult to form a conjecture of the extent of these tribes; but that they are numerous, there can be no doubt. The only Abors that border on the valley, are about the Dibong and Dihong rivers; they live chiefly on the great ranges behind the Miris and Duphlas.

The Abors are divided into an endless number of clans, and each clan or village forms a democratical republic by itself, and is governed by the laws enacted by all the inhabitants in a formal meeting. This meeting is held in the morning, and every male has an equal vote. Here the reader cannot but notice the very singular coincidence between the political institutions of these people, and those of the inhabitants of the Alps in the country of the Grisons. Though not acknowledged by them, it is evident that among the Abors, as among the Grisons, some few, either through their superior wealth, hereditary esteem, or real ability, exert a very strong influence on the rest, and can readily sway them to any measure. It might be supposed, that this would greatly facilitate the gaining of any point at issue with the Abors; but the extreme jealousy of the people, and their vigilant watchfulness to preserve their democratical rights, render it a very difficult matter to win over these influential men. It is singular to observe in these people all those different shades of extreme rudeness and civilized observance of laws, enacted and allowed by them to be necessary for the good of the community.

While many others of the mountain tribes seem superior to the Abors in some points, very few are found equally ready for a labour like that of constructing cane suspension bridges, of which there are great numbers over the rapid torrents that intersect their mountains. The skill, as well as the labour shewn in the construction of these bridges is really surprizing, and is such, as would do no discredit to more civilized nations. The canes are passed over pegs in the supporting posts, and separately stretched and fastened to groups of trees at either end; these trees are in most instances so conveniently situated for making fast the canes, as to favour the supposition of their having been planted for the purpose. There are two good main suspenders to each bridge, and on these hang elliptical coils of cane at intervals of a few yards supporting the foot-way, which is not more than twelve or fourteen inches wide; the elliptics are further connected by canes running along the sides, protecting the passenger from the danger of falling; but, though considerable stability is thus given to the whole structure by connecting its several parts, there is still a very unpleasant swinging and waving during the passage. The span between the points of suspension is frequently from one hundred to one hundred and fifty feet.

An Abor village usually consists of a hundred houses or more, built near each other on a stony slope of easy ascent: the floor of each house is made of bamboos, supported on beams driven into the ground; and the space underneath is inhabited by the cattle. In the middle of the village is the *morang*, a large building which serves as a hall of audience and debate, as a place of reception for strangers, and as a house for the bachelors of the village generally, who by their laws are not entitled to the aid of the community for the construction of a separate dwelling. It is the usual practice with these young men, at the first dawn of day, to go the round of the place, warning sleepy folks that it is time for labours to commence. Their granaries are generally built apart from the village as a security against fire.

The dress of the Abors consists principally of a *suria*, (the Asamese name for a *dhoti*, the common dress of the natives of India), made of the bark of the *adál* tree. It answers the double purpose of a carpet to sit upon and of a covering. It is tied round the loins, and hangs down in loose strips about fifteen inches long, like a white bushy beard. It serves also as a pillow at night. The rest of their dress is apparently matter of individual taste; beads round the neck are not uncommon.* Some use plain basket caps, some have the cane caps partly covered with skins, and others ornament them with stained hair. The beak of the Buceros is a favourite and striking ornament of their caps; this on the top in front, and the red chowry tail flowing down behind, gives very much the appearance of a helmet, and on the whole resembles the head dress of the Singphos. During the winter almost every man has some article of woollen dress, varying from a rudely made blanket waistcoat to a comfortable and tolerably well-shaped cloak. All the more wealthy among them have cloaks of Thibetan woollens; and scarce a man is seen amongst them without some article of the manufacture of Thibet.

The Abors are armed respectably enough; every man has a bow and quiver of arrows, a number of which are poisoned.† They also carry light spears, or the short heavy *daw*, (sword) of the Singphos.

* The beads look exactly like turquoises, and have the same hue of greenish-blue; but a close examination discovers in them minute bubbles, marking the agency of fire; they are extremely hard, and when broken have exactly the fracture of Chinese porcelain.

† The Abors frequently kill buffaloes with their poisoned arrows. They track the beast which they have successfully wounded, knowing that he will not move far before the fatal effects of the deadly poison become visible; within half an hour the noble beast staggers and falls.

They are not particular in their diet, and eat the flesh of the elephant, rhinoceros, hog, buffaloe, kid, and deer, as well as ducks and fowls; but they abhor the use of beef. They exhibit a marked predilection for fermented liquors, and large quantities are usually drank at their feasts.

Though the snows of their mountain home have narrowed their means of subsistence, and limited their intercourse to their immediate neighbours, yet they are a hospitable, and even a social race; their feasts are frequent, and all their associates are invited to partake of the good cheer; the host is in his turn a guest at the next feast, and thus a reciprocity of entertainment is insured. Nor are these hospitable rights allowed to be forgotten; the skull of every animal that has graced the board, is hung up as a record in the hall of the entertainer; he who has the best stocked Golgotha, is looked upon as the man of the greatest wealth and liberality; and when he dies, the whole smoke-dried collection of many years is piled upon his grave, as a monument of his riches and a memorial of his worth.

The trade of the Abors consists chiefly in manjit, ivory, and woollens. They also bring down occasionally a few fine large-woolled sheep, and white kid skins very neatly tanned. It appears very probable that they have a ready communication with Thibet.

Some Abors have lately settled at the foot of the hills in the district of Sadiya, where they have apparently been driven to the necessity of cultivating the fields by the desertion of the Miris, who formerly inhabited that tract of country, and were looked upon by the Abors, as their slaves and dependents.

Many of the Abor villages between the Dihong and Dibong have lately been visited by the British troops, when in pursuit of the Khamti insurgents, who in the beginning of 1839 made an attack on Sadiya. The Abors, however, appear to have maintained a strict neutrality, and conducted themselves with more propriety than might have been expected from a rude people, tempted by so powerful a party as the Khamtis in the plunder of our frontier districts; more especially as the Abors conceived themselves injured by the British government in its refusing to surrender the Miris, who have effected their escape from the authority of the Abors, and sought an asylum in our territories.

The Abors were always looked upon as the allies of the ancient Asamese government; and it is said that a large body of them, to the amount of 20,000 or 30,000, came down to assist the Bura Gohain in repelling the Moamarias, who were then devastating all the country east of Jorehat.

SECTION VI.—MISHMIS AND BOR-MISHMIS.

Hills occupied by them—various Clans—Acknowledge a common origin with the Abors—Language—the People—their Dress—Religion—Laws—Houses—Domestic Animals—Cultivation—Cane Bridges—Trade—Acknowledged Allegiance to the British Government—The Lama Country.

The Mishmis occupy those ranges of low hills that form the north-eastern boundary of the valley of Asam. Like most other tribes, they are divided into numerous clans: the principal are the Mai-Mishmis, the Taron or Digaru-Mishmis, and the Maiyi or Meme Mishmis. They acknowledge a common origin with the Abors. Their language is distinguished by several very peculiar tones, and some of its consonants are extremely difficult of enunciation. In this respect it differs from the language of the Abors, the sounds of which are easy and flowing.

The people are a small, active, hardy race, with the Tartar cast of features, and are in general excessively filthy. Their clothing is very inferior; it is made of cotton, and is of their own manufacture. The dress of the labouring men consists of a single strip of coarse strong cloth, which is as narrow as its purpose possibly permits. On occasions of ceremony, they wear a shirt which comes half way down the thigh, and is made of a straight piece of blue and red striped cloth, doubled in the middle, the two sides sown together like a sack, leaving space for the exit of the arms at the top, and a slit in the middle, which is formed in the weaving, admits in like manner the passage of the head. The hair is turned up and tied in a small knot on the crown, and this custom serves to distinguish them from the Dibong Mishmis, whom they always designate "crop haired." A narrow belt of skin over the right shoulder sustains a large heavy knife with its sheath. This knife serves for all purposes of agriculture and domestic economy.

The other apparatus appertaining to dress, consists of a broader belt worn across the left shoulder, carrying both before and behind plates of brass; these are of four or five inches diameter, and beaten in a curved or spherical form; they appear to be used rather as ornaments than for purposes of utility. A pouch of monkey's skin at the girdle is also suspended to a belt, containing tobacco, the small pipe, and the case for flint and tinder, armed on one side with a strong steel. A pipe either rudely made of bamboo or furnished with a brass bowl, imported from China through the intervention of the Lamas, is scarcely ever out of their mouths; the women, and even children of four or five years of age, are equally partakers of this luxury. The pipes of Chinese manufacture are frequently engraved with an inscription which signifies, "Made at the shop of ——— should it prove bad, please to bring it back to the maker, who will exchange it."

Most of the men carry cross-bows; the arrows for these are short, made of bamboo, and on all serious occasions are invariably poisoned. When on fighting expeditions, they use shields made of leather, which are covered towards the centre with the quills of the porcupine. Their lances are used only for thrusting; the shafts are made either from the wood of the lawn, (Caryota urens,) or that of another species of palma, *juce*. The lance-heads are of their own manufacture, and of very soft iron. Their swords are of Chinese manufacture, very long, perfectly straight, and of equal breadth throughout.

The chiefs generally use long cloaks of Thibetan woollens, or handsome jackets of the same, usually dyed red or striped with many colours. Their head dress is not remarkable; in the fields it is merely a hemispherically-shaped cap of split cane; but at home, they prefer to wear a red strip of muslin, encircling the head as a turban. Their ear-rings differ according to their wealth; those most esteemed, (and when the lobes of the ears have been sufficiently extended,) are formed of a cylinder of thin plate silver, tapering to the centre, and varying from an inch to an inch and a half in diameter.

The wives of the chiefs are habited in petticoats brought from the plains; they wear a profusion of beads, frequently a dozen strings or more, and when they are of a sort of white porcelain, which is often the case, their equipment must weigh at least ten pounds; other necklaces are of colourless glass, mixed with oblong pieces of coarse cornelian, and all of Thibetan or Chinese manufacture. The ornament of the head is a plate of silver as thin as paper, gore-shaped, and long enough to cross over the forehead.

Both sexes make use of liquor; but they do not seem to be so addicted to it as is generally the case with the other hill tribes.

Women, both young and old, mix with the men in the performance of every kind of labour, except hunting. The people live in a very promiscuous manner, so many as one hundred being occasionally accommodated in a single house.

Of the religion of the Mishmis we have no satisfactory information. Their invocations to their sylvan deities are frequent, and seem generally to be made with the view of filling their own stomachs with animal food. Whenever illness or misfortune of any kind visits them, a sprig of a plant is placed at the door to inform strangers that the house is under a ban for the time, and that it must not be entered, and sacrifices of fowls and pigs are offered to their deities.

Their laws appear to be simple; all grave crimes being judged by an assembly of Gams or chiefs, who are on such occasions summoned from great distances. All crimes, including murder, are punished by fines; but if the amount is not forthcoming, the offender is cut up by the company assembled; but the crime of adultery, provided it be committed against the consent of the husband, is punished by death; and this severity may perhaps be necessary, when we take into account the way in which they live.

Their houses resemble a good deal those of the Singphos, and are of variable size, according to the rank of the possessor. They are all built on *machans* or stages, are constructed almost entirely with bamboos, divided into compartments, and thatched with the leaf of a marontaceous plant, (arrow-root family,) likewise found in Asam; this being again covered, at least in some instances, with the leaves of a species of ratan. The leaf of the former answers its purpose admirably, both as to neatness and durability, and forms an excellent protection against the rain. In each apartment there is a square fire-place, consisting merely of earth, about which the bamboos are cut away. As no exit for the smoke is allowed, the air of the interior is dense and oppressive, and often exceedingly painful to the eyes. On the right side of the house the skulls and jaw-bones of the various cattle killed during the possessor's life time, are arranged.

Their live-stock consists chiefly of hogs, *mithuns,* (a noble and fine looking animal, intermediate between the bull and buffalo) and fowls. Of these hogs are the most common, and they are easily procurable; but they are averse to parting with their fowls, which they say is the favourite food of the deity. Their dogs are of the ordinary *pariah* kind; cats are uncommon.

Their cultivation is scanty, apparently not sufficient to supply even their wants, and carried on in a very rude way. The most favourable places are of course selected, either on the slopes of hills, or on the occasionally more level patches, and adjoining the river. The soil in almost all cases consists of a thin super-stratum of vegetable mould. Some of the villages are in possession of a good sort of hill rice; but the chief articles of cultivation are *bobasa,* (elintine cara-cana,) *gumdhan*, or Indian corn, *khonee*, (Dave spec.) and two or three more inferior grains. The villages situated at low elevations produce excellent yams, and arums of various kinds. They are unacquainted with wheat, barley, &c; nor have they even taken the trouble to procure potatoes. A small quantity of opium is cultivated principally for the purpose of selling it to the Singphos, although many of the natives themselves use it to a great extent. They cultivate a sufficient quantity of cotton for the manufacture of their own clothing, but it seems to be of inferior quality. Tobacco is in great request, but it is not regularly cultivated.

The produce of their fields is kept in small granaries, at some distance from their houses; and it is a regulation calculated to prevent quarrels, that each wife (for polygamy is allowed) has her distinct granary.

Their cane bridges are rather awkward for those not accustomed to them. A stage is erected at a considerable height above the water on either bank, and well secured with large stones and canes, made fast to the neighbouring trees; the three canes composing the suspending rope pass over well-secured supports on the stages at either end, and are separately fastened to trees, so that were one of them to fail, two would still remain. Before the stages a number of loops hang ready for use; they are made of long canes coiled like a roll of wire. The passenger inserts his hands and shoulders through two or three of these, and brings them under the small of his back; he then, or some one for him, secures the loop with great care to a waist band contrived for the purpose on the instant, and generally the spear put through the knot helps the security of the fastening, then throwing his heels over the cane, he launches forth on his adventurous passage. The weight of the body altering the curve, which so large a cane must necessarily have, however well stretched, causes him to descend at first with some rapidity, in which the hands are used rather to arrest the progress; towards the middle he is master of his own pace, and when hanging there, the cane is considerably bent from the horizontal line; now the hands are used to drag the body gradually up the inclined rope, progress goes slower as he advances, and when near the goal he appears so fatigued, that between each tug he makes a long pause. Accidents are seldom known to occur; and the canes are renewed at least every three years.

With the Lama country the Mishmis carry on an annual trade, which apparently takes place on the borders of each country. In this case, a kind of vegetable poison, *bish*, is the staple article of the Mishmis, and for it they obtain *daws*, or straight long swords of excellent metal, and often of great strength; copper pots of strong but rough make; flints and steel, or rather steel alone, which are very neat and good; warm woollen caps; huge glass beads, generally white or blue; coarse loose party-coloured woollen cloths; various kinds of cattle, in which the Lama country is represented as abounding; and salt, which is (in bulk) of a reddish colour, from being mixed up with a red earthy substance, somewhat aromatic.

With the Singphos the Mishmis barter elephants' teeth; (these animals being found in great abundance in the lower ranges of their hills,) for slaves, *daws*, and buffaloes.

With the Khamtis they appear to carry on little or no trade, though it is said that at one time they paid the Khamtis an annual tribute. With the inhabitants of the plains they engage in an extensive traffic, exchanging cloths, Lama swords, spears, *mishmi tita*, which is in very great request as a valuable febrifuge, and *gertheana*, a vegetable production much esteemed by the natives for its peculiar and rather pleasant smell, (it is used chiefly in anointing the hair,) for money, cloths, salt, and beads.

The Mishmis on the banks of the Brahmaputra have always acknowledged allegiance to the Asamese government, and during the cold season have been in the habit of visiting Sadiya in great numbers. Their hills have been visited by Captain Wilcox, and more recently by Dr. Griffiths, who found them very friendly, and willing to assist him in travelling to any part of their country. Shortly before Dr. Griffiths' visit to their hills, a party of Tartar soldiers had come across the hills armed with matchlocks, to assist in some war of one Mishmi chief against another, which tends to shew the degree of communication kept up between the Mishmis and the Lama country.

It is owing chiefly to their proximity to the Lamas that the country of the Mishmis, as being the most feasible route thither in this direction, is worthy of attention.

The Lamas occupy a small, but highly cultivated valley to the north of the Mishmi range; they are tributary to Lassa, and from all accounts, appear to be a very superior race. They are described as resembling the Chinese, whose peculiar manner of wearing the hair they adopt. Their country is very populous; the towns are all enclosed with massive stone walls, the houses are well built, and of Chinese design, and the people are well supplied with grain, the staple sort being rice. The men are of a large stature, well clothed, wearing Chinese trowsers and shoes, navigating their rivers by means of boats, and using horses, of which they possess three varieties, as beasts of burden. Their manufactures, which are numerous, are said to be very superior. They shew a determined resistance to all ingress into the interior of their country, and though a few Hindusthani *faquirs*, (mendicants,) have occasionally proceeded as far as their first town, and been treated by them with great civility, they have invariably been turned back.

SECTION VII.—THE KHAMTIS.

Descent—Political History—Language—Religion—Manners and Customs—Silver Mine—Muluks—Kujungs—Khunungs.

The next border tribes we meet with are the Khamtis. They are descended from the Bor-Khamtis, or those of the higher ranges, a powerful race, situated about the sources of the Irawadi.

On their first emigration from their native hills, they obtained permission from the Raja of Asam to establish themselves on the banks of the Tenga-pani, from whence they made several successful irruptions into Sadiya during the troubled reign of Raja Gourinath. They at length ejected the reigning chieftain, the Sadiya, Kowa-Gohain, and the Khamti chief usurping his title and jurisdiction, and reduced his subjects to dependence or slavery. The Asamese finding they could not repel the Khamtis, allowed their chief to retain the title he had assumed,—one of the highest in the kingdom,—and to govern the district of Sadiya on the part of the Asamese government.

Until the late insurrection against the British government, the Khamtis possessed many very flourishing villages around Sadiya, and appeared to be a happy people; but the ambition of two or three chiefs involved the whole in rebellion, and that district has now been entirely deserted by them; the greater part of the population having removed to Domadji.

The immediate causes of the insurrection have not been ascertained, for just at that juncture it was supposed the people had nothing to complain of: it may however be traced to the loss of political authority. The Khamti chiefs had reduced the Asamese portion of the community to the condition of serfs and slaves, and the real cause of dissatisfaction may in all probability have originated in the restoration of the Asamese to those privileges of which they had been deprived.

The Khamtis are considerably advanced in civilization, and are amongst the few tribes who have a written character. Their alphabet is evidently derived from the Burmese, while their language more closely resembles that spoken by the Siamese; nine-tenths of the fundamental words in these two dialects are the same, with but slight variations in the pronunciation, and these are confined to a few letters. Their grammatical construction is the same, and the syntactical arrangement of words is for the most part as in English.

The religion of the Khamtis is Buddhism, and their customs appear precisely the same as those of Ava. Their priests every morning hurry through the village or town, preceded by a boy with a little bell, each priest holding a lacquered box, in which he collects the offerings of the people, presented generally by the women, who stand waiting at their respective doors with a portion of their ready cooked meal.

The first appearance of the Khamti houses usually excites the surprise of those who are not accustomed to their style of building; the floor on which the family live, is completely hid under the low projecting eaves, and all that appears to view is the open and dirty ground floor, crowded with buffaloes and pigs.

Few of the women boast of much beauty; they are in general plainly dressed, and make a very neat appearance. The men turn up their hair, and form a large knot with it on the centre of the head; the women, either from the natural profusion of their tresses, or from their taking more care of them, far excel the men in the height of their topknots, which they wear nearly in the same fashion; but divide it with silver ornaments and small glass beads. Their petticoats accord better with our notions of female delicacy, than the odd dress of Burman ladies.

It is a singular custom amongst the Khamtis, that the principal amusement of their chiefs is working in metals; in which, practice renders them infinitely more skilful than the lower classes, who perhaps cannot spare much time from their labours in the fields. They readily employ themselves in fashioning ear-rings for the purpose of barter, the workmanship giving a double value to the silver. A couple of hammers and a few punches are all the tools requisite, and these they carry with them in their travelling bag. The silver is melted and poured into the hollow of a bit of bambu, when repeatedly heating it, it is beat with great patience and perseverance into plates almost as thin as paper; by a proper management of the hammer, they make it spread in the required direction till long enough to bend into a cylinder; the edges are then cut even with a pair of scissors, and the parts to be soldered are notched in a castellated form, the alternate projections inserted, and a little borax with a very thin bit of plate laid over the joint, which the application of a little heat readily unites; a curve is then given to the sides of the cylinder, when the top only is required to finish it. The top is of course a circle, and when beat thin enough, it is laid on a bed of lac softened by heat, and with blunt punches an embossed pattern is then given; both the silver and lac being repeatedly heated to prevent the latter from becoming brittle, and to soften the former sufficiently to cause it to assume readily the indentations of the punch. In this way, with the aid of sharper punches and some of small size, very pretty patterns are often given. The ordinary silver pipes of the Khamtis are of very neat workmanship.

There is a silver mine in the Bor-Khamti country, but it has never produced more than 8,000 rupees a year. It might be turned to much advantage, but the possessors are afraid of increasing its revenue, lest by doing so, they should excite the avarice of their neighbours.

There are several tribes of Khamtis on the higher ranges of the hills; but our information respecting them is very scanty.

The Muluks are said to be a distinct tribe, and their language to have no affinity with that of any neighbouring tribe. This appears very remarkable, as their number is reckoned at about five hundred houses. In former times, they are said to have been an independent people, inhabiting the plains of Hupong on the Dihing river, south of the Phungan pass. They declare, that they were plundered and dispersed by the Singphos, and that one-half of their number were carried off, and made dependent on these marauders, while the other half fled towards the Irawadi, and placed themselves under the protection of the Khamtis. Their dress is the same as that worn by the Khamtis, except that it is of ruder fashion and of inferior texture.

There is another tribe about Sadiya, known as the Kujungs; but we are ignorant in what respect they are distinguished from the Muluks. The Kujungs it appears, were made acquainted with the intended attack of the Khamtis on the lines at Sadiya, and unwilling to unite in their aggressions, the whole tribe withdrew from their villages during that eventful night. The Muluks also on that occasion, shewed their fidelity to the British government, and their chief, on refusing to join the Khamtis, was barbarously murdered.

The Khunungs inhabit the lower mountains beyond the Irawadi, and also a poorer and more savage race than those of the higher ranges. The former supply the Khamtis with salt, and possess the art of forging the *daws*, or swords, so much in request; the latter are scarcely known by name, and are said to be a wild and savage race.

SECTION VIII.—THE SINGPHOS.

Boundaries — Irruptions — altered Habits — Tribes — Classes — Language — Religion — Funeral Rites — Polygamy — Inheritance — Khakoos — their Territories — Cultivation — Manners and Customs — Burmese Singphos.

The Singphos are by far the most powerful tribe bordering on the valley. They are also the most numerous, and are scattered over the greatest extent of country. On the north, they are bounded by that branch of the Brahmaputra known as the Lohit; on the east, by the Langtang range, which separates them from the Bor-Khamtis; on the south by the Patkoi range, which divides them from the Burmese Singphos, from whom they derive their descent; and on the west, by an imaginary line drawn south from Sadiya till it meets the last mentioned mountains.

The Singphos have for several generations been the terror of the Asamese. They were in the constant habit of making irruptions into the plains, in conjunction with the Moamarias or Muttuks, by whom they appear to have been first called into Asam. They sometimes proceeded as far as the very capital itself, plundering the temples, laying waste the country, and carrying off the inhabitants into slavery. These several irruptions have won for them the low lands they now occupy. Since the British troops have had possession of the valley, these inroads have been prevented; but, impatient of such restraint, these wild people have nevertheless occasionally endeavoured to resort to their old habits. The peace of the neighbourhood has constantly been disturbed by deadly feuds amongst themselves. Their principal quarrels have arisen from a feud between the Beesa Gam, on the one side, and the Duffa Gam, now of some political notoriety, on the other. This feud has been the cause of dividing almost all the Singphos on the frontier; and even those Singpho tribes bordering on China have been involved in the hostilities to which this feud has given rise.

Latterly, however, feeling the necessity of submitting to a power which has so nearly approached them, and whose strength they now perceive they cannot resist, they have shewn an inclination to abandon their old habits of lawlessness and rapine, and to turn their attention to agriculture, now become necessary for their subsistence. The altered habits of this rude but energetic race, may confidently be expected not only to shed its influence on their own commercial resources; but likewise to extend great advantages to the future prospects of Asam. The emigration that may be expected from the misrule now prevailing in the Shyan states of Ava; the opening prospects of abundant comfort to themselves, arising from the protection of a powerful government in Asam; and the means of wealth held out to them, from the fortunate discovery, and the increasing cultivation, of that singular and highly valuable plant, which Providence has been pleased to bestow in such luxuriance on this province, are but a few of the many advantages that may be looked for, from the gradual amelioration of these people.

The Singphos bordering on Asam are said to be divided into twelve principal tribes or clans, designated after the names of their respective chiefs, or Gams. Every chieftain maintains his own separate independence, and seldom unites with any other, unless it be to punish some aspiring chief obnoxious to them all, or to make plundering excursions upon some neighbouring states. The principal clans are the Beesa Gam, Duffa Gam, Luttao Gam, and Luttora Gam; though these can exercise no powerful authority over the other Gams, their influence is acknowledged to be very considerable.

Rude as is the state of society among the Singphos, they are not without a few aristocratical distinctions. The people in general are divided into four classes, called respectively, Shangai, Myung, Lubrung, and Mirip.*

The language of the Singphos possesses many words in common with the Abor, the Burmese, and the Manipuri dialects. The intonations are similar to the Burmese, and its grammatical construction is almost precisely the same. It is peculiar for its combination of consonants, many of which would at first sight appear quite unpronounceable to a European. It doubtless belongs to the monosyllabic stock of languages.

The Singphos have no religion properly their own; but have patched up a creed from amongst the superstitions of all their neighbours, and decorated their rude temples with ruder idols of all religions.†

It is the custom of the country to bury the dead. Those of the poorer classes are interred soon after death; but the chiefs and principal individuals are sometimes not buried for years. The reason alleged for this consummation of the funeral rites is, to allow the widely scattered relations of the deceased to have time to attend, who would not fail to take deadly offence at being deprived of an opportunity of paying reverence to the ashes of the head of their family. Not knowing the art of embalming, the body after death is removed to a distance from any habitation, till decomposition is completed; after that, it is deposited in a coffin, and conveyed to the house of a deceased chief, where it lies in state, surrounded with all the insignia the illustrious individual enjoyed when alive. When all the relatives have assembled, or communicated their not being able to attend, the coffin is committed to the earth, and a mound of clay, surrounded with a curious trellis work of bamboos, is raised to his memory. If the person has died a violent death, a buffalo is sacrificed as a propitiation to their deities, and

* Vide M'Cosh's Topography of Asam.

† Vide M'Cosh's Topography of Asam.

the head of the animal is fixed to two crossed bamboos and placed near the grave; but if he has died in the course of nature, no sacrifice is considered necessary.*

Polygamy is admitted by the laws of the country, and every man keeps as many wives as he chooses, free women or slaves; and treats the offspring of both kinds without partiality.†

According to the law of inheritance, the patrimony is divided between the eldest and the youngest son; while any children that may intervene, are left to push their own fortunes as they best can. The eldest son succeeds to the title and estate, while the youngest, carrying away all the personal and moveable property, goes in quest of a settlement for himself.‡

A tribe of Singphos, known as the Khakoos, are said to occupy a valley bounded to the N. E. by the Mishmi mountains, and to the S. W. by the Mimboom range. The valley is of a triangular form, and not of any great extent; it is drained by the Tenga-pani. It is on the whole comparatively high, and may be considered as a low table land; it is incomparably the finest part of the territories inhabited by the Singphos, and, whatever may be the case with the other portions of the Singpho territories, this valley is very populous, and in a highly flourishing condition.

The chief cultivation of the valley consists of *ahu dhan*, the fields of which are numerous and extensive.

The manners and customs of the Khakoos are the same as those of the other Singphos; they are, however, represented as excelling them in treachery and cruelty. They are looked upon as a servile race, and every Singpho Gam, great or small, has his corresponding clan of Khakoos.

The Singphos of Asam are separated from the Singphos

* M'Cosh's Topography of Asam.

† M'Cosh's Topography of Asam.

‡ M'Cosh's Topography of Asam.

subservient to Burma, by the Patkoi chain of mountains. Though these two races are entirely unconnected with each other, and independent as far as concerns their respective connection with the two great paramount powers governing on either side of the mountains, yet a constant friendly intercourse is maintained between them. The Burmese Singphos occupy a very extensive tract of country on both sides of the Irrawadi, from the Patkoi mountains eastward, to the borders of China.

SECTION IX.—NAGA TRIBES.

Boundaries and Extent—Origin of the Appellation—Original Descent—Imperfect knowledge of the Tribes—Missionaries to the Nagas—Manipur—Naga Tribes—Those in communication with Asam—Salt Wells—Connection with the Government of Asam—Angami Nagas—Civil and Social State—Condition of the Women—Agriculture—Vegetable and Mineral Productions—Wars—Dress—Habitations—Amusements—Religion—Funeral Rites.

The next border tribes that come under our notice, are the Nagas. That large extent of mountainous country, bounded on the west by the Kopili river, the great southern bend of the Barak, and the eastern frontier of Tipperah, in nearly east long. 83°; on the north by the valley of Asam; on the east and south-east by the hills dividing Asam from the Bor-Khamti country in long. 97°, and the valley of the Kyendrens; and on the south by an imaginary line, nearly corresponding with the 23rd degree of north latitude, is inhabited by numerous tribes of highlanders, known to the Asamese, Bengalees, and Manipuris, by the general name of Nagas, and to the Burmese by the term of Kakhyens.

The origin of the word Naga is unknown; but it has been supposed by some to have been derived from the Sanskrit word नग्न, and applied in derision to the people, from the paucity of their clothing; but there seems little foundation for this etymological derivation, as the term has never been known to be applied by the Bengalees to either the Khassias or Garos, with whom they were far better acquainted than with the Nagas; and besides, the Garos especially are habitually accustomed to a greater degree of nudity than any of the Naga tribes with whom we are acquainted. Whatever be the origin of the word Naga, it appears that the appellation is entirely unknown to any of the hill tribes themselves. The inhabitants of these hills are divided into numerous communities or races; and they know themselves by the designations of their respective tribes only, and not by any name common to all the races.

There, however, appears to be some mark by which these tribes are distinguished from their neighbours, and some common ties by which they are all bound together as one people, though possibly at present divided into tribes by a diversity of dialects. In all probability, this common tie may have descended to all the present tribes, from the great aboriginal stock by which the hills were first peopled. Other races may from time to time have entered, and taken refuge in the hills, bringing with them their own dialects; but they may have probably amalgamated with the old stock in habits and manners, and above all, in religious superstitions; and these last especially, may form the great connecting link of all the Nagas, and the cause of separation from other hill tribes.

Though constantly at war amongst themselves, and using dialects so different that two adjoining tribes cannot converse together, except through the medium of a third dialect common to both; yet they are said to intermarry and form connexions and alliances with each other, which they do not do with tribes not belonging to the Naga community.

The Nagas also appear in general to be distinguished from their neighbours by physical conformation; for though there is much difference in this respect amongst them, yet they are in common, remarkable for extremely coarse, savage countenances, and dull, timid, heavy dispositions.

In some of their habits, all these tribes have a common resemblance. They are, moreover, all distinguished by their weapons, which consist solely of javelins or spears.

So little is known of the dialects of the Nagas, that our present information will not permit us, from this source, to form any judgment respecting their descent. From the apparent diversity in their languages, it may with probability be inferred, that many of the tribes have not sprung from one common origin. And further researches may yet prove, that while a number of the Naga tribes have emigrated from the north-west borders of China, probably during the sanguinary conflicts for supremacy, which took place between the different members of the Chinese and Tartar dynasties in the thirteenth and fourteenth centuries, others may from like political causes, have been driven into the fastnesses of these hills from Asam and Bengal, and brought with them languages very different from each other. Thus whilst some of the tribes may have dialects derived from a common source, others speak languages of a perfectly distinct stock.

A more general acquaintance with the people, and a more diligent attention to their languages, it is hoped, will not long be wanting to throw light on these interesting races. Already have two or three members of the American Baptist Board of Foreign Missions established themselves on the Naga hills, and have become so far acquainted with the language of the tribe amongst whom they have located themselves, (the Namsangiyas,) as to have been able to get up a few elementary books in that dialect, and to open a school for the education of the children. To the perseverance of these exemplary men, in the great cause to which they have devoted their lives, we shall soon be indebted for much and valuable information regarding the Naga tribes in general, and the products of the hills which they inhabit. It is further to be hoped, that by the blessing of Divine Providence, through the efforts of these excellent men, the Nagas, who from time immemorial have been the scorn and the prey of their more civilized neighbours may shortly begin to emerge from that dark barbarism which now renders the tribe of each hill an enemy to that of the next, and has hitherto prevented an Alpine tract of great natural resources and high fertility, from supporting more than a very scanty population of savages, in a state of discomfort and privation.

Within the boundaries specified as being occupied by the Nagas, is situated the rich and fertile valley of Manipur. It rests at an elevation of 2,500 feet above the sea; its extreme length is about thirty-six miles, and average breadth eighteen. The Manipuris who inhabit this valley, are not generally supposed to be connected with the great family of the Nagas. We have, however, no certain information that the Manipuri language bears no resemblance to that of any of the Naga tribes, and the probability is, that more minute researches will discover some traces of an affinity between them. The Rev. Mr. Brown of Jaipur, is of opinion, that there are some traces of a connection between the language of Manipur and that spoken by the Singphos.

The Manipuris have a written language, and are in all respects far more advanced in the state of civilization than any of the Naga tribes; which may in a great measure be owing to the advantage of their locality admitting of regular cultivation, and affording the necessary means of supporting its population in comparative comfort.*

There are but a few of the great divisions of the Naga tribes known to us; these are the Koong-juees, inhabiting the hills SW. of Manipur; the Marams to the NW.; the Laohoopas and Ungkools to the NE. and E.; and the Angamis north of the same valley. We are, however, uncertain whether these terms are correctly applied to any of these confederated tribes, or acknowledged by the people themselves.

The Nagas connected with Asam are those occupying the northern faces of the mountains now alluded to, and whose streams fall into the Bramahputra; these all pass

* For further information respecting the Manipuris, and the capabilities of their country, the reader is referred to Pemberton's Report on the North-eastern frontier.

under the general name of Nagas, while those situated on the higher ranges, are known as the Abors, or Abor Nagas.

The Nagas on the lower ranges are exceedingly jealous of the profits arising from their connexion with the province, and there is nothing which they more strenuously oppose, than the communication of the interior Nagas with the markets frequented by them; and the wish to prevent any interchange of a direct barter by the Abors with the inhabitants of Asam, has been the cause of constant wars between them. This spirit of jealousy prevails throughout all these hills, and while the Abors are debarred from access to the markets of Asam, the Nagas of the northern hills are prevented from trading with Ava or Manipur.

East of the river Namsang, and between it and the boundary of Asam, are several small Naga communities, who are now almost reduced to the state of slaves by the more powerful Singphos, by whom they appear to be greatly oppressed. Of late, however, the progress of our paramount authority has interposed for their relief. We are not aware, whether any Nagas are found further east; but it seems probable, that the Khunungs, who inhabit those mountains whence the Irrawadi takes its rise, may also be Nagas, though this general term is not applied to them.

Among those Naga tribes in communication with Asam, and who deserve more particular notice, are the Namsangiyas, the Borduriays or the Borduwarias, and the Panidawarias. These tribes are in possession of brine springs of considerable value, and further, were always supposed to pay allegiance to the Rajas of Asam.

The circumstance of the Asam government having always raised a revenue from the imported salt of the hills, and the dependence of the Nagas on the Asam markets for the exchange of salt for grain and other articles, has contributed to a mutual good understanding between the two people. The Naga hills have in consequence been always accessible to the people of the plains; whilst the Nagas have on their part, been always permitted access to the markets on the frontier.

The taxes that have been till lately levied on the Naga salt have been exceedingly heavy, and the manner in which they were imposed, led to numerous exactions on the part of the tax-gatherers. The individuals appointed to the collection of the taxes were in attendance at the springs on the hills, as well as the markets below, and tolls were levied by them both on the salt itself, and on the articles the Nagas obtained in barter for the salt.

Lieutenant Brodie, now in charge of the Sibpur district, finding the old system very oppressive to the people, abolished all the duties to which they were subject, that on the salt excepted. The tax now levied upon it consists in kind. The present receipts amount to 652 maunds 38 seers and 11 chittacks of salt, which at 5 rupees a maund, the rate at which it has been sold, yields rupees 3,264 : 13 : 4. Deducting from this the monthly expences, which amount to 120 rupees, or rupees 1440 annually, and the net return is rupees 1,824 : 13 : 4.

The salt wells in the hills are for the most part the sole property of the Nagas. In some of the wells, the former Asam government obtained a joint property, the Nagas having a right to draw the brine for a certain number of hours, and the government for an equal period. Raja Purunder Sing found this right a very profitable one, and a certain portion of his Pykes were allotted to the works. As the Pyke system has since been abolished, and it would not in all probability be so profitable under a system of hired labour, at least without some more profitable mode of boiling the brine than is now in use, the British government have not yet exercised their prerogative in these wells. To some springs below the hills the government have an exclusive right; but the jealousy of the Nagas induced them, during the weakness of the late Asam government, to fill up the wells and forcibly to prevent their being re-opened.

The Naga mode of manufacturing the salt is exceedingly rude, and the process both slow and wasteful,* so that the salt manufactured by the Nagas, can scarcely compete with that imported from Bengal. It is, however, to be hoped, that European speculators will shortly be able to introduce a far more profitable mode of manufacturing the salt, which is the more likely to succeed, as the vicinity of several coal beds will offer the means of evaporating the brine with greater facility. The Nagas themselves are at present averse to any innovations, and it is difficult to see what measures are to be taken even for their own advantage, without giving them offence.

The Naga tribes already alluded to, gave the late government considerable trouble, by the constant wars in which they were engaged against each other. Between the Namsangiyas and the Bordurias in particular, a deadly feud has long existed, which the officers of the Asam Raja far from endeavouring to quell, had till of late, by inflicting fines on both parties, made a fruitful source of gain to themselves. Mr. Sub-Assistant C. R. Strong was lately deputed on a mission to their hills, for the purpose of inquiring into the cause of their feuds, and if possible, to attempt a reconciliation. This, it is hoped, he has effectually done, by engaging both parties in a solemn agreement to abstain from further aggressions, and in future to seek for a redress of their grievances, by a reference to the British authorities.

Of the tribes of Nagas further west, we have no certain information. These tribes are allowed free access to the *hauts*, or market-places on the frontier, and most of them acknowledge allegiance to the British government. During the reign of the Asam dynasty, they were allowed the pri-

* Vide Chapter III. Natural Geography, Section I. Geology.

vilege of cultivating all the lands south of the Dhudur-Alli, at a very trifling rent; and in some parts along that frontier the Nagas possess much valuable cultivation, and a few very comfortable villages. Most of the inhabitants of these villages are composed of refugee Asamese Pykes and slaves, who found protection here from the systematic oppressions they were subjected to in their own villages.

From various causes of complaint, and chiefly, it is believed from an attempt of Raja Purunder Sing to increase the taxes already obtained from these tribes, or from a wish to bring under taxation the Nagas who had long been exempt from it, the Naga tribes between the Dikho and Disang rivers were, during the latter part of his reign, in open hostility to his government, and committed such fearful ravages on the bordering districts, as to stop all communication by the roads, and force the *ryots* to remove from the neighbourhood. But happily these disturbances have now ceased, and tranquillity has once more been restored.

To the west of the Dessai, and between that river and the Dhansiri, the hills are inhabited by numerous and peaceful tribes of Nagas, known to the Asamese by the name of Latoo Nagas. They frequent the markets of Jorehat, Kachari-hat, and the *hauts* on the Dhansiri.

Further west, and on the hills betwixt the several streams of the Dhansiri, are situated the Nagas of the great Angami community, with whom the British government have lately been brought into collision, in consequence of the constant aggressions of that tribe upon the Kachari villages in the hills of northern Kachar. These hills were transferred to Asam in consequence of these aggressions, the superintendent of Kachar not possessing so ready an access to them as is available to the authorities in Asam. The frequent atrocities committed by these tribes, at length forced upon the British government an immediate and powerful interference. Mr. Sub-Assistant Grange accordingly conducted two expeditions* against them, which it is presumed have had the desired effect. Intimidated by these expeditions, the most powerful chieftains have sent in messages, promising better behaviour, and sueing forbearance. A third mission, and which it is hoped will be final, to be conducted by Lieutenant Bigge, Principal Assistant in charge of Nowgong is now about to proceed to their hills for the purpose of negotiating with all the chiefs for terms of alliance and mutual friendly communication.

Though the Angamis are a very powerful confederation, they appear to have had no communication with the markets in Asam, from which they were probably intercepted by the Latoo Nagas, with whom they have been at constant war. Nor does it appear that the Angamis had any immediate communication even with the district of Kachar on the Jamuna. A small trade was, however, maintained with them by means of the Kacharis, and some of the Nagas of the lowest hills, who had been brought under subjection by the Angamis. The rule of the Angami chiefs seems to have been very oppressive; and many of the Nagas have been thereby driven from their own villages, to seek an asylum on the Mikir hills, to the west of the Dhansiri.

The country of the Angami Nagas had, previous to Mr. Grange's expedition, been visited by Captains Jenkins, Pemberton, and Gordon, in attempts to open a communication between Manipur and Asam. The expeditions conducted by these officers have, however, been attended with no permanent results, partly from the strenuous opposition made by the Angamis to any route being opened through their country,† and partly from the officers of the British and the Manipuri governments taking different views of the

* In the cold seasons of 1838 and 1839.

† When Captain Gordon traversed the route in 1833, a powerful coalition was entered into by all the hill tribes to arrest his progress, and he owed his ultimate success entirely to his fire-arms.

policy of the proposed measure, and not following up steadily what their predecessors had begun.

The scanty information we at present possess of the Naga tribes, is scarcely sufficient to admit of our dwelling at any length on their civil and social condition.

In all unpolished nations, the functions in domestic economy, which fall naturally to the share of women, are so many, that they are subjected to hard labour, and must bear their full portion of the common burden. Among the Nagas this is more particularly the case, owing in a great measure, perhaps, to the anarchical state of the country; or rather to the number of independent chiefs, who formerly, for the slightest offence, were disposed to wage war against each other, and the worst of all wars,—that which is covert and unsuspected. This made it necessary for the men to be always ready for an assault; and hence the custom that the women should cultivate the fields, and the men prepare for and fight in battle. In regard to the connexion of the sexes, the Nagas may boast of a propriety unknown to their more civilized neighbours. The men confine themselves to one wife, to whom they are strongly attached, and of whose chastity they appear very jealous. The women, on their part, are said to be distinguished for the correctness of their behaviour. They are in general treated with considerable kindness by the men, and are allowed to participate with them in their festivities and social amusements.

Marriages among the Nagas are not contracted in childhood, as among the Hindoos; nor do the men generally marry young. This probably arises in a great measure from the difficulty of procuring the means of paying the parents of the bride the expected *douceur* on giving the suitor their daughter to wife. Hence the youth, who wishes to espouse a girl, if accepted, agrees to serve her father for a term of years, generally limited to the period at which she may be considered marriagable. At the end of his servitude, a house is constructed for the young couple by their parents, who also supply them with a small stock of pigs, fowls, and rice. A long previous training has fully qualified the young bride to enter upon the duties of her new station; and the value of her services is generally so well appreciated, that nothing is more prompt than the vengeance of a Naga for any insult offered to his laborious partner; his spear gives the ready reply to any remark derogatory to her honour.

The agriculture of the Nagas is neither extensive nor laborious. Among some of the tribes, however, every portion of culturable land is most carefully terraced up the hills, as far as rivulets can be commanded for the irrigation of the beds; in these localities, rice forms the only object of cultivation. Arums and yams the Nagas have in great abundance, but are for the most part found wild about their villages; they have also some large capsicums, good ginger, and a few cardamum plants. Cotton is frequently grown on the sides of the hills; and with it is often seen a species of grass, (lachryma jobi,) from the grain of which the Nagas extract an intoxicating liquor by an operation that closely resembles brewing. It seems to have been one of the first exertions of human ingenuity, to discover some composition of an intoxicating quality, and there is no tribe so rude or so destitute of invention, as not to have succeeded in this fatal research. The Nagas seem as much addicted to the use of intoxicating liquors as any of the neighbouring tribes. Pigs, fowls, and ducks are abundant in all the villages, and some of the more wealthy, keep herds of cattle procured from the plains. They make no scruple of the use of beef, and in fact are by no means particular in their diet—dogs and cats, as well as reptiles and insects, are equally partaken of as food. In general, the Nagas do not use much vegetable food, and the consequence is, that most of the old people shew great and disgusting symptoms of cutaneous eruptions, scurvy, and leprosy.

In so large an extent of mountainous country as that occupied by the Nagas, the useful vegetable and mineral substances that are produced in it, must undoubtedly be numerous; but our imperfect acquaintance with their territories will admit of our particularizing only a few. Amongst the former, there are several species of laurels; that yielding cassia is known to exist plentifully in the eastern hills, whilst the plant known to us as the bay leaf, or the *tezpat* of commerce, is abundant every where. Mr. Grange in his expedition to the Angami Nagas, found the wild tea plant in considerable quantities on their hills, which the Shyans, who accompanied him, said was of excellent quality. Agar wood, the produce of these hills, was at one time in great demand as an article of commerce. A very resinous fir is also abundant in all the higher ranges, and, amongst other useful timbers, oaks of various kinds are plentiful.

The only mineral product we are acquainted with, as used by the Nagas, is salt, which we have already noticed; and as we arc awarc that salt springs exist westward on the banks of the Dhansiri at Sunkar, in the Kachar hills, as far east as the banks of the Dehing and Namsang rivers; whilst coal is plentifully found as far as we have hitherto been able to trace it, all along the lower ranges bordering on the valley, we may with great propriety suppose, that this country abounds in all the deposits of the coal formation and secondary rocks.

We have already observed, that the various tribes dispersed over the Naga mountains, are not only independent and unconnected, but engaged in perpetual hostilities with one another. Interest is not either the most frequent, or the most powerful motive of their incessant hostilities. They must in a great measure be imputed to the passion of revenge, which rages with such violence in the breast of savages, that eagerness to gratify it may be considered as the distinguishing characteristic of men in their uncivilized state.

The maxims by which they regulate their military operations, though extremely different from those which are adopted among more civilized and populous nations, are well suited to their own political state. They never take the field in numerous bodies, since such a measure would require a greater effort of foresight and industry than is usual among them. On approaching the enemy's territories, they collect their troops and advance with great caution. Even in their hottest and most active wars, they proceed wholly by stratagem and ambuscade. They place not their glory in attacking their enemies with open force. To surprise and destroy is the greatest merit of a commander, and the highest pride of his followers. If no straggling parties can be intercepted, they advance towards the villages; and if so fortunate as to remain unobserved, they set on fire the enemy's huts in the dead of night, and massacre the inhabitants as they fly naked and defenceless from the flames. When the enemy is caught unprepared, they rush upon them with the utmost ferocity, and tearing off the scalps of all those who fall victims to their rage, they carry home those strange trophies of their triumph. These they preserve as monuments not only of their prowess, but of the vengeance which their arm has inflicted upon the people who were objects of public resentment. On the death of a warrior, all the scalps taken by him during his life time are burnt with his remains.

Such a mode of warfare may be supposed to flow from a feeble and dastardly spirit, incapable of any generous or manly exertion. But when it is considered that many of these tribes, on occasions which call for extraordinary efforts, not only defend themselves with obstinate resolution, but attack their enemies with the most daring courage, and that they possess fortitude of mind superior to the sense of danger or the fear of death, we must ascribe their habitual caution to some other cause than constitutional timidity. The number of men in each tribe is so small, the difficulty of rearing new members amidst the hardships and dangers of savage life so great, that the life of a citizen is extremely precious, and the preservation of it becomes a capital object in their policy. Had the point of honour been the same amongst the feeble Naga tribes as among the powerful nations of Europe; had they been taught to court fame or victory in contempt of danger and death, they must have been ruined by maxims so ill adapted to their condition. But wherever their communities are more populous, so that they can act with considerable force, and can sustain the loss of several of their member without being sensibly weakened, the military operations of the Nagas more resemble those of other nations. They openly defy their enemies to the combat, engage in regular battles, and maintain the conflict with that desperate ferocity which is natural to men who having no idea of war but that of extermination, never give or take quarter.

The universal weapon of the Nagas is a javelin, which is usually adorned with coloured hair, and ornamented with strips of ratan of various colours. The Loohoopas make use of a long spear, and some of the eastern Nagas handle the tomahawk. The total disuse of the bow among the Naga tribes seems a very singular circumstance, especially as the weapon is common to all the surrounding hill tribes, and the advantage given them by the use of it, is acknowledged by the Nagas themselves. The steadfast retention of their own weapons of offence, may be considered as one strong mark of nationality, and an indication of a common origin; in it may also be traced the continuance of a long established custom, which could scarcely be preserved amongst tribes now so diverse, and that too, contrary to all the dictates of experience, were it not possessed of some sanctity, or consecrated in their recollection as the weapon of their forefathers. Their shield consists of a long mat, lined inside with leather or thin boards.

In general, neither men nor women make use of any superabundance of dress. To some of the tribes in the interior ranges, nature has not even suggested any idea of impropriety in being altogether uncovered, whilst those tribes that see the necessity of it, are satisfied with a very slight covering, and in some cases scarcely compatible with decency.* The cloths in use by the Nagas are made of cotton, usually woven in small breadths by the women, and dyed with various colours. The women wear a short frock, generally dyed blue, and have their necks and arms ornamented with beads and brass rings.

The war dress of the Nagas consists in a number of odd contrivances, to give themselves a fierce appearance. They bind up their legs with brogues of parti-coloured rattans, and adorn their heads and necks with bands of the same. On their heads they wear bunches of feathers intermingled with plates of brass, and the horns and teeth of wild animals; and as though their appearance were not sufficiently fantastic, they affix a bunch of hair to supply the deficiency of a tail.

The houses of the Nagas are very like large barns, built up with gable ends, and having the eaves brought close down to the ground, probably for a better protection against the severe gales with which their hills are occasionally visited; these likewise form convenient porticos for the women to sit under when engaged with their looms. In the interior the houses are divided into two or more rooms; the outer one answers the purpose of the granary, and contains large round wicker-worked bins, in which the grain is deposited, covered over with large wooden planks on which the men usually recline, basking away their time over blazing fires. The interior rooms accommodate the family and the cattle.

* Captain Jenkins mentions it as a singular circumstance in the Loohoopas, that on one occasion whilst traversing their hills, he saw the people engaged in their labours in a state of perfect nudity.

Among rude tribes in every part of the globe, the love of dancing is a favourite passion; and we find it to be the same case with the Nagas. As during a great part of their time they languish in a state of inactivity and indolence, without any occupation to rouse or interest them, they delight universally in a pastime which calls forth the active powers of their nature into exercise. All the Naga dances are imitations of some action; and though the music by which they are regulated is extremely simple and tiresome to the ear by its dull monotony, some of their dances appear wonderfully expressive and animated. The war dance is perhaps the most striking. In this the women dance in an inner circle, whilst the men holding up their weapons in their hands dance round them, beating time and singing in strains of wild and plaintive melody. The women on such occasions are neatly dressed in long dark blue or black garments, ornamented with all their finery of beads and brass rings about their necks. They move in slow and decent movements, but the men, arrayed in their full war dress, enter with enthusiastic ardour into their several parts; they exhaust themselves by perpendicular jumps and side leaps, in which they exhibit considerable agility. On the whole their gestures, their countenances, and their voices are exceedingly wild, and well adapted to their various situations.

The human mind, formed, as it is, for the reception of religious truths, is even in the rudest and most uncivilized state provided with certain ideas, which are destined, when corrected and refined, to be the great source of consolation amidst the calamities of life. Thus among the Nagas, we discern apprehensions of some invisible and powerful beings. These apprehensions, however, seem at first to be suggested to the mind rather by the dread of impending evils, than to flow from gratitude for blessings received. Hence probably originated the worship of evil spirits. Amongst the

Nagas there also appears to be some feeble pointing towards more just and adequate conceptions of the power that presides in nature. They seem to have a perception that there must be some universal Cause to whom all things are indebted for their being. They appear also to acknowledge a Divine Power to be the Maker of the world, and the Disposer of all events: Him they denominate the Great Spirit. Their ideas of him, however, are faint and confused; and of his attributes, they are entirely ignorant. Of the immortality of the soul they have some faint notions. The human mind, even when least improved and invigorated by culture, shrinks from the thought of annihilation, and looks forward with hope and expectation to a state of future existence. This sentiment of soothing consolation, resulting from a sacred consciousness of its own dignity, from an instinctive longing after immortality, is universal, and may be deemed natural. From their imperfect ideas concerning the invisible world, they suppose that they shall continue to feel the same desires, and to be engaged in the same occupations as in the present world. The Nagas have no established form of worship; they have no temples erected in honour of their deities, and no ministers peculiarly consecrated to their service. They have the knowledge, however, of several superstitious ceremonies and practices handed down to them by tradition; and to these they have recourse with a childish credulity, when roused by any emergence from their usual insensibility, and excited to acknowledge the power and to implore the protection of superior beings.

The funeral rites of the Nagas are much the same as those practised by most of the hill tribes already noticed. The following extract from the journal of the Rev. M. Branson,* who was an eye-witness on the occasion of one of these ceremonies, may convey some further information on the subject:—

* See the Missionary Magazine of the Baptist General Convention for Foreign Missions, Boston, December 1839.

"This day was the completion of the sixth month after the death of a wife of one of their chiefs. Their custom is to allow the corpse to remain six months in the house; at the expiration of which time, the ceremonies I have this day witnessed must be performed. In the morning two large buffaloes, several hogs, and a great number of fowls were killed for the occasion. About noon, numbers of Nagas from the neighbouring villages, dressed in a most fanciful manner, and equipped for battle, arrived. After beating several gongs of different sizes, so arranged as to form a sort of harmony with the music of drums, they marched to the house where the decaying corpse lay, each man bearing a shield, a spear, and a *daw.* They then commenced singing and dancing, with such a regularity of step and voice, as surprised me. They sang in the Abor tongue, and my interpreter informed me, that all their songs are borrowed from the Abors, with whom they hold daily intercourse. I was allowed to attend, in company with two of the chiefs, who interpreted to me the song, the substance of which is as follows: 'What divinity has taken away our friend? Who are you? Where do you live? In heaven or on the earth, or under the earth? Who are you? Shew yourself. If we had known of your coming, we would have speared you.' The above was first pronounced by the chorister. The whole company then answered it by exclaiming, 'Yes,' at the same time waving their huge glittering spears towards heaven, in defiance of the evil spirit who was supposed to have occasioned the death. The chorister continues, 'We would have cut you in pieces and eaten your flesh.' 'Yes,' responded the warriors, brandishing their *daws,* as if impatient for the battle. 'If you had apprised us of your coming, and asked our permission, we would have reverenced you; but you have secretly taken one of us, and now we will curse you.' 'Yes,' responded the warriors. This is the substance of what they sang, though varied, and repeated many times. The noise of music and dancing continued nearly all night. During the greater part of the following day the same ceremonies were repeated. At the setting of the sun, a large company of young women came around the corpse, and completely covered it with leaves and flowers, after which it was carried to a small hill adjacent, and burnt amid the festivities of the people. Thus closed this painful scene."

SECTION X.—KACHAR.

Boundaries—Early History—Raja Govind Chandra—Escheatment of his Territories to the British Government—Ancient Citadel—Present Inhabitants.

The country of Kachar is bounded on the west by Sylhet and Jaintia; on the north by Asam; on the east by Manipur; and south by Tripurah. It was originally divided into three portions; two of which lie on the northern side of the great mountain chain, which, sweeping round from the north-eastern extremity of the Manipur territory, forms the western termination of the Garo hills; the third division is on the southern side of this lofty barrier. These divisions were severally distinguished by the names of Northern, Central, and Southern Kachar.

The early history of Kachar partakes of the fault usually complained of in the histories of all half-civilized nations: it is much intermixed with fable; whilst the occurrences of later periods are involved in the same degree of uncertainty, from the want of regular annals. It is pretended that the kingdom of Kachar, from its foundation, (the date of which we have no means of ascertaining,) has been always governed by one family, the descendants of Bhim, the second son of Raja Pandu, a prince of the lunar dynasty, who on arriving in Kachar found it in possession of a demon, or giantess, and her brother Hirimba, from whom it is said the country takes its ancient name. Bhim, after killing Hirimba in single combat, married his sister, by whom he had a son called Ghatot Kach, alias Kartrik Chandro, who governed the country after his father's death, and from whom the kings of Kachar are said to have descended.

In 1813, the reigning prince Krishna Chundra dying, was succeeded by his brother Govind Chundra, the only surviving descendant of Bhim, the original founder of their family.

He was a weak prince, but tyrannical and avaricious. These last vices, perhaps, contributed in no small degree to facilitate his dethronement, an event which occurred in 1817, when his country was invaded by Marjit Sing from Manipur, and its eastern portion overrun by the troops of that prince, who, however, speedily retired, on learning that his brother Choorjit had advanced from Jaintia. From this period to the commencement of the year 1823, the country of Kachar was the arena on which the several Manipuri brothers, Choorjit, Marjit, and Gambhir Sing contended for supremacy. As might have been anticipated, the inevitable result of their disputes was the most serious injury to the country.

At the commencement of the year 1823, the superior energy and military talent of Gambhir Sing had secured to him the possession of the whole of Southern Kachar, with the exception of the purgunah of Ilakander, which was held by his brother Marjit. The avowed intention of the Burmese to invade this province, and its contiguity to Sylhet, rendered it an object of the utmost importance to the British government to open a negotiation with the chiefs who then ruled over it; and with this view, overtures were made to Gambhir Sing, and his brothers Choorjit and Marjit. The latter were anxious to avail themselves of the alliance; but the former held back, apparently in the vain expectation of being able to defend the usurped territory, without forming an alliance which might ultimately compromise his independence. It was in consequence determined to negotiate with the legitimate Raja, and to pension the Manipuri usurpers of his throne and country.

The events of the war led, as is well known, to the expulsion of the Burmese force by which Kachar was invaded, and to the restoration of Govind Chundra to the throne of his ancestors. In return, he agreed to pay an annual tribute to the British government of rupees 10,000.

This engagement, it is believed, was but imperfectly fulfilled, as much from the avarice of Govind Chandra, as from the devastated state in which his country had been left by the usurpers of his authority, and the visitations of the Burmese forces.

This unsatisfactory state of affairs in the southern portion of his territory, was rivalled by that of the more hilly tracts on the north; where his subjects, under a leader called Tuliram, had long successfully resisted his authority.

As Govind Chandra was now old and without issue, the magistrate of Sylhet was deputed to Kachar, to institute an inquiry into the claims of the pretenders to the succession. These were two, Tuliram already mentioned, and Govindram who was supported by the queens, and was alleged to be the Raja's natural son. The magistrate, after a careful inquiry, decided that Tuliram was the only person who had any pretensions to the succession. The feud between the Raja and Tuliram now became more bitter than ever; and Durgaram, the Raja's lieutenant in the hills, assisted by the *luskurs* of Dhurampur, waged an exterminating war against Tuliram. Mr. Scott, in July 1829, anxious to check a state of affairs so deeply injurious to the welfare of the country, obtained a written agreement from Govind Chandra, in which he assigned a tract of country in the hills to Tuliram, and bound himself not to molest him within those limits. Almost immediately afterwards, however, Tuliram was attacked by Govindram, and, as subsequently appeared, by an express order from Govind Chandra, given in direct violation of the agreement which he had signed only five months before.

On the death of Govind Chandra, Tuliram in defending himself against the attacks of Durgaram's party, put to death two men who had fallen into his hands, and who, he had reason to suppose, had been employed to assassinate him. This was represented by the party adverse to him as a breach of the treaty between him and the Raja; and the murder was further said to have been committed in a part of Kachar then under British administration. Tuliram was in consequence sent to Gowhatti, to stand his trial on a charge of murder. After a prolonged confinement, he was acquitted; and as it was considered that he could not be restored to that portion of the country from which he had been expelled by Durgaram, without again giving rise to disturbances, on the 16th of October 1834, he entered into an agreement, in which he resigned all the western portion of the country assigned to him by the previous one of July 1829, retaining the tract on the east, between the Dhansiri and Dyung rivers, and the Naga hills and the Jumuna, receiving a pension during his life of rupees 50 per mensem for the tract resigned, and paying a nominal tribute of elephants' teeth for protection, in the tract to which he was restored.

In 1830, the Raja Govind Chandra was assassinated, and there being no descendant, either lineal or adopted, the country was annexed to the British territories by proclamation, on the 14th August 1832, and the management of its affairs was entrusted to Captain Fisher, under the title of Superintendant of Kachar. Since that period the country of Kachar has been gradually returning to comparative prosperity, and once more smiles under a mild administration. It had prior to this been entirely deserted by its inhabitants in consequence of the successive devastation of the Manipuris and Burmese, and of the oppressive services exacted by the large detachment of troops which occupied the country during the war. Latterly, however, the lands along the river have again been brought under cultivation, chiefly by settlers from Sylhet. It now yields a revenue of between 30,000 and 40,000 rupees, leaving a small surplus after paying all the expenses of management.

In 1836-37, the Nagas having grievously oppressed the inhabitants of Northern Kachar, and the Superintendent being unable to afford them efficient protection, that division was transferred to the jurisdiction of Asam. The territory thus attached, may be divided into three portions: the valley of the Jamuna and Kopili rivers, heretofore known by the designation of Dharumpore, and now called the district of Jamuna Mukh; second, that portion of the country between the upper parts of the Jamuna and Myung rivers, retained by Tuliram; and third, the hilly tract between the Myung and Kopili, which was resigned by that chieftain.

The division of Jamuna Mukh has already been noticed in the remarks made on the Nowgong district. The second division is, with few exceptions, one unbroken expanse of forest. At Tuliram's place of residence, there is a little cultivation, conducted chiefly by a few Kacharis and Mikirs. There are also a few scattered hamlets along the banks of the Myung, occupied by these tribes; and towards the upper course of the Dhansiri there are a few Naga villages. Here are also a few brine springs, and the salt procured from them by the Nagas is disposed of to the neighbouring hill tribes. The third division is entirely a hilly tract, and from gentle elevations on the north, the lands rise considerably to the south as they approach the great ridge of mountains that divide the waters of the Surma, from those minor streams that empty themselves into the Brahmaputra. The Kopili river, which bounds this division to the east, is from its junction with the Myung entirely unnavigable; but the latter stream which forms its western boundary, is navigable for small canoes throughout the greater part of the year, its whole course lying in a valley, and the low elevation which separates its springs from the sources of the Jatingah which runs south, being only two or three hundred feet above the level of the Brahmaputra.

In passing through Kachar, on his route to the hills occupied by the Angami Nagas, Mr. Grange had the satisfaction of coming upon the ruins of an ancient citadel, called

Dhimapur Nuggur, situated on the banks of the Dhansiri, and said to have been built by Raja Chakardhaj, the fourth king of Kachar. The people themselves had not the slightest idea of its situation, though the fact of its existence was apparently known. "The remains of Dhimapur," observes Mr. Grange, "consist in some pillars of various patterns, a gateway, the ruined town or palace wall, and a small fort to the north, besides a few tanks both within and without the walls. The fortification is surrounded on three sides by a dry ditch about thirty feet wide, a bund and a second ditch. The gateway which faces the river, is in a tolerable state of preservation, but the inner passage or guard-room has fallen in, and lies a heap of ruins. The pillars are in three parellel rows, those of two rows are of a circular form, in the third row the pillars are square; there are ten in each row of the former, and twenty of the single row of the latter. The city walls are all in ruins, and the place itself is hid in a dense forest of trees. It is stated, that after the building of the city, Chakradhaj heard of the approach of the famous Hindusthani warrior, Kalapahar, when he fled with his effects to Mybong in the hills, where he subsequently built a fort. Kalapahar not finding his foe, pillaged the place and withdrew. On his retirement, the Asamese aware of the flight of the Raja, are said to have sent a force to possess themselves of Dhimapur; but Chakradaj not fearing his new enemy, came down from his retreat in the hills, and meeting one of the Asamese Phukans, inquired of him the reason of his approach: the answer was, that he had come merely to look at the country, and that the army had withdrawn. This answer seems to have satisfied the Raja; but whilst he and his people were engaged in their evening repast, the Asamese army came down upon them, and being unprepared to receive their treacherous foe, they were put to immediate flight. The Raja with several of his followers succeeded in effecting an escape back to Mybong, where they took up their residence, and Dhimapur was deserted. The Raja died at Mybong, as did several of his successors; but the court was afterwards removed to Kaspur in the plains."

The present inhabitants of Kachar are, with few exceptions, Bengalis, who have emigrated from the district of Sylhet, and these for the most part profess Mahomedanism. Such of the original inhabitants as still remain, are confined to the members and servants of the late royal family.

SECTION XI.—THE KHASSIAS.

Description of the Country—Jaintia—The Confederated States—Connexion with British Government—Form of Government—Disposition of the People—Amusements—Trade—Religion—Marriage and Funeral Ceremonies.

The tract of mountain territory inhabited by the Khassias borders on Kachar to the east; the district of Sylhet to the south; the Garo hills to the west; and the valley of Asam to the north. It forms an irregular parallelogram, the length of which, from north to south, may be assumed at about 70 miles, and its average breadth at 50, giving an area of about 3,500 square miles.* This area consists of three portions of unequal breadth and diversified character: the first, or most northern, is a closely wooded tract, rising from the Asam valley, and stretching by a succession of gentle undulations for 20 miles to the heights on which stands the village of Mopea, 2,746 feet above the sea, and from which the northern crest of the more elevated central plateau is seen, resting at an elevation of between four and five thousand feet above the same level. From Nunklow, which stands on the edge of the northern crest to Moosmye, which is similarly situated on the southern verge of this elevated region, the direct distance is about 35 miles. This tract, viewed geologically, consists of two portions, separated by the Boga Pani, which flows between them, from north-east to south-west. The northern portion consists, almost exclusively of granite masses, which are seen protruding through the soil at every step; and large boulders are scattered over the surface of the country in every direction. The soil is in most parts very poor, and the vegetation scanty; the barrenness of the view is, however, greatly relieved by the presence of some noble firs, which crown the

* Vide Pemberton's Report on the Eastern Frontier.

summits of the knolls, and are scattered over all the hollows which lie between the different heights. Between Moosmye and Taria Ghat, at the foot of the hills, a distance of about seven miles, is comprised the third division of this mountain tract, which consists of the steep face of the range, and, like that on the Asam side, is densely wooded. Viewed from the country below, it appears to spring almost perpendicularly from the plains to an elevation of about 5000 feet.

The tract of country thus described, is divided into a number of petty principalities, which unitedly contribute to the formation of the confederated Khassia states. But before noticing them, it may be advisable to offer a few remarks on the territory of Jaintia, which, though independent of the rest, seems in some measure connected with them. It immediately borders upon Kachar, and extends along the whole line from Asam to the plains of Sylhet. It contains an area of about 3,850 square miles, and consists of three principal divisions.

During the unsettled state in which Asam continued for some time after the Burmese war, the Raja of Jaintia is affirmed to have appropriated considerable tracts of land, which properly belonged to the former province. In 1832, four subjects of the British government were seized by the Raja of Goba, one of the petty chieftains dependent on Jaintia, and immediately bordering on the district of Nowgong in Asam; they were carried to a temple within the boundaries of Goba, where three were barbarously immolated at the shrine of Kali; the fourth made his escape to the British territories, and gave intimation of the horrible sacrifice which had been accomplished. A demand for the surrender of the culprits was immediately pressed by the British government, with the earnestness which retributive justice so imperiously demanded; but every minor expedient having been resorted to in vain, on the 15th of March 1835, Captain Lister, with two companies of the Sylhet Light

Infantry, took formal possession of Jaintiapore, the capital of the country, and the determination of government to annex the plains to the British territory was made known by proclamation.

The population of this tract of country consists chiefly of a race of people nearly allied to the Khassias, both in language and customs. There is also amongst them a large proportion of Mussulmans, and low caste Hindus of Bengal origin, distinguished, however, by some peculiar local customs and usages from the classes in the Sylhet district.

A considerable trade in cotton, iron ore, wax, ivory, betle leaf and cloths, is carried on between the plains and hills; and Jaintiapore, the capital, is the great *entrepôt* in which all commercial dealings are transacted between the inhabitants of the plains and those of the hills. The articles specified, are bartered for salt, tobacco, rice, and goats.

Of the Khassias, properly so called, it may be observed, that they present the appearance of a congregation of little oligarchical republics, subject to no common superior; yet of which, each member is amenable in some degree to the controul of his confederates.

The most important of the confederated states, are—the state of Ossimlee, the chieftain of which is more commonly known as the Nunklow Raja. The next, though in all probability the most powerful, is the principality of Kyrim. Circumstances enable this chieftain to exercise an authority far more despotic than is enjoyed by most of the Khassia Rajas, who generally have a council, without whose sanction no business of importance is undertaken. The number of villages subject to the authority of this chieftain is said to amount to seventy. Bordering upon his domain, and forming a part of the province of Kyrim, is that known as Bor-Manik's country; twenty-eight villages acknowledge submission to this chieftain. The Raja of Churra, another principality, numbers about twenty-five villages under his controul.

The next on the list is the state of Nurtung; little is known of the internal management of this domain. The principality of Nuspung, which contains twenty villages; of Muriow, containing twenty-five; of Mahram, containing twenty-four villages; and that of Ramrye, are the only others meriting notice: but little more is known of them than the sites they séverally occupy.

From about the year 1794, from which period may be dated the decline of the Asamese power, many of the tribes on the southern borders of the valley gradually established themselves in the plains, whence the paramount government was unable to dispossess them; and conscious of its weakness, was glad to compound with them for an acknowledgment of supremacy, which these tribes however spurned and disavowed whenever its exercise appeared likely to encroach on that independence of action, which they rarely permitted to be controuled. It was probably about this time also that the Khassias obtained possession of those tracts of land in the plains which they still continue to cultivate.

When the fate of war had transferred Asam to British rule, the expediency of endeavouring to open a direct communication between it and the more southern provinces of Sylhet and Kachar, did not escape the penetration of Mr. Scott. It was not, however, till 1826, that negotiations to effect this desirable object were entered upon with the Khassia chieftains.* For upwards of eighteen months after the ratification of this agreement, the most cordial understanding seemed to exist between the British authorities and their new friends; but when the most sanguine expectations of the former appeared already realized, these bright prospects were suddenly obscured by an act of the most atrocious cruelty, the cause of which is not distinctly known, but which completely changed the character of the existing

* For a particular account of this negociation, see "Memoirs of Mr. Scott," by Major A. White.

intercourse, and converted the powerful friends of the Khassias into formidable and irresistible enemies. Three or four British officers were brutally massacred, and about 50 or 60 native subjects consigned to an untimely grave. The Khassias, conscious that they had violated every pledge, which even savages are accustomed to regard with superstitious reverence, viewed with suspicion every pacific overture; and despairing of pardon, protracted a contest which their first skirmishes with our troops proved to be hopeless.

At length, however, the submission of Tirut Sing, the Raja of Nunklow, and who had been the principal culprit, was soon followed by a general pacification. The other chiefs had, with few exceptions, prior to this, adopted the sagacious policy of withdrawing from an unprosperous cause; and the few who had supported him, were glad to avail themselves of the opportunity afforded by his surrender to throw themselves on the clemency of the paramount power. All opposition having been finally overcome, and the principal chieftains having tendered their submission to the British government, it was resolved to place the whole mountain tract under the superintendence of the officer, whose skill and gallantry had so largely contributed to its pacification; and Major Lister was shortly afterwards appointed Political Agent for Khassia affairs, over which he exercises a general controul.

It has already been observed, that the form of government under which the Khassias live is republican. They acknowledge the superiority of their kings in name; a number of villages, as we have seen, profess allegiance to one sovereign, who, however, has but little authority; every village has its own chief, who obtains more than nominal respect. The office of these chiefs, requires them to administer counsel; for which reason, men of matured judgment and good sense are always selected. The number of these councillors varies in proportion to the extent and importance of the village. The business of the state is transacted at public meetings, called by order of the king, at which subjects affecting the welfare of the parties, are canvassed, opinions advanced and maintained by the king and his counsellors, and the question decided by a majority. The king usually takes up his residence in the principal village in his territory; he knows no more of the concerns of his dominions than his subjects, since every village is entitled to transact its own business, with the assistance of its chiefs. The regal power does not descend, as amongst other nations, from father to son; but from uncle to nephew.*

Imperfect as their government is, it is worthy of remark, that crimes such as would be cognizable by our law, are of very rare occurrence. Crimes detected are usually punished by fines; and in particular cases, such as murder, rape, and some cases of adultery, with death.

Disputes concerning laws or money, are settled in rather a remarkable manner. The disputing parties finding all means unavailing to bring a matter to a final settlement, determine to pass through an ordeal, which consists in being immersed in water. The party emerging first, being supposed to be convicted and rejected by the *Aquæ Deo*, loses his claim to the disputed property.

The Khassias are in general of a lively and cheerful disposition. Though laborious when actually engaged in work, they are, like most mountaineers, a slothful people. Among their bad qualities, dissoluteness of manners and drunkenness are the most prominent. But though there is much of evil, there is also much of what is good in the character of the people, which raises them above their neighbours in the scale of moral worth, considering that they are destitute of the only source from which true morality proceeds.

* For these and the subsequent remarks, we are indebted to a paper, published in the *Calcutta Christian Observer*, March 1838, entitled "A brief Account of the Khassias, by the Rev. A. B. Lish.

Amongst the amusements of the Khassias, archery may be mentioned as the chief, as well as the most interesting. Bird catching, fishing, hunting, and gambling also occupy no small portion of their leisure time.

Their trade consists chiefly in the barter of oranges, honey, iron, bees' wax, and ivory—for rice, fish, cotton, and silk, cloth and salt. Potatoes are grown to a considerable extent in their valleys, and on the declivities of their hills; and may now be considered with iron, as the staple articles of their trade.

The volatile disposition of these people naturally takes them much from home; and while they are either engaged in trading with the lowlanders, or sauntering about the hills and valleys in pursuit of amusement and pleasure, the domestic occupations devolve upon the women.

With reference to their religion it may be observed, that they believe in the existence of one Supreme Being, the Creator of the world. The minute affairs of individuals, and even the greater and more important matters of nations, they suppose to be under the superintendence of divine agents or spirits, who are likewise gods. These spirits delight in sacrifices, and all affliction is attributed to their wrath: their character is wicked; they are all evil spirits, and are always engaged in exerting their evil influences over those who do not pay them the attention they deserve; they can however be pacified by the sacrifice of a fowl or other animal.

The Khassias are not in the habit of marrying young; but usually wait till they have attained a mature age. The proposal of marriage comes from the man. He deputes a friend to the parents of the young lady, to request their consent, as well as her own, to their union. The nature of the reply regulates his conduct. If he is successful, he is allowed to visit the house, pay his addresses to her, and they mutually appoint a day on which the union is to be solemnized.

On that day the bridegroom, attended by a number of his friends, proceeds to the house of the bride, where her friends are assembled. A mutual conference takes place, in which the consent of the parents is formally asked by the friends of the bridegroom; and the bride and bridegroom are then asked if they are willing to have each other. If replies be given in the affirmative, the parties are pronounced man and wife. A feast follows, after which the friends retire, but the bridegroom remains in the house of the bride, and becomes an inmate if the bride happen to be the youngest or only daughter; if otherwise, the husband has to build for himself, and remove her to his own house, which becomes the property of the wife. Cases of separation are frequent; and both husband and wife may marry again, if they have parted from each other with mutual consent. When they have thus mutually agreed to part from each other, their friends are told of it, and some of them are requested to effect the separation by a formal ceremony, which consists in taking five *cowries*, or shells, from each party, and throwing them out of the house.

When a death occurs, there is always a great deal of grief manifested. The corpse is kept in the house four or five days, and in some cases for as many months; in such instances the body is put into the hollow trunk of a tree and fumigated. They do not bury, but burn their dead like the Hindus, though in a more decent manner. The body is carried on a bed of mats, tied to two poles, the ends of which are borne on the shoulders of four men. During the procession a funeral dirge is played on bambu flutes, which adds much to the solemnity of the scene, accompanied as it is by the groans and shrieks of the bereaved friends. Arrived at the spot, the body is taken off the bed and put into a wooden box standing on four legs, under which the fuel is placed. While in the act of removing the body from the bed to the box, it is carefully concealed from the view of the by-standers: four or five individuals surround the box, and cover it over with their garments while the body is let down. Sometimes the body is conveyed from the house in the box in which it is to be burnt. While the body is being burnt, sacrifices are offered, and offerings of betle leaf, areca nut, fruit, &c. are made to the spirit of the deceased; arrows are also occasionally discharged towards the four points of the compass. When the body is burnt, the ashes are carefully collected, put into an earthen vessel, carried home, and kept until, by the help of their oracles, the day is fixed for the removal to the family vault, which is composed simply of a tabular stone. Beneath this the ashes are placed, and on occasion of their removal from the house, those who can afford the expense have dancing and feasting, which are kept up for three or four days. The relatives do not engage in either, except to defray the expense, and superintend the proceedings. The dancers are both men and women: of the latter only such as are unmarried or widows. These dance, or rather hop, in an inner, while the men form an outer circle, and display all sorts of gesticulation, but keeping good time with the music. Sword exercise is also common on such occasions, and is the most interesting part of the proceedings. The ashes of one tribe are deposited together under one vault. The remains of a man and his wife are never deposited together, because they belong to different tribes. A husband is therefore separated from his wife and children, as the latter belong to the tribe of the mother, and their ashes are deposited with her's.

SECTION XII.—GAROS.

Nature of Country—Trade—People—Dress—Dwellings—Food—Dances—Marriages—Funerals—Religion—Connection with British Government.

We turn now to the Garos, the last of the frontier tribes we meet with in our progress along the southern boundaries of the valley. They occupy that triangular extent of mountainous country between the Khassia hills and the Brahmaputra. It may be described as one confused assemblage of hills and narrow vales, watered by numerous small streams. These hills are in general clothed with magnificent forests, among which are found an infinite variety of useful and ornamental plants. The soil is in most parts extremely good, and where the hand of man has been exerted to till and cultivate the ground, it yields a rich and abundant harvest. Cotton forms by far the principal object of culture, and it is doubtless the staple commodity of the country.* Regular markets are held once or twice a week at convenient places along the borders, where the inhabitants usually bring down their cotton, to exchange for salt, rice, dry fish, tobacco, and betle-nuts.

The Garos, like their neighbours the Khassias, are divided into numerous petty tribes, each chief of which has his vote in the assembled council, though no one of them is independent of the others. They are equally warlike with the Khassias, superior, if possible, in muscular development and bodily strength, though inferior to them in external appearance and dignity of carriage. The Khassias are more pastoral, the Garos more agricultural; the Khassia lives by the produce of his cattle, the Garo by the tillage of his hills.

* See the Trade of Asam. Chapter VI. Productive Industry.

The Garos go, men, women, and children, almost literally naked. A narrow girdle, about the middle, constitutes the whole of their dress. The hair is sometimes thrown back from the face, and fastened by a kind of brazen ornament, in a manner which gives them a fierce wild air; others cut it close, or tie it in a loose careless fashion on the crown. The women, short, squat, and masculine in features, are remarkable for their ugliness. Their dress, like that of the men, consists merely of a small girdle, seldom more than a foot wide, of a very coarse striped cotton cloth; all the other parts of the body are left exposed. Yet they seem as fond of ornament as any of the daughters of Eve, but quantity seems to have more charm for them than quality. From ten to fifteen or more brass rings, as thick as a goose quill, and three or four inches in diameter, hang in the lobe of each ear, by the weight of which it is stretched so as to touch the shoulder; while the neck is usually cased in a mass of chains, and other rude ornaments. The want of fastidiousness in the matter of dress is not necessarily followed, as more civilized people might suppose, by licentiousness. The Garos are, in the intercourse of the sexes, reputed to be far more correct than their Bengali neighbours, by whom the exposure of the person commonly observed amongst the Garos, is abhorred as most indelicate and obscene.

The houses of the Garos, like those of certain Polynesian tribes, are raised on piles several feet from the ground. They are in length from 30 to 150 feet, from 10 to 40 in breadth, and are roofed with thatch, or with mats and long grass. The props of the house consist of large timbers, and vary in number according to the size of the dwelling; over these are placed horizontal beams to support the roof. The house is divided into two compartments, of which one is left unfloored for the cattle.

The people are not at all scrupulous about their food.

Their appetite seems highly tolerant of variety. Besides the animals usually eaten, they devour cats, dogs, frogs, and snakes. Milk in every form whatever they execrate and abhor, calling it diseased matter. Of the flesh of puppies they are exceedingly fond, more especially when cooked after their savage fashion. The dog is first made to eat as much rice as it can possibly hold, it is then roasted alive, and when the rice is considered sufficiently cooked, the belly is ripped open and the entire mass is served up for eating. Men, women, and children partake largely of intoxicating liquors.

Their manner of dancing is somewhat peculiar. Twenty or thirty men behind one another in a row hold each other by their belts, and then go round in a circle, hopping first on one foot, then on the other, singing and keeping time with the music, which is animating, though harsh and inharmonious. The women likewise dance in rows, but hold out their hands at the same time, lowering one and raising the other, as the music beats, and occasionally turning round with great rapidity. The men also occasionally exhibit military exercises, like the barbarians described by Xenophon, with sword and shield, which they use with grace and great activity.

The business of marriage is generally conducted by the parties concerned. A day is then fixed for the celebration of the nuptials. It being the custom for the bride to seek the bridegroom, all those who are invited assemble on the appointed day at her dwelling, when the usual round of drinking, dancing, and singing commences. The bride is then conveyed to the nearest stream and bathed, after which the whole company moves in procession towards the house of the bridegroom, who on learning their approach feigns to fly. He is however quickly caught, and taken, like his mistress, to be bathed. His parents now commence a kind of funereal howl, and attempt to detain him by force. When this mock resistance is over, the procession returns to the dwelling of the bride, where the ceremony is completed by the sacrifice of a cock and hen, and the usual debaucheries of a savage feast.

Their funeral ceremonies are still more remarkable; the body is kept four days, after which it is placed in a small boat on the top of a pile, erected within six or eight yards of the house. The pyre is kindled by the nearest of kin to the deceased exactly at midnight, after which the company feast and make themselves merry. When the body has been consumed, the ashes are buried in the earth in the same spot where the pile was kindled, and a small thatched building, surrounded by a railing, serves to record the memory of the deceased; within this building a lamp is burned every night for the space of a month or more. If the deceased be a person of rank, the funeral pile is decorated with cloth and flowers, and the head of a bullock, sacrificed on the occasion, is burned with the corpse. At the obsequies of a superior chieftain, a large body of his followers sally forth from their hills, and having seized upon the first individual of a hostile tribe they meet with, cut off his head and burn it with the body of their chief.

Little is known of the religion of the Garos, except that it resembles that of the Khassias.

Adultery, robbery, and murder are said to be punished with death. Fines expiate all minor offences, and the money thus collected is spent in intoxicating liquor.

Shortly after the British government had possession of Bengal, its attention was drawn to the Garos by the constant reports of their aggressions on the inhabitants of the plains, and as early as 1782-83, we find Mr. Elliott deputed to the Mymensing frontier to inquire into the causes of the disturbances, and report on the pretensions of the Zemindars to duties on the trade with the hills. Mr. Elliott's deputation ended in his fixing the duties to be levied on the frontier of Soosung and Sherepore on the part of the government, the claims of the Zemindars being entirely rejected, and this led to the establishment of peace and quiet ever after. But for many years subsequent, the frontier was constantly disturbed by the attempts of the Raja of Karaibari,* (to whose estate Mr. Elliott's inquiry had not been extended,) to bring the Garos of the adjacent hills under subjection to himself, as well as by the indiscriminate retaliations of the Garos upon all the neighbouring Bengalis. The Raja kept up a number of *Burkundazes*, and at last was not only embroiled with the Garos alone, but also took possession of the lands of his neighbour of Sherepore, built fortresses thereon, and openly defied the government. After a very protracted period of contumacy, his estate was at length sold, for arrears of revenue, for the sum of 35,000 rupees; but the purchaser was many years before he could get possession of it, and spent in the attempt about 1,50,000 rupees more. These circumstances, together with other disturbances on the Garo frontier, led to the deputation of Mr. Sisson in 1815,† and on his report, the late Mr. David Scott was appointed by government a Special Commissioner to settle the relations of the Zemindars with the Garos. On this gentleman's report, the Zemindars of Rungpore were formed into the separate district of N. E. Rungpore; it was by regulation X. of 1820, put beyond the pale of the regulations, and was placed under Mr. Scott's administration. One of the first acts of Mr. Scott was to obtain

* A Mech by extraction.

† With regard to the Raja of Karaibari, who had been a tributary of the Mogul government, Mr. Sisson thought he had been hardly dealt with, and recommended the repurchase of his estate, and that he should be reinvested in it.

a small grant from the Zemindar of Karaibari for the family of the Raja then lately deceased. His surviving Ranee still resides on this grant, very much respected by the hill people. The violent spirit of the father however descended to the last of his children, a bastard son, who a few years ago was banished for life in a case of manslaughter, or murder, committed in a fit of rage. If the Ranee conceives that she was improperly dispossessed of the immense, but little valuable estate of Karaibari, it may perhaps be some consolation for her to know, that the purchase of the estate has been the ruin of the Lahouri family, who from their official connection with the authorities of Rungpore, became the purchasers of it. No sooner had the original purchaser, at great cost, obtained possession of the estate, than he died, and for fourteen years following, the sons have been embroiled in a hitherto fruitless and expensive litigation, under the Bantwarah regulations, for the purpose of dividing the estate into two portions of four and twelve anna shares, agreeable to their own agreement, in the first instance, duly ratified by the decrees of the Sudder Dewanny.

Mr. Scott in a great measure succeeded in reducing the Garos to subjection, and brought them under the immediate management of the British government by placing a range of country, which both the Zemindars of N. E. Rungpore and the Garos equally claimed, under the controul of government officers, and thus preventing any future interference of the Zemindars with the Garos. The rents of these Mehals, called the Garo Mehals, were settled with the Garos, and the profits divided between government and the Zemindars; they are still thus managed, causing no trouble as far as these Mehals are concerned. Mr. Scott also withdrew the jurisdiction of the Zemindars from the *hauts*, or market places, and placed them on a footing which has given general satisfaction to the Garos, and thus allayed a source of great discontent among them.

The higher ranges of the Garo hills are however still independent of the British government. But that extraordinary custom of burning human scalps with the bodies of their deceased still prevails, and is the cause of their committing frequent murders on the people of the plains.